The Abolitions of Slavery

From Léger Félicité Sonthonax to Victor Schœlcher

1793   1794   1848

Edited by

Marcel Dorigny

Berghahn Books

NEW YORK • OXFORD

UNESCO Publishing

PARIS

Published in 2003 jointly by the **United Nations Educational, Scientific and Cultural Organization** and **Berghahn Books**

UNESCO wishes to express its gratitude for assistance in publishing the present work from the Japanese Funds-in-Trust for International Cooperation and Mutual Understanding.

Originally published as *Les abolitions de l'esclavage* © 1995 Paris, Editions UNESCO/Presses Universitaires de Vincennes

Reprinted 1998

Library of Congress Cataloging-in-Publication Data

The abolitions of slavery : from Léger Félicité Sonthonax to Victor Schœlcher, 1793, 1794, 1848 / edited by Marcel Dorigny.
    p. cm. — (The slave route series)
    Includes bibliographical references and index.
    ISBN 1-57181-432-9 (alk. paper)
    1. Antislavery movements—History. 2. Antislavery movements—Dominican Republic—Santo Domingo—History. 3. Antislavery movements—France—History. 4. Sonthonax, Léger Félicité, 1763–1813. 5. Schœlcher, Victor, 1804–1893. I. Dorigny, Marcel. II. Series.

HT1025 .A26 2003
326.8'09–dc21   2002043990

ISBN UNESCO: 92-3-103167-8

British Library Cataloguing in Publication Data

A catalogue record for this book is available from the British Library.

Printed in the United States on acid-free paper.

Also in THE SLAVE ROUTE series

From Chains to Bonds: The Slave Trade Revisited, 2001
edited by Doudou Diène

Contents

Preface

Marcel Dorigny

THIS BOOK IS a collection of scholarly papers, originally published in French,[1] on the abolition of slavery in the French colonies, presented at an international conference held at the University of Paris VIII in February 1994. This conference, attended by some forty participants, was organized as part of a bicentenary commemoration of the first abolition of slavery, proclaimed by Léger Félicité Sonthonax in Saint-Domingue on 29 August 1793, and ratified by a decree of the National Convention on 4 February 1794 (16 Pluviôse, Year II). The commemoration was highly significant, for it prompted for the first time in France a thorough critical evaluation of the state of research into the history of the eradication of colonial slavery. In contrast to previous French colloquia that dealt almost exclusively with the slave trade and colonial societies,[2] this conference aimed at broadening these questions by considering the abolition of slavery itself in the French colonies.

The chronology adopted for the conference was largely dictated by French history: from the writings of the *philosophes* condemning the slave trade and slavery in the French colonies to the decree of 27 April 1848 permanently abolishing slavery in the French domains. Most of the contributions in this collection concentrate on the Revolutionary and Napoleonic periods. However, it was deemed undesirable to limit scholarly investigations to the French experience; indeed, the comparative approach commended itself, prompting researchers to analyse the abolition of slavery in the colonies of the American, British and Spanish nations. The goal of this academic conference, in addition to assessing as far as possible the current state of scholarship, was to encourage fresh research using not only known sources, but above all, sources still largely unexplored.

UNESCO's international *Route de l'Esclave* project shares the same purpose: to promote scientific research on the slave trade and the abolition of slavery and its vestiges in post-slavery societies until the present-day. Hence, it was possible to combine the proceedings of researchers with those of UNESCO, thereby giving this published collection of essays an undeniable international scope. The English translation of this volume will enlarge the readership for the conference, and UNESCO deserves our gratitude for taking such a constructive initiative.

Since the aim of all research is to stimulate further research, it is reassuring to note that in the seven years since the conference, a large number of publications on related topics have appeared, most of them in French. Several international conferences, indeed, have focused on the subjects of slavery and its abolition. In 1994, UNESCO organized a colloquium at Ouidah in the Republic of Benin dealing with the slave trade and the abolition of slavery, the proceedings of which were published in 2001.[3] The same research team also published a collection of studies in 1997[4] on the central figure of the first abolition of slavery, Léger Félicité Sonthonax. In December 1997, UNESCO, again in the context of its intercultural *Route de l'Esclave* programme, sponsored another international conference in Haiti to examine the Saint-Domingue slave rebellion of August 1791, the first step on the road to the initial abolition of slavery; the proceedings of that conference were published in Paris.[5] Then in 1998, which was the 150th anniversary of the second abolition of slavery in the French colonies, the Comité des travaux historiques et scientifiques held its 123rd annual congress at the University of Antilles in Schœlcher, Martinique; five volumes of the proceedings have already appeared, one of which is devoted entirely to the abolition of slavery and its aftermath.[6]

In addition to articles appearing in conference proceedings, several monographs, published in France and elsewhere, have shed light on French abolitionism. The magisterial study by Claude Wanquet, the works of Yves Bénot,[7] the research of Patricia Motylewski and Lawrence Jennings on the French abolitionist movement in the second half of the nineteenth century,[8] and the recent publication by Nelly Schmidt on the same subject all deserve to be mentioned here.[9] Moreover, Anne Girollet[10] has subjected Victor Schœlcher to a searching examination from a rather different point of view than that proposed by Nelly Schmidt in 1994.[11] The abbé Grégoire, a pre-eminent figure in the international abolitionist movement up to the beginning of the 1830s, is also better known thanks to two studies published in 2000 and 2001.[12] Moreover, the principal form taken by French abolitionism at the end of the eighteenth century should be reconsidered following the publication of the complete record of the meetings of the Société des Amis des Noirs.[13] Significantly, the role of the Church is now better understood thanks to recent work by Philippe Delisle.[14]

Several French doctoral dissertations finished or in progress have also contributed new information about anti-slavery societies, the Revolutionary struggle for the abolition of slavery both in Saint-Domingue and in France, and the manner in which the so-called indemnification of colonists was applied after the final abolition of slavery in 1848. These themes have received scholarly attention in as yet unpublished university works by Vertus Saint-Louis, Dominique Rogers, Jean-Daniel Piquet and Cecile Ernatus.[15]

This English edition of the proceedings of the international gathering in Paris comes at a fortuitous moment in the progress of French research. While the actions leading to the abolition of slavery are well known, many aspects of this story remain obscure and can only be illuminated by further research, most notably in archives. Only by the completion of such much-needed preliminary investigations can long-awaited works of synthesis be profitably undertaken. Yet however inadequate the current state of knowledge, research is proceeding apace as this present volume amply attests.

We hope that this work will contribute to a better understanding of French colonial slavery and its abolition, and enable those without a reading knowledge of French to learn about some of the research currently being done in this ever-expanding field.

Notes

1. *Les abolitions de l'esclavage 1793–1794–1848 : De L.F. Sonthonax à V. Schœlcher*, collected and introduced by Marcel Dorigny, Paris, UNESCO Publishing and Presses Universitaires de Vincennes, 1995 and 1998.
2. *The African Slave Trade from the 15th to the 19th Century*, report of the expert meeting in Port-au-Prince in 1978, Paris, UNESCO Publishing, 1979. *De la traite à l'esclavage du Ve au XVI-IIe siècle*, proceedings of the International Conference on the Black Slave Trade, Nantes, 1985, edited by Serge Daget, Paris, Société française d'histoire d'outre-mer, 2 Vols, 1988; mention should also be made of some of the published papers of bicentennial conferences on the French Revolution, with special reference to the history of the French colonies: *La Révolution française et Haïti. Filiations, ruptures, nouvelles dimensions*, published under the direction of Michel Hector, Société haïtienne d'histoire et de géographie, 2 Vols, Port-au-Prince, Editions Henri Deschamps, 1995; *Révolution française et Océan indien. Prémices, paroxysmes, héritages et déviances*, texts collected by Claude Wanquet and Benoît Jullien, Paris, Editions L'Harmattan, 1996; *Révolution française, colonisation, esclavage, libérations nationales*, Université de Paris 8, 24–26 February 1989, Paris, Editions L'Harmattan, 1990; *La Révolution française à Cuba et ses répercussions dans l'histoire, la pensée et les lettres nationales*, edited by Paul Estrade and Auréa Fernandes, Revista de la Universidad de la Habana, June 1990; *L'Ile Maurice et la Révolution française*, proceedings of the Mahatma Gandhi Institute Conference, 4–8 August 1989, texts collected by Uttama Bissoondoyal, Moka, Mauritius, Mahatma Gandhi Institute Press, 1990; *La Révolution française et Madagascar*; and, finally, *Révolutions aux colonies*, special edition of *Annales historiques de la Révolution française*, September–December 1993.
3. *From Chains to Bonds: The Slave Trade Revisited*, with a preface by Doudou Diène, New York, Berghahn Books, and Paris, UNESCO Publishing, 2001.
4. *Léger-Félicité Sonthonax. La première abolition de l'esclavage, la Révolution française et la Révolution de Saint-Domingue*, texts collected and introduced by Marcel Dorigny, Paris, Société française d'histoire d'outre-mer and Association pour l'étude de la colonisation européenne, 1997.
5. *L'insurrection des esclaves de Saint-Domingue (22–23 août 1791)*, proceedings of the international round table of Port-au-Prince, 8–12 December 1997, under the direction of Laënnec Hurbon, Paris, Editions Karthala, 2000.
6. *Esclavage, résistances, abolitions*, under the direction of Marcel Dorigny, proceedings of the 123rd Congress of Historic and Scientific Associations, Schœlcher, April 1998, Paris, Editions du CTHS, 1999.
7. Claude Wanquet, *La France et la première abolition de l'esclavage, 1794–1802. Le cas des colonies orientales*, Paris, Editions Karthala, 1998; Yves Bénot, *La Révolution française et la fin des colonies*, Paris, Editions la Découverte, 1987, *La démence coloniale sous Napoléon*, Paris, Editions La Découverte, 1991, and *La Guyane sous la Révolution, ou l'impasse de la Révolution pacifique*, Cayenne, Editions Ibis Rouge, 1997.

8. Patricia Motylewski, *La Société française pour l'abolition de l'esclavage 1834–1850*, preface by Marcel Dorigny, Paris, Editions L'Harmattan, 1998; Lawrence C. Jennings, *French Anti-Slavery: The Movement for the Abolition of Slavery in France, 1802–1848*, Cambridge, Cambridge University Press, 2000.

9. Nelly Schmidt, *Abolitionnistes de l'esclavage et réformateurs des colonies, 1820–1851*, analysis and documents, Paris, Editions Karthala, 2001.

10. Anne Girollet, *Victor Schœlcher, abolitionniste et républicain*, approche juridique de l'œuvre d'un fondateur de la République, Paris, Editions Karthala, 1999.

11. Nelly Schmidt, *Schœlcher*, Paris, Editions Fayard, 1994; see also Victor Schœlcher, *Des colonies françaises: Abolitions immédiates de l'esclavage*, preface by Lucien Abénon, Paris, Editions du CTHS, 1998 (Coll. Format).

12. *Grégoire et la cause des Noirs: combats et projets, 1789–1831*, under the direction of Yves Bénot and Marcel Dorigny, Paris, Société française d'histoire d'outre-mer et Association pour l'étude de la colonisation européenne, 2000, 192 p.; the CTHS published two award-winning works of 1841 under the title of 'The Grégoire Legacy', intended to combat colour prejudice: *Contre le préjugé de couleur: le legs de l'abbé Grégoire*, preface by Anne Girollet, Paris, Editions du CTHS, 2001 (Coll. Format).

13. Marcel Dorigny and Bernard Gainot, *La Société des Amis des Noirs, 1788–1799: Contribution à l'histoire des abolitions de l'esclavage*, Paris, UNESCO Publishing, 1998.

14. Philippe Delisle, *Renouveau missionnaire en société esclavagiste: la Martinique, 1815–1848*, Paris, Publisud, 1997, and *Histoire religieuse des Antilles et de la Guyane françaises: des chrétientés sous les tropiques? 1815–1911*, Paris, Editions Karthala, 2000.

15. Vertus Saint-Louis, 'Le nombre et le défi maritime. L'avènement de la liberté dans une société coloniale esclavagiste. Saint-Domingue 1789–1794', doctoral thesis, Université des Antilles et de la Guyane, 2000; Jean-Daniel Piquet, 'L'émancipation des Noirs dans la pensée et le processus révolutionnaire français (1789–1795)', doctoral thesis, Université de Paris 8, 1999; Dominique Rogers, 'Les libres de couleurs dans les capitales de Saint-Domingue: fortune, mentalités et intégration à la fin de l'Ancien Régime (1776–1789)', doctoral thesis, Université de Bordeaux III, 1999; Cécile Ernatus, 'L'indemnité coloniale en Guadeloupe, Martinique, Guyane, 1848–1860', doctoral thesis, Université Paris X-Nanterre 2000.

A Keynote Conference

Doudou Diène

THIS CONFERENCE IS at once a symbolic act and a commitment. The symbolic act is the support that UNESCO wishes to express for this historically and morally significant initiative of the University of Paris VIII and of the participants in this event. And it is a commitment, in so far as your meeting is an ideal opportunity to show that UNESCO is a fully committed participant in the debates and discussions about a major event in the history of mankind.

Addressing the UNESCO General Conference, President Nicéphore Soglo of Benin quoted Elie Wiesel as saying: 'The killer always kills twice, the second time by his silence.' That thought is particularly appropriate as regards the transatlantic slave trade and its underlying causes, modalities and consequences.

Major work has of course been done on this question in many centres in Africa, Europe and the Americas. But beyond the cry of the poets, it consists largely of isolated initiatives by intellectuals and researchers who felt, in all conscience, that the extreme reticence of the scholarly community did not accord with the demands of scientific objectivity and historical truth. The urgency of dealing – globally, methodically and, if possible, consensually – with an inescapable question has been rendered topical today by the debates on the issue of development and the historical factors that explain the economic and social situation of a number of countries, particularly in Africa.

For there can be no denying that the human, intellectual and cultural blood-letting of the slave trade is not unconnected to the current economic and political power relations between those who were once partners in the triangular trade. Furthermore, achieving a lasting peace, which is a fundamental objective of the United Nations system, lends urgency to the need for a new look at the question of the slave trade. The ethical principle set forth in UNESCO's Constitution, stating that 'since wars begin in the minds of men, it is in the minds of men that the defences of peace must be constructed', highlights the fact that ignorance of certain major events in history and a failure to examine them scientifically are obstacles to peace because of the unhealed wounds left by such events.

It is for all these reasons that UNESCO, in accordance with its mandate to promote intellectual collaboration, decided to launch the major international project entitled 'The Slave Route'. The Organization's aim is a dual one: to ensure that the question of the slave trade is the object of multidisciplinary study and to ensure that it enables the peoples affected, as well as the conscience of mankind, to take on board, in full awareness of the facts, a common memory and thereby create the conditions for the renewal of their current collaboration. The Slave Route project thus refers to an essential insight that the founding fathers of UNESCO wrote into the Constitution, and I quote:

> The Governments of the States parties to this Constitution on behalf of their peoples declare.... That the great and terrible war which has now ended was a war made possible by the denial of the democratic principles of the dignity, equality and mutual respect of men, and by the propagation, in their place, through ignorance and prejudice, of the doctrine of the inequality of men and races.

An International Scientific Consultative Committee, established by the Director-General of UNESCO, guarantees the scientific integrity of this project. The Slave Route project will seek, in a global perspective, to coordinate, promote, encourage and support ongoing initiatives relating to the slave trade. They include the admirable 'Links of Memory' exhibition organized by the city of Nantes: the event was a profound statement of the objectives of UNESCO in the sense in which links evoke not only the chains of slaves in the past but also the bonds that should be constructed for the future. Mention should also be made of the Gorée-Almadies memorial project in Senegal, and of the efforts of Angola, Ghana, Nigeria and other countries to restore sites of remembrance of the slave trade and reconstitute national archives on the subject.

It is to be hoped that this conference organized by the University of Paris VIII will be a significant scientific step along the Slave Route, marking out new directions for research in time to come.

Introductory Note: Slavery and Late Serfdom

Jean Bart

IS IT POSSIBLE to compare colonial slavery and mortmain, the relic of serfdom that was still to be met with in a number of French provinces in the eighteenth century? Both were abolished by the Revolution, the latter earlier and more easily than the former, and for good. But at first consideration, the two institutions differ profoundly when looked at from a legal point of view.

On the one hand, the slave was, as in antiquity, a thing, an *object*, property that was owned and which could therefore be sold just like a farm animal; on the other, the serf was a being with a legal personality who could execute deeds, in short, a *subject* of law, although in a diminished capacity.

But it is still worth considering whether, behind this fundamental difference, it is not possible to perceive some remote kinship, especially as some saw late serfdom as an intermediate stage between servitude and freedom, evidence of an untroubled evolution from a colonial-style slave system to acknowledgement of legal equality, avoiding the upheavals of instant abolition.

In French customary law, mortmain determines a set of incapacities based on descent and marriage which in particular restrict the freedom to make contracts: the man or woman subject to mortmain cannot alienate property as he or she wishes and the choice of spouse is limited, unless one agrees on marriage to surrender much of what one possesses. In addition, the whole estate of the non-free reverted to the lord on certain conditions, to the detriment of the legitimate heirs. This legal inferiority compared to free persons, which was fairly general in rural areas in the Middle Ages, survived at the end of the Ancien Régime in a few provinces in north-eastern France, and above all in Burgundy and Franche-Comté. In those areas, it was regarded – wrongly – as a vestige of slavery, an 'imperfect remnant of slavery', 'a softening wrought by time', and thus a favourable situation compared to total absence of freedom. Moreover, old-fashioned jurists took a benevolent view of mortmain as a protective institution: since those who were subject to mortmain could not sell their goods to free people, they were thus protected from bourgeois seizure of land. This was an illusory protection, as subsequent events showed. It remains that mortmain – an integral part of the feudal mode of production – was a relatively effective means of maintaining a rural labour force useful for seigniorial exploitation. And that is where the comparison with colonial slavery comes in. Those who, on the eve of the Revolution, justified the existence of late serfdom in metropolitan France did so using the same arguments as the advocates of slavery: in the name of property regarded as one of the inalienable rights of man, in this case of the master of a lordship in mortmain. The freedom called for on behalf of the last serfs was viewed as an attack on seigniorial property. The condition of individuals subject to mortmain was itself justified by the idea of an original grant: the ancestors of those who still existed in the eighteenth century had been quite satisfied to receive a few acres of land to farm, in return for just compensation for the grantor. In short, the finality and justification of these two institutions were, making all due allowance, identical.

In the course of the decades preceding the Revolution, mortmain, like many other seigniorial rights, experienced something of a revival, as those who held lordships, landowners or large-scale farmers sought to enhance their profits. In some areas, duties that had fallen into abeyance or had even been forgotten were once again being demanded from holders, which was possible because seigniorial rights could not be revoked. But this seigniorial action ran into strong opposition from those at the receiving end supported by a section of enlightened public opinion. Refusal of payment or challenges to mortmain led to many judicial conflicts. These revealed to the men of the Enlightenment the existence of the 'odious stain of serfdom'. The most celebrated trial of this type occurred in the 1770s between the inhabitants of a number of villages in southern Franche-Comté and the bishop and canons of Saint-Claude, who had inherited the temporalities of the former abbey. It was thus at the end of his life that a famous philosopher living in the neighbourhood, at Ferny, took up the cause of the 'serfs of Mont-Jura'. In order to deliver them from their serfdom, Voltaire, aided by the local lawyer Christin, published pamphlets and tracts, trying to drag his friends into the struggle.

Yet the similarity between the remnants of feudal serfdom and colonial slavery was not established. The two de facto conditions which resulted from them patently had little in common. It was no easier to establish a comparison between serfdom and ancient slavery, and yet this was done as a matter of course by the men of the Enlightenment. It is true that Voltaire felt pity for 'the sad state of twelve thousand men treated like blacks by canons and monks', but his usual reference point for lambasting the archaism of mortmain remained that of Roman slavery. Enlightenment thought, it seems, found it easier to look back in time than to cross the Atlantic.

Whatever the case, the cause of the Franche-Comté serfs was lost at law. But the movement of opinion in favour of freedom had been sufficiently powerful to influence royal legislation. By an edict of August 1779, Louis XVI, 'considering that a great number of [our] subjects, still servilely tied to the glebe, are regarded as being part of and as it were confounded with it', abolished mortmain on royal lands (where it no longer existed) and called on the lords of the kingdom to follow his example on their own lands, which the vast majority hurried not to do. Property always won out over freedom, but the days of mortmain were numbered in spite of everything. Every last vestige of personal servitude was swept away without compensation, following the vote on the night of 4 August 1789. The slaves in the Islands had to fight much longer and harder to gain a freedom that would only finally be acknowledged to them half a century later.

Part I

Resistance to Slavery in the Different Colonial Spheres (1750–1791)

Chapter 1

Slavery and Law: Legitimations of an Insurrection

Jacky Dahomay

MY ESSAY IS PECULIAR in that it is rooted solidly in philosophical problematics. Two centuries after the abolitions of slavery, what I want to do is not so much to add to historiographical knowledge as to bring out the *meaning* of events, in other words to link the past to the present. And because, in philosophy, we are continually meditating on the political-anthropological foundation of our Caribbean societies, we find ourselves again and again coming back to that period in the history of the Caribbean, as if something profoundly originary occurred there.

Contrary to what might be suggested by the title 'Slavery and Law', I do not propose here to go into the whole ongoing debate about the paradox of the status of the slave as a thing and at the same time the object of legal provisions, as was the case with the *Code Noir*. I shall try rather to understand the thing from the point of view of the slave: What meaning could his claim of law have? Natural law or positive law, civil right or citizen's right?

But to answer such questions involves above all analysing the underlying dynamic of slave insurrection from the 1790s onwards. Was it the logical consequence, the continuation, so to speak, of traditional revolts or was it, on the contrary, revolutionary in the sense that it was part of the work of the great French Revolution? To answer that question, one must reinterrogate the very idea of revolution. A conciliatory mind might simply admit that the slave insurrection ending in the enactment of abolition was the dialectical synthesis of the insurrectionary tradition of blacks and the influence of the ideals of the French Revolution. But, with dialectical solutions, at least in philosophy, there is always a risk of overlooking something important. And we wish to focus our attention on a fact that, at least to our knowledge, has hardly been addressed by Caribbean thinkers: the validity of the expression *anti-slavery revolution*. Let me explain.

Historical observation, as Moses Finley, for example, notes, shows that 'outbreaks of slave violence have been numerous in every slave society. They have also been ... shortlived and uniformly unsuccessful'.[1] That makes one stop and think, since the case of the Caribbean seems to contradict such an assertion. Did not slave insurrection there lead to the effective abolition of slavery, and, furthermore, did not the independence of Haiti in 1804 mark irreversible victory over the slave system?

The problem is thus an important one. There are only two possibilities: either what happened in the Caribbean was something out of the ordinary, in which case the complexity and originality of anti-slavery insurrection would need to be elucidated, or, on the contrary, there was no revolution in the strict sense of the word, but rather revolts within the overall framework of the French Revolution. That indeed is Finley's position: '[Only] the great revolt in Haiti was successful.' But, he adds, it 'must be viewed as a by-product of the French Revolution'.[2] If that were true, the 1789 Revolution would remain the fundamental matrix of all modern revolutions. But in that case one would also run the risk – an ethnocentric risk – of denying the very specificity of slave insurrection.

There would therefore seem to be several interesting reasons for looking at the abolitions of slavery from this angle. Thus, we might ask whether the notion of *anti-slavery revolution* has any meaning. Is the passage from a slave society to a non-slave society sufficiently significant to describe such a historical event as *revolutionary*? Moreover, the very name of this colloquy is clearly *abolitions of slavery*, not *anti-slavery revolutions* – as if slavery could only be eliminated by an abolition and not by a revolution, as if elimination could only be the consequence of abolition. That is odd. Abolition is a movement that goes from the top downwards. Law is its instrument. Revolution follows the opposite path: it institutes law.

To resolve such ambiguities we need to penetrate to the heart of events and attempt to grasp the meaning of what is at stake in the slave revolts, in the quest for human status and to understand the legitimations that may accompany it. Our argument is that there was no anti-slavery revolution in the Caribbean but, on the one hand, in the case of Haiti, an anti-colonial revolution that incorporated anti-slavery insurrections and, on the other, in Martinique and Guadeloupe, an assimilationist evolution that incorporated the earlier slave struggles. We shall explain why. And we shall see how one has the vague feeling, even today, that somewhere along the line the revolution in Haiti was blocked – which would go a long way to explain many current tragedies – and that in the French Caribbean and Guyana, despite republican assimilation, some sort of lingering unease gives the current political situation a tinge of uncertainty. We propose to bring out: (1) the foundation of colonial slave societies, (2) the repercussions of the French Revolution on the colonies and (3) the insurrectionary logic of the slaves and its philosophical-anthropological meaning.

The Foundation of Colonial Societies

Slave insurrection occurred in particular societies, and the foundation of those societies needs to be properly grasped. It is doubtless trite to observe that the colonial societies formed in America under Ancien Régime France were created in and through violence, with extermination of the Caribs and enslavement of blacks. It is however a more complex matter to grasp the implications of this for the issue of legitimation. If by legitimation we mean, first, the ratiocinations designed to justify occupation of the islands, extermination of the Caribs and the slave system – what is normally called *ideology* – we should note that though racism was already present, it was not yet the fundamental element. It would become so in the nineteenth century, after the upheaval of the political space opened up by the French Revolution. The ideology of colonial rule in the seventeenth and eighteenth centuries rested on Christianity, which justified exploitation overseas as an enterprise of evangelizing non-Christians. Slavery was a transition towards liberation.

But the justifications in this area were always being challenged, and I do not believe that colonialist ideology had been well thought through at that period. Colonialism did not yet have a fully developed, rationally thought out discourse, and that became apparent in the debates in the early days of the Revolution. Moreover, Christianity had difficulty justifying slavery, even though the Church, in fact, resolutely supported slavery. Finally, the kings of France themselves were sometimes embarrassed by the question of slavery. If a slave was a subject of the king and had to be the subject of a code, and hence in some way a subject of law, how could he at the same time be a thing? Moreover, to declare free every slave setting foot on the soil of metropolitan France meant recognizing that there was something radically 'other' about the place from which slaves came, the overseas territory, since it somehow eluded the ancestral modes of legitimation of the Ancien Régime social order.

It now remains to spell out the fundamental meaning of the word *legitimation*, which we have repeatedly used. Contrary to a widespread opinion, doubtless inherited from Marxism, the sole foundation of the social bond that holds together a community of men does not lie in an economic solidarity, an infrastructure organizing men's needs. Human life exists only because men have to give meaning and value to their presence in the world. And if they do so in the multiplicity of their cultural symbolic forms, those forms must, in the last analysis, ensure the vertical foundation of their societal order – in other words, *legitimize* political authority. We therefore understand legitimation to mean the various modes of instituting the social. We may accept with Pierre Clastres[3] that in some primitive communities or some African chieftainships, for example, modes of legitimation operate in such a way that the power that a chief is recognized as having is such that it is always denied. In the European kingdoms under the Ancien Régime, the foundation came not from the king but from above him. Power was legitimized political-theologically. With *modernity*, the legitimation of power is secularized; that is, it rests on man himself, in other words, on a basic indeterminacy, which is the whole essence of modern democracy.

What then can become of the various forms of legitimation among men of different cultural origins brought together in the artificial and violent space of the colonial slave societies in America? To the extent that colonial society was produced outside French society (distance being reinforced by the means of communication of the time), it became autonomous. What do we mean by that?

First, the social composition was not the same. There was not the same division between the nobility and the third estate. The big whites (*grands blancs*) often originated from the third estate. They ruled over slaves, something that did not occur in France. In that sense, they were at the cutting edge of modernity. That fact is vital because it gave them something in common with the North American colonies, which were also slave societies. Here we must appreciate the full implications of what Hannah Arendt is saying when she writes: '[N]o demonstrable influence on the course of the French Revolution … can equal the impact of what the Abbé Raynal had already called the "surprising prosperity" of the … English colonies in North America.'[4]

It was indeed a different labour relationship that developed, which was not without consequences on the question of the political foundation. It may be asked why another servile relationship was not established in place of slavery. But as Jacques Thibau points out: 'Would not a slavery that reproduces itself through natural increase and not through the purchase of new slaves end up as serfdom, an inadequate formula for a plantation economy?'[5] The fact is that serfdom was too archaic for a mode of exploitation that was already capitalist and modern. But it was a pre-industrial capitalism, unable to generalize wage-earning in the plantation system. The colonies found a mode that was transitional between the two, which is paradoxical since a slave is less than a serf. All this may be summed up as saying that it was modernity that instituted slavery in the colonies, a fact not unconnected with the subsequent difficulties encountered in abolishing it.

By *modernity*, we mean the advent of another epoch of world history. It was an economic, cultural and political alteration which occurred above all in European societies. While capitalism undoubtedly pre-dated this period, it became generalized as such from the sixteenth and seventeenth centuries onwards. But that was only possible because cultural changes (religious schism, weakening of tradition, emergence of the individual) favoured it. At the political level, and certainly from the time of Machiavelli, philosophical legitimations of political authority were becoming more and more secular. Finally, the French Revolution marked the culmination of this history, which is also that of the world. What this means is that there is a marked difference between ancient slavery and modern slavery. While the former is rooted in a tradition based, in Aristotle, on a certain *naturalism*, the latter is marked by its essential *artificiality*. Produced, then, by the nascent stirrings of modernity, such a slavery appears in the first place as consubstantial with modernity itself. Is that not what would make it possible to understand why the Catholic Church, even when it embraced Aristotle's arguments, found it difficult to perfect the legitimation of such a form of exploitation? Finally, is that the reason why modern republics, in Europe and North America, had so much difficulty liquidating slavery? But these are merely hypotheses.[6]

To return to the colonial societies in America, the problem then arises of the legitimation, the foundation of their societal order. But what happened very early in the colonies in America was that the traditional political-theological foundation of the Ancien Régime was eroded. Strange as it may seem, the colonies in the West Indies were present at the dawn of modernity. The

conflict pitting the colonists against the authority of the royal state was therefore deepening all the time. The terms of the conflict are well known. Malouet,
says Thibau, stressed 'the existence of a dual power in Saint-Domingue: public authority and domestic authority, with two different sets of laws, two methods of enforcing them, two different managements'.[7] There was also a dual
movement: non-recognition of the authority of priests in favour of secular
authority, and difficulty in acknowledging royal authority. It was indeed,
therefore, a matter of autonomization and a certain form of secularization of
public life that was involved.

By the same token, it is also possible to speak of a sort of deconstruction of
the symbolic institution and an attempt at recoding by Creole planters. Saint-
Domingue, in both its *nuits folles* and the everyday practices of Creole whites,
witnessed a dissolution of traditional ways and the habitual constructions of the
family, which gave life in the colonies an edge that did not exist in France. But
all that was not without effect on the status of slaves. The master's goal was to
make the slave as little a legal subject as possible, to make him a pure automa-
ton, a mechanical animal, a pure body – to relieve him, if possible, of even the
minimum of *anima* that Aristotle accorded him. But that was impossible to
achieve, which helps to understand why his greatest fear was that the slave
might take himself for a subject. This explains the ferocity and the constant
concern with repression. It was thus also natural that the slave, too, should be
obliged to seek to recode a symbolic institution, even doing so starting from the
master's religion, Christianity. The struggle between master and slave was in the
deepest possible sense a struggle to the death. The kings, slavers though they
might be, were seriously worried about the removal of any mediation between
master and slave, because it weakened the specific sphere of law. This disappearance of law Plato recounted in a quite different area – in the form of Gyges,
the possessor of a ring that rendered him invisible. He could thus do as he
wished, unhindered by morality. Michel Alexandre, commenting on Plato, is
right to say that Gyges's ring is life in the colonies![8] In psychological terms, we
know what elimination of the specific sphere of law signifies: it is perversion.
But here is not the place to analyse all the subconscious impacts of this type of
relationship on both the personality of the master and that of the slave. We propose the hypothesis that the origin of *macoutism*, hovering eternally over every
Caribbean society, also lies in the darkness of this historical period.

Whatever the case, there could be no possible liberation of the slaves.
Masters refused to accept that slaves might form a family, because to do so
would be to humanize them, and baulked at accepting their conversion to
Christianity, since that too would be to humanize them. Nor would they consider literacy. Work itself heralded death since masters had absolutely no concern with the reproduction of the slave by himself, by birth, by life. The slave
was not *Bios*; he must be entirely *Zoon*.

The Hegelian dialectic of master and slave – or rather what everyday
interpretation has made of it – cannot unfold here. Contrary to what Arlette
Gauthier says in *Les Soeurs de Solitude*, to the effect that the male slave, unlike
the female slave, can experience freedom through work,[9] work is not here the

privileged site where the slave can free himself. And the dialectic of desire here does not lead to any sort of sociality. It is the very institution of society that is referred to its nothingness. When the sphere of work, of production and consumption invades the whole social field (the sign of what some call postmodernity), the individual finds it hard to see himself as part of a work that endures. Virtue disinherits the social field and death is effectively the sole absolute master. Colonial society is therefore always traversed – and this time in a more ontological sense – by the image of death.

It is in such a death-bearing context that we must understand the slave himself. But for that we need to spell out a few more concepts. We use the expression *symbolic institution* in the sense given it by Marc Richir. It is, he says, an

> *articulation* of symbolic 'systems' ranging from language to the techniques of hunting, fishing, farming and industry by way of the rules of kinship or practices and representations portrayed as political or religious … a complex whole with no outside.[10]

But seeing this system from the viewpoint of structuralism as a 'sort of thing doing its thing all by itself' is to forget that it can always be upset by what it represses: the loss of any symbolic referent symbolically instituting the world and thus referring the subject back to his being-for-death, an experience that Richir, following a reinterpreted Kant, names the *sublime*. But for Kant, the sublime can be overcome by the discovery, beneath the starry heavens above, of the moral law within. When this mode of overcoming does not happen, the subject experiences his finitude in an absolute anguish, which is that of the very abyss of every foundation of the social. Despotism and terror (under Robespierre, for example) are a mode of escaping from this anguish, although short-circuiting it.

Phenomenologically, the slave did indeed experience this anguish and had done so ever since his capture in the slave ship. The loss of traditional symbolic referents forces him to endless recodings. But the essential precariousness of his situation means that he can never recode the symbolic in terms of a more vertical foundation of the polis, of a legitimation of political authority. It is as if a gap was being dug between, on the one side, a cultural reformulation, a symbolic restructuring enabling the slave to survive and give meaning to his presence in the world and, on the other, procedures of legitimizing political authority that remain wholly alien to him. The tragedy of independent Haiti would lie in the inability to effect an integral symbolic reunification that could give meaning to social life. For the slave, any and every system of elaborating the legal-religious would be forever marked by the dereliction of the political. That is why his revolt can only be either an exit from the system or the fury of destruction. There do remain, however, the meanders of an impossible integration or the subtle forms of what Édouard Glissant calls practices of deviation.[11] The slave will abandon his body to the master to the point of death, if need be. He has no choice. Since death is always for him meaningless as long as the sublime is hard to traverse, it is better to give it meaning by itself. Death gives meaning to death. 'Long live death!' cried the blacks of Guadeloupe, reports the historian Lacour, as they advanced, women at the head, towards Richepanse's cannon.

It may seem strange that we should insist so strongly on the nature of colonial society before introducing our analysis of slave insurrection, but we felt it indispensable for a better grasp of what we have to say on the sequence of events during the Revolutionary period in the Caribbean.

The Echo of the French Revolution

How then in such a context did the French Revolution produce its echo on the Islands? There again the matter has been well studied by historians, and we know the reactions of the various social classes and categories to news of the events of July 1789. Planters saw in them a means of countering what Yves Bénot calls 'ministerial despotism'.[12] Traders in the towns hoped to profit when these events should break the power of the planters, and in Martinique the course of events took on the appearance of an opposition between town and countryside. Mulattoes and other freemen of colour, a powerful class in Saint-Domingue, did not question the institution of slavery but sought to be recognized as equals to whites. While it is true that there were sincere patriots among the whites and mulattoes, animated by the ideals of the Enlightenment and the Revolution, we must not let ourselves be deceived by discourses. As Anne Pérotin-Dumon notes, all of these people took in of the news from France but

> little. In any event, neither the Jeu de Paume, nor the taking of the Bastille, nor the Great Fear. But only the meeting of the Three Estates, the adoption by the king of the tricolour cockade.... Alejo Carpentier has Victor Hugues say as he sails towards the islands, that the Revolution began to simplify itself as one got further away from France.[13]

The *petits blancs* were, she says, rather working for a 'colonial revolution' in the metropolitan framework.[14]

These different social classes, while open to change, since they were evolving in a society whose theological and political foundations were already shaken, did indeed want profound socio-political transformations in the framework of the French Revolution, but the spirit of the Revolution itself was totally alien to them. As James writes: 'The coarse San Domingo whites had no spark of that exalted sentiment which drove the revolutionary bourgeoisie elsewhere to dignify its seizure of power with the Declaration of Independence or the Rights of Man.'[15] Such a simplification of the French Revolution in the colonies cannot, of course, eradicate the outbursts of generosity and the noble ideals of some individuals, sailors or other transient whites, enlightened mulattoes and blacks, and there is no denying that Revolutionary ideas did penetrate the colonies. But what was their real impact on the course of events? How were they reinterpreted in a society with its own autonomous logic? To take an example among the 'Black Jacobins', while we can say that a man like Louis Delgrès in Guadeloupe drew sustenance – tragically, no doubt – from the ideals of the Enlightenment, Toussaint and Dessalines, on the other hand, remained relatively immune to such demands. Haiti's Declaration of Independence in 1804 – is it a sign? – made no mention of the inalienable rights of the human being. It is, it seems to me, not at all the truly Revolutionary spirit that presided over the sequence of events in the Islands. It is as if, in the tropics, the Revolution had always already been frozen.

It might be argued in response that the same thing happened in France, and that it was not philosophical ideas that were animating every social conflict and every popular revolt in the countryside and towns in mainland France. But to us that is a misleading way of stating the problem. The essential thing is not so much that these ideas, as they were philosophically developed, had penetrated the French masses. What was radically new and clearly seen by some observers were the fundamental shifts that occurred in the phenomenological experience of the masses, in regard to the very perception of the foundation of society and the processes of legitimation. The revolts and outbreaks of violence that spread, starting in 1789, both in Paris and in the countryside, were undoubtedly associated with poverty. But they were above all rooted in a questioning – one that was not explicit or theorized – of traditional seigniorial rights in the countryside and political authority in the towns. There was a sort of disenchantment, a gradual, even subconscious desacralization of the legal-political and religious symbolic referents that had hitherto structured the world. That is what made the French Revolution a total revolution, a mass phenomenon, and what gives it its own inescapable edge. Michelet, says Richir, had a clear grasp of the spirit that animated the people of France at the time of the festivals of the Federation that followed the Great Fear:

> Time and space, those material conditions to which life is subject, are no more. A strange *vita nuova*, one eminently spiritual, and making her whole Revolution a sort of dream, at one time delightful, at another terrible, is now beginning for France. It knew neither time nor space.[16]

And, for Richir, this 'symbolic reinstitution of the social in line with its phenomenalization in the festival only takes place, once again, in the obsolescence of the old frameworks'.[17]

There was no experience of this sort, no suspension of the world in the Caribbean. Quite the contrary, as soon as the Revolution was announced, everyone rushed into a death struggle – *petits blancs* against *grands blancs*, freemen of colour against whites, slaves against one or other of these two camps. The social bond, in its consubstantial fragility, being of a different nature in the colonies, the Revolutionary phenomenon could not have the total and radical aspect that it had in France, where what was at stake, fundamentally, was the redefinition of the ancestral social bond. But the events opened up by the Revolutionary period were extremely serious and their consequences enormous. Their violence stands apart from Revolutionary violence in the sense that it occurred in a context in which politics, reduced to its purest state, was hardly at all concerned with ethical-legal niceties. This is the framework in which slave insurrection must be situated.

Anti-Slavery Insurrectionary Logic and its Outcome

It is quite apparent that the ideas of the Enlightenment and republican ideals were transmitted to the slaves. Bénot cites the case of a mulatto, Dodo Laplaine, who was arrested, deported to Cap in late 1791, flogged and branded for having read the Declaration of the Rights of Man to slaves.[18] There were not only freemen of colour but also priests, such as Father Delahaye, vicar of Dondon, who even acted as intermediaries between Laveaux, Toussaint and the rebels. Moreover, domestic slaves overheard conversations between their masters about what was happening in France.

The insurrection began quite early, particularly in Guadeloupe throughout the Capesterre region, but 1791 was the high point of revolt everywhere, especially in Saint-Domingue. Were the insurrections then a continuation of earlier revolts and marronnage, as a nationalist vision of Caribbean history would have it, which stresses continuity and dialectics and seeks to downplay the impact of the French Revolution? I think we can answer that question in the negative. Bénot summarizes all the novelty of the insurrection in this way:

> It was from the outset a mass uprising, in the framework of a region, not as before of just one plantation. In addition, an offensive plan can be seen in it, with a military and political objective from the very first phase: the seizure of Cap … especially and against every expectation of the whites, the revolt did not die out, it proved itself capable of engaging a prolonged struggle…. That was something new, which was translated after some hesitation at the time of the difficult period of late 1791 and early 1792, by the slogan 'general freedom', meaning a radical upheaval of the system.[19]

All that seems accurate, apart from a few reservations that might be made about the expression 'radical upheaval of the system'. A large number of factors certainly appear to be true.

The traditional political and social framework of colonial society had changed. It was a society in crisis – a social crisis (serious class conflict between colonists, traders, *grands blancs*, *petits blancs* and freemen of colour) and a political crisis (weakening of royal authority). The traditional modes of legitimizing the position of each social class were undergoing total change. Slave revolts could no longer have the same impact and resounded differently on the whole of colonial society as also on the colonial state, which was in crisis in France, too. But the crisis of colonial Caribbean societies, although precipitated by that of French society, which was entering upon a revolution, was not of the same nature as the latter. There were two series of events which affected one another, which often overlapped, but which remained parallel and retained their own logic. And that makes it difficult to interpret this Revolutionary period in the Caribbean historically unless the ultimate foundation of these events is interrogated – and that is not easy.

The slave insurrections, which until then had had only a social and cultural aspect, now had a *political connotation*. For the first time, the slaves became aware that an exit from slavery was now possible, not only gradually and on an individual basis, not by marronnage as an exit from the system, but *within the system itself*. The whole problem is to know what this 'radical upheaval of the system' that Yves Bénot writes of needs to make it authentically *revolutionary*, since it is perhaps not fitting to characterize every radical upheaval of a system as revolutionary. The question is, is revolution thinkable before the advent of modernity? Were the numerous systemic upheavals in antiquity *revolutionary*? That is, if the slave revolt was political in a narrow sense, since it followed strategies and sought a social upheaval, it was not political in the strong sense of the word, that is, it did not target the state nor the taking of political power (at least between 1791 and 1794). On what processes of legitimation, then, did this slave quest for freedom base itself? What did the notions of the 'Rights of Man' or the 'Rights of the Citizen' represent for him? The, to us, incontestable universality of the Rights of Man, being part of a 'must', a *sollen*, as the Germans say, does not signify that *ipso facto* men in every age and every place could have laid claim to it.[20] So in antiquity there could be an anti-slavery struggle without it even being possible to lay claim to or to adumbrate the notion of the Rights of Man, which has to do with modern natural law. It is the relationship of the slave of African origin with this modern vision of the world that remains difficult to grasp. We should however note that, later, both under the government of Toussaint Louverture and under the presidencies of Dessalines, Christophe and many others, such a problematic would be generally absent from political power in Haiti, and it is interesting to observe with the Haitian historian Vertus Saint-Louis that the structures of a non-democratic state were put in place from the time of Toussaint Louverture himself.[21]

Finally, several surprising aspects of the slave insurrection are the reason it was so difficult to understand and remained so until the abolition proclaimed by Sonthonax. 'In 1792', notes Bénot, curiously, 'once the blacks' insurrection was victorious in the west (with the victory over the white national guard at Port-au-Prince), the rebels returned to work in the plantations.'[22] Another 'curiosity' was that despite the abolition of slavery by Sonthonax in 1793, the blacks refused to come over to his side and stayed with the Spaniards. Toussaint, says James, claimed that 'the blacks wished a King and that they would lay down their arms only when he had been recognised'.[23] But, paradoxically, instead of analysing that as an original quest for the foundation of the political, James comments by asserting that '[t]o the slave the absolute monarchy and the republic were the same if both held him in slavery'. But who can say, for example, that the slaves would not have preferred a non-slave kingdom to a republic that was also anti-slavery. It remains equally surprising that elsewhere, in other colonies and during the same period, the slaves would have demanded a king and, as in Martinique at the beginning, would have fought alongside the royalists.

Things would change later, of course, but we are here trying to grasp the causes of this 'oddness'. The explanation usually given suggests that it was normal in a first phase for slaves to have been suspicious of white and mulatto patriots, who were slave-owners, and to have taken the side of the king since, at the end of the Ancien Régime, the conflict between the king, who wanted to alleviate somewhat the condition of the slaves, and the colonists, who were defending the principle of domestic justice, had been exacerbated. It is therefore understandable that the slaves should have feared finding themselves alone, without the mediation of royal power, with slave-owning white or mulatto settlers, tempted by autonomy and domination over the slaves with no mediating rule. Furthermore, it should come as no surprise that the vast majority of slaves did not grasp the very principle of the French Revolution in those times of trouble and uncertainty.

But, relevant though they may be, such explanations cannot suffice. We need to grasp the profound meaning of all these contradictory manifestations of the slaves' revolt. In our opinion, this is where political-philosophical anthropology can help us.

It is true that the ideas of freedom and equality were spread among the slaves by those who, for lack of a better term, we shall call their 'organic intellectuals': some white Jacobins, generally transients; some priests; some freemen of colour. One is at once struck by the organization of the revolt from the very beginning, going beyond the ceremony in the Bois Caïman. The insurrection in Saint-Domingue was initially organized on the Lenormand habitation by blacks, practically all of whom were drivers.

But the principal problem is to discern what the mass of slaves internalized under the slogan 'freedom and equality'. In France, this slogan not only referred to the social question but was intrinsically inseparable from its *political* content, and there freedom was understood in its essentially political sense. For Toussaint and the slaves, however, freedom was above all *general* freedom, that is, social liberation, abolition of slavery and access to *civil rights* for all, without that necessarily being perceived as access to *citizens' rights* for all.

What that means is that we must, like Arendt, make a distinction between *freedom* and *liberation*. What gives the French Revolution its originary character is that it was not simply a struggle for liberation. Liberation may be the condition of freedom but it does not automatically lead to it. The notion of freedom included in liberation is not identical with the desire for freedom.[24] The actual content of freedom is participation in public affairs, admission to the public realm. If the Revolution had aimed only at guaranteeing civil rights, it would not have aimed at freedom but at liberation.[25]

Arendt's comments are important since they enable us to ask whether the slaves, in the years preceding 1794, were truly thinking of political freedom or merely liberation from slavery. It seems to us that while liberation requires a political strategy, along with intelligence and technical skill in action, it does not automatically imply political freedom, which is essentially democratic and supposes a legitimation of action that is based on a modern institution of the social. But could the slave have one? It is important not to read the events unfolding from 1791 to 1793 in terms of what was to happen after 1804, even if the earlier period certainly determined, especially anthropologically, the socio-political future of independent Haiti.

We need then to return to the problematic of the king in which the blacks' action unfolded. The thing is hard to explain, and for that reason, so it seems to us, any number of historical studies are content to mention the fact or pass over it or simply reduce it to a failure to understand the French Revolution. We suggest the following explanation.

The slave was traversing a contradiction. He felt (and this was not necessarily conscious knowledge) that action for liberation deserved legitimation. It could only operate from a proper base, and that base was a pre-colonial vision of the institution of the social and of political authority. Since the majority of slaves were *bossales*, that is, born in Africa, the symbolic and legitimizing reconstruction did not start ex nihilo. We may be certain that it linked up with a problematic of African chieftaincy or kingship, whether or not we understand it in the sense given it by Pierre Clastres: avoidance of the institutionalization of political rule in state power.

A second possibility is that this process of legitimation may operate from something novel. But can we say that the problematic of modern natural law was already accessible to people from cultures that were not at all modern in their principles, even if it is true that the individuals who composed it had been detribalized by the slave trade and atomized (individualized?) as commodities on slave habitations? We may therefore suppose that there was a reworking of a religious vision of the world, articulating society on an originary and transcendent foundation, one that was religious and not secular, that is, proceeding from a re-enchantment of the world. This would explain the importance of the religious ceremonies that presided over the insurrections.

But all of these attempts seem to us to suffer from fundamental shortcomings. The first – the problematic of chieftaincy – is hardly to be realized in a society whose economic and social mechanisms are already largely modern, as we showed in the first part of this chapter. The second is marked by the fragility peculiar to a stage of symbolic reconstruction. It is surely wrong to regard voodoo as being at the origin of the slave insurrection. Everything suggests that the slaves were attempting to combine syncretically several forms of religious representations, including Christianity and even Islam,[26] and several forms of political representation, including republicanism.

The result is, in our view, that the slaves were bound for the time being to miss the profound meaning of the democratic foundation and the spirit of the French Revolution, since they had experienced the sublime in servitude, because they were moved by a compulsion to repeat or return to pre-modernity while at the same time their frameworks of existence were modern and they vaguely felt that the ideals of the French Revolution had something to say to them. It was a very harsh contradiction which would be resolved historically in the French-speaking Caribbean in two ways: by the Haitian experience and by assimilation.

In Haiti, the state would often be in the hands of a president for life or even a king (Christophe). The great mass of Haitian peasants, a majority of them *bossales* at the time of independence, would return to a problematic of avoidance of the state (or running away from it), leaving it in the hands of the Creole (black and mulatto) minority. But such a political power would never be founded authentically on a mode of legitimation deriving from modern natural law, against a philosophical background of the Rights of Man. Such a power was clearly in a problematic of chieftaincy, but a chieftaincy that was no longer of an African type. It had to operate with a minimum of the rationality of modern political power, having to ensure the resumption and development of the plantation economy and operate in the world capitalist market, at the same time as the peasant masses were developing a counter-plantation culture. The state so created would always be a bastard state, a political monstrosity, neither altogether old nor altogether modern, a state reduced to its most simple expression (its sole truly developed institution being the army), whose political-anthropological foundation had miscarried and which, in consequence, must always give death to be seen. Such in our view is the death-bearing essence of *macoutism*, the particular despotism produced in the Caribbean. It was only at the end of the regime of Jean-Claude Duvalier that we witnessed on the part of the Haitian peasants a resolute and massive quest for citizenship and effective participation in the formation of the law. It was quite simply a demand for *political freedom*, as if, two centuries after 1789, it was a matter of effectively accomplishing the Revolution.

As for the French Caribbean and Guyana, we could speak with Josette Fallope of a veritable 'assimilationist revolution'. After 1848, the slaves, by now overwhelmingly creolized, would aim for political freedom but would do so while allowing state power to remain in the hands of others, that is, the colonial metropole.

Conclusions

Reflection on these historical events, when it opens up more widely to political-anthropological problematics, shows that the Caribbean, because of its history, offers us the image of tragic societies in which modernity somehow is always ill-assumed. The peoples of our regions exist in their cultural particularities only because the slaves had to carry off an unheard-of accomplishment: to continue to survive while embarking on *integral* symbolic modifications (something which was not the case for slaves in antiquity), and to do so in a relatively short time. What have we inherited from that and inherited outside any simplistic historical determinism? What then of our 'historiality'?

Our discussion also aims to show, against an allegedly Marxist simplifying interpretation and also against a triumphant liberalism, that the French Revolution, at least in its essential foundations, harboured inescapable principles and that, at bottom, the ideas of freedom and equality are still not accomplished – as if the Revolution has not ended, and will it ever? The slave insurrection, at the dawn of this Revolutionary period, traversed what was a becoming of modernity, that is, of the new political-anthropological order that was being established. To reflect on it is to contribute also to an analysis of other possibilities, essentially negative ones, of modern republics, both the colonialist and imperialist adventures and the horror of the concentration camps.

Finally, against reductive differentialisms, if there is indeed one requirement to remember, it is that no liberation (whether social or national) is possible if it is not articulated on the idea of political freedom in the strong sense, that is, on founding principles that, even though they were able to flourish, through all the hazards of history, in a given culture, nevertheless belong to the human species as such.

Notes

1. M. Finley, *Ancient Slavery and Modern Ideology*, Harmondsworth, Penguin Books, 1983, p. 114.
2. Ibid., p. 115.
3. P. Clastres, *La Société contre l'État*, Paris, Éditions de Minuit, 1974 [Eng. trans., R. Hurley, *Society against the State*, Oxford, Basil Blackwell, 1977].
4. H. Arendt, *On Revolution*, Harmondsworth, Penguin, 1973, p. 23.
5. J. Thibau, *Le Temps de Saint-Domingue*, Paris, Éditions J.-C. Lattès, 1987, p. 63.
6. See on this subject the thoughts of L. Hurbon in 'Esclavage moderne et État de droit' in *Genèse de l'État moderne en Méditerranée*, Collectif publié par l'École française de Rome, Rome, 1993, and also 'État et religion au XVIIe siècle face à l'esclavage au Nouveau Monde', in *Peuples méditerranéens*, Nos. 27–8, 1984.
7. See J. Thibau, op. cit., p. 30.
8. M. Alexandre, *Lectures de Platon*, Paris, Bordas, 1966.
9. A. Gautier, *Les Soeurs de Solitude*, Paris, Éditions Caribéennes, 1985.
10. M. Richir, *Du sublime en politique*, Paris, Payot, 1991, p. 14.
11. E. Glissant, *Le Discours antillais*, Paris, Éditions du Seuil, 1981 [partial Eng. trans. J. M. Dash, *Caribbean Discourse: Selected Essays*, Charlottesville, University Press of Virginia, 1992].
12. Y. Bénot, *La Révolution française et la fin des colonies*. Paris, Éditions de La Découverte, 1987.
13. A. Pérotin-Dumon, *Être patriote sous les tropiques*, Basse-Terre, Bibliothèque d'histoire antillaise, 1985, p. 121.
14. Ibid., p. 225.
15. C. L. R. James, *Les Jacobins noirs*, Paris, Éditions Caribéennes, 1983, p. 58 [Eng. orig., *The Black Jacobins*, London, Secker and Warburg, 1938, p. 50; 2nd rev. ed. New York, Vintage Books, 1963].
16. M. Richir, op. cit., p. 15 [J. Michelet, *Historical View of the French Revolution*, Eng. trans. C. Cocks, London, H. G. Bohn, 1860, p. 393].
17. Ibid.
18. Y. Bénot, op. cit., p. 139.
19. Ibid., p. 141.
20. On the difficulty of understanding the relationship between the universality of the Rights of Man and cultural differences, see our article 'Que peut être une fondation universelle de normes', in Cahiers de Philosophie Politique et Juridique, *Tradition et argumentation*, Université de Caen, 1992.
21. V. Saint-Louis, 'Régime militaire et règlement de culture', *Chemins Critiques, Nationalisme*, Vol. 3, Nos 1–2, Port-au-Prince, CIDIHCA, December 1983.
22. Y. Bénot, op. cit., p. 158.
23. C. L. R. James, op. cit., p. 38 [Eng. orig., p. 99].
24. H. Arendt, op. cit., p. 29.
25. Ibid., p. 32.
26. On this, see the article by G. Barthélemy, 'Propos sur le Bois Caïman', *Chemins Critiques. 1771–1991, Qui a peur de la démocratie en Haïti?* Vol. 2, No. 3, May 1992.

Chapter 2

Forms of Resistance in Bourbon, 1750–1789

Prosper Ève

ONE OF A slave's concerns is becoming free. Wherever colonial slavery reigned and for so long as it reigned, slaves forged weapons to contest this system in their own way. Bourbon, which was institutionally and definitively colonized after 1664 and gradually opted for slavery in the 1680s,[1] is no exception. After a little over half a century's experience of this system in this food-producing island – where the internal order of each habitation was the responsibility of its master, who would brook no external interference in his affairs – slave resistance had taken on its own peculiar features. It was not something in which the majority was involved. Most of those who found themselves taken to Bourbon were unable to make use of the sea because it was by sea that they had been torn from the land of their birth and their kin, and locked up in this unknown island. Only the Malagasies, who had made the shortest journey (800 kilometres), found it easy to turn to the sea to recover their freedom. As slaves could not move about freely, the only place in Bourbon with which they were really familiar was their master's habitation. Thus, they endeavoured to show themselves to best advantage so as to make their life as bearable as possible. In order to meet certain needs, they did of course break a few rules, but with no awareness of upsetting social peace. The fate and behaviour of domestic slaves and talented slaves were different from those of field slaves. Those who demonstrated their willingness to adapt to the dominant economic and social model and thereby reached positions of responsibility as drivers or watchmen, thinking that they were on the narrow path that led to manumission, were condemned to offer daily proof that they truly merited their master's confidence. Those who belonged to smallholders with fewer than five slaves eking out a wretched living, being often in a situation of relative independence, would do nothing that might make their fate worse. As for Creole slaves, they could not dream of somewhere other than Bourbon, since that was where they had been born. It was certainly not from their ranks that the greatest challenge could arise. Yet resistance took a wide variety of forms.

The major form of resistance was marronnage, the most serious crime of all, according to Louis XV's edict of December 1723. It made such a mark on the island that many place names were derived from it when it was at its height (1700–50): Mafate, from the Malagasy 'maha-fat', which gives death; Cilaos, from the Malagasy 'tsilaosa', the country where cowards do not go; and Mahavel, from the Malagasy 'maha-velona', which gives life. Some places retain the memory of famous maroons (Dimitile, Matouta, Caverne à Cotte, Piton d'Anchain), or attest to their presence in days gone by (Ilet Marron, Brûlé Marron, Ravines des Cafres, Plaine-des-Cafres). And then there are the legendary figures who haunt the collective imagination: Anchaing and Héva,[2] Mario,[3] Mafate, Bâle and Diampare.[4] The researcher can get a pretty accurate idea of the extent of marronnage from statements made by masters,[5] reports on the capture of maroons,[6] statements made by heads of detachments on their return from pursuits,[7] a few reports of maroons killed in the woods[8] and a number of file dockets of maroons and sentences pronounced by the Conseil supérieur.[9] While marronnage was the route most favoured by slaves at odds with their environment, it must be acknowledged that some of the female maroons were carried off by force by maroons when they attacked coastal habitations, while others had simply followed their partners.

Other major forms of resistance, alongside marronnage, were the refusal to conceive, which involved a good number of black women and forced masters to spend money to ensure the survival of their holding and the continuation of the system, and acts of resistance associated with the defence of their cultural identity (religion, music, dance and so forth), which the ruling group did not perceive as a direct threat.

There were other forms of resistance that also worried masters and those responsible for keeping order and social peace, but they were minor in the sense that few slaves engaged in them. First was flight by sea. It was different from marronnage since in this case the authorities were prompt to take steps to deal with masters' negligence. Then there were plots. Here the research is relatively well documented, as rulers outdid one another in nipping plots in the bud and punishing those responsible. Finally, there was suicide.

Major Forms of Resistance

Marronnage

IMPORTANCE AND REASONS FOR THIS CHOICE – Between 1725 and 1749, 199 *grands marrons* (slaves who had run away long before) were caught by hunters, of whom 125 were killed in the woods and 74 captured, representing 62.8 and 37.2 per cent respectively, and between 1750 and 1765, 506 *grands marrons* were hunted down, of whom 145 (28.7 per cent) were killed in the woods and 335 captured (66.3 per cent).[10] At the beginning of the period of royal government, fewer and fewer heads of detachments were going into the woods to pursue them, but that does not mean that *grand marronnage* had become a minor matter. If it had, Crémont in 1772 would not have regretted the sort of embourgeoisement of Creoles that was turning them away from this activity. 'Many colonists', he says, 'have taken to wearing shoes, and as soon as a shoe has been put on a Creole's foot, he is no longer up to hunting down maroon blacks.'[11] Between 1766 and 1788, 352 maroons (90 per cent) were taken (slightly more than in the previous period), and 39 (10 per cent) were killed. These figures do not give an overall idea of this form of marginality because there are often gaps in the documentation, especially for the *petits marrons*, that is, those who had left their master's habitation for the first time, were not taken in by experienced maroons and lurked about not far from the habitation, lacking the courage and energy to face the hilly, wooded, unpredictable terrain, before giving themselves up a day or two later or being taken by a passer-by. The maroon's path was such an obstacle course that his first attempts had to be abandoned. Of course, for the master, every slave who was not found was a maroon. But what are we to think of Louis Jean, aged 3, whom Pierre-Robert Técher came to declare a maroon on 26 February 1782?[12] If this master was telling the truth, how are we to explain the flight of such a young child? If he was not, was he using this statement to conceal a terrible crime? Generally, little black boys and girls – except for those born in the woods – manifested their rejection of the system by running away when they were about 8 to 12 years old. Thus, Cotte, who ran away on 5 October 1736 for the first time at the age of 12, gave herself up the next day. She ran away again on 9 October 1738 and, when she was retaken four days later, received 100 strokes of the lash. She ran away for the last time on 1 June 1743 and was killed at age 28, on 17 June 1752 by François Damour *fils*.[13] She was not the only one to suffer such a fate. The treatment meted out to slaves and the break with their original cultural environment certainly caused trauma among the most thoughtful, especially as masters in Bourbon, from a very early date, saw the advantage of dividing in order to rule and favoured dispersing ethnic groups. Slaves were imported from different cultural areas: India, Madagascar and the east coast of Africa (Sofala, Mozambique, Ibo, coast of Zenguebar, islands of Quiloa and Zanzibar).

Slaves' adaptation to the reality of Bourbon does not appear to have posed any problems in terms of food and housing. The few criticisms made in the area of food concern not its quality but only its quantity. François, interrogated on 26 June 1776, said that 'his master is too wicked and does not give him enough millet to eat'.[14] Mathieu, a first-time maroon, arrested after two months, said at his interrogation on 11 April 1776 that 'his master mistreats him too much and refuses him food to eat, that if he was a good master, he would be happy to serve him'.[15] Marie, an Indian woman, confirmed on 30 November 1787 that her master, Sieur Servant Moreau, 'is too bad and gives her only one meal a day'.[16] Moreover, the *grands marrons*, organized in a band in camps, did not baulk at growing maize and cassava, despite the fact that they were monotonous staples in the daily ration of slaves in the habitations. However, their food was slightly more varied and abundant, since they also planted *songes*, sweet potatoes, and the forest offered them honey as well as papaws and palm-cabbages. Slaves built their own houses after the style of their old country shortly after their arrival. Their walls of straw and wood were reproductions of their original huts. Their calabashes and earthenware pots were their ordinary everyday utensils. That being the case, masters cannot be accused of being tyrannical because their slaves' huts were squalid.

Farming methods varied from one habitation to the next, but generally speaking they were hard for the slaves to bear and required them to make enormous efforts in order to adapt. In their home countries they were not all used to working the land. Those who had been engaged in farming had not necessarily grown the same crops as in Bourbon. Africans, used to hunting, fishing and warrior activities, and, for some, slash and burn farming, doubtless improvised to make the most of the land in Bourbon and grow rice, wheat, maize and tobacco. Without training and with rudimentary tools, the new slave had to show himself productive and motivated, with little more to guide him than a few words of advice from a driver or some old slave, the master being very keen on results. Coffee, the main cash crop in Bourbon from the 1710s to the beginning of the nineteenth century, required land clearing and heavy physical work at and after harvest-time. At that time, the island was in the earliest stages of its development, and slaves were engaged in the laborious work of land-clearing, road-building and carrying water. Work, which no slave could escape, was organized and had to be performed regularly, without fail, on pain for the slave of being reprimanded and punished by a vigilant and zealous driver. To justify his marronnage, Dominique replied laconically on 26 June 1776: '[M]e no able.'[17] What did he mean if not that he lacked the resources to blend into the Bourbon mould, to be the model and docile slave that the colony so needed?

In any case, agriculture was not the only sector of activity that precipitated a reflex of resistance among some slaves. Repeated punishment forced fishermen who did not bring back enough fish or big enough fish to run away. In 1787, Félix,[18] Pedec[19] and Narcisse[20] found themselves in that situation. A slave assigned to a particular task that did not correspond truly to his capacities might choose the solution of marronnage. François, a slave belonging to Sieur Mangueret, who had been assigned to do the cooking, ran away because he could not face being beaten.[21] It was clearly these blows, so generously distributed by masters and drivers, that led workers who were on the receiving end, or who feared that they were about to receive them, to resist or run away, despite the risks involved. The edict of December 1723 provided for the cutting-off of ears and branding with the fleur-de-lis if the slave's absence lasted a month, a second branding and cutting of the hamstring for a second offence, and death for the third.[22] Laurent, a maroon from 7 April 1754 to 15 July 1754, and then from 22 November 1754 to 22 May 1756, explained his actions by saying that 'his master is too bad. He has him punished severely for the slightest faults'.[23] After his fifth running away on 27 November 1755, Manuel admitted at his capture on 6 February 1756 'that he had run away because he missed the roll-call of blacks and because his driver, without regard to the fact that he was sick, wanted him to ground coffee day and night, which he could not bear'.[24] François, interrogated in 1757, after having run away four times since 1754, revealed 'that he went there ... to get away from the ill-treatment of his master who used to hit with him with a stick every day'.[25] Thomas and Pauline, his wife, captured after a marronnage of more than a month, agreed 'that they went away because their master beat them too much and for no reason'.[26] At his interrogation on 26 October 1757, Jouan could not have been more precise in expressing his dismay. 'His master maltreated him too much', he said, 'and it was all the same to him whether he died from the blows or with the help of justice.'[27] Resistance was also the fate of those who lost money or something belonging to their master. That is what happened to Gaëtan,[28] Colle[29] and many others. Those who were unjustly accused of stealing and who had been unable to convince their master of their innocence had no other solution than to run away so as not to face their master's wrath. Jupiter, a maroon for the third time, confessed on 21 June 1773 that 'his comrades having eaten some maize that he was looking after, he was afraid of being beaten by his master'.[30] In 1776, following a theft of maize on his master's habitation, Télémaque was so severely flogged that he ran away; he was retaken after two months of marronnage.[31] Augustin, whose master had lost a boar, ran away because his master had promised him two hundred strokes of the lash if he failed to find it straightaway.[32] His master having accused him of having stolen a clove tree, Charles ran away.[33] Those who contravened some custom or other of the habitation preferred to use their own devices to avoid punishment. Romain, a maroon for a year, acknowledged when he was taken 'that he had gone out for a walk without permission one Sunday, and that, fearing a flogging, he did not dare return'.[34] Barbe, a slave belonging to Sieur Pierre Valentin, went to relax at the house of one Baptiste, a free black, without her mistress's permission. As she had spent a night outside, she no longer dared to return home for fear of being flogged.[35] Avril confessed 'that he had been with his master's gang of blacks threshing maize and had fallen asleep in the kitchen, and that not being with the other blacks in the morning to go to work, he was afraid of being chained and so he left'.[36] It was not, as some have rather hastily written, laziness that was the reason for their decision. In 1776, the case of Pierre-Louis, a slave belonging to Sieur de Villecourt, speaks volumes. One Sunday he went to work on his own account to get some money together, and the driver having flogged him when he came back, he ran away soon after.[37]

THE MAROON, A HUNTED DESERTER – Relations between resistant slaves and loyal slaves were difficult. On 25 December 1750, Joseph de Guigné de La Bérangerie informed the clerk of the Conseil supérieur that three of his slaves who had been watching his flocks had found in the Ravine à Jacques an *ajoupa* housing a black, a negress and a black boy. The black having sought to defend himself, they warded off the blows by striking him with a spear, of which he died.[38] Like the official maroon hunters, collaborating slaves opted for the easy way out of putting the maroon where he could cause no harm. Could three of them not have overcome this slave, who cannot have been tremendously strong, without using their spears? On 17 January 1751, Alexis, a Creole slave belonging to Claude Mollet, having learnt that maroons had caused damage on several habitations, took himself up to the heights of his master's habitation and, on reaching the Ravine d'Arnauld, he found in a cave Laurent, a maroon black belonging to François Ricquebourg. When Laurent attempted to flee, he hit him with the spear and then stabbed him several times with a knife and took him to the district prison.[39] On 22 April 1751, Augustin, belonging to Sieur Deheaulme, watchman of the habitation, having surprised a maroon stealing a head of bananas, took off after him with his dogs. When he described his feat, Augustin spelt out that, armed with a knife, the maroon had jumped on him, and he only had a small stick. In the hand-to-hand fight that followed, he succeeded in grabbing the knife and killing him.[40] Had this watchman not reversed the weapons? Who is he trying to convince that a watchman could decide to pursue a maroon armed only with a small stick? At the beginning of May 1755, after noting the disappearance of a large number of fowl, four slaves belonging to Joachim Lautret decided to go and visit the heights of the habitation and arrested two maroons whom they presumed to be the thieves.[41] On 6 December 1766, René Duguet warned the clerk of the Conseil that Jouan, a slave belonging to Antoine Gubillon, had attacked his slave Gaspard, who had been sent to bring home a negress belonging to François Gonneau, with a blow with a stick on the right hand when he saw him attempt to catch her when she had slipped his clutches. Jouan had also told Gaspard that Théodore, a slave belonging to René Duguet – who captured him in marronnage and had him punished by cutting off his ears and branding him with the fleur-de-lis – was firmly awaiting the opportunity to take his life as he no longer cared about his own.[42] Resistants sometimes had the last word. Sieur Louis Maunier, having a negress who had run away, sent one of his blacks to find her. When he reached the heights of Sieur Hyacinthe Ricquebourg's habitation, he met two maroon blacks. They grabbed him, questioned him, tied him up, lit a fire, held his left leg over the flames until it was burned, and then left him.[43] But their victory was short-lived. After such outrages, they were caught, and had to face two charges. On 27 October 1751, François was sentenced to receive two hundred lashes and to carry a forty-pound chain for life at his master's for having stabbed the slaves Cupidon and Alexandre who were trying to arrest him.[44] Noël, who had dared hit back at Sieur Gabriel Grosset's blows and speared him a few times, was to have his wrist cut and then be hanged and strangled to death.[45] The hunters were so anxious to wipe out the rebels that their aggressiveness drove the *grands marrons* to hide farther and farther away, in the most inaccessible places. Until the 1760s, most of these were at the headwaters of rivers – the Rivières des Marsouins, des Roches, du Mât, des Galets, Saint-Étienne, du Rempart – at Bras de la Plaine, in pays Brûlé. In the 1770s and 1780s, they took refuge on the tallest peak, Piton des Neiges, 3,069 metres high.[46]

Nothing could break the determination of true resistants. The repression unleashed by the royal government had no educational value. Among the *grands marrons* sentenced for the first time, some did not have their ears cut off because there was no one to carry out the sentences, but only received lashes. Conversely, those sentenced a second time all suffered their punishment. Yet many third-time maroons were sentenced by the Conseil supérieur to a violent, spectacular and terrifying death, if they had escaped death at the hands of a hunter. Some *grands marrons* eked out their lives above the habitations and came to scrounge on their own master's habitation or on neighbouring ones. If they committed these robberies by breaking and entering and if, in addition, they were carrying weapons or attacked a freeman or killed a slave, then even for a first offence they did not escape the death penalty.

The hunt for resistants was a lucrative activity, so they were not safe anywhere. Whites, whether organized into detachments or not, and free or slave collaborators could hunt them down like ordinary wild animals, in the name of law and order. In January 1750, Hilaire Touchard, finding himself near the habitation of Paul Laval, saw a slave. He called on him to stop. When he failed to do so, he shot him dead.[47] Richard, a free Creole, having gone fishing on 12 December 1787 in the headwaters of the Rivière des Galets with two comrades, found four Malagasy slaves in the Plaine des Chicots; he managed to capture two of them, whom he took to the prison.[48] In September 1780, Geneviève, a Creole slave who had run away for the first time after losing her mistress's money, was retaken by a soldier near La Redoute.[49] The hen house that Maho, a slave belonging to Sieur Girard, was guarding was visited in the night of Sunday 29 May 1785, and the next morning with two of his master's slaves and one belonging to Sieur Antoine Maunier, he went to find the thieves' tracks. Armed with his master's gun, he explored the heights of the habitation with the other members of his team and ended up discovering two maroons. He killed one and wounded the other.[50]

Masters and loyal slaves saw in the resistant, whatever his age and physical strength, an extremely dangerous individual. If he came face to face with them, any maroon who still had the slightest desire to stay alive was well advised to obey commands to stop. If not, a shot would ring out. So strong was the fear among the hunters that they really did very little to bring back those they discovered alive. The reports of heads of detachments on their return from activity are so similar that the reader could easily believe that they were in fact performing a ritual. Until 1752, these chaps with their guns rarely made proper pursuits. They even fired on a maroon child who was running away. They were so intimidated by his presence that they seem to have had no other solution than to kill him. On 31 January 1752, François Mussard at the head of a detachment found along the arm of the Étang du Gôl a camp of eight wretched huts made of leaves that could accommodate about fifteen maroons. He visited it with his men and found a little black boy about 11 years old and a little girl about 9. As these children tried to run away when they saw them, two riflemen opened fire. Pierre Técher killed the little boy and Silvestre Grosset wounded the little girl.[51]

MAROONS, A PUBLIC DANGER EXPLOITED WHEN IN A POSITION OF WEAKNESS – Maroons were dangerous because they attacked habitations. Raids by maroons were frequent in the first half of the eighteenth century, but they continued after that. Some slaves who cut loose by running away to the inland parts of the island formed themselves into bands and sought to organize their life. To build their camp and engage in farming, they needed tools. As they could not make them, they took them where they could find them, on the habitations in lowland areas. They organized raids. On occasion, they carried off one or two negresses and brought back some meat, too. Hunters would seize the tools in the camps when they passed through, and the surviving maroons had little choice but to go back and look for others. Thus, on 29 February 1750, Sieur Patrice Droman declared that maroons had attacked his habitation in the heights of Sainte-Marie the night before. They had stolen several of his cooking pots, axes, long saws and other household utensils, killed a Cafre and taken away a Malagasy negress, Agathe.[52] In the night of Thursday to Friday 4 June 1750, at about 8 o'clock, maroons attacked the habitation of François Garnier in the heights of Saint-Paul. They killed the Malagasy negress Soye and wounded Francisque, whom they carried off with them. They made off with the canvas of two mattresses and one of a palliasse, two pigs, two axes, an adze, four picks, six scrapers, a bill hook, a cooking pot, a pewter plate and four pewter spoons, a sugar bowl, four goblets, five flasks, a brass coffee pot, thirty chickens and five sticks of tobacco.[53] On 22 March 1765, Claude Garnier reported that fifteen maroons had made an incursion on his habitation, wounded a black and carried off an eighteen-year-old Malagasy negress named Rosalie.[54] On 7 August 1775, Mr Henry Paulin Panon Desbassyns declared to the notary Jean-Baptiste Larabit that on the night of 5–6 August, several maroons had visited his habitation in the Grande Ravine. They had forced their way into the watchman Gaëtan's hut, manhandled him, and then carried off the negress Thérèze, aged 35.[55] The latter was found in the woods two days later, killed with two knife cuts in the throat and stomach.[56]

Resistants inspired fear because they were armed. On 14 September 1750, before the clerk of the Saint-Paul district, Pierre Dejean, a slave belonging to Sieur Delanux, Mananque, affirmed that on his return from Saint-Denis, he had met coming down from the Grande Chaloupe three slaves, one carrying a very large iron spear, the second an iron one and a wooden one, and the third a wooden one. Seeing himself surrounded, he threw down his calabash full of syrup and took to his heels.[57] Resistants had more than just spears: they also had guns and lead shot. In October 1751, when François Mussard discovered on the Îlette à Cordes a camp of thirty wooden huts that could accommodate fifty blacks, he ordered the blacks in his detachment to go through the camp with a fine toothcomb. In a small cave they found two guns in working order, in the trunk of a tree a double-barrelled gun with shot and four quarters of powder in a horn, eleven iron cooking pots, axes, spades, billhooks and iron spears. They took them all away with them.[58] When their camp was attacked, the maroons had not been able to use these weapons, seized in raids and carefully concealed, because they were not to hand, nor did they know exactly when the hunters – who had a liking for attacking at dawn – were going to appear and launch their attack. Their camp was well guarded by a look-out and by dogs which gave the alarm, but when the hunters arrived, they were taken by surprise and had no choice but to get away as fast as possible. Sometimes, to hold up the advance of a detachment climbing a cliff, the maroons would roll stones and throw them down on them, but they would be forced to abandon their positions to escape the gunfire.[59] Only the nimblest of them had any chance of getting away. Those most threatened preferred to end their lives by throwing themselves over a rampart rather than surrender. But some were panic-stricken and would throw themselves on their knees to beg for mercy. Dogs were very useful to the maroons to warn of the presence of hunters. On 15 June 1752, the head of a detachment, Patrice Droman, stated that in an attack on a camp at Bras de la Plaine, his men had killed thirty-one dogs.[60]

Once he had been retaken, a resistant sometimes showed his determination by refusing to reveal the reason why he had run away. Knowing that what a slave had to say only had any weight with a magistrate when it suited him, Mathèse on 5 July 1776, Leveillé on 21 June 1787 and Crabe on 3 May 1787 replied ironically 'Just like that!' to the question 'Why did you run way?'[61]

A resistant who had been wounded found himself in a very unhappy situation. Hunters would take advantage of his weakness to apply pressure on him to reveal the whereabouts of other camps. They would promise him that he would surely be pardoned. The case of Taffique, a Malagasy slave belonging to the Morau estate, is very clear. He had run away the first time for seven days, from 21 to 28 February 1756, a second time for three days, from 24 to 27 February 1765, and then a third time on 1 December 1765; he was not tried when he was taken in May 1768 by François Mussard's detachment. Acting on the orders of Sieur Crémont, president of the Conseil supérieur, he was handed over to Sieur Cerveaux, one of the members of the detachment, as 'this black could greatly help us discover the maroon camps in the woods'. Marie Siavel, a negress belonging to Sieur Duboishardy, who was pregnant by Taffique, was granted to Sieur Cerveaux.[62] But what are we to think of the statements made by the head of a detachment, Jean Dugain, on 3 June 1758, when he asserted that as he moved on the Rivière des Remparts, Mac, a wounded maroon, described to him the camps that he knew of and offered to act as his guide? Dugain hastened to accept the offer, had the marooon tied up and made him walk in front of the detachment: 'Having led them near to a certain cave in the upper Rivière des Remparts and having assured them that this was the place where his comrades were, at that very moment, the said blacks' dogs began to bark very loudly. The detachment rushed to try and immediately surround the cave from which there were two exits through which the blacks were getting away.'[63] Had Mac deliberately made this proposal, or was it forced on him by the head of the detachment? It is difficult to know one way or the other. But, by tying Mac up to carry out this dirty deed, the detachment proved that it had no confidence in him. If that is the case, then how far can he be said to have been the instigator of this proposal? In an attack on a maroon camp in the Rivières des Galets on the Îlette des Lataniers by François Mussard's detachment in December 1752, three slaves caught in the cross-fire knelt in front of the hunters and begged for mercy. In his statement, soon after this scene, the head of the detachment was emphatic that he had asked the black Samson the position of the Laverdure camp a first time and that he had

had a negative response. When he repeated his question with the promise of getting him pardoned, the maroon immediately replied

> that he could take him there and would do so when asked.... When they reached the bottom of the Rivière Saint-Étienne, they found a different camp from the Laverdure one. He asked if could go and look for those who were inside. Mussard having agreed, he went in to distract them and prevent the dogs from barking. Meanwhile, the detachment took up positions around the huts and arrested the occupants.[64]

In this particular case, the sudden turnaround occurred long after the application of any pressure.

Did hunters not dangle in front of wounded resistants the possibility of treatment that might reduce their sufferings to get them to make a confession? Some of what the hunters said makes this a plausible hypothesis. François Mussard and his men had set out on 21 October 1751 from Saint-Paul and arrived on the Îlette à Cordes on 26 October. Having observed huts on a rampart, they took that direction and met a black man, a negress and a black boy aged about 9, who fled as soon they saw them. Unable to outrun them, the head of the detachment gave orders to his riflemen to fire on the two adults and pursue the child. The woman was killed and the man wounded. Mussard wanted to know if they were alone and plied the wounded man with questions. The man told him that on the other side of the little island there was a camp where fifty blacks were living and another smaller one with ten maroons a league away.[65] It would seem that Mussard is not telling us the whole truth about what happened. It is rather worrying that when he questioned the young slave captured by Antoine Cerveau, he did not get the hoped-for replies. 'Seeing that the little black did not want to reply and kept beating about the bush at everything he asked him', he called a halt to his interrogation.[66] Why would a wounded adult maroon agree to betray his brothers when a child kept quiet? There can be little doubt that it was the treatment promised by the hunter and the fear of being hit again and then being abandoned to die if he refused to co-operate that drove him to make his confessions. Not knowing how serious his condition was and unaware that a seriously wounded maroon was never brought back to base until the early 1750s because he hampered the hunters' movement through the woods and river beds, Samson did not see the trick and played into their game.

Once captured, *petits marrons* were returned to their master, and it was up to him to punish them, while *grands marrons* were tried by the Conseil supérieur, which enforced the edict of December 1723 in all its rigour until 1775. The ordinance of 4 May 1775 provided for appeals, and in some cases, the punishment laid down and inflicted in the first instance was reduced. *Grand marrons* were now sentenced to serve for life in His Majesty's galleys with a chain round their neck weighing from 25 to 30 pounds and be branded with the letters 'GAL' on the cheek and each arm. Maroons who were hamstrung were first taken to the hospital where they remained until completely healed, and then handed back to their master.[67] Thus, in 1787, the Malagasy Lundy – who did not understand French, did not know to whom he belonged, had deserted his habitation for two months because a slave had whispered to him that 'in the woods you don't have to work at all' and did not know the punishment awaiting him – was sent back to his master on appeal after receiving thirty lashes at the hands of the man responsible for carrying out punishments.[68] The Malagasy Ferla, who also did not understand French and explained his running away by saying 'that he followed the path that a friend had shown him to go into the woods', was returned to his master,[69] as was Julie, a slave belonging to Isidor Robert, whose 'mistress made her life a misery when she was pregnant'.[70] Saturne, who had been on the island for three years and had run away because his master punished him every day, received fifty lashes after running away for the first time.[71]

Did they suffer only the punishments laid down by the civil authorities? Some scepticism is in order, in light of the statement of Isabelle, a slave belonging to Sieur Calvert, on 15 July 1775. She had run away for just two days for the first time, not for a month, and yet her master had her ears cut off: 'The white who had taken her took her to the prison at Sainte-Suzanne from where she was brought here by whites with whom there was a black belonging to her master Calvert who had her ears cut off.'[72] When some tongues were loosened because the interests of the powerful were at stake, the fate meted out to some of these resistants comes through in the language used. Thus, on 19 November 1752, André, Sieur Lambert's driver, asserted that on the 15th, at about 8 o'clock in the evening, some slaves belonging to his master having arrested the maroon Laurent, a slave belonging to Sieur Saint-Léger, on their habitation, he had ordered that Laurent be tied to a picket and flogged before he took him back to his master. Jolibois, Mr Bosse's driver, claimed that he had met this slave on the 16th on his way to Mr Galenne's to have a second chain put on his feet. Sieur Saint-Léger's blacks, who were escorting him, were driving him along under a hail of blows from a peach-wood stick. A certain Sans Façon, an ex-soldier and Sieur Saint-Léger's driver, was also maltreating him. To escape the blows, Laurent had flung himself into La Saline ravine. Coming back from Mr Galenne's, Laurent had been 'carried trussed up, bound by the feet'. In the conflict between these two masters concerning the pains felt by Laurent in his head and chest, Sieur de Saint-Lambert blamed Saint-Léger's slaves and not his own.[73]

Refusal to Conceive

This type of resistance involved a good many negresses. They might not have been able to break their irons, but they did not want to bear the responsibility of having put a human being into slavery. To reduce, if not eradicate, resistance by slaves, the royal government had decided that slaves should be converted to Catholicism without being taught to read and write. The Lazarists who worked in Bourbon after 1714 did not institute a religion on the cheap for them. They taught the same morality of everyday life to free and slave alike. They instructed them that conception should occur only in the framework of a family bound by the sacred ties of marriage, when the slave was not master of himself, and that procreation was the purpose of marriage. For them, 'to baptize an adult slave without marrying him at the same time is to condemn the neophyte to concubinage and immorality'. But such a project had little chance of success in so far as masters could not renounce their right of ownership and their authority by allowing a slave woman to leave the habitation to follow her husband, or to ensure a balance between the sexes on their habitation. According to the work of R. Bousquet, in both Saint-Paul and Saint-Denis, the rate of illegitimate births within the slave population rose between 1700 and 1739. In Saint-Denis, it rose from 12.5 per cent of total births in 1700–9 to 32.5 per cent in 1710–19, 40.5 per cent in 1720–9 and 53 per cent in 1730–9, and in Saint-Paul from 5.7 per cent in 1700–9 to 38 per cent in 1710–19, 37.2 per cent in 1720–9 and 59.4 per cent in 1730–9.[74] Our own research shows that this trend became even more marked in the second half of the eighteenth century. It rose to 43.5 per cent in Saint-Paul in 1740–9, 52.7 per cent in 1750–9, 68 per cent in 1760–9 and 93.4 per cent in 1770–9.[75] While the priest asked the father's name for illegitimate children and succeeded in getting it in 80 per cent of cases and entered it in the written certificate, they were still illegitimate.

Elsewhere, action by the clergy made little progress. In Saint-Benoît, right from the time the parish was established, the illegitimacy rate was over 75 per cent of total births. From 1734 to 1743, it reached 78 per cent and from 1744 to 1752, 75.3 per cent.[76] In Saint-Pierre, from 1728 to 1737 it was 66.3 per cent, from 1748–57, 70.2 per cent.[77] Between 1730 and 1739, the average number of children per union in Saint-Paul and Saint-Denis was between 2.27 and 2.32 children as against 5.6 on average per family among the whites of Saint-Paul: 'The slave population adopted a Malthusian behaviour as the earlier the age of marriage, the lower the age of the mother at the last birth.'[78] It limited births by delaying the conception of the first child: fewer than 15 per cent of slaves in Saint-Paul conceived their eldest child in the first year of marriage as against 43.14 per cent among whites. While slaves married in the first half of the eighteenth century, they were able within that framework to express their rejection of servitude by limiting births.[79] This was an attitude that went against the interests of masters and administrators. Through marriage and a high birth rate, the former would have liked to have slaves cheaply, and the latter to reduce Bourbon's dependence in the area of slave recruitment. Under the monarchy, Bellecombe and Crémont attempted to encourage marriage and the birth rate among slaves by rewards. In 1769 a piece of blue cloth was given to Dorothée, a slave belonging to Mr Panon, 'in consideration of the two twins that she bore for three consecutive years … and to encourage her to continue on the same path'.[80] Their proposal to grant freedom to black couples who had presented their masters with ten slaves shows their desire to combat slave resistance, even though the initiative failed. Generally, the number of pregnancies was reduced by suckling, which rendered three women in four temporarily sterile, by natural sterility or sterility acquired before the age of menopause, and above all by the poor conditions of birthing. Negresses achieved this result by practising abortion. The author of a memoir on Bourbon in 1785 attributed the failure of the policy of trying to raise the birth rate primarily to that fact: 'The principal cause is that most of these women destroy the fruit of their womb not wanting to bring into the world children as unhappy as themselves.'[81] Slave society may have been permissive, but the survival of slavery rested essentially on the slave trade. It is the slave trade that accounts for the increase in the slave population, which represented 80 per cent of the overall population between 1765 and 1789, rising between those two dates from 21,047 to 37,894.

Forms of Resistance in the Area of Religion and Culture

In the religious domain, masters undermined the work of Westernization and contributed, despite themselves, to the success of the battle waged by slaves to cling to their ancestral culture and resist slavery. By converting the slaves, the clergy ensured the unity of the faith, it is true, but in so doing it altered their beliefs, and fought everything that smacked of superstition. The clergy served the interest of the state and the masters. The clergy alone could teach slaves the hierarchical pattern of society in which the king was superior to his subjects, the master to his slaves, parents to children and men to women. The clergy alone could advise them to be grateful to those who were their superiors and make them accept that they had a moral obligation to stay in their place because it was God who had placed them there. Hell was used to terrify those who did not resign themselves to their status and sought to rebel. It also served as a hope of revenge since it was where God would send bad masters and oppressors. The clergy alone could make them accept, too, that all misfortunes – epidemics, sickness, poor harvest, poverty, natural disasters – originated in men's sins.

To succeed in its mission among the slaves, the clergy had to get to know their language and count on the unfailing collaboration of masters. In Bourbon, the vast majority of colonists had little time for Christian teaching, since by strengthening the slaves' unity, Catholicism threatened also to strengthen their capacity to foment plots. They thus unwittingly facilitated slave resistance. Since the colony needed labour, most of the new slaves were no longer children and arrived with their own culture solidly implanted. The clergy who converted them were not acting on a *tabula rasa*, so they did not always achieve their objectives. It was difficult to get adults to accept that baptism was a spiritual remedy, giving life to the soul and having no effect on physical health. Adults tended to believe that their comrades who had died after receiving baptism had lost their lives because of that sacrament. They saw it as a sort of poison or spell, and 'they only resolved to accept it in the way that criminals accept their punishment', observed Father Caulier.[82] According to a letter from the poet Parny dated 19 January 1775 to his friend Bertin, some slaves refused to convert so as not to admit the possibility of punishment after death, which would keep them in slavery: 'I saw one recently who had been torn from his country seven months before; he was starving himself to death. As he was about to die and very far from his parish, I was asked to baptize him. He looked at me smiling and asked me why I was pouring water over his head. I explained it to him as best I could, but he turned over saying in bad French:

"[A]fter death, everything is finished, at least for us Negroes; I don't want any-thing to do with another life, as I shall still be a slave there.'"[83] Others refused to save their lives by embracing Christianity when they learnt that their tor-mentors, too, were hoping to go to heaven. Most put their own interpretation on the clergy's message. At the end of the eighteenth century, the volcano was seen by them as an infernal kingdom in which the Evil Spirit reigned, the slaves white and the masters black.[84] By night, round the fire, the old men would tell stories of *gniangs*, revenants who delighted in making the lives of the living a misery,[85] and other tales in which they mocked the powerful of the land. As when the slaves were in marronnage, they could once again express themselves, and it is sometimes possible to get a glimpse of the value they attributed to the sacraments they had received and to certain rites. In June 1758, Germain Guichard took a maroon negress carrying a child aged between 3 and 4 months. When questioned, she said that her name had formerly been Françoise and that she was Catholic and married in the eyes of the Church. In the woods, she had taken the name of Reine Fouche and had married again the black Mauzac according to their traditions.[86] When some maroons replied to the investigating magistrates that they did not know whether they were Christians, either they had not yet been baptized and their ignorance of the meaning of the word was obvious, or they had been baptized and attached no importance to the ceremony – or they were cheeking the magistrates. Eugène Dayot's writings on the customs of the maroons show that in the woods they expressed their magical thinking. In *Bourbon Pittoresque*, before undertaking a raid on a coastal habitation, the maroon chiefs hold a meeting. Mafate, a wise man opposed to this type of action, consults his *sikydis*, and then advises Diampare and his men to be extremely careful, since the great Zanaar (God) is not happy. Diampare, refusing to let his men down after this prediction and detesting the ascendancy that Mafate has over them, claims to discover a trick by the old man in the way in which he interprets his *sikydis*. He has a discus-sion with him in private and calls on him to come up with an argument to restore his men's confidence. Mafate is forced to retract his prediction. He mentions the omission of a funerary rite to explain to them God's passing anger. They have forgotten to honour the sacred *vazemba*, that is to throw a branch taken from the nearest tree on the mound where the body of one of their number is buried.[87]

As regards health, the black power of the slaves was able to superimpose itself on the white power of the masters. Whether from negligence or because of financial difficulties, masters rarely fulfilled their duty of caring for slaves. They thus forced them to turn to those who had healing knowledge, arousing the indignation of official medicine. In 1768, an ordinance was issued out-lawing the activities of slaves who treated the sick without seeking permission from the king's doctor or surgeon established in each district. But these seden-tary healers, hidden away in the habitations and aided by the complicit silence of masters who would not or could not spend money to care for their slaves, were difficult to track down. The authorities' efforts to eliminate them from the healing network were a failure. At the beginning of the nineteenth century,

Billiard could write: 'The blacks, particularly the Malagasies, know the virtues of a large number of simple persons, like those to be found in the mountains of Madagascar. Among them are some healers who have sometimes been able to keep alive sick individuals given up for lost by the doctors; but it is true that there is always a little sorcery in their medicine.'[88]

On each habitation, white owners also tolerated the songs and dances of African and Malagasy slaves because they did not deem them harmful to the maintenance of social order. Yet these cultural expressions allowed the slaves to have an existence, to forget their status, to feel themselves men among men, to reconstitute an Africa and a Madagascar of their own in this island, and to use their own words to condemn the system and their daily misery. They sang in the fields or as they carried litters. They sang at night, at religious festivals and at the new year. Through these songs and dances they were simply seeking to get closer to their ancestors and to please them. What Father Labat observed for the Antilles is certainly equally true for Bourbon,[89] if we remember these words by Évariste de Parny in Book I of the Elegies:

Another fate seduces the unhappy Negro
Seized by a trader from the deserts of Africa
Bent under a despotic yoke
In a long slavery he languishes enchained
But, when welcome death has put an end to his misery
He flies once again joyously to the land of his fathers
And this happy return is followed by a meal.

In order to enjoy their deceased relatives' protection, on the anniversary of their death, a near relative must indeed prepare a small meal, get a few friends together, say a few words in praise of the deceased, recall his qualities and ask those present to remember him in their prayers so that he might obtain rest for his soul. To end this festival, the drum must sound out loud. The silence of the sources in Bourbon on these funerary rites is not surprising in view of the fact that they had to be conducted inside the huts behind closed doors and must have been looked upon by the masters with the contemptuous condescension of their alleged intellectual superiority. The Black Code dictated that 'songs and drums must stop at 11 p.m.'. Billiard notes on this point: '[H]ow many times did I not fall asleep to the songs of the blacks, the melancholic sounds of the *vali* and the *bobre* which often continued into the middle of the might?' In addition to the *bobre,* or musical bow, and the *vali,* or Malagasy harp, the slaves also used the *encive*, a sea conch, to call to one another and to accompany their singing. But on the habitation, they would put anything to use as an instrument: their songs were beaten out by the thumping of 'heavy pounders' with which they broke 'the tough dried pulp surrounding the coffee bean'.[90] The Africans' most colourful dance was the *sega*, an extremely sensual dance, according to travellers' reports. The whites who watched them spoke of what they saw. They were amused by the sight of the outrageous doings of some of the dancers, in particular those fitted out with a variety of feathers or who imitated this or that bird, whereas the slaves had only one thing in mind – to make Africa or Madagascar come back to life, and to break through the chains of slavery in their own way. If the Malagasy's music is presented as melancholic and his dance as more serious than that of the African,[91] in expressing himself, he too was no less showing his desire not to lose his culture and not to submit entirely to the institution of slavery.

Minor Forms of Resistance

Flight by Sea and Plots

A minority of slaves saw flight by sea, at night, as the best way of putting the greatest possible distance between themselves and the slavers in order to become free again. The poet Parny, in a letter to his friend Bertin dated 19 January 1775, writes about this type of resistance:

> Their homeland (Madagascar) is two hundred leagues from here. But they imagine that they can hear the crowing of the cocks and recognize the smoke of their friends' pipes. Sometimes up to twelve or fifteen of them escape at once, take a pirogue and abandon themselves to the waves. They almost always leave their lives there, and that is little enough when you have lost your freedom.[92]

Flight by sea worried the civil power and the masters, not because of its destabilizing power, but because for the owners it represented a total loss.

From the very earliest years of slavery, the colony was faced with this problem. In 1704 Governor de Villers adopted measures for keeping watch on canoes to put a stop to this type of resistance, in which the Malagasies were experts. But it still continued all through the second half of the eighteenth century, even though those engaging in it knew that they might be swept away by waves at any moment. Before setting out they performed rites to secure the protection of the gods.[93] For those wishing to take this way out, a lot of thinking and a minimum of preparation were involved. The crossing took several days, and they had to select a boat and lay in provisions and water. On the night of 3 August 1752, Sieur François Baillif at the Repos Laleu decided to visit his black camp about midnight. To his amazement, he discovered that most of his slaves were not asleep but were instead holding a meeting. He concealed himself, listened and understood that they were in the process of formulating plans to seize Mr Desforges' pirogue. Baillif watched them in the days that followed and found them excited on Sunday the 6th. Hidden near a hen house, he saw one of his drivers, Jérôme Bayonne, who was wearing an old skirt of blue cloth and was carrying a gun and a packet. He asked him to stop, but the slave fled under the coconut trees. Baillif went to alert his brother Michel, and together they went to visit the pirogue. They found Antoine, the boss, asleep in his hut and four oarsmen placed on board. They waited on the seashore until 2 a.m. Seeing no black lurking around, they looked over several places before going home. At Sieur Dejean's five or six slaves were cooking their meal, at Hyacinthe Ricquebourg's some were awake, at Pierre Hibon's several huts were lit, while at Michel Baillif's the blacks had already prepared two pots of maize, another one of rice and two calabashes of water, and the blacks who were awake were moving from hut to hut. On Monday morning, Rosette, a maroon slave belonging to René Baillif, was arrested. She replied all innocently to explain her running away – that she had to leave that very night in Mr Desforges' pirogue; that the leaders of the enterprise were Bayonne, Timoléon, a Cafre belonging to Baillif, and Laurent, a Malagasy belonging to François Ricquebourg; and that twenty-eight slaves were involved. Armed with this information, René Baillif decided to arrest Bayonne and took him to Saint-Paul to be imprisoned.[94]

The Conseil supérieur punished those taken just as they were about to put their plan into operation in an exemplary way, in order to deter as many slaves as possible from doing anything similar. In 1753, Manombre and Louis who wanted to take a rowing boat belonging to the Company, were sentenced to receive two hundred lashes each and to carry the chain for life.[95] Between 4 and 15 November 1754, five owners from Saint-Paul came to declare their pirogues. One of them, Jacques Martin, had lost his on 25 June 1754.[96] On 16 December 1764, the bourgeois René Cousin revealed to the clerk of the Conseil supérieur the existence of a plot to desert and to seize a canoe in which his black François, a Malagasy, was an accomplice. As soon the scheme was exposed, François escaped, taking with him the negress Roze and her child Judith. Hunted down at once, he stabbed himself several times in the stomach and chest with a knife when he was arrested.[97] Between 25 and 31 March 1769, seven owners from the Repos Laleu, who had lost a total of thirteen slaves during the night of 23–24 March, suspected that the escapees had embarked in a six-oar pirogue that had recently been lost, which had belonged to Sieur Delanux Véronge and which had been chained up near Athanaze Touchard's house.[98] It was one Thérèze, a slave belonging to François Baillif, taken up as a runaway on 25 March on the estate of Mr Reinaud, who denounced her companions because they had not allowed her to leave with them, due to a wound she had in her leg.[99] She was certainly disappointed. Nevertheless, by confiding in her master, she was not driven by a thirst for revenge. She simply wanted his clemency.

On 20 July 1769, Crémont signed an ordinance in which he required that pirogue owners should moor them solidly and declare them within a month. This regulation was deemed inadequate in practice and was amended on 1 March 1772. A fine of £200, and for a repeat offence £500, was laid down for any pirogue owner who had not beached it at night. The owner of an improperly guarded pirogue had to reimburse the owner of runaway slaves the value of those slaves, if their master was able to establish the negligent party's guilt.[100] That did not prevent de Courcy having to regret the theft of three pirogues between April 1778 and April 1779, one in the Rivière d'Abord, and two in the Repos Laleu.[101] At the beginning of March 1781, four slaves belonging to Antoine Desjardins informed him that in the night of 25–26 February, three of his blacks had embarked in a pirogue stolen from the beach at Saint-Gilles belonging to Sieur Gonneau de Montbrun. They confessed to Desjardins that 'they were in the plot, that they had planned to rendezvous on the beach to embark and only fear had made them stay, being afraid of the quantity of blacks who wanted to get into the pirogue'.[102] During the night of 26–27 October 1788, three Malagasy slaves belonging to Venant Dejean left his habitation at Saint-Paul. When on the 30th he learnt of the theft of the small pirogue belonging to Sieur Dennemont, he immediately suspected that they were responsible for the theft and that they had already left the island.[103]

Once the escapees by sea had got off from the island's coasts, they no longer represented a permanent danger for the whites. Conversely, those who plotted against the whites prevented them from sleeping peacefully. The least rumour was exploited by the masters to demand better defence of their security from the civil authorities. Many slaves concealed behind a permanent smile and an obsequious servility an impatience for vengeance that sometimes resulted in crime or revolt. Plots were rather uncommon on Bourbon between 1750 and the eve of the Revolutionary period, but there were plans in abundance. On 2 August 1756, Sieur Ricquebourg stated that he had learnt of the existence of a cabal of blacks, and had arrested four men and four women and found lead on them. In the night of 1–2 August 1756, about 9 o'clock, Arsène Maillot set out in pursuit at Ravine des Chèvres of a black and three negresses who had come from Bras-de-Chevrettes (heights of Saint-André). On arresting them, he learnt that they had a rendezvous first at Mrs Justamond's with their leaders, the Cafres Jouan, Petit Jean, Laurent and Charlot, and that they were then to go to Dame Bachelier's, at Ravine des Fugues. Jouan, who was the man behind their move, played on their belief in the supernatural to make himself credible and galvanize his troops. Among the twenty-one slaves who made up the band, some had made the journey from Saint-André to Sainte-Marie on foot. Charlot, who was carrying a pistol when he was arrested, said that 'Jouan, a Mozambique Cafre, had promised them that as soon as they reached Jean-Louis, he would lift them up into the air and make them fly like birds to go to his country.... If it had been for anything else, no one would be mad enough to follow him'. The investigators of this affair, who were unable to determine the true purpose of the gathering, gave some credence to this argument, since they asked the guilty parties: 'In the meetings, did not Jouan make horns dance to do his divining?' Charlot, for example, replied: 'Yes, they were little horns as big as fingers. He passed himself off as a sorcerer.'[104] Since this gathering had not occasioned the deaths of any whites, Jouan and Charlot were sentenced on 1 April 1757 to 200 lashes, to be branded with a fleur-de-lis on the right shoulder and to carry a chain for life. All of the others were to receive 200 lashes.[105]

Over this period, only a single plot aimed directly at whites was discovered. On 15 May 1779, Mr de Launay informed Mr de Courcy that the blacks of the Saint-André quarter had formed a plan to kill all of the whites attending mass on Whit Sunday. A counter-attack was organized by the commander of the Saint-André quarter, Mr Welmant. Every militia officer in the surrounding area went to his house, and all of the owners of habitations were discreetly warned to be on their guard. Sixty soldiers of the garrison backed by reinforcements from the Île-de-France regiment came to help the people of Saint-André. In this way, Mr Welmant was able to surround part of the assembled black band. They surrendered without offering the least resistance, except for the leader of the band, who was disarmed by a sword blow to the face. Only a black guarding a hen house was killed by the rebels. In total, thirteen slaves were arrested and detained in prison. On 27 May 1779, the mayor of Saint-André informed Mr de Saint-Maurice that it was only a scare. The habitants had deliberately exaggerated the facts. The thirteen blacks arrested were only guilty of having wanted to steal and perhaps set fire to a few huts and hen houses. The tranquillity that reigned in the quarter was clear proof in his eyes that this plan did not involve all of the slaves. The Conseil supérieur, informed of the affair, found it more serious than the municipality of Saint-André, certainly in order to make anyone who might be thinking of fomenting a plot think twice before acting. It imposed the following punishments on eight of the thirteen arrested. Two were sentenced to be broken alive, burned and their ashes thrown to the winds, and two others to be hanged, burned and their ashes thrown to the winds. This second category included a pregnant negress who was to be executed only after she had given birth. Seven others were sentenced to be whipped, branded and sent to the galleys for life, one got off with a year on the chain and the last was condemned to witness the execution of the others with those who had not been hanged.[106]

Suicide

Suicide by hanging or drowning, used by slaves to show their exasperation at repeated punishments and the fear of likely punishments and their rejection of injustice and humiliation, sounded as an alarm signal. But masters always judged themselves blameless, and did not try to analyse the significance of the message. Gaps in our documentation are so large as to make it impossible to assess the scale of this phenomenon. Between 1744 and 1766, only eighteen reports on the discovery of the bodies of suicides have been preserved and for 1767–88, forty-two. But, even though they must be treated with circumspection, shot through as they are with the prejudices of all involved, the explanations they give are sometimes valuable. They show us how ill-equipped the system was for children. Jupiter, aged 12 in 1780, hanged himself, while Manuel, a slave, asserted that 'his master had a really soft spot for him, being the first one he had bought in the islands'.[107] Télémaque, aged 10, sent by his master to get a whip from a neighbour, hanged himself from a mango tree. The master said: 'We have to suppose that the little black was afraid that [the whip] was for him, but he had not done anything to me, and I am at a loss to understand the reason for his fear.'[108] The system was ill-equipped for old people, too, who saw no end to their troubles. On 13 December 1778, Pierre, aged 60, was found hanged. According to his master, Sieur Paul Stéphen, Pierre 'was tired of living, he was always moaning, he used to say sometimes when he was bringing a packet that it would be better not to live. He had never imagined that getting old was so unpleasant'.[109] Suicide usually expressed rejection of the situation of suffering in a society where violence ruled.[110] Beyond merely challenging the system, some must have harboured a desire for vengeance and sought through their gesture not simply to strike a blow at the masters' economic potential but also to punish their tormentors, if we accept what G. Debien says: '[S]uicide among animist peoples is a means of returning in the guise of spirits to torment those who offended you and drove you to suicide.' This is a credible hypothesis, since it was rare for a master to say anything bad about the memory of a suicide. Sieur Broutin's bursar had nothing to criticize Larose for, yet in August 1787, Larose opted for suicide.[111] Joseph, too, was an obedient servant who had never been beaten. He hanged himself in January 1788.[112] Aza, aged 15, was said to be lazy. His master stated all the same, after Aza's suicide in 1788, that he was an obedient servant and that he did not know the real reason for what he had done. Even his comrades said that the evening before at supper, 'he did not seem to have any bad thought in his head'.[113] Magistrates' obsession with the corpses of those who had chosen suicide so as not to have to answer for their deeds before the Conseil supérieur was designed to make it impossible for them to appear before the ancestors and to provide proof that slaves had no rights and above all not the right to choose how and when to die. It also reflected the will to desacralize death and discourage the fascination that it exercised over slaves. In 1779, Bernard, one of those involved in the Saint-André plot, committed suicide in prison. His body was condemned to be tied by the feet behind a cart with the face against the ground, dragged on a hurdle through the Saint-André quarter, hanged by the feet to a gallows, exposed for twenty-four hours and then thrown onto the rubbish dump.[114]

Conclusions

In the second half of the eighteenth century, the philosophical spirit that was articulated around a number of fundamental principles – such as criticism of religious fanaticism and exaltation of tolerance, confidence in observation and experience, critical examination of every institution and every custom, and definition of a natural morality – won over increasing numbers in France.[115] The work of the *philosophes* won support for the view that there is no human dignity without freedom of thought, no social order without tolerance. Anti-slavery took off. The most resounding condemnations of slavery came from Montesquieu in *L'Esprit des lois* (Chapter 5, Book 15) in 1748, Voltaire in his *Essai sur les mœurs* in 1756[116] and Father Raynal in his *Histoire philosophique et politique des établissements et du commerce des Européens dans les deux Indes* in 1770.

In Bourbon colonial society, which owed its prosperity to slavery, slaves, when confronted with the abuses committed by masters, did not simply lie down and accept their fate, despite their division and the difficulties of organizing. By taking refuge in the forests, getting off the island, committing suicide, refusing to conceive or falling back on their ancestral culture, some showed that they were not a resigned, consenting and satisfied flock, and gave in their own way a lesson on a theme in vogue in France at that time: freedom. As rulers thought only of their economic success and as, in their mind, that success was linked up with maintaining slavery, they vigorously fought the forms of slave resistance that were deemed most harmful to the system. Their conservatism prevented them from decoding and fully appreciating the message being sent by those slaves condemned in principle to silence and obedience. So as not to precipitate their death, masters did not dare utter the word 'freedom'. In Bourbon, the eighteenth century did not end in 1789.

Notes

1. On this question see J. Barrassin, 'L'esclavage à Bourbon avant l'application du Code Noir de 1723', *Bulletin de l'Académie de la Réunion*, Vol. 17, 1957, pp. 5–53; and J. Mas, 'Scolies et hypothèses sur l'émergence de l'esclavage à Bourbon', in *Économies et sociétés de plantation*, Saint-Denis, Publications de l'Université de La Réunion, 1989, pp. 109–58.
2. A. Vinson, *Salazie ou le Piton d'Anchaine*, Paris, 1888.
3. Archives of the parish of Saint-François Xavier (Rivière-des-Pluies): Papiers concernant la pose de la Vierge Noire.
4. E. Dayot, *Oeuvres choisies*, 2nd ed., Saint-Denis, Lougnon, 1977.
5. ADR, Co 950–954 (1751–1764) and 37 C, 1767–1788.
6. ADR, Co 968–973 (1752–1766) and 37 C and 38 C, 1767–1788.
7. ADR, Co 993–1009 (1750–1767) and 45 C, 1772–1777.
8. ADR, Co 1010–1011, 1755 and 1767.
9. ADR, Co 1028–1037 (1752–1766), Co 2526–2532 (1750–1768), Registres des arrêts du Conseil supérieur.
10. J. Barrassin, 'La révolte des esclaves à l'Ile Bourbon au XVIIIe siècle', in *Mouvements de populations dans l'océan Indien*, Paris, 1974, p. 388.
11. J. M. Desport, *De la servitude à la liberté. Bourbon des origines à 1848*, Saint-Denis, Océan, 1989, p. 67.
12. ADR, 37 C, Déclaration de Pierre-Robert Técher du 26 février 1782.
13. ADR, Co 995, Extrait du registre de marronnage, Côte malgache.
14. ADR, 37 C, Interrogatoire de François du 26 juin 1776.
15. ADR, 37 C, Interrogatoire de Mathieu du 11 avril 1776.
16. ADR, 37 C, Interrogatoire de Marie, Indienne, du 30 novembre 1787.
17. ADR, 37 C, Interrogatoire de Dominique du 26 juin 1776.
18. ADR, Co 1030, Procès de Félix, esclave du Sieur Leclerc de Saint-Lubin (1756).
19. ADR, 37 C, Interrogatoire de Pedec du 27 janvier 1787.
20. ADR, 37 C, Interrogatoire de Narcisse du 17 novembre 1787.
21. ADR, 37 C, Interrogatoire de François du 18 août 1787.
22. A. Lougnon, *L'Ile Bourbon pendant la régence*, Paris, 1956, pp. 257–61.
23. ADR, Co 1034, Procès de Laurent, esclave de Paul Payet, 1756.
24. ADR, Co 1033, Procès de Manuel, esclave de Bidot Duclos, 1756.
25. ADR, Co 1036, Procès de François, esclave de Pierre Hibon, 1757.
26. ADR, Co 998, Déclarations de retour (1755).
27. ADR, 37 C, Interrogatoire de Jouan du 26 octobre 1787.
28. ADR, 37 C, Interrogatoire de Gaëtan du 16 novembre 1787.
29. ADR, 37 C, Interrogatoire de Colle.
30. ADR, 37 C, Interrogatoire de Jupiter.
31. ADR, 37 C, Interrogatoire de Télémaque du 12 avril 1776.
32. ADR, 37 C, Interrogatoire d'Augustin, esclave de Sieur Rozière du 19 juillet 1787.
33. ADR, 37 C, Interrogatoire de Charles du Sieur Brunac.
34. ADR, 37 C, Interrogatoire de Romain du 28 mai 1787.

35. ADR, 37 C, Interrogatoire de Barbe du 20 avril 1787.
36. ADR, 37 C, Interrogatoire d'Avril du 2 octobre 1787.
37. ADR, 37 C, Interrogatoire de Pierre-Louis du 13 février 1776.
38. ADR, Co 993, Déclaration du 25 décembre 1750 de Joseph de Guigné.
39. ADR, Co 994, Déclaration d'Alexis, esclave de Claude Mollet du 17 janvier 1751.
40. ADR, Co 994, Déclaration d'Augustin, esclave du Sieur Deheaulme du 24 avril 1751.
41. ADR, Co 998, Déclaration de quatre esclaves de Joachim Lautret, mai 1755.
42. ADR, Co 1068, Déclaration de René Duguet du 6 décembre 1766.
43. ADR, 45 C, Déclaration du Sieur Maunier du 1er septembre 1783.
44. ADR, Co 2527, Arrêt du Conseil supérieur du 27 octobre 1751.
45. ADR, Co 2527, Arrêt du Conseil supérieur du 10 octobre 1753.
46. ADR, 38 C, Interrogatoire de Jacques du 1er octobre 1782, 37 C, Déclaration d'Honoré Lauret du 1er juillet 1788, de Joseph Grosset du 19 juin 1785, de Louis Carron du 29 décembre 1785, 45 C, Déclarations d'Edme Cerveau des 21 août 1780, 22 juillet 1782, 20 octobre 1782, Déclaration de Joseph Grosset du 8 mars 1780.
47. ADR, Co 993.
48. ADR, 45 C, Déclaration du 12 décembre 1787.
49. ADR, 37 C, Interrogatoire du 12 décembre 1780 de Geneviève.
50. ADR, 37 C, Interrogatoire de Maho du 1er juin 1785.
51. ADR, Co 995, Déclaration de François Mussard du 31 janvier 1752.
52. ADR, Co 968, Déclaration de Patrice Droman du 29 février 1750.
53. ADR, Co 993, Déclaration de Paul Lauret du 16 juin 1750.
54. ADR, Co 972, Déclaration de Claude Garnier du 22 mars 1765.
55. ADR 45 C, Déclaration de Paulin Desbassyns du 7 août 1775.
56. ADR, 45 C, Déclaration de Patrice Droman du 7 août 1775.
57. ADR, Co 993, Déclaration de l'esclave Mananque du 14 septembre 1750.
58. ADR, Co 995, Déclaration de François Mussard du 31 octobre 1751.
59. ADR, Co 995, Déclaration de Patrice Droman du 15 juin 1752.
60. ADR, Co 995, Déclaration de Patrice Droman du 15 juin 1752.
61. ADR, 37 C, Interrogatoires de Mathèse du 5 juillet 1776, de Leveillé du 21 juin 1787 et de Crabe du 3 mai 1787.
62. ADR, 38 C, Extrait du registre du greffe de Sainte-Suzanne, Taffique, esclave de la succession Morau.
63. ADR, Co 1000, Déclaration de Jean Dugain du 3 juin 1758.
64. ADR, Co 995, Déclaration de François Mussard.
65. ADR, Co 994, Déclaration de François Mussard du 31 octobre 1751.
66. Ibid.
67. This provision was copied from one adopted in Martinique on 3 January 1764.
68. ADR, 37 C, Interrogatoire de Lundy du 4 janvier 1787.
69. ADR, 37 C, Interrogatoire de Ferla du 4 janvier 1787.
70. ADR, 37 C, Interrogatoire de Julie du 28 juin 1787.
71. ADR, 37 C, Interrogatoire de Saturne du 14 février 1787.
72. ADR, 37 C, Déclaration d'Isabelle, esclave du Sieur Calvert du 15 juillet 1773.
73. ADR, Co 995, Déclaration du 19 novembre 1752.
74. R. Bousquet, *Les Esclaves et leurs maîtres à Saint-Paul et dans le quartier sous le vent des origines à 1735*, Mémoire de DEA, Université de La Réunion, 1992, p. 67.
75. ADR, GG Saint-Paul 1740–1779.
76. ADR, GG Saint-Benoît 1734–1753.
77. ADR, GG Saint-Pierre 1728–1757.
78. R. Bousquet, op. cit., p. 148.
79. R. Bousquet, op. cit.
80. ADR, C 20, Lettre de Crémont à Poivre du 2 novembre 1769.
81. C. Wanquet, *Histoire d'une révolution, La Réunion (1789–1803)*, Vol. 1, Marseilles, Jeanne Lafitte, 1980, pp. 47–8.
82. Archives des Lazaristes (Paris), Vol. 1506 (1746–1773), pp. 91–2.

83. E. de Parny, *Oeuvres*, Lettre de Parny à Bertin de janvier 1775, p. 431.
84. J. B. G. M. Bory de Saint-Vincent, *Voyage dans les quatre principales îles des mers d'Afrique pendant les années IX et X de la République (1801 et 1802)*, Paris, Vol. 1, pp. 181–3 [Eng. trans., *Voyage to, and Travels through the four Principal Islands of the African Seas, performed by Order of the French Government, during the Years 1801 and 1802*, London, R. Phillips, 1805, p. 132].
85. A. Billiard, *Voyage aux colonies orientales pendant les années 1817, 1818, 1819 et 1820*, Paris, 1822, pp. 119–20.
86. ADR, Co 1000, Déclaration de Guichard, 1758.
87. P. Ève, *Ile à peur. La peur à Réunion des origines à nos jours*, Saint-André, Océan, 1992, p. 326.
88. A. Billiard, op. cit., p. 100.
89. P. Pluchon, *Histoire de la colonisation française*, Paris, 1991, Vol. 1, pp. 428–9.
90. C. Wanquet, 'Aspects culturels de la société réunionnaise du XVIIIe', in *Mouvement des idées dans l'océan Indien occidental*, Saint-Denis, 1985, p. 420.
91. Ibid., p. 421.
92. E. de Parny, op. cit., p. 431.
93. P. Ève, op. cit., p. 73.
94. ADR, Co 995.
95. ADR, Co 2527.
96. ADR, Co 1062, Déclarations de Jacques Martin, Jean-Baptiste Grimaud, Thomas Elgard, Pierre Baillif et Bernard Lautret des 4, 5, 7, 11 et 15 novembre 1754.
97. ADR, 37 C.
98. ADR, 45 C, Déclaration de Jean Arnoye du 25 mars 1769, d'Adam Baillif du 25 mars 1769, de Michel Baillif du 29 mars 1769, de Jacques Mercier du 31 mars 1769.
99. ADR, 45 C, Déclaration de Thérèze du 25 avril 1769.
100. P. Ève, op. cit., p. 72.
101. ADR, C 20, Lettres à Nairac et Pignolet, avril 1778, 8 et 16 octobre 1778, 27 mars et 26 avril 1779.
102. ADR, 45 C, Déclaration d'Antoine Desjardins du 3 mars 1781.
103. ADR, Co 1035, Déclaration du Sieur Ricquebourg du 2 août 1756.
104. ADR, Co 1035, Dossier de plusieurs esclaves accusés de complot contre la sureté de la colonie.
105. ADR, Co 2528, Arrêt du Conseil supérieur du 1er avril 1757.
106. P. Ève, op. cit., pp. 79–80.
107. ADR, 28 C, Levée de cadavre d'un esclave du Sieur de Jouvancourt du 1er octobre 1780.
108. ADR, 28 C, Levée de cadavre d'un esclave du Sieur Savignan 22 avril 1787.
109. ADR, Levée de cadavre d'un esclave du Sieur Savignan 22 avril 1787.
110. P. Ève, op. cit., pp. 126–8.
111. ADR, 28 C, Levée de cadavre d'un esclave du Sieur Broutin du 23 août 1787.
112. ADR, 28 C, Levée de cadavre du 26 janvier 1788.
113. ADR, 28 C, Levée de cadavre du 7 mai 1788.
114. ADR, I B 6, Arrêt du Conseil supérieur du 7 août 1779.
115. R. Chartier, *Les origines culturelles de la Révolution française*, Paris, Éditions du Seuil, 1990, p. 28 [Eng. trans. L. G. Cochrane, *The Cultural Origins of the French Revolution*, Durham, N.C., Duke University Press, 1991].
116. J. Meyer, J. Tarrade, A. Rey-Goldzeiguer and J. Thobie, *Histoire de la France coloniale, des origines à 1914*, Paris, Éditions Armand Colin, 1991, pp. 186–8.

Chapter 3

Resistance to the Slave Trade in African Trading Posts

Harris Memel Foté

I SHALL DEAL here with resistance in the African trading posts on the African Atlantic coast in the narrow sense – that is, what was happening on the coast, in the hinterland, in the islands and on the boats anchored off the coast. The European slave trade system established in Africa from the fifteenth to the eighteenth centuries was built on the assumption that capitalist companies, backed by monarchical states and blessed by the Christian Churches, should ally with African polities, the first link in the trading networks.

But this alliance did not go unchallenged. The concept of 'resistance' refers to the attitudes of refusal and the hostile actions of free and captive Africans and, as we shall see, of African slaves. These hostile actions of all sorts – whether by individuals or by groups, spontaneous or organized, traditional or novel – may have been unable to destroy or repel the system, yet they succeeded in slowing it down, hampering its development and limiting its effects and its exactions through escapes, revolts and violence to others or to oneself.

Using the barely examined available documents and chronicles, in particular ships' logs, we can broadly distinguish two periods of resistance with different features, traditional in one case, novel in the other. From these we can detect both an anthropological and a historical signification.

First Period: Fifteenth to Sixteenth Centuries

Resistance to the establishment of the slave trade system was very traditional in character. The system was started by peopling several islands planted with sugar cane (Sao Tome, Canary Islands, Cape Verde), allying with African rulers, erecting forts and winning converts to Christianity.

The first feature of this resistance was that it preceded what I have called alliance. Resistance preceded alliance since the Portuguese slave trade was from the outset a conquest, using predatory violence to produce captives in the strict sense, and hence resulting in uprootings.

The second feature was that it was traditional. As news of this violence spread from the islands to the mainland, and from north to south, the societies used old modes of resistance to oppose being uprooted. The same traditional frameworks (the village, the camp, the kingdom or the ethnic group) were involved in all of the countries attacked (Arab, Berber or black countries). There was the same participation in this resistance by all groups in society (chiefs, masses, men and women, old and young); the same traditional defence strategy (moving people away, ambushes, counter-attacks); the same materials, tools and traditional weapons (including bows and poisoned arrows, spears and swords); and the same ethic of courage and honour, through which individuals made their marks as heroes.

The third feature was continuity. From the second half of the fifteenth century, once the slave trade had become an industrial business, a trade in gold and a trade in human beings, and although former resisters and chiefs who had resisted captivity joined the system, resistance continued, on both the ideological and the political level. At the ideological level, there was the accusation that Africans made against Europeans of cannibalism; there was the European legend of 'bad people', meaning people hostile to the system or to its methods; there were traditionalist factions that refused to condone their kings' decision to become Christian (in the Congo, for example). In the political domain, there were still unbeaten chiefs who did not want to yield to the system. There was a refusal to allow forts to be built, for example, at El Mina in 1482.

The fourth feature was that something new was happening. In areas where the system had already taken off, there was innovation: a sort of class struggle emerged. At the same time, the peoples in the hinterland changed status and in turn became resistants in relation to the coastal peoples. By the second half of the century, there were two types of response. On the one hand, there were slave revolts in the island societies that had become slave societies properly so called. For example, in Sao Tome the slaves, allied with peasants indigenous to the region, rose in rebellion against the colonists in 1540, 1574 and 1595. At one point, the slaves controlled the island under the authority of their leader Amador. On the other hand, in addition to this emerging class struggle, there was the invasion of the coastal peoples by peoples from the interior. For example, the Congo, a Christian state, was invaded by the Jagas, a stateless people, who destroyed churches, drove the king from his capital and occupied the territory.

Whatever the novelty of the alliance between slaves and peasants, in Sao Tome resistance at the time had two major weaknesses, which are a reflection of traditional economies and which explain the failure of the Jagas in the face of the subsequent Portuguese counter-attack. One of these weaknesses was of a political nature: resistance was local, ethnic, compartmentalized. The other weakness was their largely archaic, rudimentary technology, which was powerless before firearms.

Second Period: Seventeenth to Eighteenth Centuries

Resistance to the spread of the slave trade system became better equipped but remained inadequately organized politically during this period. Expansion at this time was fuelled by the discovery of new sources of raw materials in the Americas, the increase in the number of powers engaged in world competition, advances in technology that increased the tonnage of vessels and developed the firearms industry, and above all the adaptation of coastal societies to fulfilling the role of middlemen. Between 1600 and 1800, over 8 million slaves were exported.

The intensity of resistance then shifted and spread from the coast to the interior, from politics to religion, and extended the class struggle from the islands to the ships. This movement was geopolitical, while resistance continued on the coast with the seizure of hostages, pillaging and the burning of trading posts. The main focus of struggles, naturally not without ambiguities, shifted to the pressure brought to bear by animist military states in the interior on the coastal states that were already more or less Christian, for example, in the Congo, the royal state of Queen Anna Nzinga in the seventeenth century, or in Ashanti or Dahomey. So there was pressure on the coast and also a wider spread sociologically; some advocates of political and economic reform borrowed sacred language and proposed radical solutions. Such was the Christian nationalist prophetism of Dona Beatrix, who has been called the 'Congolese Joan of Arc', who wanted a free, prosperous Congo and a decolonized Church. Such too were the *djihad*, equipped with firearms – the Muslim revolutionaries in West Africa who dreamed of theocratic, multiethnic, quasi-national, just states that would ensure free trade in cereals and protect the faithful from slavery. We might cite the cases of Nasir al-Din or Abdul Kader Kane in Futa Tooro, Malik Sy in Bundu and Karamoko Alfa in Futa Jallon, West Africa.

The class struggle spread from the islands to the ships. In the islands, the number of slave struggles increased – Cape Verde (1661), Sao Tome in alliance, as noted above, with indigenous peasants (1616, 1693, 1709, 1734) – but above all, on the ships there were countless escapes, drownings, suicides, murders and revolts. On the 1,327 voyages of Nantes vessels between 1707 and 1793 in Jean Mettas's list, more than seventy declared revolts failed. The slaves who threw off their shackles and attempted, with few or no firearms, to overcome the crew, were killed or drowned, thereby making the rest cower.

The successful revolts, numbering at least seven, led to three types of liberation. Firstly, there was liberation by an outsider: local chiefs boarded the ship, seized the crew and freed the slaves. Secondly, there was liberation by an alliance of local people and revolting slaves: the former on the coast saw the latter in revolt on board a ship and in difficulty because the crew was using firearms. They came to the aid of the rebels and freed them. And thirdly, there was liberation by the slaves themselves – bold and technologically and organizationally new. That happened on *La Maîtresse* at Princes Island in May 1751, the *Henriette* on 26 February 1768, *La Diane* in July 1773, *Le Bienfaisant* in 1777 and *Le Docile* in 1788, for which we have evidence. Once masters of the ship, the slaves raised anchor and sailed away.

* * *

Over both periods, instances of resistance by free Africans, captive Africans or African slaves had two significations, one anthropological and the other historical. They reveal not only the state and level of development of societies and cultures through the personality and actions of the protagonists, but also the limits imposed on particular societies and cultures by compartmentalization and technological underdevelopment. By the same token, they demonstrate the irreversibility of an economy preparing for the later radical dependency that followed on 'thingification' and deracination – in other words, an economy preparing for colonization.

Chapter 4

Slave Resistance in the Seventeenth and Eighteenth Centuries in the French Colonies in America, and Chiefly the Windward Islands

Léo Élisabeth

IS IT NOT the case that all those things that create rights – daily bread, house and garden; family, religion or pleasures, inseparable from meetings and even associations; medicine, inseparable from poison and witchcraft; mixing and emancipation, sure signs of integration – is it not true that they all generate some form of resistance that for a colonial society is reflected in the perception of a danger? We shall limit ourselves to the often intertwined themes of marronnage – slaves escaping – plots and revolts. What could be more natural than rejection of the slave order in the name of those aspirations that impel virtually all of mankind to feel free and equal? Beyond that universal aspect, what role did racial or ethnic references as well as autonomy play in resistance? We shall leave aside the study of types of marronnage and maroons, and start with the general development of marronnage, examining the interrelationship between the marronnage-plot-revolt triptych and the perception that contemporaries had of danger. We will then analyse the environment and the solidarities and some aspects of the forms of resistance associated with integration, including in that a discussion of the levels of perception of ideals.

Movements over Time and the Perception of Resistance

Since plotters may have wanted simply 'to get from their masters what they were worth',[1] we felt it possible to study the marronnage-plot-revolt triptych by examining how the first term evolved. In Martinique there were 9 per cent of maroons in 1665, falling to 2.4 per cent per cent in 1708, 1.2 per cent in 1726 and 0.4 per cent in 1784. Guadeloupe reported 1.9 per cent in 1726, 1.2 per cent in 1773, 2.1 per cent in 1782 and 1.8 per cent in 1783.

What value can we put on the figures when resistance was likely to be apprehended through the prism of danger? For Martinique in 1665, the figure of 300 or 400 maroons given by Father du Tertre seems excessive.[2] Runaways were dispersed in groups numbering twenty to twenty-five, and we doubt whether a single person, Fabulé, could command fifteen or twenty groups. Several hunts yielded only six or seven captures. Having surrendered and become a bounty hunter, Fabulé brought back 'quite a number' of his former companions, which does not really enlighten us. As regards the danger, at Prêcheur, the three slaves belonging to the widow of Fabulé's master found themselves facing eight whites, four of whom, it is true, were children. Of the ninety-four house-owners, only forty-eight owned slaves. For 177 slaves working, the company had 200 militiamen. Finally, the inhabitants were more concerned about their allocation of tobacco than they were about these maroons. Already, in 1656, in Guadeloupe, similar disorders had aroused little concern. People railed against the Amerindians with the hope of seizing their lands, but only a single Dutchman, driven out of Brazil and very hard up, came forward to hunt down rebels allegedly seeking to destroy all whites.[3] Individual cases could move people. In November 1681, the Conseil supérieur of Martinique deplored the large number of maroons and their depredations.[4] Governor General Blénac opened an enquiry. In December, six companies reported that they had none. The other six reported twenty-five. All that fuss for 0.2 per cent of runaways suggests that the figures did not take into account those who had been retaken or who had returned, and when, in 1708, intendant Vaucresson[5] railed against 500 to 600 runaways, he was doubtless exaggerating.

Nevertheless, we think we can accept the trend indicated, since whereas the absolute figures and percentages diminish for Martinique, the resistance reflected by these figures is not identical in Guadeloupe, where generally higher absolute figures and rates rose between 1773 and 1783. Between 1708 and 1728, the total number of slaves doubled in Martinique. In Guadeloupe, it rose practically fourfold. Between 1753 and 1788, the increase was 13 per cent in Martinique and 110 per cent in Guadeloupe, and, from the time of the Seven Years' War, the latter island had more slaves than Martinique. Thus, while Guadeloupe was becoming more Africanized by leaps and bounds, Martinique was increasingly creolized, and we therefore incline to attach more importance to the correlations between massive imports and marronnage – already noted by Father du Tertre – than to the propensity to run away of certain ethnic groups. Moreover, in 1672, when the colonists decided that running away became serious only after a full year's presence in the country, they interpreted marronnage by newcomers as something almost normal. They believed that, as with creolization, getting used to a place would reduce this form of resistance.

Another embarrassing question remains: do not the labels 'maroon' and 'rebel' cover complex images? Was the individual being hunted as a maroon always conscious that he was in breach of the law? Was he not often more concerned to defend a freedom he had won, de jure or de facto? In the combats mentioned in the seventeenth century by Father du Tertre, the eagerness of the blacks, whom the Caribs had welcomed before selling them to the Spaniards, is suspect.[6] Since these orange-red fighters had not been assimilated in a few days, are we not here dealing rather with those who would come to be called 'Black Caribs'? Father Labat believed that they had escaped from Barbados. The *ordonnateur* (quartermaster-treasurer) Mithon thought they had come from the French and English islands.[7] But in 1722, Father le Breton – who had made long stays among them between 1693 and 1701 – insisted that it was improper to describe them as slaves, and thought that they came from Spanish slave ships that had been shipwrecked before French and English colonization,[8] an opinion endorsed by J. P. Moreau.[9] After the expedition of 1719, French vocabulary moved on. They were neither Africans nor Caribs nor Creoles since they lived in tribes, and they were called 'Black Caribs' at least from 1749.[10] Richard Price, however, opts for marronnage.[11]

Another category was that of individuals returned to slavery in the Islands after a stay in Europe. In 1663, du Ruau Palu, agent of the Compagnie des Indes, became concerned about it.[12] In 1704, Mithon gave details of a case.[13] One Louis had been carried directly to France, and had stayed there for more than fifteen years and was legally free. Sent back to Martinique as a slave, he rebelled and refused to perform his duties. In the Islands, the local ordinance of 15 August 1711 subjected emancipations to the authorization of the administration in order to prevent disputes. On 24 October 1713, the king approved it but banned any retroactive effect, which, in 1723, did not prevent slaves from being recovered who had been freed in about 1708.[14] People who were de facto free found themselves in equally complex situations. Thus, in France, following the edict of October 1716, the administration ordered a search for maroons who were legally free. Freemen reduced to slavery by foreign powers experienced similar problems. In 1698, fifteen freemen belonging to Guadeloupe, taken up in 1696 and sold to Antigua, were reclaimed.[15] Of some twenty escapees from that island, five were viewed as maroons by the English and freemen by the French.

Some motivations are far from clear. What really happened in Grenada to justify the establishment of a provostal court in 1726?[16] In the island of St John's in 1734, was the revolt not provoked by the arrival of the new Danish masters? Is there not some analogy with what happened in St Kitts after the eviction of the French in 1702? What value is to be put on the accusation of a plot designed to massacre all whites which recurs particularly just before Christmas and Easter? In 1656, Father du Tertre accused forty maroons, including women and children, of having wanted to massacre all of the whites in Guadeloupe, keeping their women for themselves. Dessalles took up the same theme in 1789.[17]

On 28 July 1710, Governor Gabaret announced that 200 slaves were planning to burn down Saint-Pierre and the neighbouring estates.[18] Thirty had already been arrested. Tried by the provostal court – doubtless because there was no evidence – several were burned and others broken on the wheel. Two leaders had fled. Despite their denials and the protection of their masters, they were later executed. The following year, the new Governor General Phélypeaux concluded that the accusations had been false.[19] In August 1789, illicit meetings followed by refusals to work set off a merciless repression in Saint-Pierre. But in November, when the agitation had spread to fifteen rural parishes and led to the assassination of a white overseer, 'something which has not been seen for twenty years',[20] and then in December spread to French Guyana,[21] the word 'plot' was not used. As in the repression in Antigua described by D. B. Gaspar,[22] did not revolts often occur simply because the administration and justice had so decided?

Did moments of intense legislative activity or the recurrence of maroon hunts correspond to an exceptional danger? In Martinique in 1671, the publication of a tariff of bounties suggests rather that hunting maroons was not very attractive.[23] Masters were then authorized to cut their hamstrings. But in May, an inhabitant was prosecuted for having beaten a woman to death and burned the private parts of a man. On 20 June 1672, the Conseil supérieur of Martinique laid down a sentence of death for those who, after being on the island for a year, remained maroons for longer than three years.[24] Governor General Baas made it compulsory to declare maroons and added a hierarchy of punishments.[25] In 1677, the Conseil supérieur of Martinique laid down that only the courts could order mutilation.[26] Since that principle was repeated in the edict of March 1685, does not this legislative activity reflect a determination to limit the powers of masters?

Environment and Solidarities

Distance was a factor in marronnage, as the maroon needed to know that food was available in areas where he might take refuge. But such considerations did not weigh absolutely, otherwise no one would have been able to keep a slave in Guyana. In Guadeloupe, marronnage increased as more and more land was occupied. In order to survive, the fugitives did not move too far away from their garden or, at least, stole from others' gardens while awaiting their own harvest. What seems to have been a more decisive factor was the reception they got.

Should we regard the colonized space and, beyond that, Europe, as being out of bounds to maroons and rebels? Some learnt of the privilege of the soil in France, and so tried their luck. The question of their being sent back, which had been mooted since October 1691,[27] was settled by the edict of October 1713, which legalized temporary slavery in France. For the administration, France was no longer an asylum. For the courts, the problem was more complex.

In the Islands, the question seemed settled by the convention signed with the British in St Kitts on 1 May 1627. Each side agreed to return runaways, whether they were slaves or indentured servants. There seem always to have been problems in enforcing this article, renewed for the last time on 16 November 1686. The war of words resumed in 1690 with Antigua[28] and St Kitts.[29] The removal of the French from the latter island in 1702 put an end to attempts to find procedures for exchanging runaways. The French administration refused to return those who had run away to rejoin their former masters.[30] In 1707, thirty-two slaves, previously belonging to Frenchmen, arrived in

Guadeloupe claiming religious reasons. Intendant Vaucresson demanded their release.[31] After 1711, runaways could change masters by being sold for the benefit of the king or by being given as a gift to administrators.[32]

In the absence of a convention, relations with Puerto Rico proceeded in this latter framework. According to Gaspar,[33] the problem appeared as early as 1664 with the arrival of four fugitives from the island of St Croix in Puerto Rico, where the Spanish governor left them free. The Spanish rulers confirmed this approach in 1680, 1693, 1740, 1750 and 1798. By 1714 there were already such large numbers of maroons in Puerto Rico that they formed a separate grouping in a suburb of the town of San Juan. St Eustatius, a Dutch island, and St Thomas, a Danish colony, applied similar policies. Yet it was Puerto Rico, the most distant of them, that was the focus of attention. The cedula of 1750 caused a big stir in the northern islands of the archipelago. In 1752, fifty slaves from Guadeloupe attempted to land in Puerto Rico,[34] and the subsequent development of this affair revealed that in the previous two years, sixteen had succeeded in taking refuge there. Twenty-four others were reported in 1753, seven in 1771.[35] With regard to Venezuela, the situation appears to have been more complex. In his apologia of 1681, Father Épiphane de Moirans recalled that he had first brought trouble on himself by taking on the defence of blacks from St Vincent who had been sold by the Governor of Cumana.[36] Conversely, since 1721, the French Governor of Grenada had been accusing his Spanish counterpart, de la Marguerite, of harbouring runaways.[37] By 1728, there were over 120 of them.[38] Had something really changed, or was it a matter of a different interpretation?

In the Guyanas, the first complaints were made in 1721 by residents of Surinam.[39] The following year, a black from French Guyana took the opposite route.[40] Was this something new, or was it the expression of a new sensibility? While at that time residents did not have the right to cut off the ears of a fugitive, a colonist had to go into exile for killing a maroon.[41] Was the danger not being exaggerated in 1718 when there was talk of panic in Cayenne?[42] When a security scare took hold in 1722, the governor authorized owners to open fire.[43] On the other hand, fugitives from outside were so welcome that the governor wanted to take them for himself.[44] After 1754, the maroons of Surinam began to move into French Guyana.[45] At least from 1762, they appeared as people with whom one could reach an understanding.[46] The war they had been waging against Holland in 1768 did not raise any concern. In 1774, attempts were being made to win them over.[47]

In the south, in 1732, the Governor of Para was still refusing to hand back runaway slaves claimed since 1729.[48] The King of Portugal ordered their return,[49] and twenty-five were sent back in 1735.[50] Other claims are reported in 1753 and 1766.[51] In 1767, when the Portuguese refused to allow a French mission to enter their territory, seven of their fugitives were confiscated for the King.[52]

The failure to proceed against important people for concealment of maroons should not be allowed to blind us. In France, the case of Marshal de Saxe, who was recruiting the slaves of others without paying a penny, is not an isolated case. Ships' captains were doing the same thing. For the residents, an example may be taken from the 1710 revolt. The principal accused found refuge, board and clothes in the house of his master, a militia officer.[53] In short, a dangerous maroon was rather one who caused a loss within the colony where he had his residence, and the harbourer could only be a *petit blanc*: a soldier or the master of a foreign vessel, and above all a non-white.

The Caribs were the first to be accused. In 1654, after clashes in Grenada and St Lucia, they attacked Martinique.[54] It was said that they would have quickly withdrawn if they had not been aided by runaway blacks. This alliance was again referred to in 1651–7,[55] but two expeditions did not encounter any in the community houses. Yet these blacks, described as maroons, reappear orange-red as Caribs, who in October 1657 agreed not to receive them any more. In 1678–9, Blénac repeated this accusation.[56] He ordered the arrest of fifteen Caribs from Dominica and threatened to hang them if they did not hand over the blacks that they had taken. Might they not have bought them? With regard to the people of St Vincent, viewed as those friendliest to the runaways, the Governor General, thwarted in his desire for vengeance by the twelve to eighteen months that it would take an expedition to be successful, resorted to calumny. For three centuries, readers believed that Father Épiphane de Moirans, en route to the Spanish colonies of Venezuela, had been murdered by the blacks of St Vincent who were transporting him.[57] In 1704, the subdelegate Mithon accused them again of harbouring maroons.[58] In 1714, intendant Vaucresson raised the stakes.[59] Five years later, to secure pardon for his participation in the 1717 revolt, Dubuc mounted an expedition against them. While he was in St Vincent, a delegation of blacks was negotiating in Martinique. Accused of harbouring large numbers of runaways, they admitted only three, a figure that may well not have been far from the truth.[60]

Should we accept the contrast suggested by some writers between the attitude of the mulatto as the enemy of the Negroes and that of the free Negro as a receiver of maroons? In Martinique, in 1665, when Governor Clodoré had no one to turn to but former fugitives commanded by one of their own, Fabulé,[61] it meant that Africans were hunting down Africans. In the eighteenth century, the burden once again fell on the militiamen of colour. To that end, after 1726, mulattoes and free blacks were incorporated into separate companies. The freeman of colour was regarded as dangerous, or at least useless, and he was forced to justify his usefulness by hunting maroons, and so the compulsion was a pretence. The fact is that whatever particular shade of colour they were, maroon hunters were rather men who were serving for their freedom. For in order to obtain the administrative authorization and, if possible, exemption from payment, male candidates had no other choice. Since others were earning more money and honour simply looking after their own businesses, light-skinned men did not seek to enter the constabulary of Saint-Domingue.

The notion of the free black hiding maroons does not stand up any better. In 1678, Blénac published an ordinance against those concealing them. In 1679, free blacks were mentioned. By analogy with the capitation affair, which began in 1683, we cannot accept the idea that the mulattoes were not targeted.[62] One case suffices: in 1678, Blénac accused the 'free blacks', perhaps for no more reasons than the Caribs, and proposed to deport them to Saint-Domingue. But in 1681, he took a position against intendant Patoulet by taking up the cudgels on their behalf.[63] On 20 January 1683, Patoulet allowed his hatred to erupt with the now classic arguments: debauchery, laziness, concealing maroons.[64] However, the fine of 300 livres provided for against freedmen concealing maroons by Article XXXIX of the edict of March 1685 (the *Code Noir*) was not directed only at free blacks. In 1704, Mithon returned to the themes developed by Patoulet to call for the loss of their freedom.[65] Ignoring family or racial ties and the spirit of resistance, he claimed that the 'free blacks' were making the maroons work in their gardens and sharing the fruits of their raiding with them. His proposal, approved on 10 June 1705, was applied to all freedmen.[66] In 1711, Governor General Phélypeaux repeated the same accusation to legitimize the ordinance of 15 August, subjecting all emancipations to prior administrative approval. Finally, the 'we Negroes' of the petition of 28 August 1789 covered slaves of all colours and, in that of the 29th, the divergences were above all at the level of the demands expressed by the freedmen in favour of mulatto slaves.[67]

In 1710, the judges overlooked the collusion. Are we to believe that, despite the *ponches de tafia* (rum punch), the dances were performed in such silence that the owners – the Ursulines of Saint-Pierre – and their neighbours were unaware of this *gaoulé* bringing together at least two whites and a free mulatto with slaves from different African ethnic groups as well as Creoles? In 1789, the way the judges meted out different punishments to different people masked the coming together of people of a broad range of racial and social backgrounds, whatever divisions might have existed in other spheres. In flight, Father Jean-Baptiste, a Capuchin, was not pursued. Nor was another white man who was compromised. The free mulatto Louis Genty was dismissed with the warning to be more careful in future. The free black Alexis René, who was said to be the writer of the letter sent on 29 August to Governor General Vioménil, signed 'The whole Nation', was released after agreeing to co-operate with the authorities, according to Dessalles. With the rural slaves absolved, it only remained to deal with the urban ones. Were they all really slaves? The references made in the letter of the 29th to mulattoes being better treated than blacks in the militia suggest the presence of people serving to obtain confirmation of their freedom. In addition, on 11 September, an ordinance provided for better supervision of men who were de facto free, of whom there were many among the workers in the port of Saint-Pierre, since 'they are all facing difficulties meeting their basic needs, and are behind the disorders that are disturbing society'. In short, assessing resistance faces problems that are not always apparent.

Associations, Demands or Plots?

The decline of marronnage seems, at least in Martinique, to run counter to the aspiration to freedom. Was there not a shift to other forms of resistance? What was actually being judged in 1710? A small group of maroons, located on the intendant's estate, caused a hue and cry about an attack that had been nipped in the bud. The fact that the militia had just distinguished itself by its lack of zeal in hunting them down allows us a glimpse of marked divergences between the administration and the residents. The former opted for strict application of the rules. The latter preferred to allow safety valves to work. Slaves from Saint-Pierre had formed an association, though it was an offence punishable by death for slaves belonging to different masters to meet.[68] Apart from the inevitable 'sorcerer', charged with selling 'cordons' (belts) that made it possible to fight without being wounded or to come back after running away without being punished, they had equipped themselves with a hierarchy copied from the dominant society: governor, intendant, captain, major, maitre d'hôtel and so on. The same features were to be found in Antigua in 1736 and, later, in other slave societies.

In August 1789, the insurgents claimed what they believed was already the law. The 1787 hurricane, the 1788 earthquake and the side-effects of the wheat crisis in France led to price rises and shortages at a time when unemployment was hitting the 'day Negroes' in the port of Saint-Pierre. For a year, slaves had been witnessing the rows between planters and traders, the emigration of freedmen protesting against the increase in their head tax, and the pre-Revolutionary discussions. In that context, Condorcet's letter requesting the inclusion in the cahiers of an 'examination of the means of destroying the slave trade and preparing the destruction of slavery' was interpreted all the more tendentiously because it was being repeatedly said that 'the Nation is free'. People were referring to the white, mulatto or black nation. But the slaves who referred to themselves as 'the nation' understood that they had been emancipated.[69]

In the town of Saint-Pierre, freedom seems to have been perceived at a conceptual level, well beyond primary reactions. In the Fort Church, the 'Negroes' priest', Father Jean-Baptiste, allowed them a glimpse of the end of slavery. The freemen of colour had disappointed them since their main concern was the rapid freeing of mulattoes. Discussions with militia officers and with Clarke, the doyen of the Conseil supérieur, and with the intendant left them convinced that only the masters were opposed to implementation of the royal decision. These notables had been easy to approach. Thus, one of the accused was a mulatto belonging to Clarke. Two others were slaves belonging to Lejeune de Montnoël, an officer in the militia. Governor General Vioménil having expressed sympathy with the people of colour, both slave and free, the idea took hold that he would be coming to Saint-Pierre on Sunday, 30 August, for the festival of St Louis. The conspirators had convinced the slaves from the town and the nearby estates to go in large numbers to meet him, in order to protect him, so that he could proclaim the law. That was why there was the meeting and the subsequent marronnage. The threats made on 28 August enabled Dessalles to distort this intention into a plot aimed at killing all of the whites, except for a few who would be kept as valets or concubines.

In Guyana, too, the slaves talked together, bandying about the famous theme of massacring all whites. Here in the countryside, more elementary representations could be glimpsed behind the word 'freedom': not to be subject to any constraints in their dances and the sale of the produce of their gardens.[70] The notion of equality appeared when one of these slaves said to his mistress: 'We're all equal now, we can eat together – just think of that.' Was this a repetition of the August movement and its extension to Guyana? In August in Saint-Pierre, the demand for equality barely went as far as the mulattoes. By December, we can see looming over both colonies Article I of the Declaration of the Rights of Man, not yet officially published, but read in the churches.

The oldest model of resistance was being replaced by other models in which integration was an aspect of resistance. Did not getting rid of all whites mean above all getting rid of inequality? In the seventeenth century, as in 1710 and 1789, convivial meetings figured prominently in the imaginary. They help in perceiving a black identity that was wider than that conveyed by the description 'Black Caribs'. At least in the 1770s, the 'Black Caribs', perceived in addition as coming within the French orbit, were enjoying genuine solidarities in the world of freemen and blacks in Martinique in their revolt against the British. The 'whole Nation' and 'we Negroes' of 1789 also went beyond the African tribal framework, already obsolete in 1710. Above all, without an external event, namely, the Revolution, would the masses not have continued to daydream about a very few racial, economic or cultural concerns, marked with that syncretism which we know as *créolité*?

Notes

1. A.N. Col. C8A 115, f. 210. Judgement of the Conseil supérieur of Martinique, 30 November 1815.
2. J. B. Du Tertre, *Histoire générale des Antilles habitées par les Français*, Paris, Th. Jolly, 1667–71; reprint, Fort-de-France, Horizons Caraïbes, 1973, Vol. 3, p. 179.
3. J. B. Du Tertre, op. cit., Vol. 1, p. 496.
4. A.N. Col. F3. f.651.
5. A.N. Col. C8A. f.362. 22 August 1708.
6. J. B. Du Tertre, op. cit., Vol. 3, p. 179, Vol. 2, p. 499.
7. A.N. Col. C8A 16.f.119. 10 November 1706.
8. Father Le Breton, 'Relation historique de l'isle de Saint-Vincent', *Annales des Antilles* (Martinique), No. 25, 1992, p. 37.
9. Jean-Pierre Moreau, *Les Petites Antilles de Christophe Colomb à Richelieu*, Paris, Karthala, 1992, p. 176.
10. A.N. Col. C8A. f.252. 8 November 1749.
11. R. Price, *Maroon Societies: Rebel Slave Communities in America*, New York, Anchor Books, 1973.
12. A.N. Col. F3 31.f.84. 30 November 1673.
13. A.N. Col. C8A 15.f.347. 20 November 1704.
14. A.N. Col. C8A 32.f.268. 17 November 1723.
15. A.N. Co. C8A 10.f.255. 6 October 1698, letter from Governor General d'Amblimont.
16. A.N. Col. C8A 35.f.145. 27 September 1726. f.197. 9 July 1726.
17. F. R. Dessalles, *Historique des troubles de la Martinique pendant la Révolution*, presented by H. de Frémont, Fort-de-France, Société d'histoire de la Martinique, 1982, p. 25.

18. A.N. Col. C8A 17.f.236
19. A.N. Col. C8A 18.f.297. 24 May 1712.
20. A.N. Col. F3 30.f.116.
21. A.N. Col. F3 22.f.495. 23 December 1789.
22. D. B. Gaspar, *Bondsmen and Rebels: A Study of Master-Slave Relations in Antigua*, Baltimore, Johns Hopkins University Press, 1985.
23. M. de Saint-Méry, *Loix et constitutions des colonies française de l'Amérique*, 6 Vols, Paris, by the author, 1784–1790, Vol. 1, p. 248.
24. Ibid., p. 264.
25. Ibid., p. 268. Ordinance of 23 August1673.
26. Ibid., p. 306.
27. A.N. Col. B 14.f.312.
28. A.N. Col. C8A.f.255. 24 October 1698.
29. A.N. Col. C8A 10.f.261. 28 November 1698.
30. A.N. Col. C8A 15.f.347. 20 November 1704.
31. A.N. Col. C8A 15.f.235. 24 July 1707.
32. A.N. Co. C8A 18.f.125. 8 July 1711.
33. D. B. Gaspar, op. cit., p. 205.
34. A.N. Col. C8B 10.f.56. 13 May 1752.
35. A.N. Col. C8A 72. 18 September 1773.f.170 et seq.
36. E. de Moirans, 'La liberté des esclaves ou défense juridique de la liberté naturelle des esclaves [Servi liberi seu naturalis mancipiorum libertatis justa defensio]'. Translated and presented by R. Lapierre, *Mémoires de la Société d'Histoire de la Martinique*, No. 6, 1995.
37. A.N. Col. C8B 7. f.115. 8 November 1721. C8A 245.f.287. 23 July 1725. C8A 35.f.145. 25 September 1726. At the time Grenada claimed it was being threatened by the maroons. In 1725, a provostal court pronounced twenty-four death sentences.
38. A.N. Col. C8B8.f.63. 12 June 1728.
39. A.N. Col. C14 7.f.15. 22 July 1712.
40. A.N. Col. C14 7.f.105. 11 October 1712.
41. A.N. Col. C14 8.f.85 11 August 1714.
42. A.N. Col. C14 11.f.40. 8 October 1718.
43. A.N. Col. C14 13.f.11. 11 January 1722.
44. A.N. Col. C14 9.f.36. 10 January 1716.
45. A.N. Col. C14 23.f.47. 10 May 1754.
46. A.N. Col. C14 25.f.318. 7 October 1762.
47. A.N. Col. C14 35.f.234.
48. A.N. Col. C14 14.f.46. 24 June 1732. f.310. 21 October 1729.
49. A.N. Col. C14 16.f.83. 1732.
50. A.N. Col. C14 16.f.50. 4 May1735.
51. A.N. Col. C14 22.f.8. 20 March 1753. C14 34.f.331. 18 July 1766.
52. A.N. Col. C14 35.f.271. 15 July 1767. C14 37.f.91. 13 May 1768.
53. A.N. Col. F3 247.f.382 et seq.
54. J. B. Du Tertre, op. cit., Vol. 1, p. 464.
55. Ibid., p. 496.
56. A.N. Col. C8A 2.f.79. 5 September 1679. 1 October. f. 131. 23 September. f.213. 22 September.
57. A.N. Col. C8A 2.f.206. 18 September 1679.
58. A.N. Col. C8A 16.f.119. 10 November 1704.
59. A.N. Col. C8A 20.f.50. 30 December 1714.
60. A.N. Col. C8A 26.f.204. 5 September 1719.
61. J. B. Du Tertre, op. cit., Vol. 2, p. 179.
62. Starting in 1696, the challenges initiated by the 'Negress' Magdeleine Berne – in reality a 'capress' (offspring of a Negro and a mulatto) – show that some of her children were mulatto women married to whites.
63. A.N. Col. C8A 2.f. 189. 23 September 1678. F3 248.f.221. 3 December 1681.

64. A.N. Col. F3 246.f.766.
65. A.N. Col. C8A 15.f.220. 12 June 1704. f.224. 29 June. f.267. 30 August.
66. A.N. Col. B26.f.116.
67. A.N. Col. C8A 89.f.69 and 70.
68. For Y. Debbasch, such associations did not come out into the open before 1793. See 'Les Associations serviles à la Martinique au XIXe siècle, contribution à l'étude de l'esclavage colonial', in *Études d'histoire du droit privé offertes à Pierre Pelot*, Paris, Dalloz, 1959, pp. 1–12.
69. A.N. Col. C8A.f.152. Letter of 13 November 1789. In 1850, Etienne Rufz de Layison noted that 'the African still calls his brother from Africa, my nation, nation me', *Études historiques et statistiques sur la population de Martinique*, Vol. 1, p. 147, St Pierre, 1854.
70. In these circumstances, the demand for three days of freedom a week seems somewhat belated.

Chapter 5

The Church and Slavery in Eighteenth-Century Saint-Domingue

Laënnec Hurbon

Historical Gaps

Missionaries with an interest in archives[1] provide an abundance of information about the life of the clergy but do not dare tackle the problem of slave
revolts, nor for that matter the role of the Church at the centre of such events.
A. Gisler's work (1965) does indeed deal with the theology and ethics that
inspired the action of missionaries in the seventeenth and eighteenth centuries, but it is not concerned with the participation of priests in the revolutionary movements that engulfed Saint-Domingue between 1789 and 1804.
Conversely, G. Debien (1974) devotes a long chapter to missionaries and slavery in his *Histoire de l'esclavage aux Antilles*, yet merely hints at the contradictions confronting the Church once it claimed to be engaged in the work of
evangelization. More recently, historians[2] have focused on the role of voodoo,
an African cult reworked by the slaves, in rumours about the poisoning of
colonists or in the maroon camps. The debates on the mobilizing force of
voodoo in the great slave insurrection of 1791 have had the effect of obscuring any interrogation of the role of the Church during the Revolutionary
period. Everything conspires to demonstrate that we already know everything
there is to know about the negative role of the Church: first, the clergy owned
slaves; second, the role of the clergy was to act as an ideological police agency,
given how long slavery had endured, and it was closely watched by the administration; and third, fear of the radical direction taken by the French Revolution after the Civil Constitution of the clergy drove the Church to withdraw
into itself and avoid any involvement in the anti-slavery revolts.

Our aim here is to show that the debate is not as simple as it appears.
Many eyewitness reports suggest that the Jesuits, driven out of Saint-
Domingue in 1764, prepared the ground, at least indirectly, for the slave uprising. Again, in the North province of Saint-Domingue, the majority of priests
went over to the insurgents. We shall attempt to look at these two aspect – the

Jesuits and the direct participation of priests in the insurrection – but we shall ask why Catholic historiography has obscured the positive role of numerous missionaries during the Revolutionary period in Saint-Domingue, whereas the Church has always claimed, since the event, that it had co-operated through its 'spiritual' work, in the abolition of slavery.

The Jesuits and the Cause of the Slaves

When Father Labat reached Saint-Domingue for his visit at the end of the seventeenth century, he did not conceal his disappointment at the situation of the Church. Guadeloupe and Martinique already had fifty years of missionary work behind them. Churches had been built, parishes were functioning more or less normally and priests were universally respected. In Saint-Domingue, however, the situation was quite different. In the church at Le Cap where he celebrated mass, Father Labat observed that

> no one thought of performing his devotions.... I cannot help saying that I was much scandalized by the *little* respect shown by the people for their religion. I thought I had been transported to a new world when I thought of our inhabitants in the Windward Islands and I compared their devotion, their exactitude in approaching the sacraments, their respect for their pastors and their modesty in the church to the extraordinary and licentious manners of these people. They came to church laughing and chaffing each other as if they were about to see some show or entertainment.[3]

Other travellers confirm Father Labat's impressions. The church of Port-de-Paix, for example, was built of wood and still open on all sides. Two Capuchins alone served it and scarcely had time to visit the estates. Monks, Dominicans and Carmelites worked in the North, living in poverty. In the South there were a few Dominicans, but for example in Acul, Petit-Goave, the residents had to club together to establish a living. Father Labat records that on his arrival in 1704, there were only eight parishes under Le Cap, and that the first task of the Jesuits who landed with him was to repair the churches, 'open on all sides and delivered over day and night to all sorts of profanations by man and beast'.[4] The slaves were baptized en masse – there were, in truth, only 9,000 of them in 1700 – but their religious instruction was reduced to very little: the *Credo*, the *Pater* and the *Ave Maria*.

Finally, it seems that it was with the Jesuits that the Church first began to put down roots in Saint-Domingue, but that implantation owed a great deal to the experience acquired in the first steps taken by the missionaries in Guadeloupe and Martinique. As the estates were created, and the sugar industry took off, thus intensifying the slave trade, it was felt increasingly that a religious establishment was needed. But this initially concerned those who were then called the 'habitants', that is the colonists and whites in general. These latter were less concerned about the religious life of the slaves. Administrators and missionaries often complained about the way in which the planters left their slaves bereft in terms of religion. It seems that only the baptism of slaves was tolerated. Whites were content simply to break in the freshly landed slaves to work on the plantations and in the gangs. Saint-Domingue had 9,000 slaves in 1700, 24,000 in 1713 and 110,000 in 1739. This indicates that the colony prospered with remarkable speed, the commercial and political circumstances being positive. In a very short time, Saint-Domingue became the centre for exchanges between Europe and America and largely overtook Martinique and Guadeloupe in the development of the sugar industry. There were 1,138 sugar mills in 1713, and 1,450 in 1759. In the North alone, 70,000 slaves were at work. At Le Cap, each year, 500 ships left for the ports of La Rochelle, Nantes, Bordeaux and Marseilles. Colonization had therefore now become essential for the development of France, and it was in that context that the Jesuits were entrusted with the task of evangelizing Saint-Domingue. But it must straight-away be added that the whites saw it simply as a matter of setting up the structures of the Church: building monasteries, charitable institutions (hospitals, orphanages), schools for girls and schools for boys. When Father Margat (a Jesuit missionary) spoke in his letter to the Procurator General of the Order in 1743 of succour offered 'to all the poor', he did not claim to be speaking of the slaves. The category of the poor included only whites who had come to make their fortune in the Islands, but who had met only with disappointment. Almost 600 of them were received into the Maison de Providence des Hommes. If people had taken the trouble to look after them earlier and not leave them destitute and sick, he reported, 'we would have preserved in the area under Le Cap alone more than 30,000 colonists whom poverty and despair had caused to die'.[5] Similarly, a Maison de la Providence had been opened for 'poor aged women', meaning white women reduced to begging. As regards parish administration, Father Margat again stressed: 'Only four priests are permanently resident in Le Cap. The parish priest, who has a vicar under him, is for the white residents of Le Cap. There is a priest for the Negroes who also ministers to sailors.' In ceremonies on Sundays and festivals, a clear distinction was made between the mass for the whites and 'the mass known as the Negro mass', which required 'an explanation of the Gospel and religious instruction proportionate to their capacity'.[6]

But conflicts arose between the Church and the colonists when the missionaries took it into their heads to pay some attention to the slaves. Yet those same missionaries owned slaves, either as domestics or as slaves on their plantations. There was thus apparently no reason to fear any real solidarity between the missionaries and the slaves, at least during the first half of the eighteenth century. Priests were needed for baptisms, which, by recording slaves, made possible some oversight of planters' assets and, above all, some monitoring of the behaviour of slaves in relation to their masters. Religious instruction had been taken more seriously in the seventeenth century, but it was now regarded as a danger. Now that slaves had become numerous and had been broken in to work at a brutal pace in the gangs, they needed to be subjected to closer surveillance. The world of the estate, the unit of production which counted sometimes up to 150 slaves, was strictly a circumscribed universe.

Managers had not the least wish to allow their slaves to go to catechism or to tolerate (religious) marriage, or even to grant slaves enough time to honour their dead. Missionaries complained about such negligence on the part of the colonists, but reproached them only for their religious indifference. The truth is that the colonists were pursuing a well-thought-out strategy. For them, slaves needed only to be taught docility by the missionaries, as the Church might threaten the very foundations of the institution of slavery on which the wealth of the colony rested. A letter from the Governor of Martinique to the Minister of the Navy, dated 11 April 1764, stressed the need to keep the blacks in the greatest ignorance in order to safeguard public order and for 'the security of whites'. The action of the Jesuits in favour of blacks thus came very rapidly to be seen as suspect. Father Boutin, parish priest of Le Cap, was on the receiving end of all manner of petty harassment from the administration for having pressed masters to send their slaves to mass and to catechism, and, above all, for having been willing to grant their dead a religious funeral. Masters saw this as awakening in blacks a feeling of equality with whites. It was better, said the Governor of Martinique in his letter, to treat the slaves like animals. But how was it possible to overcome the contradiction of simultaneously demanding the evangelization of blacks, which was one of the justifications of slavery? That contradiction was bound to become more acute as large numbers of slaves themselves began to take too great an interest in Catholic ceremonies. First, in 1733, the Conseil supérieur of Le Cap took aim at a Jesuit who had the bright idea of saying in a sermon that 'the blacks revolt against the whites and in so doing avenge God and that the time is not far off'. This surely indicates that the suffering of the blacks on the plantations and in the gangs was attracting attention, since it precipitated desertions, which led to a hardening of the punishment system. The Jesuits would therefore have been accused of being traitors to the cause of the colony for having shown tolerance towards maroons by welcoming them into churches. But what primarily drew down the wrath of the authorities was the work of evangelization itself. By creating, for example, a society called 'the slavery of the Blessed Virgin', the Jesuits seemed to be encouraging blacks to see their duty of absolute obedience to masters as a matter of degree. Indeed, so many slaves were to be found in that 'society' that an esprit de corps gradually took root among them. On 29 December 1752, a letter from the Minister of the Colonies rejected the whole project as indicative of an excessive hold by the Jesuits over the slaves which might eventually lead to revolts.[7]

After the Makandal affair – Makandal being a maroon slave known for his magical practices who specialized in the systematic poisoning of whites – the Jesuits were suspected of being too lukewarm in providing the co-operation expected of them in finding those guilty. In 1758, the colonists had captured Makandal and condemned him to death. When he was on the pyre, he had managed to escape and, from then on, slaves believed him to be invulnerable. Even after he had been retaken and executed, Makandal remained a legend, and all practices of poisoning and evil sorcery now bore his name. A collective hysteria gripped the colonists who hunted among the slaves for the accomplices of

Makandal, the leader of the revolts in the 1750s. There were numerous trials, but the imprisoned slaves consistently refused to denounce their comrades. However, the colonial administration was convinced that the Jesuits were behind the slaves' stubbornness in such an attitude of defiance. In a letter written from Cap-Français on 24 June 1758, bearing the title *Relation d'une conspiration tramée par les nègres de l'Isle de Saint-Domingue*, we read that a young imprisoned 'Negress' stated at her trial 'that the Jesuit father, who had come some time earlier to hear her confession, had forbidden her, on pain of eternal damnation, from revealing her accomplices, and [bid her] rather to suffer any tortures that might be inflicted on her'. Further on, we learn that 'when the governor was informed of the conduct of the Jesuit father, he caused him to be forbidden entrance to the prisons. It was also forbidden to all the reverend fathers and this article is enforced very strictly'.

The various complaints made by planters, managers and administrators against the Jesuits eventually won out. Under cover of the hunt for Jesuits unleashed by the government in metropolitan France, the Order was banned in Saint-Domingue in 1763. The property of the missionaries was confiscated on the spot and placed under the control of the churchwardens. Institutions, plantations, sugar mills and slaves – the Jesuits owned some, too, as we have seen – were resold to honour the debts contracted by the Order in illicit trading with other Caribbean islands. But we need to remember how this campaign of persecution against the Jesuits began. The Jesuits had long been suspected of constituting a religious society totally at the service of the Pope and little concerned with national interest, and had never inspired much confidence in the royal court in France. In 1682, in a charter written under Bossuet's patronage, Gallicanism was already expressing its determination to limit the domination of the Roman Church over the affairs of the nation-state. At the end of the reign of Louis XIV, the Jesuits were held responsible for the papal bull *Unigenitus* against Jansenism, which had some support in a parliament inclined to challenge the King's absolutist style. It was in such a context that Madame de Pompadour, the King's mistress, sought to wreak vengeance on the excessively strict Jesuit confessors at court by fuelling suspicions against the Order. Jean Lacouture correctly notes: 'Many logs were thus piling up at the foot of the Jesuits' stake in France.'[8] It was in fact not difficult to light the fire, thanks to the scandal caused by a Jesuit, the Society's purchasing agent in Martinique, who was trafficking in the Islands' produce for the benefit of the Order's works, even though such trafficking was forbidden by canon law. The fire took all the faster because the Jesuits were made the scapegoats for all of the difficulties encountered by the royal court in its determination to impose its absolutism. For example, rumours were put about that the Jesuits were behind Damiens's attempted regicide in 1757. Beyond these facts, which were, all in all, rather unconvincing as a justification for hunting down Jesuits, we must detect that the real debate was situated at the political level, because for the French state it was a matter of asserting its sovereignty against papal power represented by the Jesuits and of vigorously defending its own narrow interests. In Saint-Domingue and the other French-ruled islands, Gallicanism would play well, the Jesuits having been regarded, because of the trust the slaves had in them, as the colonists' chief enemies.

Let us stop and take a quick look at the intent of the Jesuits' action in favour of slaves. The Jesuits clearly remained far removed from any notion of abolition, having been slave-owners themselves. But on at least two levels their actions served the cause of the slaves and indirectly prepared the way for insurrection. First, their ultramontane position was undermining the bases of Gallicanism by relativizing the King's authority in ecclesiastical matters. It should be understood that at the end of the seventeenth century, a mere religious justification of slavery could prove to be very fragile.[9] The *Code Noir*, promulgated in 1685, sought precisely to give legal bases to the institution and thereby to make the state the ultimate foundation of slavery. In other words, the more the state took away from the master the possibility of having absolute power over the slave, the more the institution of slavery was likely to endure. The Jesuits' ultramontanism was bound, in such a context, to be seen as a threat in the colony. Second, on the strictly religious level, the Jesuits, by appointing *curés pour les nègres*, were providing the slaves with opportunities to meet and equip themselves with symbolic reference points that strengthened their bonds of solidarity. Even a devotion such as that to the Blessed Virgin was welcomed by the slaves, who interpreted it as further means of turning the duty of obedience to masters into a form of marronnage. Religious instruction was also fostering among slaves a sense of equality with whites. It is true that efforts were made to stress that this equality was on the spiritual level, but slaves were bound to translate it into concrete liberation. Finally, the lack of tolerance that the Jesuits showed towards African magical-religious practices led to the recycling of those practices at the very heart of the slaves' Catholicism. It is thus not surprising that the evangelization proposed by the Jesuits should have been sought out with fervour, even with passion, by slaves, once they embarked on a struggle to the death against the slave system.

Control of the Clergy on the Eve of the Revolution

When the Jesuits left Saint-Domingue in 1763, a seminary for the colonies was established in France, with the aim of training priests who would unfailingly serve the institution of slavery. The truth was that in the Islands, secular priests and religious continued to be criticized for their laxity towards the slaves. What travellers and also administrators called the decline of the morality of the colonial clergy – many of whom were said to be living in concubinage with Creole women – derived above all from the interest they took in mitigating the harsh treatment meted out to slaves. Not that the clergy did not themselves have wealth and slaves just like the colonists, but the task of evangelization created an insurmountable contradiction: it offered equality – if only in the next life – with whites. While there was no real decline in religious observance as a consequence of the departure of the Jesuits, what did happen was that the clergy were subjected to the closest surveillance.

On the one hand, it was recognized that there was a need to depend on the Church to contain the slaves and limit any recrudescence of marronnage, while, on the other, the dangerous character of evangelization was stressed again and again.[10] Thus, for example, for the Marquis de Fénelon, a colonial governor, religious instruction was an absolute necessity but was a dangerous means in the hands of priests because, he said, they had a hold on the 'Negroes' through instruction and confession. 'If a revolution were ever to happen in the colonies', he wrote, 'which is not mere fantasy, it will only come about through the monastical orders.... The security of the whites surrounded on their estates by negroes handed over to them, requires that they be kept in the most profound ignorance.'[11] Similarly, Malouet, an administrator, opposed the creation of a bishopric in Saint-Domingue. 'How would it be', he declared, 'if they [the 'Negroes'] saw a bishop respected by every order in the colony, clothed with every mark of his dignity, speaking to their masters with authority? They would take him for a God and the prelate would be the sole master of the inhabitants and the estates.' But curiously, at the same time, Malouet recognized that 'religion is the strongest barrier against a slave revolt'.

Only close control of the clergy's activities could – for lack of anything better – reassure the colonists. The *Règlement de discipline pour les nègres adressé aux curés des îles françaises d'Amérique*,[12] in 1777, was seen by the colonists as setting limits to the preaching and religious instruction offered to slaves. To remedy the slackening of religious life in the colonies, the document stressed that religious instruction must serve 'public safety, the interests of masters and the salvation of souls ... in the interest of the State and the Church'. Consequently, the most important thing was not to get the slaves to be fasting or mortifying themselves or even indulging in 'abundance of prayers and pious practices', since 'the continual work to which they are subjected takes the place of all that'. It was enough, then, to bind them to fulfil the duty attached to their estate and thus to make them accept internally their condition as slaves. On the means of instructing the slaves, the document recommended, given the little time that priests had with up to 10,000 slaves in their care, to divide them up in the churches into those baptized, those married and catechumens, and to make the most instructed responsible for organizing prayers and catechism. Similarly, the priest would have to make regular visits to the estates so as to prevent 'poisonings and suicides'. The regulation remained extremely close to the reality of slavery, which the author knew well, since he had spent twenty years in Martinique as a missionary. Poisonings and suicides, to which he added abortions and marronnage, were treated in this document as 'capital vices' and 'crimes', since they were subversive of the institution of slavery. A. Gisler, who has made a detailed study of the *Règlement de discipline*, sees it as an attempt to get a grip on the colonial clergy and redirect their activities in terms of the psychology of the slave, especially to deter him from any thought of revolt. The apostolic prefect invoked not only the slaves' passion for religious practices, but also 'their vulnerability to the contempt of their companion', in particular through the proposal for a humiliating 'penitential discipline', the exact tenor of which it is worth recalling:

We felt that the establishment of a penitential discipline was the sole means of securing among the Negroes the correction of certain vices which reprimands, threats and the harshest punishments cannot make them confess. We are not unaware of how the Christian religion does not know either violence or constraint but it does have the discipline of penalties that it can impose to punish the wicked ... for how can we contain within the bounds of duty people of such a gross character, so faithless and so inclined to evil, if religion did not impose on them a sort of punishment that hits them more than the chastisements themselves?

Concretely, the blacks denounced by their masters would have to kneel at the church door every Sunday and holy day during prayers and catechism for three or six months or even a year, depending on the seriousness of the offence. For the pardon, after signs of repentance: 'On Easter day, it being supremely a day of grace, we exhort masters to grant pardon to such of their slaves as arrive penitently.' On the penitent slaves, kneeling in the centre of the church, 'the priest, wearing his surplice and stole, shall pronounce the following words: for the runaway Negroes, faithless and wicked servants ... we condemn you to ...'.

Despite regulations designed to strengthen control over the clergy in the years immediately before 1789, slave revolts were becoming more numerous, marronnage was spreading, and there were more and more cases of poisoning. The administrators and colonists once again held the missionaries responsible for the growing lack of security in the colony. In 1781, a new royal ordinance declared that any priest suspected of disturbing public order would be sent back to France. Moreover, each apostolic prefect was required to examine the conduct of missionaries and to make a report thereon to the Governor General, as if this latter now had the real authority over the behaviour of the clergy. It is time now to look at the issue of the participation of priests in the great slave insurrection of August 1791.

The Clergy and the Insurrection of 1791

Rarely, if ever, has the problem of the participation of the clergy in the insurrection of August 1791 in Saint-Domingue been looked at in depth, yet it is the subject of various reports, including those of the anonymous author of *Histoire des désastres de Saint-Domingue* (1795) and Garran-Coulon (1796–9) and those addressed to Propaganda by Father Julien de Bourgogne (2 September 1797) and Charles Tarbé (*Rapport sur les troubles à Saint-Domingue*, 29 February 1792). Recently, in an article entitled 'Notes sur le clergé du Nord et la révolte des esclaves en 1791' (1992), Father Antoine Adrien has endeavoured to open up the debate on the attitude of the colonial clergy to the slave revolt in the North, although with the greatest caution. The evidence that he adduces is very important. I shall summarize it here. It makes it possible at once to abandon the current view that the clergy was wholly committed to the cause of slavery. Such a view was, it is true, already dubious, for administrators and colonists had never stopped criticizing the conduct of missionaries and proposing that they be subject to the strictest control. The expulsion of the Jesuits in 1763 must have been a source of at least temporary relief for the colonists. But what still remains an enigma for many contemporary observers is the admittedly scandalous behaviour of some priests with little interest in their own apostolic task and preoccupied with enriching themselves just like colonists, when they did not consort openly with Creole women, while those same priests opted to take the side of the rebellious slaves once the troubles came. It needs explaining. For the moment, we shall attempt to clarify the role of some missionaries in this insurrection, which was to result in the abolition of slavery in Saint-Domingue.

First, there were some priests – at least three – who were executed by the colonists for having gone over to the rebels. The best known is Father Philémon, the parish priest of Limbé, the parish where the insurrection broke out. He is described as a barbarous minister, a 'rogue', who had committed the 'crime' of allowing the slaves to seize white women who had come to seek refuge in the presbytery during the night of the insurrection. Garran-Coulon's report shows how much the colonists were taken by surprise by the scale of the revolt, which they regarded as acts of brigandage:

> Father Philémon, parish priest of Limbé, who was with the rebel Negroes from the beginning of the revolt as their pastor, or, more exactly, parish priest of Petite-Anse and their instigator, committed more than one crime. No sooner had they seen the flames devouring their rich possessions than the inhabitants of Limbé, as I said before, felt they could no longer put off seeking a safe haven; almost all had gathered in the presbytery; as the danger became more urgent, they were forced to move down to the shore where rowing boats awaited them and to abandon all they held most dear in the world to the discretion of a barbarous enemy. Then the rebels, absolute masters of the district, could not wait to fall on all the unfortunate women scattered and isolated on their estates. They sent them to the presbytery of the parish where Father Philémon was made their guardian. But how these unhappy women suffered both from the brigands and from that wretch Philémon! Each of them was the object of their infamous recreations, and even the young among them were not exempt from this abominable attitude! After making them work all day long in the garden or the kitchen, commanded by Negresses, they were shut up in the church where Father Philémon, as in a seraglio, came in the evening to select one with whom he would spend the night and handed the rest over to the brigands who fell on them in a crowd and took advantage of their weakness. This infamous traffic, tolerated by a minister of religion, went on for the space of two months.[13]

We can see here that Father Philémon was accused of every crime for throwing in his lot with the slaves. From the presbytery at Limbé to the rebel camp, a single bloc was now formed to respond to the colonists' reprisals, which were not long in coming. The profound involvement of Father Philémon in the insurrection is clear, since he spent two months among the insurgents, undoubtedly providing them with a great deal of valuable information on the enemy. We do not have further details about what Philémon did, but we do at least have the report of his capture and execution, which suggest that he was given almost as much responsibility as Boukman in the insurrection:

Father Philémon, parish priest of Limbé, tried and convicted of having maintained the Negroes in their revolt and having corresponded with their various leaders, as well as with the Spaniards, was hanged at four-thirty in the afternoon, Boukman's head being hung on the gallows to mock the intimate link that had existed between him and this leader.[14]

Then there was the case of Father Cachetan, parish priest of Petite-Anse, who was accused of having held white women and children prisoner and of having agreed to put himself at the service of the rebel slaves:

The clergy has disgraced France, contributing to our own disgrace. You shall judge of it by the conduct of a minister of religion. Father Cachetan ... who, like all the inhabitants of his district, could have withdrawn to Le Cap as soon as the insurrection broke out, preferred to remain among the rebel Negroes to preach the gospel of faith to make them persevere in an insurrection which he saw as holy and legitimate. He solemnly consecrated the Negro Jean-François and the Negress Charlotte king and queen of the Africans and leaders of the revolt. Thus, when the army seized the camp, seeing that he would soon be punished for his crimes, he took a lot of persuading to leave his presbytery. He made so bold as to say that he was tranquil among his parishioners (the Negroes) and that if his house had been damaged, it was only by whites. This unworthy minister of religion ... was incarcerated the day after his arrival in Le Cap.[15]

Barbé de Marbois, the anonymous author of L'histoire des désastres de Saint-Domingue, reports that Father Vasquez was an accomplice in the massacre of the French at Fort Dauphin in 1794. Father Delahaie, parish priest of Dondon, is known to have campaigned with Sonthonax in favour of the general emancipation of the slaves.[16] According to Madiou, Father Delahaie died at Le Cap in 1803, drowned by Rochambeau. Father Adrien maintains that at least four priests (and not three, as Father Cabon reports) must have been executed by the colonists and that overall, sixteen priests out of a total of twenty-four in the apostolic prefecture of the North followed the cause of the rebel slaves. This count by Father Cabon, who cannot be suspected of sympathy for this attitude on the part of the missionaries, is based on numerous reports, including those of Father Constantin, the apostolic prefect, Father Julien de Bourgogne (in a letter to Propaganda in the Vatican), Barbé de Marbois and Charles Tarbé. Similarly, in the convent of Notre Dame du Cap, nuns described complicitously the dances of the slaves as they went to attack the town of Le Cap. It seems indeed that the insurrection was not altogether a surprise for the priests and nuns who had close contacts with the slaves. Garran-Coulon's report also highlights the cases of priests who acted as negotiators between the colonists and the rebel slaves. Thus, Father Bienvenu, parish priest of Marmelade, was taken prisoner in an insurgent camp, as he was proposing to the slaves to negotiate with the enemy. Father Cabon rightly argued that 'the parish priests divided between the two parties: some, those in localities where whites were in control, held out for the whites, the rest followed the rebel bands'.[17]

But can we say that the clergy was chiefly responsible for the insurrection? When Garran-Coulon wrote 'It is not to the aristocracy alone that we should attribute the cause of our disasters; the clergy brought about France's misfortune, and thereby contributed to our own', he seems to be suggesting that the clergy had a driving role in the insurrection. The bitterness with which he describes the action of priests on the slaves' side shows very serious disappointment on the part of the colonists about a clergy from whom they expected more support. 'Scoundrels', 'bandits' and 'barbarians' are some of the names he uses to describe priests, blaming them for atrocities (crimes, rape and the killing of children) committed by the insurgents. There were two reasons for him to blacken the behaviour of the clergy as much as that of the slaves: on the one hand, he needed to show how far the colonists were in danger and win support from the metropole; on the other, it had to be shown that the blacks by themselves had no taste for freedom and thus that they had been pushed into insurrection by a dissolute clergy. Conversely, to maintain that only the priests had given the slaves an education in freedom would be to exaggerate the role of the clergy. Such an argument can only be advanced with the aim of obscuring the no less important role played by voodoo in the organization of the insurrection.

How then are we to explain that such a large number of priests in the North province supported the insurrection of 1791? First, the monks, Capuchins, were part of the lower clergy whose demands were known in the metropole and who thus had an interest in the overthrow of the Ancien Régime. Second, they were tired of the petty annoyances of the colonial administration, and so opted for the cause of the rebel slaves. But there is more: the Capuchins in the North had almost all had the time to swear allegiance to the Civil Constitution of the clergy. Rome would have had to accept their collective secularization on 23 July 1791. Everything thus tends to indicate that their commitment on the side of the slaves was not the result of opportunism.

But this commitment on the part of the Capuchins in the North does not give grounds for speaking of a change of attitude by the Church towards slaves. At most it must be acknowledged that there was a deep division in the Church in the midst of the turmoil of the revolution in metropolitan France as in the colonies.[18] In the south of Saint-Domingue, where the revolts were not so intense but where the slaves' demands were firm, the religious do not appear to have advocated insurrection. On this aspect, Antoine Gisler's thesis on the Church's role in propping up slavery is not refuted. Rome never supported the slaves' right to rebel, any more than it approved the French Revolution and the Civil Constitution of the clergy. The problematic of the Rights of Man and the Citizen, as it had been inaugurated in 1789, was rejected en bloc by the Church, which had clearly seen that it was a direct blow at its privileges in the Ancien Régime.[19] It was not until Vatican II that there began to be a change in the position of the Church on human rights, but there again, Father Grégoire, fervent defender of abolition based on the principles of fundamental universal human rights, remained schismatic vis-à-vis Rome. While Toussaint Louverture was seeking to make permanent the abolition of slavery – achieved in August 1791, proclaimed by Sonthonax in 1793 and ratified by the

Convention in 1794 – the only means he could find of reintegrating the Church into Saint-Domingue society was to appeal to the clergy who had taken the oath. Father Grégoire was to supply him with precisely twelve priests who accepted the Civil Constitution of the clergy.[20]

One last question must be addressed here, before we conclude. How was the Christian doctrine received by the slaves? It has often been suggested that the slaves could not by themselves, from their own culture, have an ideology of human rights that could drive them to revolt, and that only Christianity gave it to them. To pose the problem in that way is to imagine the slave masses as totally isolated from the rest of Saint-Domingue society and enclosed in traditions imported from Africa that had stayed unchanged. But what actually happened was rather that the slaves had been abruptly plunged into a modern context, the context of slavery based on profitability, which is to be observed in the Americas. The African ethnic groups were broken up in the horror of slavery and the blacks had to re-create a new cultural system. What Christianity offered – and that, moreover, is one of the factors explaining the slaves' infatuation with Catholicism – was not only symbolic reference points favourable to the development of solidarity, but also props for the reconstruction of lost or forgotten African traditions. That was how it was possible to reconstitute voodoo at the heart of Catholicism, the sole religion tolerated. This capacity of slaves in struggle to play on the very contradictions intrinsic to the slave system that imposed a controlled Christianity is evidence of their determination in their insurrection and the rationality that they used to attain their objectives.[21] In the last analysis, we cannot, in my opinion, state that the insurrection of 1791 was due uniquely to Christianity or the doctrine of 'spiritual' equality internalized by the slaves, nor solely to voodoo, which provided the site where the revolts fomented. The insurrection seems rather to have rested on Christianity *and* voodoo, both symbolic bases that made it possible to cement and consolidate the action of the slaves, as a solidary group determined no longer to be outsiders in the colonial space. The problematic of universal human rights that was abroad among the mulattoes, as it was among a clergy muzzled by the administration, easily filtered down to the drivers, domestic slaves and maroon leaders to the point that the least breach in the slave system might open the floodgates to a slave insurrection.

Notes

1. For example, Mgr Jan (1955) who in his work on the parishes and congregations in Saint-Domingue describes the life of the clergy in the eighteenth century; or J. Rennard (1954).
2. Such as P. Pluchon (1987), but without throwing any real light on the debate on the sources of the insurrection of 1791.
3. Father Labat (1742), Vol. III, p. 232 [*Memoirs of Père Labat 1693–1705*, p. 148]. On religious life in Saint-Domingue in the eighteenth century, see G. Debien (1974), p. 268 et seq.; H.-J. Sosis (1971), p. 194; A. Gisler (1965); and L. Peytraud (1897).
4. Mgr. Jan (1955), p. 31.
5. Ibid., p. 35.
6. Ibid., p. 36.
7. Cited by G. Debien (1974), p. 286.
8. J. Lacouture (1991), Vol. I, p. 447 [*The Jesuits* (1996), p. 274].
9. See L. Peytraud (1897), pp. 191–2, on the ruling of the Conseil of Le Cap of 18 January 1761. This ruling banned meetings of slaves in churches where domestics and workers set up meetings between noon and 2 o'clock. The Jesuits were accused of giving runaway slaves refuge in churches. The same ruling ended by forbidding slaves from serving as beadles, vergers or catechists, or from going from house to house preaching, so suspect did their infatuation with the Catholic religion seem in the eyes of the colonists.
10. I have attempted elsewhere to show in what way the state had been the ultimate guarantor of modern slavery in the Americas.
11. Letter from the Marquis de Fénelon, 11 April 1764.
12. Cited by A. Gisler (1965), p. 172.
13. See A. Gisler (1965), p. 185 et seq.; and G. Debien (1974), pp. 288 et seq.
14. See J. Thibau (1989), pp. 311–12; see *Boston Independent Chronicle*, 8 December 1791.
15. See J. Thibau (1989), pp. 311–12.
16. Ibid., p. 309.
17. Father Delahaie is again mentioned in Garran-Coulon's report, as a negotiator between the insurgent slaves and the colonists, but he is later found alongside Toussaint Louverture. See Y. Bénot, 'Un épisode décisif de l'insurrection: la prise de Dondon (10 septembre 1791)', *Chemins Critiques*, Vol. 2, 1992, pp. 97–112.. Similarly, Barbé de Marbois (1795) reports that Father Delahaie had close relations with Biassou, who was expecting from him a 'plan of conduct' and 'a code of law for governing his nation'. See Adrien (1992), p. 54, note 2.
18. Eyewitness accounts of the life of the clergy in Saint-Domingue in the eighteenth century, such as those of A. S. Wimpffen (recently republished by P. Pluchon), speak of 'parish priests tranquil in their presbytery' who 'are consuming quite a considerable income', who preach little or who are irregular (pp. 222–4); see also F. Girod (1972) and C. Frostin (1979) or H.-J. Sosis (1971), who stress the depravity of the clergy on the eve of the Revolution. But what seems relevant to us is much more the division of the clergy between those who opted for the side of the rebellious slaves and those who placed themselves at the service of the colonists or who fled with them.
19. Cabon (1933), p. 35.
20. Cabon (1933, p. 65) mentions at the same time that former missionaries had to leave Saint-Domingue with the abolition of slavery. Three bishoprics (West, South and Samana) were created by a decree of the National Council realized under the leadership of Father Grégoire.
21. On the political and religious issues of the Civil Constitution of the clergy, see the excellent work of T. Tackett (1986) and the articles in *Concilium* on the Revolution and the Church, by Cholvy, Plongeron, Comby and Menozzi (1989), which all show how far the struggle against the ideals of the French Revolution had been a point of honour for the Church.

Bibliography

ADRIEN, A. 'Notes sur le clergé du Nord et la révolte des esclaves en 1791'. In: *Évangélisation d'Haïti 1492–1992*. Port-au-Prince, 1992.

BÉNOT, Y. *La Révolution française et la fin de colonies*. Paris, Éd. La Découverte, 1987 and 1992.

———. 'Un épisode décisif de l'insurrection: la prise de Dondon (10 septembre 1791)'. *Chemins Critiques*, revue haïtiano-caraïbéenne, Vol. 2, 3 May 1992, pp. 97–112.

CABON, A. *Notes sur l'histoire religieuse d'Haïti. 1789–1860*. Port-au-Prince, Petit séminaire collège Saint-Martial, 1933.

CARTEAU, E. *Soirées bermudiennes*. Borduaux, Peltier-Lavalle, 1802.

CHOLVY, G. 'La Révolution et l'Église. Ruptures et continuités'. *Concilium*, Vol. 221, 1989, pp. 54–5.

COMBY, J. 'Liberté, égalité, fraternité: principes pour une nation et pour une Église'. *Concilium, revue internationale de théologie*, Vol. 221, Paris, Beauchesne, 1989, pp. 21–30.

DEBIEN, G. *Les Esclaves aux Antilles françaises (XVIIe–XVIIIe siècles)*. Basse-Terre and Fort-de-France, Société d'histoire de la Guadeloupe et de la Martinique, 1974.

FROSTIN, C. 'Méthodologie missionnaire et sentiment religieux, en Amérique française au XVIIe et XVIIIe siècles'. *Cahier d'Histoire ...*, 1979.

GIROD, F. *La Vie quotidienne dans la société créole: Saint-Domingue au XVIIIe siècle*. Paris, Hachette, 1972.

GISLER, A. *L'Esclavage aux Antilles françaises (XVIIe–XIXe siècles)*. Freiburg (Switzerland), Éditions Universitaires, 1965.

GOURRAN-COULON, J. P. *Rapport sur les troubles de Saint-Domingue*. Commission des colonies, Paris, Imprimerie Nationale, 1797–99.

GROS. *Isle de Saint-Domingue, Province du Nord, Précis historique*. Paris, 1793.

HURBON, L. 'État et religion au XVIIIe siècle face à l'esclavage au Nouveau Monde'. *Peuples Méditerranéens*, Vols 27–8, 1984.

———. 'Esclavage moderne et État de droit'. In: H. Bresc and C. Veauvy (eds), *Collectif Genèse de l'État moderne*, Rome, École française de Rome, 1993.

JAN, Mgr. *Le Cap français*. Vol. 1. Port-au-Prince, Editions H. Deschamps, 1955.

LABAT, J.B. *Nouveau voyage aux Isles de l'Amériques*. 2 Vols. The Hague, 1742 [*Memoirs of Père Labat 1693–1705*, Eng. trans., abridged by J. Aden, London, Constable and Co, 1931].

LACOUTURE, J. *Jésuites I Les Conquérants*. Paris, Seuil, 1991 [Eng. trans. J. Leggatt, *The Jesuits*, London, Harvill Press, 1996].

MARBOIS, Barbé de. *L'histoire des désastres de Saint-Domingue*. Paris, Garnery, 1795.

MENOZZI, D. 'L'importance de la réaction catholique à la Révolution'. *Concilium*, Vol. 221, 1989, pp. 83–94.

PEYTRAUD, L. *L'Esclavage au Antilles françaises avant 1789*. Paris, Hachette, 1897.

PLONGERON, B. *L'Abbé Grégoire ou l'Arche de la Fraternité*. Paris, Letouzet Editions, 1989.

PLUCHON, P. *Vaudou, sorciers, empoisonneurs de Saint-Domingue à Haïti*. Paris, Karthala, 1987.

RENNARD, J. *Histoire religieuse des Antilles françaises des origines à 1914*. Paris, 1954.

SOSIS, H.-J. 'The Colonial Environment and Religion in Haiti: An Introduction to the Black Slave Cults in Eighteenth-Century Saint-Domingue'. Ph.D. diss., Columbia University, 1971.

TACKETT, T. N. *Religion, Revolution and Regional Culture*. Guildford, 1986.

THIBAU, J. *Le Temps de Saint-Domingue: l'esclavage et la Révolution française*. Paris, Éd. J.C. Lattès, 1989.

WIMPFFEN, A. S. de. In: P. Pluchon (ed.), *Haïti au XVIIIe siècle: Richesse et esclavage dans une colonie française*. Paris, Karthala, 1993.

Part II

Was There a Demand for Abolition in Western Thought in the Eighteenth Century?

Chapter 6

British Abolitionism, 1787–1838

James Walvin

Birth and Growth of the Abolitionist Spirit

At first sight, the British abolition movement was totally successful in a relatively short time. Within twenty years of the movement's initial creation in 1787, the British Atlantic slave trade had been abolished. Later, when the movement had been revitalized after 1825, slavery in the British colonies themselves was abolished between 1834 and 1838. No one in 1787 would have dared to hope that they would succeed so quickly and so thoroughly. But, of course, they were aided by forces they could scarcely understand, see or predict. What enabled the abolitionist movement to succeed were forces transforming British life in conjunction with seismic changes among the slaves in the colonies. The abolitionist movement in Britain has often been credited with being solely responsible for bringing the British slave system down. Modern historians do not seek to deny its importance – or to minimize its contribution – when they look for a much broader explanation for the end of the British slave system.

First, it is important to understand why the abolitionist movement alone, taken in isolation from other factors, has received so much praise in the historiography of abolition which, until 1945, simply took it at its word, relying on what the abolitionists had themselves said of their actions. The most prominent abolitionists (notably Thomas Clarkson and William Wilberforce) were great publicists, for themselves and their campaigns, throughout their public life. Indeed, it was part of their goal to establish in the British mind that they and their followers were the personification of the drive to end slavery. It was also an era which saw the unfolding of history and contemporary politics in personal terms, in terms of individuals locked in combat – great figures engaged against a background of epic struggles. This image, assiduously promoted by the abolitionist propaganda machine, portrayed abolitionists as Good versus Evil (slave-owners). It proved an effective ploy. Moreover, after abolition in 1838, it was an image which was perpetuated by successive generations of historians anxious to portray abolition as the triumph of divinely inspired men over the forces of darkness.

For over a century, this view of history in which Good – and religion – triumphed over Evil remained intact. It was, of course, difficult to argue against that simplification without appearing to strip slavery of its gross immorality. And that, in a way, was a result of the work of the abolitionists, for what they did, so quickly and so brilliantly, was to capture the high moral ground. They had ensured for themselves a morally unassailable position which could not be gainsaid. They were men – and women – of an exemplary religious devotion, who sought to carry on through God's will in their fight against a slave system that they accused of being irreligious. Needless to say, the story was much more complex than that. Yet it needs to be stressed that the triumph of abolitionism helped to establish the abolitionists' own interpretation as the definitive explanation for the ending of British slavery. This mythology, so long dominant, has been challenged in the years since 1945.

The origins of the British abolition movement were rooted in the influence of Enlightenment writing (most notably Montesquieu) and the development of British non-conformity. The majority of members of the first abolitionist group in 1787 were Quakers. Quaker groups had been created across the face of Britain from the early eighteenth century, and they gave the abolitionists an immediate national network. When the movement's speakers travelled round the country to make speeches, they found local sympathizers who saw to their accommodation, organized meetings and got the public out. They were also – and crucially – a literate constituency. Thus, when the Revolution broke out in France, the national abolitionist network was already well organized, with the grass-roots support of the religious non-conformists. Moreover, many of these activists were influential and prominent men whose authority was unimpeachable and who could, accordingly, secure respect and a hearing in their locality.

This embryonic network was galvanized, like much else, by the impact of 1789. The vocabulary of abolition was transformed by the vernacular of the French Revolution, as slogans such as the 'Rights of Man' and 'Liberty, Equality, Fraternity' entered deeply into the everyday political vocabulary of Britain. At least until 1791, the changes in France were a source of energy and inspiration for British abolition, as they were for the radical movement in Britain. The British often looked to Paris and, seeing the old regime under constant attack, seemed to draw inspiration from those methods and seek in them hope for thoroughgoing change in their own country. These same changes, of course, also strengthened defenders of the established order. While abolitionists and radicals saw in them an added reason to demand reform, for the same reason defenders of the existing order were encouraged to dig in against all change.

Nevertheless, initially it seems that the Revolution in France acted as a fillip to major groups in Britain to step up their efforts to secure reform. The abolitionists were able to capitalize on the mood for reform by gathering remarkable numbers of signatures on abolitionist petitions, which they submitted to Parliament. They issued cheap and plentiful tracts, simple publications which presented abolitionist arguments in a direct, crisp format to a British reader-ship which was (at least in towns and cities) much more widespread than any-thing the government feared. We cannot tell how many people read this abolitionist literature, but we do know that it was consumed in taverns, cof-fee-houses, private homes and public meeting places by the millions. This led to a remarkable outpouring of this cheap literature – by both abolitionists and radicals – which met a growing demand among readers.

Between 1787 and 1789, there was an explosion of interest in the argu-ments being advanced by abolitionists. The abolitionists' opponents – the West Indian planters, the Atlantic merchants and bankers and those with interests closely tied to the slave empire – were clearly taken by surprise. For more than a century they had thrived, unchallenged by questions of morality, because they had brought such amazing prosperity to Britain. There was no denying the growth of the mother country and of cities such as Glasgow, Bris-tol, Liverpool and, of course, London; the magnificent homes and palaces built with wealth derived from the slavery of blacks; the charm of London and Bath, often linked to the profits of the same system – all that and much else besides were confirmation of the value and infallibility of the Atlantic slave trade system. The profits of black slavery were there for all to see. Whatever moral doubts about slavery may have existed, they remained the preserve of a minority. Moreover, the incalculable suffering which the British slave empire had brought forth was far away in Africa, on the Atlantic crossings and in the American colonies. There were, of course, thousands of Britons who knew what slavery really meant, most notably those men who worked on the slave ships and in the slave colonies, or those military and government officials who had spent part of their careers in the slave colonies. But they, too, stayed silent.

This is a key point. For over a century, from the establishment of the Eng-lish colony of Jamaica in 1655, Britain had benefited from the influx of wealth from its slave colonies without bothering too much about the inhu-man and immoral horrors that underpinned the system. Then, after 1787, there was an enormously rapid and unexpected change. First, the Enlighten-ment ideals for the first time called into question the morality of slavery. A hint of doubt as to the inhumanity of the institution began to emerge in edu-cated circles. The events of 1789 transformed that doubt into a basic objec-tion. From the ideals of the Revolution, there emerged a key debate on the justification of slavery. But this criticism, supported by the self-assured abo-litionists, confronted the massive obstacle of self-centred economic interest. The slave lobby's case was simple and apparently irrefutable. The wealth that poured into Britain's major slave ports was massive and irreplaceable. Were the slave trade to end, it would bring the wealth pouring into British ports to a halt. That, they argued, would cause Britain to suffer massive economic loss. How could they be answered?

For their part, the abolitionists adopted a different tack after 1787. Their basic premise was to attack the slave system of the Caribbean by ending the Atlantic slave trade. If new supplies of Africans were no longer available to the planters – if they had to rely on existing slave populations for their labour force in the islands – the planters would be obliged to treat their slaves better. And if their treatment of slaves improved, the health of the population would improve, the population would flourish and, before long, a black peasantry would emerge which would provide the opportunity of free labour, rather than slave labour. It was, of course, a highly speculative venture. But it had the benefits of being specific and manageable. With such an argument, it became possible to convince Parliament to modify the way that the transatlantic trade was organized.

From 1792, the abolitionists had lodged the issue of abolition inside Parliament. Thereafter it was subject to the whims and unpredictabilities of parliamentary moods and accidents. Indeed, had Wilberforce been a better manager of votes, it is very likely that Parliament would have passed abolition before 1807. There intervened, however, war between Britain and France, the slave revolution in Haiti and a domestic attack on British radicalism. From 1792 onwards, a growing body of opinion, inside and outside Parliament, feared demands for change because they seemed to be influenced by France and because they threatened to duplicate the disasters that the French had experienced in Saint-Domingue. The slaves themselves had begun to play an obvious and undeniable role in the debate about their own future. This was to be the turning point in the story of British abolition.

Initially, after the declaration of war, British Members of Parliament – and all the organized interests which supported them – recoiled from the idea even of discussing the end of the slave trade because it seemed likely to threaten a reprise of events in Haiti. It seemed, they claimed, madness to debate abolition when in the Caribbean there was a convulsion among slaves in the French colony which threatened to prove contagious. Indeed, planters throughout the region were deeply alarmed about the spread of slave insurrection from one island to another. They monitored movements between the islands and watched with horror as Haiti swallowed up a British army, which had set out to establish British rule there. The outcome was an effective end to realistic prospects for ending the British slave trade for a decade. Ultimately, it took the ending of Pitt's regime and the brief period of peace between Britain and France before abolition made further headway. But when it did, in 1806, it rapidly passed through Parliament. By 1807 the British had ended their Atlantic slave trade.

Thereafter – indeed for more than a century – the British embarked on a new crusade: to persuade the rest of the world to follow their own self-righteous lead. Although they had been the leading slave traders in the eighteenth century, they now turned their backs on it and fully intended to make others follow their example. Invoking morality and Christianity, but using the power of the Royal Navy and the diplomatic muscle of the Foreign Office, the British set about imposing abolition on the rest of the world. Needless to say, few people were impressed by this remarkable, almost St Paul-like conversion, and other European nations viewed it differently. The French had good reason to doubt British sincerity, the Spanish and the Portuguese still had empires that demanded fresh Africans, and the new United States of America was unhappy to follow the lead of its former colonial governor. But this did not deter the British from pursuing what they regarded as their divinely appointed mission. Few of the British stood back to question the curiousness of their posture – slave poacher turned abolitionist gamekeeper.

At the end of the Napoleonic Wars, the British used the Congress of Vienna meetings in 1814–5 to promote the case for abolition, with varying degrees of success. They were also able to apply pressure through their ships and their diplomacy. In effect, abolition became a permanent objective of British foreign policy for the rest of the nineteenth century. In the eighteenth century, when they were the leading slave trading power, they were Africans' main scourge, but now they had taken upon themselves the role of saviours of those very same Africans and other peoples, whom they claimed to protect from the threat of slavery. This role caused intense irritation to other powers, most notably the French and the Americans. But British naval power – buoyed up by expansive industrial wealth and reinforced by major international possessions – enabled the British to cloak their action in the guise of a pious mission to safeguard virtue against the threats of Evil. Opponents were inclined to see it in more down-to-earth terms.

British self-interest was no longer served by the slave trade. But if they sought to promote freedom, the new forms of economic prosperity that came with it suited, of course, a broad range of British interests. Freedom meant free trade, free labour, the free movement of capital – in effect, the freedom of an ascendant British economy to invest, exploit and control, as best it could within the constraint of a new economic world system. Whereas, by and large, the era of slavery was one in which the theory of mercantilism reigned – closed systems controlled by and for the mother country – British economic ideology in the nineteenth century demanded freedom. Of course, this economic ideal had severe limitations. Nonetheless, it stood in marked contrast to the dominant ethos of the previous century. Freedom, not slavery, was the leitmotif of British Atlantic trade and business in the nineteenth century.

After the British abolition of the slave trade in 1807, there was a brief respite before the abolitionists renewed their attack – this time on slavery itself. The gap was understandable. First, the war consumed all energies and diverted all demands for reform. But perhaps more importantly, it was essential to wait and see what results were produced, in the Caribbean by the ending of the slave trade. By the early 1820s, when the first census returns from the slave islands had yielded reliable data, it was clear that the slave population was in decline. This is exactly what the planters had predicted, but it was merely a phase of a natural cycle, lasting only until young slaves, who had been children when abolition was passed, entered their child-bearing years. From the mid-1820s, the slave population began to pick up and grow, slowly but steadily. In the meantime, planters, faced with a possible decline in their slave labour force, began to reorganize their slave gangs. One result was that house slaves and those who might have expected improvements found themselves labouring in the fields. These reorganizations – necessary for the planters – served to increase discontent among the slaves.

There were other powerful forces for change among the slaves. First and foremost, they were rapidly and universally converting to Christianity in the British islands, notably to dissenting churches (Baptists and Methodists). With the end of the slave trade, African-born slaves began to die off and were replaced by Island-born slaves, and ever more of them were Christian. This had dramatic results that had long been feared by the planters but were generally unexpected by the missionaries. A few years later, in the reign of Queen Victoria, following the abolition of slavery, the British tended to see in the liberation of the blacks the triumph of Christianity that had been previously thwarted by slavery. We do not need to go to that extreme to acknowledge that conversion to Christianity introduced qualitative changes in the life of slaves. For a start, it gave slaves an ideological unity that they had previously lacked. More than that, it gave them a direct bond with a growing band of abolitionists in Britain. In the past, the ill-treatment suffered by the slaves had been held up as the means of keeping 'uncivilized' Africans in their place. But the maltreatment of black Christian slaves took on the appearance of a cruel persecution that was quite unnecessary. Non-conformists in Britain were outraged to hear stories about the punishments inflicted on their black co-religionists. Thus, in an unusual twist, black and white came together as never before.

It was in the Caribbean islands that black Christianity produced its most fundamental changes. First, the new chapels provided slaves with a meeting place away from the plantations. They also offered a forum for the emergence of powerful black preachers, steeped in the imagery and vocabulary of the Bible. With their charismatic qualities, they would become the recognized leaders of the local black communities. They told their black followers of the promise of a better life to come, of redemption, salvation and the promised land. They talked of crossing the Jordan, of escaping from the house of bondage, images that had a very definite meaning for the slaves. The Old Testament, in particular, was replete with imagery of direct relevance for people in bondage, awaiting salvation and freedom. Black Christianity deeply impressed visitors to the islands with its fervour, its noise, its enthusiasm. But its most impressive impact remained unnoticed at first, for it was crucially important in focusing the slaves' attention on their condition and raising their hopes of salvation to come.

Black church leaders demanded a salvation in the here and now. More and more slaves were unprepared to wait for the distant prospects of heavenly salvation. This expectation, whose intensity varied from island to island, was expressed in a variety of ways. Its most potent expression took the form of major slave rebellions – in Barbados in 1816, in Demerara in 1823 and then, most seismic of all, in Jamaica in 1831–2. The causes were local, of course, but everywhere there were the same sources that we have just mentioned: the reorganization of the slave gangs and the consequent feeling of disappointed hopes, and the ideological impact of Christianity, which brought people together. Running like a descant through it all was a rising sense of unease, in Britain about the processes needed to keep slavery in place. Each slave uprising was put down using a level of violence that shocked opinion in Britain. What had been accepted as obvious in the seventeenth and eighteenth centuries now aroused grave concern and indignation. The British were sickened by the idea of the collective killings, torture and massacres that were needed to maintain slavery. The question was asked: If slavery could be kept in place only by violence on a truly medieval level, was slavery worth it? Here we touch on the other crucial element. Britain itself was changing.

By the mid-1820s the British had lurched into the first phases of major urbanization and industrial growth. A growing proportion of the people found themselves living in an urban habitat, where political organization was easier and where the printed word could circulate more freely and readily. Popular literature swirled through British towns as never before. The abolitionists took advantage of this situation to flood the country with their writings. Millions of tracts and pamphlets advocating the freedom of blacks were put out by local abolitionist groups and carried all over the country. For those who were interested, there were lectures on the abolitionist circuits. Tens of thousands turned up to listen to the abolitionist case. Indeed, the only restraints on abolitionist lectures was the physical capacity of the meeting places. In all this women played an increasingly notable role. Thus, the printed and the spoken word swept up the British people in the movement.

From 1825 abolitionists turned once again to the petition as an expression of opinion. Thousands of petitions, with millions of signatures, flooded into Parliament, at first demanding a whole raft of improvements for slaves, and then calling for outright abolition. MPs were lobbied in their constituencies; they were in effect threatened that unless they supported abolition in Parliament, abolitionists would direct their powerful armies of supporters against the MP in any future election. Thus, a groundswell of abolitionist sentiment was built up, in the country at large and within Parliament. The process was completed in 1832 by the reform of Parliament. Though they inaugurated a system still far from democratic, the reforms swept away many of the old pro-slavery MPs, replacing them with men in favour of abolition. The abolition campaign had yielded good returns in its attention to constituency politics.

Thus, after 1832, it was only a matter of time before Parliament decided to end black slavery. It was disliked at home and in Parliament and, of course, was hated by its victims throughout the slave islands. It was not merely coincidental that Britain ended slavery at the moment it found its broader economic interests switching. Although industrialization was still in its infancy in 1834, the shift towards a different conception of the world that underlay the movement was already well under way. By the late eighteenth century, it was clear to many commentators (most notably Adam Smith) that the restraints on trade necessary to support the old slave empire were ultimately damaging. The argument took a different form among the small-time investors and speculators who had previously been the typical backers of the slave system because of its fabulous profits. Men and women with spare cash to invest found that profits were higher, and certainly less speculative, in house building or in home investments than in slave ships and slaves. It was not so much that slavery became unprofitable, but rather that other forms of economic activity were more attractive, less risky and more easily controlled.

Parliament brought slavery partially to end in 1834; it was finally terminated in 1838. Thereafter, Britain used its abolitionist impulses – all mixed up as they were with its self-interest and diplomatic gains – as a principal instrument of its foreign policy. Abolition became a key factor in that cultural imperialism which became the hallmark of the British for a century and more. Indeed, the Anti-Slavery Society still operates with its headquarters in London.

The temptation of modern scholars is to see the abolition of the British slave system merely as a function of broadly based economic and social changes in Britain and the Caribbean. In part, this is a healthy antidote to the older school, which thought in terms of personalities and religion. Yet there has been a danger of undervaluing the abolitionist movement and its prominent leaders. In truth, they played a crucial role, for they acted as a catalyst, capitalizing on those broader changes, often unconsciously. It was, after all, Parliament that abolished the slave trade and slavery. We need to know how and why that political change took place. The difficulty facing future historians is to explain the precise mix and the exact juncture between the specifically political factors and the broad economic generalities. Though it seems doubtful that any future study will revert to an explanation focused on the abolitionists themselves, it would be wrong to marginalize them.

Chapter 7

The Enlightenment and Slavery in North America in the Eighteenth Century

Èlise Marienstras

> Slavery is one of those Evils that it will be very difficult
> to correct. Of all Reformations those are the most diffi-
> cult that ripen where the Roots grow as it were in the
> pockets of Men.[1]

THIS BITTER, FRANK OBSERVATION comes from a New Englander who was a convinced opponent of slavery but who, like many of his contemporaries, saw
anti-slavery as an almost impossible cause.

Surprise is sometimes expressed that it took the French Revolution five
years to apply to the slaves in the colonies the principles laid down in the Declaration of the Rights of Man. In America, it was eighty-nine years after the
Declaration of Independence, which asserted that 'all men are born equal' and
have 'the inalienable right to life, liberty and the pursuit of happiness', and
seventy-seven years after the adoption of the Bill of Rights that slavery finally
disappeared from the territory of the United States in the bloodbath of the
Civil War and that this abolition, through the adoption of the Thirteenth
Amendment, had the endorsement and protection of the Constitution.

The banning of the slave trade in 1808 and the freeing of all the slaves
in the mid-nineteenth century were the end-result of an intermittent struggle that unfolded in two very different phases, separated by several decades.
The first, which preceded and accompanied the American Revolution, bore
the imprint both of the Enlightenment and of a variety of religious trends.
This movement rather ran out of steam at the end of the eighteenth century,
and it remained an open question whether it had failed or was simply marking time before it rebounded between 1830 and 1860 in a more concerted,
radical and aggressive way.

Here we shall be concerned only with the first phase of the anti-slavery
movement, a first stage, it is true, in the liberation of American blacks, but also
a moment that reveals the extreme contradiction between the values declared

at the founding of the United States and the mindset and social and economic constraints of the time.

There is no doubt that nationally, the first anti-slavery movement failed in its aims, since, despite the principles set out during the Revolution, the federal Constitution adopted in 1787 implicitly acknowledged the existence of perpetual and hereditary slavery in the territory of the United States. As to the local successes of the abolitionist movement, it is rather difficult to determine how significant they were: among the Northern states, only New Hampshire adopted radical and immediate emancipation measures in its 1776 constitution. Most states, such as Pennsylvania or New York, envisaged a moratorium and gradual emancipation, with the children of slaves remaining in servitude until the age of twenty-eight after the adoption of the Pennsylvanian constitution of 1780, and twenty-one in the state of New York. In Massachusetts, despite a popular will demonstrated since the 1770s by petitions from rural counties, the drafters of the constitution refused to commit themselves explicitly; it took a judicial decision in 1783 for the state constitution to be understood as an emancipationist document.[2]

Until the 1760s and 1770s and the events that led to the American War of Independence, anti-slavery sentiments were mainly expressed rhetorically or in very general terms, which contrasted any form of servitude with the freedom of nature. The period of conflict between the colonists and the Crown provided the occasion for the advocates of abolition to focus more closely on the slavery of American blacks and the slave trade. During the war, opponents of slavery stepped up their activities, leading some to hope that the independence of the former colonists would be accompanied by the emancipation of the blacks. For a few years, there was a link between the fate of Americans and the fate of slaves. But after the establishment of the United States, the anti-slavery voice weakened and became timidly limited to the Northern states, which had the fewest slaves. And, finally, it is very clearly the introduction of the institutions of the federal republic that marked the end of an abolitionism that had had its high point in the last third of the eighteenth century. The movement would re-emerge in the second third of the nineteenth century to take its place on the national stage and in the great political debates.

Between the end of the eighteenth century and the years 1830–60, the issues concerning slavery had changed considerably, the United States having in the interval undergone a remarkable economic transformation that sharpened interregional tensions between the South, dominated by 'king cotton', and the North, which had gradually rid itself of the contentious issue of slave-owning. But by the mid-nineteenth century, many of those who may be described, more accurately than their elders, as abolitionists would inherit the questionings as well as the values of the Revolutionary period, and it was often in the name of the principles enshrined in the eighteenth-century Constitution that they would combat slavery in the nineteenth. Only then would the contradictions peculiar to an America that was both revolutionary and slave-owning be tackled head-on and noisily. The first anti-slavery movement had often glossed over the contradiction between its own demands: hoping to rid the nation of an evil that was undermining its values, but refusing to envisage a multiracial republic, it equivocated with the natural rights that it otherwise laid claim to, and thereby rendered itself powerless to push abolitionism to its logical conclusion. The ambivalence of the Enlightenment opponents of slavery reflected in a way that of the institution with which they were confronted.

Peculiarity of English-Speaking Enlightenment America

Slavery was introduced into the English colonies by stealth at the beginning of the seventeenth century. It took root there and developed empirically, only being sanctioned after the event and without debate by the laws of the various colonies. Only Georgia publicly debated the issue before taking the decision in 1750 to admit slaves, despite the fact that the colony had been founded in 1732 on the principle of freedom.[3]

In the course of the eighteenth century, slavery became the core institution of the Southern economy, but still remained far from being the peculiar regional institution that it became in the nineteenth. For an entire century it was the dominant feature in a network of production and trade that embraced the whole of the British colonies and, for a while, the United States. At the time of the Revolution, there were slaves, in varying proportions, all down the Atlantic coast, and all together they accounted for 20 per cent of the total population.

Here we need to stress how far, in the context of the Atlantic Enlightenment, the situation of American opponents of slavery and the slave trade differed from that in which pamphleteers and philosophers in France and Britain were writing. For the metropolitan abolitionists, slavery was a faraway, almost abstract evil about which one could think humanistically and universally.[4] American abolitionism was dealing with a local and general situation. The peculiarity of the American situation struck foreign visitors. Thus, the Marquis de Chastellux, visiting the American colonies during the War of Independence, wrote:

> ... in the midst of the woods and rustic tasks, a Virginian never resembles a European peasant: he is always a free man, who has a share in the government, and the command of a few Negroes. Thus he unites in himself the two distinct qualities of citizen and master, and in this respect clearly resembles the majority of the individuals who formed what were called *the people* in the ancient republics.[5]

It was not simply colonial economic issues and *a fortiori* those of the South, but also the colonists' sense of identity and, after the Revolution, the very definition of the American nation that were tied up with the existence of slavery. As they took root and developed, the British societies in the New World had driven to their margins or their depths those who were different, whether they were indigenous or of African origin.[6] The need to isolate themselves to protect their identity as civilized, Christian, European whites, already very noticeable among the British colonists, became more marked after 1776 when, now independent, they had the task of creating the nation. In addition to philosophical considerations of natural rights and humanism and universalism, American opponents of slavery or the slave trade were thus compelled in the last third of the eighteenth century to raise political, economic and cultural questions that directly involved their fate.[7]

The powerlessness of opponents of slavery to make the Enlightenment and the Revolution coincide with the emancipation of blacks was also due to political and institutional factors. In the late colonial period, it was the colonies' subordination to the Crown that stood in the way of the few American attempts to put a stop to the slave trade. The Americans, while being personally involved in the slave system, were also colonists, subjects of the King of England. Despite the autonomy that the colonies enjoyed, their laws had to be approved by the British Crown. In 1771 in Massachusetts, and the following year in Virginia, bills outlawing the importation of Africans or imposing an import tax on them were disallowed by the royal veto or that of the King's representative. Thomas Jefferson recalled this in his original draft of the Declaration of Independence in 1776, blaming the Crown for what he described as an inhuman traffic.

Jefferson's colleagues deemed this clause too compromising for the future of the new nation, and it was removed from the final text of the Declaration.[8] The executive power might appear to stand in the way of ending the slave trade, but it was the weakness of the central government that, after the Revolution, enabled supporters of slavery to retain their institution. In reaction to the 'tyranny' experienced at the hands of the central government, each of the federal states after the Revolution enjoyed a broad measure of autonomy. Decisions about citizenship and free or unfree status were within their remit. This meant that while some states in the North and some mid-Atlantic states were able to outlaw slavery in the wake of the Declaration of Independence or in the following decades, not only Southerners, but also, under their pressure, federal bodies would leave it to the mechanisms of the economy to keep the institution alive or kill it off. So long as slavery survived, the Constitution, strengthened on this point by the Fugitive Slave Act of 1793, protected property in slaves.

The chief concern of the drafters of the Constitution was to establish a united nation that was fair to all the signatory states, and it was they who enhanced the political weight of the slave-owners through the notorious 'three-fifths clause': three-fifths of the blacks in each state would be added to the total number of the white population which served as the basis for electing members (whites and slave-holders) of the House of Representatives.[9]

Finally, the Constitution forbade Congress from legislating on the importation of slaves for twenty years. But it is striking that once that period had elapsed, in 1807, Thomas Jefferson, then President, secured from Congress a ban on the importation of slaves into the United States.

The drafters of the Constitution were all signed-up adherents of the Enlightenment. They had varying degrees of familiarity with Locke and Montesquieu, and some had read anti-slavery tracts. But those delegates to the Constitutional Convention who refused to sign the final text in September 1787 were not taking a stand about slavery. They were above all protesting against the shortcomings of the Constitution on individual rights – those of whites, not those of blacks. The opponents of slavery gave in to *raison d'état*, narrowly understood, which demanded this concession to the slave-owners. The pressure of realities seen as insurmountable made the most ardent abolitionists yield. The following year, when the Constitution was sent to the states for ratification, a few voices were still raised to denounce its iniquitous racial character, but they did not affect the result of the vote.[10]

In the face of such disappointing results for the first wave of American abolitionism, it is difficult to blame or ignore it. We should first of all note the few successes it achieved despite everything in the earliest years of the American republic, and, to gain a better understanding of the reasons for its temporary failure, we need to appreciate the external and above all internal contradictions confronting it.

Religion and Slavery

Although it came into being in an altogether different environment, the American anti-slavery movement drew on the same sources as the British movements: religious convictions in the traditional and new sects, the 'Great Awakening' of an egalitarian evangelism, the principles and ideals of the Enlightenment, the features of which differed hardly at all from one side of the Atlantic to the other. The Enlightenment saw its fulfilment in the American Revolution, and it was then that the internal contradiction that had previously lain concealed within it burst out into the broad light of day.

The equivocation was already quite manifest in the various religious sects that had got a foothold in the American colonies. At the time of the introduction of the first slaves in the first half of the seventeenth century, no Church had protested. The act adopted by the Warwick assembly in Rhode Island in 1652, which outlawed servitude for life 'of any man white or black' in that colony, was never enforced. On the contrary, the colony of Rhode Island became one of the chief centres of the slave trade. Both in Puritan New England and in Anglican Virginia or Maryland, which was briefly Catholic, ministers and the most fervent believers acquired African servants and traded in them. The Bible was the anchor of the conviction that slavery was legitimate, so long as it affected foreign peoples, pagans and captives.

Thus, many Pequot Indians defeated in the 1637 war waged against them by the United Colonies of New England, and then the Wampanoags who survived King Philip's War in 1676 were quite legitimately sold to the equally Puritan Caribbean island of Providence, as well as to the Azores, Portugal, Spain, the Spanish West Indies and Virginia.[11] In the seventeenth and eighteenth centuries, the colonies of Virginia and North and South Carolina enslaved the Cherokees, the Catawbas and the Tuscaroras defeated in numerous conflicts between the Indians and the colonists. The Indians were sometimes given to the soldiers in lieu of pay, but they were generally sold away for reasons of security.[12]

The enslavement of Indians, however, was a marginal matter. It was blacks, purchased or kidnapped in Africa, or imported from the Caribbean after a period of seasoning (a period of breaking them in to the very harsh conditions of slavery in the colonies, which made it possible to select the strongest),[13] who soon came to be seen as the servile class in colonial societies. For the New England Puritans, slaves were goods like other goods, listed, for example by Cotton Mather, following his cattle, his house and his children, as proof that he was a 'visible saint', 'blessed by God in his fruits'.[14] Few Puritans paid any heed before the middle of the eighteenth century to the harm caused by slavery to both masters and victims. In 1700, an isolated voice was raised in Massachusetts, that of Samuel Sewall, Judge of the Superior Court of the province, who relied on biblical genealogy to show that slavery was contrary to nature and that, while blacks might indeed be inferior to whites, all men nevertheless are 'of the same blood':

> It is most certain that all Men, as they are the Sons of *Adam*, are Co-heirs, and have equal Right unto Liberty, and all other outward Comforts of Life. GOD *hath given the Earth unto the Sons of Adam, Psal., 115, 16. And hath made of one Blood all Nations of Men*.... So that Originally, and Naturally, there is no such thing as Slavery. *Joseph* was rightfully no more a Slave to his Brethren, than they were to him....[15]

Other Puritans, paying little heed to such words and finding contrary arguments in the Bible, refrained from condemning slavery in the name of their beliefs. In the mid-eighteenth century, Jonathan Edwards, Samuel Hopkins and Ezra Stiles, who denounced the slave trade, belonged to a later generation, won over to the 'New Lights' of the Great Awakening and more exposed to the principles of the secular Enlightenment than to the strict Congregationalism of their ancestors.

It was among the various Quaker groups that the first real protests appeared. The first collective stand that has survived was issued by the monthly meeting of the Mennonites of Germantown, Pennsylvania, in 1688. In this colony, where, before it was taken over by William Penn, the Dutch had already introduced the slave trade and black slavery, slavery quickly became a difficult subject of a debate for the Friends. To the question, 'Now what is this better done as Turkes doe?' they replied:

> yea rather is it worse for them, wch say they are Christians.... Now tho' they are black, we cannot conceive there is more liberty to have them slaves, as it is to have other white ones. There is a saying, that we shall doe to all men, licke as we will be done our selves: macking no difference of what generation, descent, or Colour they are.... Here is liberty of Conscience, wch is right & reasonable, here ought to be lickewise liberty of ye body, except of evildoers, wch is an other case.... This mackes an ill report in all those Countries of Europe, where they hear off, that ye Quackers doe here handel men, Licke they handel there ye Cattel; and for that reason some have no mind or inclination to come hither.... These are the reasons why we are against the traffick of mens-body.[16]

Political considerations and an implicit sentiment of wrong were mixed together for the four signers of this first Pennsylvanian petition. They had no need to rely on biblical precepts. The humanist cause had been heard and would be taken up in other petitions that for decades would remain without effect. The Pennsylvania Quakers and those who migrated farther south continued to grow rich by trading in and exploiting Africans. It was not until the middle of the century that Benjamin Lay, John Woolman and Anthony Benezet embarked on a determined crusade against slavery and had an impact on the governing bodies of the Society of Friends who, in difficulties with the Governor of Pennsylvania and losing influence in the colonial assembly, decided to outlaw slavery from the sect. Despite their close relations with the London Quakers, whose opposition to slavery was total, it was only in 1780 that the last Quaker slave-owners left the Society of Friends.

To the arguments of their predecessors, Woolman and Benezet added an egalitarianism peculiar to Quakers but which was also spreading in other dissenting religious movements. John Woolman's pamphlets of 1754 and 1762 were directed mainly at the Society of Friends in the colonies. Woolman recalled that all men share in the inner light and that freedom is a gift from God to all His children. With his usual stylistic simplicity, he reversed the terms of the problem. Far from focusing on some alleged natural inferiority of Africans, he was the first to stress the importance and danger of racial prejudice, the cause and not the effect of the inferiority of blacks:

> Placing on men the ignominious Title SLAVE, dressing them in uncomely Garments, keeping them to servile labour, in which they are often dirty, tends gradually to fix a Notion in the Mind, that they are a Sort of People below us in Nature.... Through the Force of long Custom, it appears needful to speak in Relation to Colour. [Our judgment is distorted by] the idea of Slavery being connected with the Black Colour, and Liberty with the White.[17]

Anthony Benezet also denounced the racial character of slavery. A tireless correspondent and pamphleteer, his *Historical Account of Guinea* converted the Englishman Thomas Clarkson to abolitionism and inspired his *Essay on the Slavery and Commerce of the Human Species*. It can be said that Benezet was the founder of the first international anti-slavery movement. In Philadelphia, he welcomed both blacks and whites into his school, and in 1770, he opened the first 'African school'. He was pragmatic as well as committed, and attacked the slave trade more strongly than Woolman, knowing that it would be easier to suppress than slavery. Benezet also appealed to the cultural conscience of whites. Depriving the blacks of freedom, he wrote, was also a source of internal corruption for their owners.[18]

All of these principles – natural freedom, equality of souls, the corruption of slave society – were the arguments of dissenters coming out of the religious Great Awakening or the more secular Enlightenment who would attack slavery from the 1770s.

The movement of the Great Awakening, which spread from England to the Northern and middle American colonies and then to the Southern ones between 1740 and 1760, can hardly be separated from the American Enlightenment movement. This is not the place to discuss the influence of the former on the American Revolution, which broke out ten years after the movement had died out. But in their common assertion of natural freedom and equality, both the religious and the secular movements had an impact on black slavery.

The collective name of the Great Awakening should not suggest the idea of a single uniform movement. Although it was everywhere an evangelical movement, in the colonies even more so than in England, it had numerous variants; it gave rise to a variety of sects; in some places it affected rather the enlightened élites (as among the rationalist Congregationalists or the Arminian clergy of New England), in other places, it addressed isolated farmers in the back country; or again it won over both blacks and whites, slaves and freemen. It was the awakening of faith and a new reading of the Bible that aroused an aversion to slavery and, above all, to the slave trade. The emergence of the ideology of man's 'benevolence' opened up people's minds to the idea of a natural goodness of Africans, their primordial innocence and perhaps their natural equality with whites.[19] Despite the 'enthusiastic' practices of some evangelical movements in the mid-eighteenth century, they can be said to have been echoing the Enlightenment movement in their shared references to a natural order, natural equality among men, and the supremacy of reason and free will. Some were spontaneous, others more mystical. All argued for the superiority of individuals over institutions. Most, such as the Baptists, gave to every inspired man the right to become a preacher and to all men the right to pray together. It was out of the Great Awakening that the black churches came, created after the new Baptist and Methodist sects had initially accepted the presence of blacks alongside the white flock, even going so far as to allow blacks to be preachers.

But out of all this protean activity, which was indeed often populist in nature, no truly abolitionist movement arose. In most sermons, it was spiritual equality that was asserted, slavery being one of the evils present here on earth but which the sects emerging from the Great Awakening forbore to attack directly. While they spoke and above all acted subversively with regard to clerical institutions, they affected social institutions only indirectly. It was the American Revolution – more precisely, the independence movement in the colonies, inseparable from the Enlightenment, which reached its peak in America in the last third of the century – that had an immediate impact on thinking about slavery.

The Enlightenment and Slavery

Americans were active participants in all the schools of thought that marked the Enlightenment. For Benjamin Franklin, Benjamin Rush or Samuel Hopkins, for Thomas Jefferson, George Washington, John Adams or Ezra Stiles, for Deists or practising Christians, naturalist *philosophes* or fervent clergymen, precursors of the Revolution or direct actors and leaders, the liberation of man from the darkness and chains of the past was the common cause of Americans.

The names of these men from a variety of backgrounds are associated with a line of thinking about the practice of slavery from which none of them was able to diverge without some degree of ambiguity. Of all these individuals, only one, John Adams, never owned slaves. Benjamin Rush, a well-known doctor, refused the post offered to him in Charleston, South Carolina, so as not to live 'in a country where wealth was accumulated through the blood and sweat of the black slaves'.[20] But it was only in 1784, after having a dream about the horrors suffered by enslaved Africans and their 'liberator', Anthony Benezet, that he threw himself into the work of the Pennsylvania Abolition Society. Even then, he waited another seven years before freeing his own slave.[21]

The precursor of the Enlightenment in America, Benjamin Franklin was never a supporter of slavery. He promised his five slaves that they would be freed after his death, never thinking that they might easily die before him. He waited, however, until he was president of the Pennsylvania Abolition Society and the drafting of the 1787 Constitution to express himself publicly on the subject. Until then, he limited to his correspondence with his European friends his thoughts on an institution which he said conflicted with the equality of mankind and made white children lazy and insolent. A single document, written in 1751 and published in 1754, had recorded his position on slavery. In this paper, *Observations Concerning the Increase of Mankind*, for which he went down in history as 'the first American demographer', he had already protested against the slave trade and slavery. The reasons he advanced were economic and demographic, the cost of a slave being in his eyes higher than that of a wage labourer, and the whole world being already well enough populated by darker-skinned people without America 'darkening itself' too by the further importation of Africans. For the English edition of 1758, Franklin altered a phrase contained in the previous edition, 'almost every Slave being *by Nature* a Thief',[22] to read 'every Slave being from the nature of slavery a Thief'.[23]

Franklin's opportunism was an idiosyncrasy. Some of his contemporaries, Pennsylvania Quakers, Southern men of letters or men devoted to the cause of freedom in the North, were more committed and more consistent. While it remained the concern of a minority, the movement against slavery was no longer marginal after the end of the Seven Years' War in the 1760s. A voluminous anti-slavery literature was published in the twelve years between the Seven Years' War and the American War of Independence, a period during which the gulf between the colonists and the mother country deepened.

The concordance in time is no accident. It was quite clearly the constitutional and ideological debates, together with the economic conflict with the Crown, that provided the opportunity to raise the problem of slavery in the colonies. Black slavery and the metaphorical, and ultimately political, deprivation of the colonists could not be separated. Was it possible to demand liberation for the British colonists without thinking of the Africans chained in very real servitude? The question was raised early on by a small number of people, then more and more widely till it had an impact on the most diverse circles. One of the earliest essays to make the link between the liberating ideology of the colonists and the need to free the blacks was *Rights of the British Colonies,* published in 1764, by James Otis, a Boston attorney. Protesting against the strengthening of the English Navigation Acts, Otis asserted: 'The

Colonists are by the law of nature free born, as indeed all men are, white or black.... Does it follow that tis right to enslave a man because he is black?... Can any logical inference in favour of slavery be drawn from a flat nose, a long or short face?'[24]

Otis was the first of many pamphleteers to rest the colonists' arguments in favour of their own autonomy on two types of rights: one, a natural right, as established by their favourite authors, Montesquieu in *The Spirit of Laws* and Adam Smith in his *Theory of Moral Sentiments*, and the other, constitutional law, the right of the British to vote for their own taxes and more generally to enjoy natural freedoms. It was natural right that prevailed in anti-slavery writings, the authors almost always making the parallel between their own desire 'to free themselves from the chains of English tyranny' and the right of blacks to be free in a continent dedicated to freedom. Reference to the slave status of blacks in America enabled the colonists to broaden the scope of their own demands and to base the metaphor of their own 'enslavement' on the reality of another one. Like the Africans reduced to slavery, the colonists had to be freed of their chains, not only because they enjoyed the rights of British subjects but because as men they enjoyed the natural right to freedom.

In the years that followed, while Britain became ever more demanding and the colonists ever more unwilling, the question of slavery occupied a growing place in public thinking and debates. Thus, in the midst of the emerging debate with the British Crown, the colonists of Massachusetts found the occasion to denounce the enslavement of blacks. In 1767, the Massachusetts General Court debated a bill 'to prevent the unwarrantable & unusual practice ... of inslaving Mankind in the Province'.[25] In 1770, Reverend Samuel Cooke devoted most of his election sermon to the sin of slavery. In 1773, the issue of abolition was the subject of the Harvard College commencement debate.[26]

In the middle colonies and even in the South, the leaders of the colonial movement were waging two campaigns. The greatest leaders of the Revolution – George Mason, Patrick Henry and Edmund Pendleton in Virginia, Caesar Rodney in Delaware, Luther Martin in Maryland and Benjamin Rush in Pennsylvania – spoke in terms hostile to slavery to such good effect that at the meeting of the Continental Congress in Philadelphia in 1774 to organize the common resistance to the mother country, the association for the boycott of British ships that it set up there declared that it would boycott any vessel engaged in slave trading. In 1776, Edmund Pendleton, George Wythe and, it seems, Thomas Jefferson laid before the Virginia Assembly a bill to free the slaves and send them to settle the territories in the West. In 1783, Thomas Jefferson would propose that Virginia ban the introduction of new slaves into the state.

It was thus not simply a matter of utilitarian rhetoric. A shift was occurring from the notion of personal sin and the threat to salvation formerly advanced on religious grounds to the idea that slavery stained colonial society with a collective crime for which the punishment was political oppression. The anti-slavery movement swelled during the War of Independence, permanently basing itself on natural rights, which henceforth constituted one aspect of the rebels' republican ideology. The 'virtue' of the American republic, such as it had been declared in July 1776, required not only that the nation be free of the corruption of the old monarchical European nations, but also that it purify itself of its own shortcomings and that its citizens be industrious, modest and devoted to the common weal. Maintaining a category of men in dependence on a section of American citizens constituted in the eyes of men as in the eyes of God a crime the collective character of which was more and more frequently stressed as the victory of the rebels loomed larger. The Marquis de Chastellux, faithfully echoing what he heard people saying in Virginia, notably Jefferson, rang the changes on the 'fault' denounced by his hosts as contrary to natural rights, but he saw in it also a political effect. Through the fault of the hereditary system, he wrote:

> The national character, the very spirit of the government, will always be aristocratic. Nor can this be doubted when one considers that another cause is still operating to produce the same result. I am referring to slavery, not because it is a mark of distinction or special privilege to possess Negroes, but because the sway held over them nourishes vanity and sloth, two vices which accord wonderfully with established prejudices.[27]

Seen as corrupting the masters, whose vices were incompatible with republican principles, and as hurting the education of children who would become bad citizens, slavery was no longer, following the Declaration of Independence, simply blamed on the Crown. Intent on creating a nation and securing its international recognition, the former colonists seemed to be taking up their responsibilities. Slavery might have been initiated by the mother country, but it was now an American reality, not only in the area of individual ownership but in that of social and even national responsibility. It might even be said that it was in the issue of slavery that for the first time an American national consciousness was expressed, a bad conscience, when the crime of owning and exploiting men was perceived as a sin or a hindrance to the establishment of a democracy.[28] In the struggle being waged by the colonists for their independence, slavery, said American patriots spontaneously, was a fault that would receive its punishment. The Americans could not expect deliverance from their calamities 'till we put away the evil of our doings'.[29] Benjamin Rush spoke of a 'national crime' which would lead to a 'national punishment'.[30] And even Thomas Jefferson, the ambivalence of whose position we shall see presently, feared a bloody civil or racial conflict in the nation's future if the question of slavery was not resolved. In the years of the War of Independence, anti-slavery sentiments were thus widely shared, sometimes for ideological reasons, sometimes for economic reasons (the war having led to a stagnation of trade) or sometimes for considerations of foreign policy.

> It is true that this opinion, which is almost universally accepted [Chastellux writes rather excessively], is inspired by different motives. The philosophers, and the young men who are for the most part educated in the principles of sound philosophy, consider only justice and the rights of humanity. The fathers of families, and those who are principally concerned with their interests, complain that the maintenance of their Negroes is very expensive....[31]

It was these various considerations, nicely observed by the French visitor, that led Virginia in 1783 to repeal the 1723 law that outlawed individual manumission. Maryland in 1787 and Delaware in 1790 also took steps to facilitate manumission by masters. The number of freedmen grew quite rapidly: in Virginia their numbers rose from 1,800 in 1782 to 13,000 by 1801, while in Maryland their numbers rose from 8,000 in 1790 to 20,000 in 1801. Manumissions were often explicitly motivated by revolutionary principles and Christian morality.

Yet no states in the South and certainly no state in the lower South, South Carolina and Georgia, adopted measures for the total abolition of slavery in their territory. And it was chiefly pressure from the states of the lower South that led to the Constitutional Compromise of 1787, as a result of which slavery persisted until the Civil War. The most recent historical writing on the United States stresses the fact that slavery in the United States was to the very end a national affair and not simply a Southern one.[32] Backed by enlightened leaders of Virginia and Maryland, Northerners need not, it seems, have taken account of threats to secede from Georgia and South Carolina. Those two states lacked the economic and military resources to form a separate nation in 1787. Moreover, the problem of compensating slave-owners was not insoluble: compensation by the federal government was something that could be considered, and indeed was at one point contemplated before the drafting of the Constitution. It could have benefited from the vast revenues from the Western territories recently acquired by the federal government. Governor Morris, representing Pennsylvania at the Constitutional Convention in 1787, proposed 'a tax "for paying for all the Negroes in the U. States" rather than to "saddle posterity" with a Constitution that legitimated slavery'.[33] The members of the Convention rejected the principle of federal taxation, and subsequently the revenue from the sale of the western land was devoted, as Alexander Hamilton suggested, to repaying the war debts of the states. By then there was no further consideration of the matter of federal compensation for slave-owners.

Thus, as the time approached for the crucial choice, the natural rights as somewhat vaguely set out in the Declaration of Independence – vague both as to their application and to their universality (should the equality of man be extended to all men, or only to men of the white race?) – and the priority to be given among those rights to property remained very much in the balance. If property won out unambiguously, it was also and above all because alongside the freedom necessary for all men, there was the problem of equality between the 'various sorts of men' and above all their living together on a footing of equality in a single nation.

Slavery, Race and Nation

In 1799, when George Washington, the great Virginia planter, hero of the War of Independence, 'Father of the Nation' and the first President of the United States, died, his slaves were freed as provided in his will. For the second President,

John Adams, who lived soberly in Massachusetts, the question did not arise. Conversely, when the third President of the United States, Thomas Jefferson, died in 1826, all his slaves except five were sold at auction to pay the vast debts he bequeathed to his descendants. Of all the slaves that he had ever owned, only eight, 2 per cent, were freed, some while he was still alive, the rest by will.

Should we follow the old history and excuse the private Jefferson because of his financial problems on the grounds that in his public life he was regarded by English abolitionists as the hope of a free world to come?[34] Or should we doubt his sincerity and view as hypocritical his defence of equal natural rights? Is there a contradiction, an inconsistency between the private man and the public man? Or, as some contemporary historians think, were ambivalence, caution, pusillanimity and even racism stronger than the desire of a man of the Enlightenment to see the disappearance of an institution damaging to his dream of an 'empire of freedom'?[35] And in the last case, it remains to assess how representative Thomas Jefferson's attitude and thought were in the young nation.

On his Monticello estate, Thomas Jefferson was a paternalist planter. He rarely had his slaves whipped, and even then rather for the example than as a systematic punishment. He provided correctly for their sustenance and saw that they lived in conditions best suited for optimum productivity. It was also to set an example that he sold recidivist runaways, demonstrating that he knew how to use family separation as a punishment.

It was not for lack of rationality in the organization of work and in the employment of workers that the Monticello plantation was an economic failure, but rather because of a series of strokes of bad luck and, above all, because of the excessive lifestyle that its master strove to maintain throughout his life. Slaves were necessary to that lifestyle. They constituted the 'children' of the Jefferson household, giving the owner of the estate the stature of a patriarch.[36]

Towards them, Thomas Jefferson showed a kindly acknowledgement, apparently making no connection between the general principles that he asserted in public life and the situation of his own workers. Neither in 1770, when, as a lawyer (but not as a landowner), he pleaded for Samuel Howell, a slave whose great-grandmother was a white woman who had been condemned to slavery for having a child by a black man, whom Howell thought ought to be freed because 'according to the law of nature, we are all born free',[37] nor in 1774 when he wrote in his pamphlet *A Summary View of the Rights of British America* that 'the abolition of domestic slavery is the great object of desire in those colonies',[38] nor even after 1783, when voluntary manumission was made easier in Virginia, did he make any effort to free his slaves, but rather continued to have runaways hunted down. Whereas George Washington refused to traffic in slaves, Jefferson sold or bought scores of slaves as his needs required.

Thomas Jefferson visibly never sought to reconcile the ideals expressed in the Declaration of Independence with the reality of being a slave-owner, nor later when he was Governor of Virginia and, later still, President of the United States at the head of a slave society. According to recent studies of Jefferson, it is clear that the public man himself was only prudently and occasionally anti-slavery and that he was 'guided by his racist feelings, his interests as a proprietor and his programme for building a white republic, made up of small white farmers and a natural aristocracy, who alone could serve freedom and benefit from it'.[39]

Having failed in his younger days to secure the adoption of a law allowing manumission in Virginia, Jefferson's later legislative proposals concerning revision of the criminal law in Virginia, which he describes in detail in his *Notes on the State of Virginia*,[40] sought to soften the criminal law for whites, but to tighten the old slave code, even increasing the number of cases punishable by dismemberment and hanging. In 1779, in a bill on the naturalization of immigrants, he ruled out access to citizenship for free blacks. Finally, he suggested to the assembly of his state that any manumitted black who did not leave the state within a year should 'be out of the protection of the laws', as would the white mothers of black children.[41] The Virginia Assembly did not go along with him, and it was only much later, in 1803, that it decided to expel free blacks.

As a member of the United States Congress, as President and then as adviser to his successors James Madison and James Monroe, Thomas Jefferson, contrary to appearances, was no bolder in his anti-slavery policy. Paul Finkelman points out that even the Plan of Government for the Western Territory, which Jefferson presented in 1785, would have banned slavery only after 1800, that is at a time when in Kentucky and Tennessee the slaves already there in 1785 would have increased to such numbers that a ban would have been impossible.[42] In 1803, he made no proposal to ensure the abolition of slavery in Louisiana, the vast territory he purchased from Napoleon. And in 1820, in the face of the national division precipitated by Missouri's request to enter the Union as a slave state, the 'fire bell ... filled [him] with terror' for the future of the Union and democracy. 'I regret', he wrote at that time, 'that I am now to die in the belief, that the useless sacrifice of themselves by the generation of 1776, to acquire self-government and happiness to their country, is to be thrown away by the unwise and unworthy passions of their sons.'[43]

Yet Jefferson was not wholly devoid of hostility to the institution itself. Above all, he felt that it besmirched the characters and manners of slave-owners and that his generation was bequeathing to the next one a major disagreement as to the nature of the republic and the nation. Concerned throughout his life with the succession of the generations and the responsibility of the old to their descendants, convinced like Thomas Paine that 'the earth belongs to the living', he was appalled at the prospect of leaving debts when he died and deliberately left it to the children of the revolutionaries to settle a situation that he himself refused to deal with.

Among his contemporaries, other thinkers and politicians were more resolute on the necessity of abolishing slavery, but most, as could be seen in the North, advocated proceeding gradually such that, as an abolitionist in New Jersey wrote indignantly addressing himself to blacks, 'we will not do justice unto you, but our posterity shall do justice unto your posterity'.[44] Thanks to the gradual emancipation adopted in the Northern states, the costs of compensation were transferred from the slave-owners to the children of their slaves, who worked to earn their freedom.[45]

Postponement to better times, when attitudes would be more favourable to a liberation of the black race and when the cost of freedom would have been compensated by their labour, also accorded with the ideology of progress shared by Jefferson and his contemporaries. In the evolution of mankind, slavery represented a regrettable stage, it was true, but one that was temporary and to which time would inevitably provide a solution.

However, Jefferson's evolutionism and a certain determinism were not the only factors in his unwillingness to opt for outright and immediate abolition. His own conception of natural law led him to say in the Declaration of Independence, that 'all men are born equal'. But when he came down to concrete matters and examined the 'the races of black and of red men ... [that we have under our eyes] as subjects of natural history', he advanced it 'as a suspicion only, that the blacks, whether originally a distinct race, or made distinct by time and circumstances, are inferior to the whites in the endowments of both body and mind'.[46]

Jefferson's caution was his custom. Conscious of the burden of responsibility that his status as a liberal philosopher and statesman gave him in the nation and the world, he did not want to shock anyone. He admitted that he had no scientific proof, but his argument was part of what Joyce Appleby describes as the Jeffersonian conception of natural rights: 'The assertion of an underlying uniformity in the face of conspicuous human differences had enabled the Jeffersonians to enlist nature in the war against hierarchical society ... but the association of the right to life, liberty and the pursuit of happiness with a uniform human nature bode ill for those deemed naturally different. Where traditional society recognized a variety of statuses, ethnic groups and regional identities, Jeffersonians obliterated that variety in the celebration of all free men, except where, as Jefferson wrote, "the difference is fixed in nature".'[47]

To admit to citizenship men whose colour 'and not their circumstances' had made them inferior to the white citizens of the United States would be to threaten the very foundations of the republic that he had powerfully contributed to creating and 'pollute' the nation 'freely chosen' by free contracting parties.[48] Whereas it was the age of environmentalism, Jefferson persisted in asserting, using Roman examples to prove his point, that the quasi-beast-like character of American slaves – their disposition to sleep when they had nothing to do; their lack of imagination, caution and forethought; their ignorance of the 'delicate mixture of sentiment and sensation' that love is; their lack of 'the circumstance of superior beauty [that] is thought worthy attention in the propagation of our horses, dogs, and other domestic animals' – is not due to their servile state but is a matter of nature, and counts among the organic characteristics that blacks improve when they have mixed children, but which then contaminate the white race.[49] At the time of the Missouri question in 1820, Thomas Jefferson, uneasy about the threat Congress was causing to hang over 'the right of States to make laws regarding slavery', revealed his chief concern. If Congress took upon itself the right to eliminate slavery in the South, he wrote at that time, 'all the whites south of the Potomac and Ohio must evacuate their States'.[50] That whites and freed blacks should live together side by side was something he felt to be impossible, blacks being incapable of being full citizens and democratic principles ruling out the possibility of second-class citizens being part of the polity. The democratic republic of which Thomas Jefferson dreamed did not allow for participation by races deemed to be inferior.

All through his career and after his return to Monticello, when he withdrew from public life, Jefferson clung to the view that it was impossible for blacks to participate in the republic and that they therefore had to be expelled to some other place once they had been emancipated, preferably to virgin lands where they would gradually, with the help of the American government, become used to the exercise of freedom and government, and especially where they would be 'far removed from the possibility of mixing with whites'. It was chiefly due to his influence, but also because his views and what Winthrop Jordan calls his 'derogation of the Negro'[51] were widely shared in both North and South, that the American Colonization Society was founded in 1816 which sought, with little success, to remove freed blacks to Africa. Yet it was also in support of the words of the Declaration of Independence, drafted by Thomas Jefferson, that more and more slave abolition societies were founded in the Northern states and as far south as Virginia.

There are several reasons that account for the desire to see the free blacks leave and for the hesitation about freeing all the slaves in the United States. One constant reason dating from the colonial period and continuing after independence in the Northern states that had abolished slavery must not be overlooked: Americans feared above all that their societies would become 'mixed' and the citizens be 'different by nature'. Thus, in 1764, in the same pamphlet in which he lambasted slavery as a rhetorical figure of the oppression experienced by colonists and as a real fact of life for Africans, James Otis had advanced as evidence of their virtue the 'purity' of colonial societies. The North American continent, he wrote, was not inhabited, 'as people in England imagine, by a bastard mixture of English, Indians and negroes, but by free white British subjects'.[52] After independence, in Massachusetts, Connecticut and New York State, freed blacks saw themselves being increasingly excluded from citizenship and public bodies.

Thomas Jefferson's ambivalence was that of his time, but we can also say that it was that of the history of English-speaking America over the long term. It created a situation whereby '[i]n the nineteenth century, abolitionists used Jefferson's words as swords; slaveholders used his example as a shield'.[53]

For the slaves and their freed brothers, those chiefly concerned by abolitionism, there was no ambivalence. In the face of rising abolitionism, blacks, slave or free, did not remain inactive. Some historians even argue that 'the American Revolution represents the greatest slave uprising in our history'.[54]

The uprising, if we accept the term, was not immediately directed at the masters. It took the legal form of petitions for the freeing of individuals, for general emancipation or for the elimination of the slave trade, the indirect form of running away from plantations at the call of the British authorities who promised freedom, and the cultural form, the 'national', one might say, of the creation of a 'nation within the nation' – a community of refuge for blacks who, despite their freedom, found themselves refused equality in the American nation.

In the various petitions sent to the assemblies of the colonies and later the Northern states from the beginning of the conflict between Britain and the colonists, we can observe, among those blacks who, by various means, had access to the speeches and conversation of whites, or who were able to read the pamphlets of American patriots, the constant reference to the principles of natural rights alleged by the Americans in favour of their cause. Petitioners were not asking to be given their freedom; they were demanding it as a right: '[T]he more we are Convinced of our Right ... to be free ... we can never be convinced that we were made to be slaves.'[55]

No one doubted that the right of blacks to be free derived from the fact that God had created all the nations of the earth of one blood. Refusing to resort to physical violence or even really verbal violence during the War of Independence, blacks vigorously asked 'whether it is consistent with the present Claims, of the united States, to hold so many Thousands, of the Race of Adam, our Common Father, in perpetual Slavery. Can human Nature endure the Shocking Idea?'[56] In their petitions to state legislatures, in the articles that they got published, at the rituals which they initiated, blacks took up as their own the terms of the Declaration of Independence and the Puritan revolutionary typology of the chosen people. They felt that they had a greater right legitimately to identify with the Hebrews than did the colonists, since they had, like Joseph, been sold into slavery and, like Moses, they were hoping to be saved from Pharaoh's chains. Thus, Americans saw themselves deprived of their own arguments, unless, by liberating the blacks, America remained true to its mission.

Despite the 'Toryfication' of those blacks who dug a breach in the institution of slavery by running away and joining the British armies, the struggle of those who remained on their plantations or in the Northern states was not intentionally subversive. Some, like the poet Jupiter Hammon of Long Island, did not seek freedom here on earth and advised their brothers to exercise patience. But the most militant ones reminded Americans of their Revolutionary principles, calling on them to restore 'the Natural Right of all Men' and cease to be 'chargeable with the inconsistancey [sic] of acting themselves the part which they condemn and oppose in others ...'.[57] During the War of Independence and the early years of the national era, blacks thus made themselves the conscience of America, an America in which they claimed to be active participants. 'Let your Petitioners rejoice with your Honours in th[ei]r Participation with your Honours of that inestimable Blessing, *Freedom*',[58] they pleaded, asking 'our Government' to be fair and act in accordance with universal morality. Apart from the leaders of those slaves in the South who took the side of the Tories, most black leaders adhered to the ideology of American independence, adopted its terms to the letter and based their hopes of liberation on their confidence in a just America purified of its original sin. The American patriotism of these blacks has often been noted.[59] Their rapid disillusionment, when discrimination and even persecution spread in the free Northern states, led them to hesitate between the possibility of a return to Africa and the self-segregation of black institutions, such as schools, Masonic lodges, mutual help associations and above all black Churches.

The impracticable idea of a return to Africa was soon abandoned, but the black institutions that developed despite the pervasive hostility in the Northern and middle states and underground in the Southern states were the springboards for an unbroken struggle against slavery. The victims of slavery and their ethnic brothers would not yield, in the first decades of the nineteenth century, to the defeatism that affected American citizens. It was largely due to this persistent determination that abolitionism resurfaced on the political stage in its second and last phase. Those who took over then from the men of the Enlightenment would be Quakers, evangelicals but also reformers whose inspiration, contrary to what a contemporary historian claims, would draw both on the secular principles of the rights of man and on those of equality in God's eyes.[60]

Notes

1. Mathew Ridley to Miss Livingston, n.d., cited in D. J. MacLeod (1974), p. 75
2. See L. Litwack (1961); A. Zilversmit (1967).
3. The main purpose of the founders of Georgia, with James Oglethorpe, was to attack the system of imprisonment for debt, common in England. See A. L. Higginbotham, Jr. (1978).
4. There were probably barely more than a thousand slaves in England at the end of the eighteenth century. Laws and legal precedents concerning the status of labourers, and in particular of black slaves imported from the colonies, were vague and often contradictory. At the time of the Somerset case, which ended in 1772 with the discharge of the plaintiff and which finally laid to rest doubts about the lawfulness of slavery in England, a comment made in 1640 was bandied about: 'England was too pure an air for slaves to breathe in.' On several occasions in the course of the century, legal cases highlighted the incompatibility of the English Constitution and slavery. See D. B. Davis (1975), pp. 470–2.
5. F.-J. de Chastellux (1980).
6. E. S. Morgan (1975).
7. D. B. Davis (1966); D. B. Davis (1975); W. D. Jordan (1968).
8. C. Becker (1956); P. Finkelman (1993), pp. 181–221.
9. S. Lynd (1967), Chapter 8.
10. In January 1788, Luther Martin, Attorney General of Maryland, campaigned against ratification of the Constitution. He criticized it in particular for the article preventing Congress from taking any action for twenty years on the question of the slave trade. See L. Martin (1788) as cited in G. B. Nash (1990), pp. 142–5.
11. A. W. Lauber (1913 [1979]), 126–53.
12. Ibid. See L. Greene (1942).

13. Therein lies part of the explanation for the difference in life expectancy of slaves in the Caribbean and slaves in the mainland colonies. See R. W. Fogel and S. L. Engerman (1974), pp. 22–7.
14. See H. W. Haynes (1889), pp. 191–5.
15. 'The Selling of Joseph a Memorial, by Samuel Sewall' (1700), cited in G. Moore (1866), pp. 83–4. See also D. B. Davis (1966), pp. 342–6.
16. '"Protest" of the Germantown, Pennsylvania, Quakers against Slavery' (1688), as cited in S. W. Pennypacker (1880), pp. 28–30.
17. J. Woolman (1762); D. B. Davis (1966), pp. 483–93.
18. T. E. Drake (1950); G. B. Nash and J. R. Soderlund (1991).
19. D. B. Davis (1966), p. 367.
20. Letter to Barbeu Dubourg, 23 April 1773, in L. H. Butterfield (1951), Vol. 1, p. 77. In 1773, he published in Philadelphia 'An Address to the Inhabitants of the British Settlements in America, Upon Slave-Keeping', a virulently anti-slavery pamphlet.
21. G. B. Nash, op. cit., pp. 32–3.
22. L. W. Labaree (1961), p. 229.
23. Ibid.; G. B. Nash and J. R. Soderlund, op. cit., p. xi.
24. J. Otis (1764), p. 29.
25. Cited in L. S. Gerteis (1987), p. 8.
26. See G. B. Nash, op. cit., pp. 9–10.
27. F.-J. de Chastellux, op. cit., p. 355 [Eng. trans., p. 435].
28. Luther Martin, Attorney General of Maryland, said in 1788 that 'slavery is inconsistent with the genius of republicanism, and has a tendency to destroy those principles on which it is supported, as it lessens the sense of the equal rights of mankind, and habituates us to tyranny and oppression'. Luther Martin, op. cit.
29. Reverend Samuel Hopkins, quoted in D. B. Davis (1975), p. 294.
30. Ibid., p. 292.
31. F.-J. de Chastellux, op. cit., pp. 360–1 [Eng. trans., p. 439].
32. See G. B. Nash, op. cit., Chapter 2. This is a revision of the traditional historiography of the constitutional treatment of the question of slavery, initiated by James Madison's Notes during the Constitutional Convention and developed, for example, by S. Lynd, op. cit.
33. Cited by P. Finkelman (1987), p. 193.
34. See, for example, his correspondence with the English radical Richard Price, an ardent supporter of the American revolutionists and an opponent of slavery, in J. P. Boyd (1953), pp. 258–59, 356–7.
35. For a survey of the historiography of slavery and abolitionism at the time of the American Revolution, see G. B. Nash, op. cit.; I. Berlin and R. Hoffman (1983); and P. S. Onuf (1993).
36. See L. C. Stanton (1993), pp. 147–80.
37. Cited by I. Rhys (1993), p. 89.
38. In P. S. Onuf, op. cit., Vol. 1, p. 130.
39. P. Finkelman (1993), pp. 181–221.
40. T. Jefferson (1955 [1781]), pp. 144–5.
41. J. P. Boyd, op. cit., Vol. 2, pp. 470–3.
42. Even this proposal, however, was too advanced for the other Southern delegates such that the law, finally adopted in 1787, covered only the territories in the north-west between the Ohio and the Mississippi.
43. Cited by P. Finkelman (1993), p. 211.
44. D. Cooper (1780).
45. G. B. Nash, op. cit., p. 34.
46. T. Jefferson, op. cit., p. 143.
47. J. Appleby (1993), p. 11. See also T. Jefferson, op. cit., p. 138.
48. T. Jefferson, op. cit., p. 141: 'The improvement of the blacks in body and mind, in the first instance of their mixture with the whites, has been observed by every one, and proves that their inferiority is not the effect merely of their condition of life.'
49. Ibid., pp. 138–9.

50. Thomas Jefferson to Albert Gallatin, 26 December 1820, in P. L. Ford (1892–9), Vol. 10, p. 177.
51. W. D. Jordan, op. cit., p. 481. What is most striking in the section of the *Notes on the State of Virginia* devoted to blacks is Jefferson's horror of mixing, a horror that had more to do with the eventuality of a mixed-race nation than with individual cases. He put no obstacles in the way of one of his slaves marrying a white artisan. And in the 1800 presidential campaign, he himself was accused of a liaison with a slave, which had resulted in the birth of several very light-coloured children. Historians and novelists who have looked at this story and found no proof have deduced that either Jefferson was an arrant hypocrite or on the contrary that in reality he liked blacks. The anecdote is of little importance if we consider the fact that his slave Sally Hemings, a mulatto herself, seemed to him to be an exception to the ugliness of the black race which he denounced and also that he was above all motivated in his *Notes* by his status as a public figure rather than by his private life, Jefferson made no link between these two spaces, the private space and the public space. On this subject see the excellent chapter by J. Lewis (1993), pp. 109–46.
52. J. Otis, op. cit., p. 24.
53. P. S. Onuf, op. cit., p. 418.
54. G. B. Nash, op. cit., p. 57.
55. 'The Petition of the Negroes in the Towns of Stratford and Fairfield [Connecticut] ... who are held in a State of Slavery', 11 May 1779, as cited in H. Aptheker (1951), pp. 10–12.
56. Ibid.
57. Prince Hall (1777), as cited by S. Kaplan (1973), p. 184.
58. 'The Petition of the Negroes in the Towns of Stratford and Fairfield.'
59. See the classic work by B. Quarles (1961).
60. J. Appleby, op. cit., writes: 'It is not surprising that the antislavery movement that finally led to abolition came from America's Evangelical Christians who spoke the language of sin and damnation, not that of nature and rights.'

Bibliography

APPLEBY, J. 'Jefferson and His Complex Legacy'. In: P. S. Onuf (ed.), *Jeffersonian Legacies*. Charlottesville, University Press of Virginia, 1993.

APTHEKER, H. *A Documentary History of the Negro People in the United States.* New York, Citadel Press, 1951.

BECKER, C. *The Declaration of Independence.* New York, Knopf, 1956.

BERLIN, I.; HOFFMAN, R. (eds). *Slavery and Freedom in the Age of the American Revolution.* Charlottesville, 1983.

BOYD, J. P. (ed.). *The Papers of Thomas Jefferson.* Vol. 8. Princeton, Princeton University Press, 1953. [24 volumes to date]

BUTTERFIELD, L. H. (ed.). *Letters of Benjamin Rush.* 2 Vols. Princeton, Princeton University Press, 1951.

CHASTELLUX, F.-J. de. *Voyages dans l'Amérique septentrionale dans les années 1780, 1781 et 1782* [1st pub. Paris, 1788], Paris, Librairie Jules Tallandier, 1980, p. 301 [revised Eng. trans. Howard C. Rice, *Travels in North America in the Years 1780, 1781 and 1782.* 2 Vols. Chapel Hill, University of North Carolina Press, 1963, p. 397].

COOPER, D. 'A Farmer', 'To the Publick'. *New Jersey Journal*, 20 September 1780.

DAVIS, D. B. *The Problem of Slavery in Western Culture.* Ithaca, NY, 1966.

———. *The Problem of Slavery in the Age of Revolution, 1770–1823.* Ithaca, 1975.

DRAKE, T. E. *Quakers and Slavery in America.* New Haven, Yale University Press, 1950.

FINKELMAN, P. 'Slavery and the Constitutional Convention: Making a Covenant with Death'. In: R. Beeman, S. Botein and E. C. Carter II (eds), *Beyond Confederation: Origins of the*

Constitution and American National Identity. Chapel Hill, University of North Carolina Press, 1987.

————. 'Jefferson and Slavery: "Treason against the Hopes of the World"'. In: P. S. Onuf (ed.), *Jeffersonian Legacies*. Charlottesville, University Press of Virginia, 1993.

FOGEL, R. W.; ENGERMAN, S. L. *Time on the Cross: The Economics of American Negro Slavery*. Boston, 1974.

FORD, PAUL L. (ed.). *The Writings of Thomas Jefferson*. 10 Vols. New York, Putnam's, 1892–9.

GERTEIS, L. S. *Majority and Utility in American Antislavery Reform*. Chapel Hill, 1987.

GREENE, L. *The Negro in Colonial New England*. New York, Columbia University Press, 1942.

HAYNES, H. W. 'Cotton Mather and His Slaves'. *Proceedings of the American Antiquarian Society*, New Series, Vol. 6, October 1889, pp. 191–5.

HIGGINBOTHAM, A. L., Jr. *In the Matter of Color: Race and the American Legal Process – The Colonial Period*. New York, 1978.

JEFFERSON, T. *Notes on the State of Virginia* [written in 1781]. William Peden (ed.). Chapel Hill, University of North Carolina Press, 1955.

JORDAN, W. D. *White over Black: American Attitudes towards the Negro, 1550–1812*. Chapel Hill, 1968.

KAPLAN, S. (ed.). *The Black Presence in the Era of the American Revolution, 1770–1800*. Greenwich, Conn., New York Graphic Society, Ltd., 1973.

LABAREE, L. W. (ed.). *The Papers of Benjamin Franklin*. Vol. 4. New Haven, Yale University Press, 1961. [32 volumes to date]

LAUBER, A. W. *Indian Slavery in Colonial Times within the Present Limits of the United States*. New York, Columbia University Press, 1913 [Williamstown, Mass., 1979].

LEWIS, J. '"The Blessings of Domestic Society": Thomas Jefferson's Family and the Transformation of American Politics'. In: P. S. Onuf (ed.), *Jeffersonian Legacies*. Charlottesville, University Press of Virginia, 1993.

LITWACK, L. *North of Slavery: The Negro in the Free States, 1790–1860*. Chicago, 1961.

LYND, S. *Class Conflict, Slavery and the United States Constitution*. Indianapolis, 1967.

MACLEOD, D. J. *Slavery, Race and the American Revolution*. London, 1974.

MARTIN, L. 'Genuine Information'. *Maryland Gazette*, 22 January 1788 [as cited in G. B. Nash, *Race and Revolution*, Madison, Madison House, 1990].

MOORE, G. *Notes on the History of Slavery in Massachusetts*. Boston, 1866.

MORGAN, E. S. *American Slavery, American Freedom: The Ordeal of Colonial Virginia*. New York, 1975.

NASH, G. B. *Race and Revolution*. Madison, Wis., Madison House, 1990.

NASH, G. B.; SODERLUND, J. R. *Freedom by Degrees: Emancipation and its Aftermath in Pennsylvania*. New York, 1990.

ONUF, P. S. (ed.). *Jeffersonian Legacies*. Charlottesville, University Press of Virginia, 1993.

OTIS, J. *Rights of the British Colonies Asserted and Proved*. Boston, 1764.

PENNYPACKER, S. W. 'The Settlement of Germantown, and the Causes Which Led to It'. *Pennsylvania Magazine of History and Biography*, Vol. 4, No. 1, 1880, pp. 28–30.

QUARLES, B. *The Negro in the American Revolution*. Chapel Hill, 1961.

RHYS, I. 'The First Monticello'. In: P. S. Onuf (ed.), *Jeffersonian Legacies*. Charlottesville, University Press of Virginia, 1993.

STANTON, L. C. '"Those who labor for my happiness": Thomas Jefferson and His Slaves'. In: P. S. Onuf (ed.), *Jeffersonian Legacies*. Charlottesville, University Press of Virginia, 1993.

WOOLMAN, J. *Considerations on the Keeping of Negroes*. N.p., 1762.

ZILVERSMIT, A. *The First Emancipation: The Abolition of Slavery in the North*. Chicago, 1967.

Further Reading

BENDER, T. *The Antislavery Debate*. Berkeley, 1992.

BROOKES, G. S. *Friend Anthony Benezet*. Philadelphia, 1937.

BURNS, R. (ed.). *Am I not a Man and a Brother? The Antislavery Crusade of Revolutionary America, 1688–1788*. New York, 1977.

CURRY, L. P. *The Free Black in Urban America, 1800–1850: The Shadow of a Dream*. Chicago, 1981.

DAVIS, D. B. *Slavery and Human Progress*. New York, 1987.

DUBERMAN, M. B. (ed.). *The Antislavery Vanguard: New Essays on the Abolitionists*. Princeton, 1965.

DUMOND, D. L. *Antislavery: The Crusade for Freedom in America*. Ann Arbor, 1961.

FINKELMAN, P. *The Law of Freedom and Bondage: A Casebook*. New York, 1986.

FRANKLIN, J. H. *Racial Equality in America*. Chicago, 1976.

FREY, S.R. *Water from the Rock: Black Resistance in a Revolutionary Age*. Princeton, 1991.

GEORGE, C. V.-R. *Segregated Sabbaths: Richard Allen and the Rise of Independent Churches, 1760–1845*. New York, 1973.

GREENE, J. P. *All Men Are Created Equal: Some Reflections on the Characters of the American Revolution*. Oxford, 1976.

HARDING, V. *There is a River: The Black Struggle for Freedom in America*. New York, 1981.

KETCHAM, R. *North of Slavery: The Revolution in American Thought, 1750–1820*. New York, 1974.

MACCOLLEY, R. *Slavery and Jeffersonian Virginia*. Urbana, Ill., 1964.

MILLER, F. J. *The Search for a Black Nationality: Black Colonization and Emigration, 1787–1863*. Urbana, Ill., 1975.

MILLER, J. C. *The Wolf by the Ear: Thomas Jefferson and Slavery*. New York, 1977.

MULLIN, G. W. *Flight and Rebellion: Slave Resistance in Eighteenth Century Virginia*. New York, 1972.

NASH, G. B. *Forging Freedom: The Formation of Philadelphia Black Community, 1720–1840*. Cambridge, Mass., 1988.

POLE, J. R. *The Pursuit of Equality in American History*. Berkeley, 1978.

ROBINSON, D. L. *Slavery in the Structure of American Politics 1765–1820*. New York, 1971.

SODERLUND, J. R., *Quakers and Slavery: A Divided Spirit*. Princeton, 1985.

STANTON, W. *The Leopard's Spots*. Chicago, 1960.

WIECEK, W. M., *The Sources of Antislavery Constitutionalism in America, 1760–1848*. Ithaca, 1977.

WINCH, J. *Philadelphia's Black Elite: Activism, Accommodation, and the Struggle for Autonomy, 1787–1848*. Philadelphia, 1988.

WOOD, P. *Black Majority: Negroes in Colonial South Carolina from 1670 through the Stono Rebellion*. New York, 1974.

Chapter 8

Is Slavery Reformable? Proposals of Colonial Administrators at the End of the Ancien Régime

Jean Tarrade

AT THE END of the Ancien Régime, colonial administrators, appointed by the King and the Secretary of State for the Navy, were chosen from among the nobility in the case of governors, and from among members of provincial *parlements* for intendants and among commissioners of the navy as *ordonnateurs* (quartermaster-treasurers) for junior posts.[1] These administrators, often ignorant of colonial realities when they arrived, lived in practice in the closed world of the *grands blancs*, proprietors of rich *habitations* (estates) and owners of *ateliers* (gangs) of black slaves. Very often they themselves became owners of estates by purchase, inheritance or marriage, even though it was in principle forbidden. They naturally came to share the colonists' mentalities and did not question slavery. We may take the cases of the Marquis de Bouillé[2] and of Guillemin de Vaivre, himself intendant of Saint-Domingue and later intendant-général of the colonies until June 1792, who held similar positions under the Consulate and was the man who re-established slavery in the colonies.[3]

Winds of Change

Yet by the middle of the century of the Enlightenment, some administrators were already becoming, to varying degrees, sensitive to the philosophical ideas whose major works were published in the period between the peace of Aix-la-Chapelle (1748) and the Treaty of Paris (1763). Under the Choiseuls, those who were won over to the new ideas corrected them in the light of contact with colonial realities. The Marquis de Fénelon, appointed Governor in 1763 to take charge of Martinique, which had been returned by the British, gave a good summary of the changes that were occurring when he wrote to his minister:

> I arrived in Martinique with all the prejudices of Europe against the severity with which negroes are treated and in favour of the teaching owed them by the principles of our religion.

The severity had revolted me and went against every human right; the ideas of slavery did not in my heart balance out the affecting spectacle of human creatures just like us except for the colour of their skin, being treated like animals. Barbarity – in every colony there are inhabitants who push severity to that point – seems to me a horror. But a harsh, indeed a very harsh discipline is an indispensable and necessary evil, I feel it and am convinced of it.

As to education – I should terrify every saint of the clergy of France if my opinion were to get out of the sanctuary of your office – this is a duty by the principles of religion, but wise policy and the strongest of human considerations go against it.

Education may give the negroes a first opening, which might lead to other consequences, to a sort of reasoning. The safety of whites, who are fewer in number, surrounded on their habitations by these people, abandoned to themselves, demands that they be kept in the deepest ignorance.[4]

The intendant who accompanied Fénelon was himself a *philosophe*: Paul-Pierre Le Mercier de la Rivière had already governed Martinique from 1757 to 1762 and was sent there again after the peace. In his major work, *L'ordre naturel et essentiel des sociétés politiques*, published in 1767, he curiously overlooks the specific case of colonial slavery and remains at the level of philosophical generalities: 'Once we recognize the physical necessity ... of living in society, we see obviously that it is absolutely necessary and consequently just that every man be *solely* owner of his person and of the things that he acquires by his endeavours and his labour.'[5] Like the members of the Constituent Assembly twenty years later, he asserted the principle of the individual freedom of man but refused to draw the logical conclusion concerning black slaves in the colonies.

The influence of the ideas of the *philosophes* in governing circles rose steadily in the following decade. Turgot's brief tenure at the navy (1774) and the false news of the freeing of the slaves, a rumour probably intended to discredit him (1776), helped to speed up the process. This can be seen in the work on the second version of the Committee on Colonial Legislation.[6] Whereas the first Committee established by the Duke de Choiseul, in which the moving spirit was Émilien Petit, was composed wholly of lawyers, the one established by Sartine was made up chiefly of practitioners – former colonial administrators. Among them were two intendants who would play a key role: Philippe-Athanase Tascher, intendant of Guadeloupe in 1771 and later of all the Windward Islands, who returned to France in 1777 for health reasons, and Alexandre Jacques de Bongars, intendant of Saint-Domingue from 1766 to 1771 and again from 1781 to 1785. This committee did a substantial amount of work, especially between 1778 and 1781. But when, after the Treaty of Versailles (1783), Marshal de Castries proposed to carry out the necessary reforms one after the other, Vaivre caused every proposal by the committee regarding the status of slaves and free people of colour to be blocked.

Yet the influence of the new ideas was such that signs of change became apparent both in the colonies and at Versailles. There was a concern with improving the management of plantations, both to raise production and to limit abuses in the treatment of slaves. Of course, there were always good masters concerned about how their blacks were treated, but the advance of humanitarian and philanthropic ideas under the influence of the sensibility deriving from Jean-Jacques Rousseau went hand in hand with a clear conception of where their interest lay: properly fed and relatively well-treated slaves were more productive than those on estates where cruel, despotic and avaricious masters, overseers or drivers were in charge. But, as Vaivre was able to see for himself, too many plantation owners were absentees, living in France on the income from their estates entrusted to attorneys or overseers who often ran them into the ground and took little interest in what happened to the slaves. This led to the ordinances, adopted on 3 December 1784 and 23 December 1785, that allowed the administration to manage estates whose owners were absent and to ensure that slaves were properly treated.[7] These ordinances were, with the Castries version of the *Exclusif mitigé*, one of the main reasons for the colonists' opposition to the Revolution.

The Committee on Legislation and the former administrators had also become fully aware of the catastrophic numerical imbalance between whites and slaves, which would make a slave revolt particularly dangerous, especially in Saint-Domingue, where the gap was overwhelming: in 1788, there were 27,717 whites and 21,808 free people of colour as against 405,564 black slaves. Allowing for *libertés de savane* (a limited form of freedom that permitted some slaves freedom of movement on the estate) and purely fiscal fraud, the true number of slaves was probably over 500,000.

Insurmountable Problems

At the time of the American War of Independence, colonists and administrators alike were particularly sensitive to this numerical imbalance between slaves and whites, especially in Saint-Domingue, fearing a slave revolt comparable to those in Dutch Guyana (Surinam) and Jamaica. Examples such as these caused Lescallier to write that far from being stupid as the colonists asserted, the blacks were capable of courage and organizing ability. This fear was aggravated by the example of the young United States, where some states outlawed slavery and the slave trade. This obsession with revolt came on top of the old belief in poisonings, a survivor in Saint-Domingue of the terror aroused in 1756 by Makandal, although Bouillé – speaking of the Windward Islands – mocked these fantasies as a product of the colonists' 'gullibility'.[8] Yet the fact remains that the existence of bands of black maroons kept the unease alive. On the other hand, during the War of Independence, troops of royal hunters had been raised that had taken part in operations on the American coast. Administrators, especially the frequent acting ones, had increased the numbers of slave manumissions, not hesitating to give signed blank certificates granting freedom to their office clerks for whom their sale was an extra source of income.[9] Concerned about this, Castries condemned the excessive number of manumissions granted and called for regular statistics.

The result was a confrontation between two conceptions: on the one hand, the traditional principle, with strict maintenance of the gap that had been established between black slaves and white colonists, and on the other hand, the necessity that had now become apparent of relying on free people of colour to help the whites put down any slave revolt.

The problem was set out starkly in the instructions given to Governor Bellecombe and intendant Bongars in 1781, a document which reflects the ideas of the Committee on Legislation, it being the usual practice for new administrators to be associated with the drafting of the King's memoir that would act as their instruction:

> It was thought that, in a country where there are fifteen slaves for every white, it would be impossible to put too much distance between the two species, and impress on the Negroes too much respect for those to whom they are subjected. This distinction, strictly observed, even after manumission, has been regarded as the principal link in the subordination of the slave, because of the resulting opinion that his colour is condemned to servitude and that nothing can make him equal to his master.

This document reproduces earlier instructions but is directly followed by new considerations:

> The most thoughtful people however today consider the people of colour as the strongest barrier against any trouble from the slaves. This class of men, in their opinion, merits respect and favours, and their opinion leans in favour of moderating the current contempt with which they are treated and even putting an end to it. This delicate issue calls for deep reflection.[10]

The administrators were asked to consult local bodies (Conseil supérieur, Chambers of Agriculture) and welcomed the approach of the quadroon Julien Raimond, the owner of a coffee plantation in the south of Saint-Domingue, who in 1783, in the name of the free landowners, offered to participate in the proposal made by the colony to offer a vessel to the King.[11] Raimond was well received by the administrators, and even introduced to the Minister in 1785. Consulted by Castries that year on the instructions intended for their successors in Saint-Domingue – La Luzerne and Marbois – Bellecombe presented his conclusions on the question raised in 1781: 'Whether the infamy attached to slavery is to be continued however far removed individuals are from the slave generation.' Bellecombe observed that for the old inhabitants, it would never be wiped out for them, but that those without prejudice were against this mark of infamy. For his part, he proposed setting a term to this proscription, but thought that that would be dangerous in a country where everything rested on the superiority of one race over the other. He also referred to the mixing of the races in the Spanish part of Saint-Domingue[12] as well as the danger of discontent on their return of the 'misallied', who had come to study in France and were looked down on in the colony. Castries noted his decision in the margin of Bellecombe's observations: '[N]ot approved.'[13] Earlier, consulting Bellecombe on a memorial from Raimond, Castries indeed spoke of 'unjust prejudice' and of the affecting situation of these free men and added 'the matter is infinitely delicate and merits the most serious examination'.[14]

What we can see, then, is that royal administrators were aware of the need for some limited changes in the status of free people of colour and for improvements in the lot of slaves. While such ideas were gaining some ground in the minds of the rulers in Versailles, they did not go much beyond that, as all were aware of the realities on the spot. In the instructions drawn up in 1788 for the new Governor of Saint-Domingue – Du Chilleau[15] – La Luzerne, the Governor of Saint-Domingue having succeeded Castries as Secretary of State for the Navy, raised the question whether free men could be admitted into the class of whites when the external signs of their origins had disappeared. He replied prudently:

> ... Perhaps it might be right, as has been suggested, to prohibit any research into the origin of individuals whose colour would differ not at all, or hardly at all, from that of the nation, but before promulgating a law on the subject that justice and humanity alike demand ...,

he wished to have the opinions of the Conseil supérieur, the colonial assembly once it was established and the most worthy inhabitants whom they would consult. It seems difficult to have any illusions about the outcome of such a consultation, since the major obstacle was the intransigence of the colonists, who did not want to hear any talk of even the least change in the slave regime. More and more they made it a matter of skin colour, refusing to accept equality with those having the least drop of black blood – and they were masters at detecting the least hint of blackness.

We are far indeed from Sartine writing in 1776, but for a special case, that of the freemen of Gorée settled in French Guyana: 'It is slavery and not colour that indelibly marks Negroes.'[16] It was the jurisconsult Moreau de Saint-Méry who reflected most absurdly and most systematically this obsession of the colonists by calculating all the possible categories from 128 parts of white or black blood, that is over seven generations. It is, in the strictest possible sense, madness.[17]

Administrators to the Fore

We now need to look at the case of three administrators who, in very different ways, wrote important works on this problem: Malouet, Poivre and, above all, Lescallier, the only one to put forward a plan for the gradual abolition of slavery. The writings of these three royal administrators provide concrete examples of the various stands taken by these men placed at the interface of new ideas and the concrete realities that they had to manage.

The first of these administrators, Pierre-Victor Malouet, is well known because of his role in the early days of the Revolution,[18] the publication in Year X of his *Collection de mémoires et correspondances officielles sur l'administration des colonies* and the *Mémoires* published by his grandson in 1868. Malouet is interesting for two reasons, as a royal administrator and as the owner of an estate in Saint-Domingue, which came to him through marriage. However, only a brief comment is necessary because of the excellent article by Michèle Duchet, 'Malouet et le problème de l'esclavage [Malouet and the Problem of Slavery]' in the proceedings of the colloquy on Malouet organized at Riom in 1989 by Jean Ehrard and Michel Morineau.[19]

Michèle Duchet has admirably brought out the ambiguities of the man, a new colonist discovering the realities of slavery on his estate in Saint-Domingue. Appointed Commissioner of the Navy – *ordonnateur* – in French Guyana, Malouet was given the task of examining the possibilities of carrying out the utopian colonization plans put forward by Baron de Bessner, an individual with good connections in Parisian society, who suggested this time using the Indians and maroon blacks of Surinam, a proposal the illusory character of which soon became apparent to Malouet.[20] He much preferred examining, with the engineer Guisan, the methods used by the Dutch in Surinam to drain lowlands. He stood aside from the developing ideas about slavery going on in governing circles. In him, the colonist had won out; his idea of reforms consisted simply in asking masters to treat their slaves well, without gratuitous cruelty, and to take good care of what happened to them. Naturally, since his writings were published after the drama of the Saint-Domingue revolt, they were marked by the dominant ideas of the colonist milieu, and it is evident that he had become an even stronger supporter of slavery than ever.

With Pierre Poivre, *philosophe* and botanist, Commissioner General of the Navy acting as *ordonnateur* in the islands of France and Bourbon, rewarded with the title of intendant for his introduction of spice plants, we have a different case. As a *philosophe,* he sharply condemned slavery. Slavery, he wrote, 'degrades man and after debasing the slave, it tends to enervate the master, to corrupt him, to chain him under the shameful yoke of pride, harshness and every vice'.[21] While blaming the Compagnie des Indes for having introduced slavery into those islands which it had administered until their recent retrocession to the King (1764 de jure, 1766 de facto), he accepted the fait accompli. Speaking with the voice of his times, he vehemently condemned masters forgetful of their duties towards their slaves. He felt it necessary to soften their fate through the teaching of religion, not forgetting that he had started out at the Lazarist Society of Foreign Missions. He wrote:

> Our simple religion, by adopting them among the number of its children, will return them beyond what they have lost. Its consoling truths will enable them to bear patiently the harshness of their fate.... Despite the horrors of slavery, they will be able to be happy, by retaining that precious freedom of the soul that only vice can take away.... The same law [the *Code Noir*] also requires masters to promote marriage among their slaves, and that they feed them, clothe them and treat them humanely.[22]

Poivre went on to denounce the corruption of morals brought about by slavery and recalled the ban on manumitting children born of concubinage between masters and slaves. One of the factors determining his attitude was the need to ensure the defence of the island against the British enemy, who, to make matters worse, were heretics. His writings, notably on the right of property, often shocked Versailles, which led to a ban being placed on their publication in France.[23] In terms of concrete application, Poivre had the occasion to set out his policy in the case of Madagascar: he thought that what was needed was to 'Frenchify' the inhabitants and not to make slaves of them.[24] But when he needed slaves for the King's works, he did not hesitate to seek permission to trade with the Portuguese in Mozambique to procure some.[25] In so doing, Poivre proved himself a worthy representative of the royal administrators of the 1760s: as a *philosophe,* such as Le Mercier de la Rivière, he condemned slavery in principle as contrary to natural law, while accepting it as a reality. He sought simply to improve the lot of slaves on the basis of the *Code Noir,* which contained provisions in favour of slaves that the vast majority of colonists omitted to implement. It is worth noting in passing that for this *philosophe,* as was generally the case with his contemporaries, the 1685 *Code Noir* was seen, despite what we view as the odious nature of some articles – such as Article 44, which declares that slaves are 'chattels' – rather as a protection against abuses by masters (such as, Articles 22 to 26 regarding food and clothing). In reality, the fact was that, far from Versailles, the colonists did as they wished and did not implement that sort of article. Poivre's example inclines us to support the analysis by Philippe Hesse at the Nantes colloquy in 1985 and not the interpretations of Sala-Molins, which were rightly refuted by Michèle Duchet.[26]

The most typical of the royal administrators who were sympathetic to reforming the lot of slaves was Daniel Lescallier, Commissioner of the Navy. With his case we can compare concrete action on the ground with the systematic exposition of a proposal for reform published in 1789. During the American War of Independence, Lescallier was employed in conquered Grenada, and then appointed *ordonnateur* in Demerara, a Dutch colony reconquered from the British in 1782 and which he returned to the Dutch in 1784. He was then appointed in May 1785 to serve as Commissioner General of the Navy, as *ordonnateur* in French Guyana, where he remained until May 1788, at which date he returned to France without permission. A month before his departure, on 12 April 1788, Governor Villebois noted that while relations between them were normal, Lescallier's principles were 'easygoing'.[27]

Lescallier advocated encouraging the emancipation of slaves. The colony was too poor, he felt, for it to be possible to set too high a tax on manumissions straightaway. At his request, the Secretary of State approved a decree by the Conseil supérieur, which decided that for three years the tax would be set on a case-by-case basis by the administrators after consultation with the Dean and the Procurator General of the Conseil supérieur and the Commandant of the district affected.[28]

Lescallier also supported the experiment undertaken by the Marquis de Lafayette on the estates *La Gabrielle* and *Saint-Règis* that he had acquired for that purpose in French Guyana and whose management he entrusted to an engineer and geographer, Henri de Richeprey. The latter's task was to develop the culture of cinnamon and cloves brought from the Île-de-France and to ensure the evangelization of the slaves on those estates. He abolished corporal punishment for them, granted them a wage and applied to them the legislation that applied to whites. Richeprey died on 9 February 1787, and Lescallier was appointed to continue the experiment.[29] On his return to France, he published in 1789 a work of seventy-one pages, entitled *Réflexions sur le sort des Noirs dans nos colonies,* in which he developed his ideas at length.[30] His project offers the best picture of the conceptions of enlightened administrators on the eve of the meeting of the Estates-General. After challenging the received idea that blacks are stupid or that it is impossible to grow anything in the West Indies without blacks and without slaves whose current state is 'infinitely preferable, it is said, to that of our peasants', he adds: '[T]he colonists (who are almost all in favour of maintaining slavery) put a lot of passion into supporting a cause that seems personal to them; the others (who are a small number of people who for the most part have no interest in the colonies) show the greatest zeal in favour of relieving suffering humanity.' Starting from there, he observes

> that the estate whose management is the most reasonable, the least arbitrary, and on which the Negroes are taught their catechism, where an attempt is made to instil some manners in them, where they have a little property and a sort of social existence, is also the one that brings in the most constant revenues to its owner, and the less unhappy the Negroes are the richer their master gets. The supporters of slavery acknowledge as much themselves.

Starting from these everyday observations, he goes further. He states first that a sudden and unlimited emancipation must be avoided, as it would be dangerous – above all, for the new Negroes unaccustomed to the Europeans' language or ways of doing things. For that, an end needs first to be put to the slave trade, which is inhuman and cruel. His experience of the colonies makes him think of giving freedom to blacks gradually with an end-point which '… would not be very far off'. Lescallier suggests beginning by sending to work in the fields or freeing domestic slaves, artisans and workers, whom it would always be possible to hire later, and also '[f]reeing the whole race (at least that yet to be born) of mulattoes and mixed bloods'. As for the mass of blacks working in the fields, he envisaged a progressive system of at least nine years to reach a new status or *Code Colonial,* replacing the *Code Noir,* which, through a system of growing rewards, would enable the families of blacks to be freed successively by purchase, thanks to the savings made from their profits.

The conclusion summarizes the exposition of the gradual means proposed opening with a stark assertion: 'Slavery is a vicious and unjust institution; the slave trade is an even more damnable barbarity.'

In conclusion, we may note that for thirty years the problem of slavery had been among the concerns and projects of governing circles in Versailles. Through the inevitable shifts over time (period of Choiseul – the 1770s – period of Castries) and because of differing personalities, royal administrators generally hoped to improve the lot of slaves. Those who were advocates of reforming the system itself were very prudent, since they were prisoners of the dominant mentalities among the colonists whom they were administering. Saint-Domingue was the key colony in all this both because of its economic importance and because the memory of its 1769 revolt was still very much alive. It is moreover not surprising that the experiments and the most advanced projects emanated from the administrator of that unhappy colony of French Guyana, the privileged terrain of every reform attempt and every utopia since 1763.

To the initial question asked: is slavery reformable? we therefore reply that all the administrators wanted it to a greater or lesser degree but that the predictable resistance of the colonists explains the prudence of their behaviour. Only the Convention in Pluviôse, year II, would attempt to realize the necessary reform through total and immediate abolition but in the context of a situation that had become tragic, fully realizing the fears that this radical solution inspired in royal administrators before 1789.

Notes

1. J. Tarrade, 'Les intendants des colonies à la fin de l'Ancien Régime', in *La France d'Ancien Régime (Mélanges Pierre Goubert)*, Toulouse, Privat, 1984, pp. 673–81.
2. François-Claude Amour, Marquis de Bouillé (b. 1739; d. London, 14 November 1800). In 1768 he married Marie-Louise de Bègue, whose family fortune lay in Guadeloupe, whence his appointment as Governor of that colony.
3. Jean-Baptiste Guillemin de Vaivre (Besançon 1736, Paris 1818), intendant of Saint-Domingue (1774–1780), intendant-général in August 1783, resigned 21 June 1792, head of the Office for the Colonies (Fructidor Year VIII, 1807), *maître des comptes* (1807–1817).
4. Archives Nationales, Colonies, C8A 66 f° 33–4, Fort-Royal, 11 April 1764, Fénelon to Choiseul.
5. P.-P. Le Mercier de La Rivière, *L'Ordre naturel et essentiel des sociétés politiques*, 1767, 511 pp., Paris, Collection des Économistes, 1919, 405 pp. Quotations on pp. 14 and 10 respectively.
6. J. Tarrade, 'L'administration coloniale en France à la fin de l'Ancien Régime', *Revue historique*, Vol. 219, 1963, pp. 103–23.
7. G. Debien, *Les Esclaves aux Antilles françaises*, Basse-Terre-Fort-de-France, Sociétés d'histoire de la Guadeloupe et de la Martinique, 1974, 531 pp., pp. 471–95.
8. Arch. Nat., Col., C8A 82, f° 40–2, taken from Bouillé's 'Mémoire' on his administration, 1777.
9. Ibid., C9A 152, 27 September 1782, Bellecombe and Bongars to Castries.
10. Ibid., C9B 29, minute on the Mémoire pour servir d'instruction pour Bellecombe et Bongars (sent on 15 October 1781).
11. G. Debien, *La Société coloniale aux XVIIe et XVIIIe siècles,* Vol. 2: *Les Colons de Saint-Domingue et la Révolution – Essai sur le club Massiac*, Paris, A. Colin, 1953, 414 pp. See pp. 36–40.
12. D. L. Ropa, 'La société coloniale de Santo Domingo à la veille de l'occupation française', *R.F.H.O.M.*, Vol. 46, 1959, pp. 56–198.
13. Arch. Nat. Col., C9C 6, Observations sur les instructions pour La Luzerne and Marbois, M. de Bellecombe, n.d. (=1785).
14. Arch. Nat., Col., B 193, f° 105 v°, Versailles, 17 February 1786, Castries to Bellecombe.
15. Arch. Nat., Col., C9A 160, 1 August 1788, mémoire-instruction for Governor Du Chilleau.
16. Arch. Nat., Col., B 156, Versailles, 16 June 1776, Sartine to the administrators of French Guyana, Fiedmont and de la Croix.
17. M. de Saint-Méry, *Description ... de la partie française de Saint-Domingue*, 3 Vols, Paris, Édition Blanche Maurel and Étienne Taillemite, 1958, 1,565 pp. See Vol. 1, pp. 85–102.

18. J. Egret, *La révolution des notables – Mounier et les Monarchiens*, Paris, A. Colin, 1950, 244 pp.

19. J. Ehrard and M. Morineau (eds), *Malouet (1740–1814)*, Actes du Colloquy de Riom, Puy-de-Dôme, 1990, 205 pp. See pp. 63–70 for Michèle Duchet's paper.

20. J. Tarrade, *Le commerce colonial de la France à la fin de l'Ancien Régime*, Paris, P.U.F., Publications de l'Université de Poitiers, Lettres et Sciences humaines, XII, 1 and 2, 1972, 892 pp. (thesis for doctorat d'État).

21. P. Poivre, *Oeuvres complètes précédées de sa vie* (by Dupont de Nemours), Paris, 1797, including *Voyages d'un philosophe*, citation p. 219.

22. Ibid., pp. 220–1.

23. Arch. Nat., Col., B 134, f° 5, 17 January 1769, Praslin to Sartine.

24. Ibid., C5A 2, 20 July 1768, Poivre to Praslin.

25. Ibid., C4 18, 30 November 1767, same to same.

26. P. Hesse, 'Le Code Noir: de l'homme et de l'esclave', in *De la traite à l'esclavage. Actes du Colloque international sur la traite des Noirs, Nantes 1985*, 2 Vols, Nantes-Paris, C.R.H.M.A., (Université de Nantes) and S.F.H.O.M, 1988, Vol. 2, pp. 185–91; M. Duchet, op. cit., p. 69; L. Sala-Molins, *Le Code Noir*, Paris, P.U.F., 1987. The papers of the colloquy on 'Esclavage, colonisation, libérations nationales', Université de Paris 8, February 1989, Paris, Éditions de L'Harmattan, 1990, pp. 104–11, set out the sixty articles of the *Code Noir* (as an appendix to Samuel Mack-Kit's paper).

27. Arch. Nat., C14 62, f° 11/12, 12 April 1788.

28. Ibid., B 196, f° 593, Versailles, 19 August 1787, Castries to Villebois and Lescallier. Ibid., C 62, f° 34–5, Cayenne, 7 January 1788, text of the final ordinance. See J. Tarrade, 'Affranchis et gens de couleur libres en Guyane', *Revue française de l'histoire d'outre-mer*, Vol. 49, 1st quarter 1962, pp. 80–116, especially pp. 87–90.

29. E. Taillemite, *La Fayette*, Paris, Fayard, 1989, 623 pp., pp. 125–6.

30. Published by EDHIS in *La Révolution française et l'abolition de l'esclavage*, a facsimile reproduction of the 1789 edition. The following quotations come from pp. 11–13, 16, 38 and 67.

Chapter 9

Slavery before the Moral Conscience of the French Enlightenment: Indifference, Unease and Revolt

Jean Ehrard

HERE WE SHALL not be dealing with learning. My intention is not to add to the work of Michèle Duchet, Yves Bénot, Carminella Biondi and others by unearthing unknown texts or documents. What I should like to do is to react to the groundless accusations made in recent years about colonial slavery and Enlightenment philosophy by putting well-known texts into perspective. My purpose is not to idealize the French eighteenth century, but to attempt to understand an attitude that it seems to me can be summed up in three words: indifference, unease and revolt. Let us examine each element one by one.

Indifference

Firstly, indifference. Naturally, a distinction has to be made among different periods: the century was not all of a piece, and there was a great difference between the Regency and the pre-Revolutionary period. After 1760 and above all 1770, writings on colonial slavery are far more numerous than in the first half of the century, before *The Spirit of Laws*, and there was undoubtedly at that time a growing realization of the seriousness of the matter. Yet compared to the great debates that pervaded the century, the problem remained marginal. Writings on the issue of slavery are a fraction of those on philosophical and religious polemics, controversies over the French 'constitution' and the prerogatives of *parlements* or even discussions of the freedom of trade in cereals. In the 72,000 articles in that monument of the Enlightenment, the *Encyclopédie*, I have been able to find only thirty-three explicit references to the slave trade and slavery.[1] Even if, as is likely, I missed some articles, the impression would still be that, overall, interest was rather limited.

Why this lack of interest? Precisely, and first of all, because there were many other subjects that were more current and closer to home competing with blacks in the colonies in emerging public opinion. I am thinking, for example, in addition to the controversial matters mentioned above, of the great work of reassessing productive labour morally and socially that was being developed from the time of abbé Saint-Pierre to that of the *Encyclopédie*,[2] and beyond, a work too concerned with celebrating labour to linger long over the fate of workers, whether white or black. We must remember, too, the distance, both geographical and mental, between France and the Antilles, and recall – it is not superfluous – that the eighteenth century had not invented either photography or television and that no written word will ever have the emotional impact of a shock image. Are we who receive such images evening after evening terribly worried about buying certain cheap goods from Asia and South America when the media tell and show us, at least now and again, how they are made? All the more reason why the exotic had on Voltaire's contemporaries its well-known effects of embellishing and prettifying. And then, how could people spend too much time thinking about the human cost of sugar and indigo when in France itself violence was an everyday affair, popular violence, violence in the streets, violence by the state – and the Church – in hunting people down and judicial procedures and public punishments? In contrast to these accustomed horrors, in Versailles, Paris or the great ports along the Atlantic, colonial exploitation offered its most smiling face. It was not its 'drivers' brandishing their whips that were met at court and in the salons, but beautiful women toying with little black boys dressed in red, and the elegance and wit of a Dubucq or a Malouet.

At least two other considerations, intellectual in this case, should be added to those above. The first is that the basic notions were not at all cut and dried. In the eighteenth century, a clear distinction was not always made between slavery and serfdom. Antoine Furetière's *Dictionnaire Universel*, which ran to many editions, defines the serf as 'one who is a slave' and finds nothing more to say about serfdom (*servage*) than this gallant comment: 'Old word which used to mean slavery, servitude, and which is now used to describe the captivation, the attachment of a lover to his mistress.' In the *Encyclopédie*, the same article 'Servage' borrows the beginning of the definition from Furetière, regretting that a useful word has fallen into disuse, but without further distinguishing between serf and slave. On the other hand, the precision of the jurist, in this case Boucher d'Argis, can be seen in the article 'Serf' (serf), which does avoid confusion: 'The state of serfs is midway between that of freedom and slavery.' Similarly, the article 'Esclave (Jurisp.)' (Slave (Jurisp.)), by the same author, refers to the early days of the French monarchy: 'In addition to the true slaves there were in France many serfs, who occupied a place midway between Roman servitude and freedom.' But the long article 'Esclavage' (Slavery) – ten columns – by the Chevalier de Jaucourt takes the reader from ancient slavery to colonial slavery by way of serfdom without clarifying the difference. But there were indeed still many serfs in eighteenth-century Europe, and a few in France. In his 1775 memorial in favour of those in Franche-Comté, Voltaire uses the words serfs/slaves, servitude/slavery interchangeably.[3] Is this simply a matter of style intended to render the condition of the *mainmortables* in the

Jura even more dramatic, or the sign of loose definitions? In any case, it would be a safe bet that for most enlightened opinion, and perhaps even for specialists in the history of law, the equivalence that Jaucourt was happy to accept did not create any problem. Montesquieu himself, so learned in both ancient and medieval history, uses the words 'slavery' and 'servitude' interchangeably in his *Esprit des Lois* (Spirit of Laws). The furthest he goes is, when writing on the colonate or serfdom, to specify 'glebe slavery' (XIII, 3).

Such vagueness of definition was bound to make the institution of colonial slavery seem quite ordinary and dilute the shocking nature of it. But for that scandal to become intolerable required much more than a less imprecise terminology: it required the invention of doctrinal references on which to rest a clear and unequivocal condemnation. When the Church approved or kept quiet, it was necessary to give philosophy the means to criticize its complicity or make up for its silence. It is simply not possible to discuss the manner in which the eighteenth century tackled the problem of slavery by assuming or pretending to believe that the key ideas of the Enlightenment were constituted and widespread from its very beginning. We repeat, they were not de facto from the outset, but rather an invention – the object of laborious maturation and perilous dissemination, both spread over time. It is not by chance that the first decisive challenge to the principle of colonial slavery appeared only with the *Esprit des Lois* towards mid-century.

Unease

Even this relatively late appearance occurred in a context of unease that lingered until the Revolution, but was, it seems to me, the dominant feature of the years between 1750 and 1770: it is an unease very apparent in Montesquieu himself and also in the *Encyclopédie*. Without going into detail about Montesquieu's thought, I will simply recall the gap between the sharpness of the philosophical condemnation of slavery in Book XV of the *Spirit of Laws* and the timidity of the practical conclusions drawn from it. It is a contrast between the luminous rigour of the argumentation that motivates, in Chapter 2, the rejection in principle – freedom is inalienable: before Rousseau and, on this precise point against Locke, Montesquieu was the first to write it – and the extreme embarrassment of the author when it comes to answering the question 'Then, why slavery?'. For here we have slavery declared both against nature and natural (XV, 7), without our knowing very clearly – and Montesquieu admits that he is certain of nothing – whether the climatic constraint is or is not, in his opinion, irremediably inevitable. I have tried to show elsewhere[4] what this hesitation tells us about the crisis then beginning to engulf the 'all's well' optimism that had been the Enlightenment's initial response to Christian pessimism. But we also need to remember how that theoretical embarrassment, indicative of a need for thought and not of insufficient thought, made worse by a split between 'mind' and 'heart', led to a liberating illumination: 'Because the laws were badly made men were found to be lazy;

because those men were lazy, they were reduced to slavery' (XV, 8). This paragraph, which contradicts the first line of the same chapter, does not exist in the manuscript in the Bibliothèque nationale. Its sudden appearance confirms the tense character of an ongoing process of thought, a tormented quest also evidenced for other chapters of Book XV, both the 1757 additions and the manuscript erasures.[5]

It will come as no surprise, knowing how much the *Encyclopédie* owes to Montesquieu, that a similar embarrassment is to be found in its pages. Of the just under fifty articles examined wherein the subject matter might call for mention of black slavery, fifteen fail to mention it, twenty mention it neutrally – a silence that speaks volumes on such a question – ten condemn it more or less vigorously and three support it (see summary table). At the extremes, there are on the one side Jaucourt with 'Égalité naturelle' (Natural Equality), 'Esclavage (Droit nat)' (Slavery (Natural Law)), 'Liberté naturelle' (Natural Freedom), if the article is indeed his, 'Marron' (Maroon), 'Stampe' (Brand), 'Traite des nègres' (Slave Trade), and Diderot, with 'Humaine espèce' (Human Species), Damilaville with 'Population', the author of 'Trente-six mois' (Thirty-Six Months) and, for 'Usure' (Usury), Faiguet who however accepts temporary slavery. On the other, the engineer Le Romain – a colonial – with 'Nègres (commerce)' (Negroes (Trade)), if the article is to be attributed to him, and 'Nègres considérés comme esclaves' (Negroes Regarded as Slaves), as well as the unexpected backing of Jaucourt who, in the article 'Rio-Negro' (Géo Mod.), himself finds extenuating circumstances, at least for the Portuguese in South America:

> They trade much in slaves, and they must do them [*sic*] within the limits laid down by the laws of Portugal, which only allow a person to be deprived of his freedom if his situation is being made better, by making him a slave: such are those unhappy captives destined for death, and to be served up to their enemies among the nations that engage in this barbarous usage.

The argument from African barbarity is precisely one of those used by Le Romain to give himself a clear conscience: the wretched blacks, subject to the most terrible violence in Africa 'find in America a gentleness that makes animal life much better than in their own country' ('Nègres considérés comme esclaves' [Negroes Regarded as Slaves]). Moreover, would they deserve a different fate? The same author, in an article in which the word 'slave' does not even appear, notes that they are a 'vicious', 'treacherous' and 'lazy' species on whom sensitive souls would be wrong to waste their pity ('Sucrerie, Habitation' [Sugar Mill, Estate]). More than a hint of racism thus hovers over the generous enterprise of the *Encyclopédie*. What a contrast with the article 'Traite des nègres' (Slave Trade), in which Jaucourt waxes furious against 'a traffic that violates religion, morality, natural laws and every right of human nature'. Everything can be found in the *Encyclopédie*, including two very different ways of reading Montesquieu: that of D'Alembert, who in Volume V, in his 'Analyse de *l'Esprit des Lois*', seems quite content to go along with the idea that slavery is an effect of the climate; and that of Jaucourt who, in the article 'Esclavage'

#	Headings	Author	Explicit ref.	Against	For	Neutral	Notes
1	Acara	Diderot	+			+	
2	Angola	Diderot	+			+	
3	Assiente	Mallet	+			+	
4	Cacao	Diderot	+			+	
5	Calinda						
6	Captiverie	Mallet	+			+	
7	Code Noir		+			+	Boucher d'Argis?
8	Colonie	Forbonnais		+			
9	Commandeur		+			+	Reference to colonies
10	Commerce	Forbonnias		+			
11	Coton	Diderot		+			
12	Cotonnier	Le Romain		+			
13	Égalité Naturelle	Jaucourt	+		0		Slavery in general
14	Esclavage (droit nat.)	Jaucourt	+				
15	Esclavage (metteur en oeuve)		+			+	
16	Esclave (jurisp.)		+			+	Boucher d'Argis?
17	Habitation (comm.)	Mallet	+			+	
18	Humain espèce	Diderot	+				
19	Indigo	Le Romain?		+			
20	Indigotier		+				
21	Liberté naturelle	Jaucourt?	+		+		
22	Loango	Jaucourt		+			Indigenous slavery
23	Manioc	Le Romain	+			+	
24	Marron	Jaucourt	+		+		
25	Monnaie de comptes modernes						
26	Nègres (hist. nat.)	Formey		+			
27	Nègres Blancs		+			+	
28	Nègres (commerce)		+			+	
29	Nègres considérés comme esclaves	Le Romain	+			+	
30	Pièces en fait de monnaie		+			+	
31	Pièce d'Inde		+			+	
32	Pièce (comm. d'Afrique)	Jaucourt	+			+	
33	Population	Damilaville	+		+		
34	Rio Negro	Jaucourt	+			+	
35	Stampe	Jaucourt	+				
36	Sucre	Le Romain					
37	Sucrerie (edifice)						

#	Headings	Author	Explicit ref.	Against	For	Neutral	Notes
38	Sucrerie (habitation)	Le Romain					
39	Sucrier	Le Romain					
40	Tabac (hist. nat.)	Jaucourt					
41	Tabac (culture du)	Jaucourt					
42	Tabac (ferme du)	Jaucourt					
43	Tête de Nègres						
44	Toque	Jaucourt					
45	Traite de Nègres						
46	Trente-six mois						
47	Usure	Faignet		+(?)			Accepts temporary slavery
48	Ver de Guinée						
49	Analyse de L'Esprit de Lois	d'Alembert					
			34	16	10	4	

(Slavery), reconstructs Book XV in order to eliminate the author's hesitations and make the condemnation more resounding.[6] The fact is that the *Dictionnaire Raisonné* never aimed to propose a body of doctrine about anything, but rather to get people thinking. The *Encyclopédie* is at once a data bank and a debating platform. Its most useful role in the formation of the anti-slavery movement was certainly to have made an unspoken malaise into an open confrontation.

Nothing is ever healthier than transforming an embarrassment into a public debate. Such a debate was all the more desirable because it did not come down to a confrontation between moral idealism and realism or even cynicism. It was not a situation with, on the one hand, the avengers of humanity, and, on the other, dry accountants totting up the profits of the slave trade and colonial exploitation. Were they good? Were they bad? The dividing line went through consciences. The author of the article 'Nègres (Commerce)' (Negroes (Trade)) is not insensitive to the despair of blacks torn from their homeland. And when Jaucourt (in 'Tabac, fermes du' [Tobacco, Taxing of]) sets out to calculate the beneficial economic and demographic effects that would result from tobacco plantations in Louisiana, he does sing the praises of freedom of a trade that 'everywhere sows abundance and joy …', forgetting that those benefits were not evenly shared. All of the encyclopedists shared the one system of values, more or less. While the question of slavery made the assumptions and contradictions of that system partly visible to them, it does so wholly to us.

No one is totally free of prejudice, not even those who claim to be fighting it. So it was in the eighteenth century with the assumption of the superiority of the white man, which was at once both combatted and reinforced by the spirit of the Enlightenment. For while that spirit did open itself up to faraway civilizations, it was no less imbued with the sentiment of European pre-eminence: the 'Discours préliminaire' of the *Encyclopédie* is a paean to modern Europe, in which D'Alembert sets out recent advances in the sciences and the arts. A few years later, in 1756, the *Essai sur l'esprit des moeurs et l'esprit des nations* laid out in 164 chapters a panorama of universal history looked at afresh, which went from ancient China to the century of Louis XIV. Both the Far East and the Middle East have their place in it, and so does America, but black Africa is the only region of the known world – about which, it is true, little was yet known – not to be treated separately, apart from the chapter devoted to Christian Ethiopia. From comments about it scattered all through the work, however, two themes emerge: the scandalous cupidity, which led Europeans to treat men like 'beasts of burden',[7] and the genetic inferiority of blacks. Voltaire was convinced 'that in every breed of men, as in plants, there is a certain principle by which they are differenced'. And he goes on: 'Nature has subordinated to this principle those different degrees of genius, and those national characters which so seldom vary. It is this that renders the negroes slaves to the rest of mankind.'[8]

What Voltaire was theorizing about, many others were innocently thinking. The first black hero of fiction arrived from England in 1745: he possessed all the moral virtues, all the physical qualities of a white man, 'except for colour', and this exceptional individual is betrayed by his own people.[9] Forty years later, the young Virginia and her friend Paul will take pity on the fate of a poor black maroon woman, but this compassion will not make them question the servile condition of old Domingue any more than it will deter Paul from dreaming of a prosperity made from the labour of 'many blacks'.[10] And when the two adolescents play with Domingue and Marie the mime of the shepherds of Madian, it is Paul who fights off the wicked shepherds, whose role is, of course, played by the two slaves.[11] Thus, the idyll carries the stamp of an innocent racism.

Yet racial prejudice – and one can hardly be surprised that it should not spare the eighteenth century when it is so widespread today – is not the sole, nor even the chief, cause of the *philosophes'* embarrassment when faced with colonial slavery. That was due, above all, to a conflict of values: on the one hand, the idea of the Rights of Man, on the other, the conviction that intellectual and social progress assumed economic progress, and hence the development of trade. It is well known that the literature of the century, from the *Lettres philosophiques* to the *Histoire des deux Indes*, tended to contrast warrior adventures and the virtues of peaceful trade that brought enlightenment and liberty. The merchant thus became the emblematic figure of the new spirit. There was a share of deliberate illusion in this, even a slightly suspect vagueness: who would swear that there was never a single slave in the holds of Mr Vanderk's vessels?[12] Yet this new moral mythology was not simply mystification. It is true that the triangular trade that enriched French ports along the Atlantic at the expense of Africans was the element driving the beginnings of economic growth in France. What would its textile industry have been without the cotton and indigo of the islands? And without modern industry, there would have been no creation or circulation of wealth, no work for the poor, little urban development, more poverty and less enlightenment. It is easy to see that the conflict was one between values, and not only between generous ideas and powerful interests. To remove the contradiction, other models of development needed to be invented, for example, the physiocratic model, whose promoters were being wholly consistent when they declared themselves abolitionists.[13]

Revolt

However that may be, the fact remains that in the early 1770s, embarrassment was tending to become rejection. This can be seen in 1771 with Saint-Lambert and above all Mercier, in 1773 with Bernardin de Saint-Pierre, in several writings by Diderot and in successive editions of the *Histoire des deux Indes*. Before long, the baton was taken up by the generation of Condorcet (1781) and Brissot (1786). And then the debate moved openly from the domain of philosophy and ethics to that of politics. But while the protests mounted, we must take care not to exaggerate their scope, for there were several sorts of revolts. The most widespread, far from new, was emotional and affective. Always underlying other forms of rejection, it is indispensable and nothing could be done without it; but in itself it is quite inadequate to inspire a project of liberation. From Father Labat's *Voyage aux Isles* (1722) to Voltaire's *Candide* (1759) and in many later writings, indignation focuses on the ill-treatment inflicted on blacks. But to claim to mitigate their lot – if only because the servile labour force was capital to be conserved – or to denounce the excesses of bad masters who do not even respect the injunctions of the *Code Noir* is not to contest the legitimacy of the institution. To make such a radical challenge required, of course, a reasoned, argued rejection, such as Montesquieu's refuting one after the other the pro-slavery arguments and showing that 'the law of slavery', because it gives everything to the master and nothing to the slave, is 'contrary to the fundamental principle of every society' (*Esprit des Lois*, XV, 2). In that sense, it matters little that in the *Contrat Social* Rousseau should make no allusion either to the slave trade or to colonial slavery. The third chapter of Book I, which takes up and expands – *contra* Grotius – Montesquieu's argument, owes its universal scope to its abstract quality: 'These words, slavery and law, are contradictory; they are mutually exclusive.' Can there be a stronger condemnation of the *Code Noir*?

For the emancipation of the slaves in the colonies to become a philosophical demand, the idea of liberty had to be generally accepted. It was also necessary – and this was not self-evident – that the demand for liberty should prevail over the other key idea of the century, the idea of property. On the eve of the Revolution, that battle, the most difficult one, was not by any means won, but at least it was joined. Voices were raised to say man is not a thing. Already, in 1772, Diderot was writing in the *Correspondance Littéraire*: 'A man can never be the property of a ruler, a child the property of a father, a wife the property of a husband, a servant the property of a master, a black the property of a colonist.'[14] Freedom is not divisible. It is through that conviction that the emerging abolitionist movement owed its impetus to the Enlightenment.

One last distinction needs to be mentioned here. In the last fifteen or twenty years of the Ancien Régime, an abolitionist movement was beginning to work on public opinion, appearing even in the ranks of the administration, though senior officials, such as Malouet, were working effectively there to defend the interests of colonists.[15] But no one proposed abolishing slavery overnight. No one took up the cry of Chevalier de Jaucourt: 'May the European colonies be destroyed rather than make so many individuals unhappy!'[16] Inspiration, rather, came from the conviction that it ought not to be impossible to reconcile retention of the colonies with the rights of blacks through measures providing for gradual emancipation, over a more or less extended period of time and accompanied by negotiations among the slave-trading powers for the suppression of the slave trade. Such, for example, is the reforming project in Book XI of the *Histoire des deux Indes*, similar to that advanced by Condorcet a few years later: the aim was for reforms, not revolution. We need therefore to be circumspect in interpreting the apparently messianic announcement by L.-S. Mercier in Chapter 22 of *L'An 2440*, and then by Diderot-Raynal, in two new editions of the *Deux Indes* (1774 and 1780), of the advent of an 'avenger of the new world' who would exterminate the colonists, or at least replace the *Code Noir* with a no less terrible *Code Blanc*. Neither Mercier nor Diderot, enthusiastic but peaceful philosophers, were men of blood, and if they felt that carnage was coming, they surely did not wish it.[17] Once the event happened, these texts could be read as a prophecy of the insurrection led by Toussaint Louverture, but when they were published, and in their original context, they were simply warnings to enact reforms in order to avoid chaos. Was that something insignificant, a lucidity of no consequence? History needs Cassandras, even if at the time – alas! – Cassandra is always wrong, whether the truth comes from the gods or, as here, from the simple enlightenment of reason.

Notes

1. J. Ehrard, 'L'Encyclopédie et l'esclavage colonial', in *La Période révolutionnaire aux Antilles*, presented by Roger Toumson, Faculté des Lettres et Sciences humaines, Université des Antilles et de la Guyane, Fort-de-France, 1988, pp. 229–39. A third of the summary table that was to accompany the article was omitted. I feel it is useful to include it here.
2. J. Ehrard, 'Aspects de l'idée du travail dans l'*Encyclopédie*', in *L'Eta dei Lumi* (Mélanges Franco Venturi), Naples, Jovene Editori, 1985, Vol. I, pp. 285–300.
3. Text cited by R. Pomeau, *Politique de Voltaire*, Paris, A. Colin, 1963, pp. 215–19.
4. *L'idée de nature en France dans la première moitié du XVIIIe siècle*, Paris, S.E.V.P.E.N., 1963, Vol. I, pp. 499–502, and Vol. II, pp. 735–6.
5. See G. Benrekassa, 'Montesquieu et le problème de l'esclavage: ce que nos apprend l'étude du manuscrit du Livre XV de *L'Esprit des Lois*', *Bulletin de la Société Montesquieu*, No. 3, 1991, pp. 4–10.

6. See J. Ehrard, 'L'*Encyclopédie* et l'esclavage: deux lectures de Montesquieu', in *Enlightenment: Essays in Memory of Robert Shackleton*, Oxford, The Voltaire Foundation, 1988, pp. 121–9.
7. Voltaire, *Essai sur les moeurs* [1759], ed. R. Pomeau, Paris, Garnier, 1963, Vol. II, p. 328 [Eng. trans., Chapter 122, p. 215]. See ibid., pp. 360 and 379–80.
8. Ibid., p. 335 [1759 edn, p. 215], also pp. 305–6 [a section omitted from the English translation of 1759]; and for the albinos, p. 419: 'Nature has perhaps placed them after the negroes and the hottentots, above the apes, as one of the degrees which descend from man to animal.' Is the Negro himself fully human? In order to situate Voltaire's attitude in the context of his period, the reader should consult the major work by M. Duchet, *Anthropologie et histoire au siècle des Lumières*, Paris, Maspero, 1971.
9. A. Benn, *Oroonoko or the Royal Slave*, 1688 (French translation by La Place, Amsterdam, 1745) (in the French version the name is simplified to Oronoko). See the chapter that C. Biondi devotes to this novel in *Les Esclaves sont des hommes. Lotta Abolizionista e letteratura negrofila nella Francia del Settecento*, Pisa, Goliardica, 1979, pp. 86–108. As Biondi observes, the sympathetic admiration that the individual inspires does not involve any questioning of the legitimacy of slavery: Oroonoko himself deems it normal to enslave prisoners of war.
10. J. H. Bernardin de Saint-Pierre, *Paul et Virginie*, edition established and presented by J. Ehrard, Paris, Gallimard, 'Folio', 1984, p. 212 (1st edn, 1788) [Eng. trans., J. Donovan, *Paul and Virginia*, London, Penguin, 1988, p. 112].
11. Ibid., p. 150 [Eng. trans., p. 67]. On Bernardin's contradictions see the introduction by Y. Bénot to his edition of the *Voyage de l'Isle de France*, Paris, La Découverte/Maspero, 1983, pp. 16–18.
12. M. J. Sedaine, *Le Philosophe sans le savoir*, Paris, 1765. One could ask more such rhetorical questions: How did 'the good Tanié', the hero of *Ceci n'est pas un conte*, the unhappy lover of the treacherous and covetous Reymer, get rich in Saint-Domingue? See J. Ehrard, 'A propos d'un silence: Diderot, l'indépendance américaine et l'esclavage colonial', in M. R. Morris (ed.), *Images of America in Revolutionary France*, Washington, D.C., Georgetown University Press, 1990, pp. 54–5.
13. Although the thesis, supported by Mirabeau and Dupont, that slavery was not profitable was rejected by Turgot, as demonstrated by Philippe Steiner in his essay in this volume.
14. 'Fragments échappés du portefeuille d'un philosophe', 7, in *Oeuvres complètes*, ed. R. Lewinter, Paris, Club Français du Livre, 1971, Vol. X, p. 77. The attribution of the passage to Diderot has been confirmed by the work of G. Goggi, 'Diderot', in *Mélanges et morceaux divers*, Siena, 1977, p. 315.
15. On the project for gradual emancipation presented in 1779 to the Committee on Legislation for the colonies by Baron de Bessner, former Inspector General and soon to be Governor of French Guyana, a project opposed by Malouet, see M. Duchet, op. cit., pp. 129–35, 154–8, etc. The project affected only French Guyana.
16. 'Traite des nègres' [Slave Trade], article by L. Jaucourt in *L'Encyclopédie*, 35 Vols, Paris, 1751–80. The author, however, immediately adds: 'But I believe that it is false that the suppression of slavery would lead to their ruin. Trade would suffer for a while … but many other advantages would arise from suppression. Let the blacks be made free and in a few generations this vast and fertile country will have inhabitants without number.… It is liberty and industry that are the real sources of plenty.…'
17. On the nuances of these texts, see J. Ehrard (note 12 above), 'A propos d'un silence', p. 57.

Chapter 10

Mirabeau and the Société des Amis des Noirs: Which Way to Abolish Slavery?

Marcel Dorigny

THE SOCIÉTÉ DES AMIS DES NOIRS, founded in Paris on 19 February 1788, was the first organized French abolitionist society. It was respected, had regular statutes, now and again elected a president and secretary who were well-known public figures, and, finally, had its own financing, which gave it independence. While the existence of this society is well known, its detailed history has yet to be written for want of sufficient primary sources, at least in the current state of publications.[1] The internal history of this first French abolitionist movement, however, is not the subject of this essay, which has a more modest aim – to explain how it got a hearing, made its existence known and, above all, informed public opinion about its programme and its manner of operating.

The fact is that the Société des Amis des Noirs could not hope to have a journal of its own to spread its ideas and programme. The press under the absolute monarchy was tightly controlled by the administration, and the various colonial lobbies were sufficiently powerful to bring pressure to bear on the Ministry concerned and render nugatory any attempt by the Amis des Noirs to obtain a licence to publish a periodical. To get around this obstacle, the society resorted to indirect means to publicize its position and its struggle. The publication of works, especially translations of English titles, was one of those means, as censorship was less vigilant towards books than it was towards periodicals. But above all, the society enjoyed the constant support of Mirabeau, one of its first members. Whatever may have been his political twists and turns, before and during the Revolution, Mirabeau continues to be closely associated with the first French abolitionist movement, and there can be no doubting the sincerity of the anti-slavery commitment of the man who was yet to become the great tribune of the Constituent Assembly.

Mirabeau's contribution to the dissemination of the arguments defended by the Société des Amis des Noirs took three successive main forms: first, making available to the society a journal almost wholly removed from the constraints of censorship; second, advocating parliamentary action in the autumn of 1789, in close collaboration with Thomas Clarkson, one of the chief promoters of the London Committee for the Abolition of the Slave Trade; third, intervening with the Jacobin Club in Paris in an to attempt to secure its support for the programme of the Amis des Noirs in favour of abolishing the slave trade.

The first thing that Mirabeau did was to make available to the Amis des Noirs an exceptional instrument of propaganda in the context of the 1780s. Through his multiple connections in a wide range of milieux, he had secured tacit authorization to bring out in Paris a journal not subject to the pettifogging control of the censorship of the Bureau de la Librairie – on the sole condition that it publish only information from England and translated from English newspapers. Such was the origin of the curious periodical known as the *Analyse des papiers anglais*, published by Mirabeau starting in November 1787.[2] This was the instrument that Mirabeau made available to the Société des Amis des Noirs to publish accounts of its meetings, some of the correspondence it received and many other items about its activities. Better still, a reading of Mirabeau's paper demonstrates that it was the instrument used to prepare French public opinion for the creation of the Société des Amis des Noirs. Thus, the *Analyse des papiers anglais* not only was the unofficial organ of the society after it was set up, on 19 February 1788, but also was an integral part of its creation, and for that reason we cannot fail to regard Mirabeau as one of the inspirers and co-founders of the Société des Amis des Noirs, on a par with Clavière and Brissot. It is true that the paper became the unofficial mouthpiece of a society whose goals were not dissimulated by the editor, contrary to the commitments he had made to his ministerial protectors. But who could then seriously think that a person such as Mirabeau would honour such commitments and exclude from his journal the French debates, limiting himself to British politics alone?

The *Analyse des papiers anglais* published more than fifteen articles devoted to debates on the colonies and especially the issue of the abolition of slavery, systematically highlighting the actions of the Société des Amis des Noirs, after skilfully preparing people for the formation of that society. Number 16 of the journal, dated 21–24 January 1788, published a first article entitled 'Varia on Slavery' including 'an extract from Paley's *Principles of Moral and Political Philosophy*', which provided the pretext for a long tirade by Mirabeau against the slave trade and slavery in America. This was followed by an appeal in favour of the abolition, gradually and by law, of this barbarous practice, which did not even have the advantage of being profitable to the economy of the countries that had wandered into it. The article ended with this assertion: '[T]he crime is simply an accounting error.'[3] Number 19, dated 31 January– 1 February 1788, published Granville Sharp's 'Plan for the Total Abolition of the Slavery of Negroes in British Possessions'; Sharp was one of the founders of the London Committee. Publication of this document was immediately followed by a letter from Brissot and Clavière, 'À Messieurs les rédacteurs de l'Analyse des papiers anglais', which announced the foundation in London of a Committee for the Abolition of Slavery and the Slave Trade and called for the formation in Paris of a similar institution: '[We] intend to publish very shortly a Prospectus with the aim of inviting all friends of humanity to join with us, and in it we shall set out the means necessary for the formation of that society …'.[4] Then, in support of that appeal, was published the full text of a resolution adopted by the London Committee on 27 August 1787, expressly naming Brissot de Warville as the English Committee's spokesman in Paris and earnestly recommending that he 'would set on foot and promote to the utmost of his power a similar Institution in that Country for the purpose of effecting the abolition of the Slave Trade …'. This same resolution also made Clavière a member of the English Committee, giving him responsibility for the same task as Brissot in France.[5] Mirabeau's paper was indeed the channel through which the French educated public learned of the existence of the English Committee and above all of the personal links that had been formed between it and a small core of French or French-settled publicists and businessmen. Thanks to the *Analyse des papiers anglais,* the Société des Amis des Noirs could come into being on a foundation prepared in advance by the publication of information.

It was again this same paper that publicized the formation of the Société des Amis des Noirs. Number 25 of Mirabeau's paper, dated 19–22 February 1788, published: 'Speech pronounced on 19 February 1788 in a society of a few friends, gathered together in Paris, at the request of the one formed in London for the abolition of the slave trade.' The full text of the speech made by Brissot that day was then published in Numbers 25 to 28 of Mirabeau's paper. The last part of the speech inaugurating the Société des Amis des Noirs was accompanied by this notice to readers:

> The need to enlighten people on the important matter of the abolition of the slave trade and slavery impels us to believe that we would be performing a true service to the public by offering it the collection of everything that has appeared and will appear in England on this matter. We initially assumed we would be able to insert the major part of it in this journal; but we have been overwhelmed by the quantity of material, and shall limit ourselves to publishing letters, information and details of parliamentary debates, reserving all the rest for an Appendix, or Supplement to this journal, which will be chiefly devoted to developments in this interesting question. This collection will comprise several volumes; it is impossible for us to say how many of them there will be now….[6]

In reality, this programme for translating English works on the slave trade and slavery corresponded to one of the main points in the programme of the Société des Amis des Noirs, as Brissot had just outlined in his inaugural speech; Mirabeau was thus putting his paper forward as editorial support for the new society's educational campaign. The collaboration of the *Analyse des papiers anglais* with the Société des Amis des Noirs was subsequently faithfully pursued: in each issue of his paper Mirabeau gave the question of the slave trade extensive coverage, announced meetings of the Amis des Noirs, reported their main resolutions, and so forth. In fact, until the appearance of the first issues of Brissot's *Patriote français,* starting from the end of July 1789, Mirabeau's paper provided a platform for the Amis des Noirs. In the general framework of a press regime subject to prior control, this organ enjoying semi-freedom of expression constituted the sole possible means of publicizing the aims of the French abolitionist society.

An indirect effect of the almost exclusive role played by the *Analyse des papiers anglais* in the dissemination of anti-slavery ideas, although perhaps unintended, is worth stressing. The tacit permission granted to Mirabeau for his paper assumed respect for the original project: to disseminate news from England and nothing else. Even though we know how lightly Mirabeau treated this constraint, it is still quite obvious that the articles on the slave trade and slavery, and indeed on other subjects, were almost always obliged to make some reference to British news on these matters. Passing by London, Liverpool or Glasgow was an almost compulsory rhetorical device to get into what for the French reader was the meat of the matter – the rise of anti-slavery in France. It cannot be denied that this obligatory reference to England, apart from the fact that it reflected an undeniable Anglophilia on the part of the Amis des Noirs in Paris, accentuated the role of the London Committee in the French anti-slavery movement and had the effect of making Brissot, Clavière and other Amis des Noirs 'English agents', an argument seized on by the colonists to discredit French abolitionists. This charge that the Amis des Noirs associated with enemies of French interests, sacrificed to English greed, would remain a constant feature of the colonists' counter-attack, both during the Revolution and long after, under the Restoration and the July Monarchy in particular.[7] The place granted the Société des Amis des Noirs in a paper that made no secret of its admiration for English freedoms was bound to lend credence to the notion of British manipulation, even a British stranglehold over French abolitionist ideology. Amis des Noirs and 'anti-French party' rapidly and enduringly became synonyms in the view of the defenders of the colonial system.[8]

The second way in which Mirabeau contributed to the Société des Amis des Noirs consisted in active preparation of the parliamentary attack to secure from the Constituent Assembly the immediate abolition of the slave trade. We know that as early as Necker's speech on 5 May 1789, the Amis des Noirs intervened to secure, first from the Ministry and then from the Assembly itself, a radical measure to that end,[9] but the role of Mirabeau and Thomas Clarkson in the affair is less well known.

Clarkson was in regular correspondence with the French abolitionists, Brissot and Clavière, in particular. In addition, he was among the most active in the battle being waged by British abolitionists to secure the passage through Parliament in London of a law providing for the immediate abolition of the British slave trade. Until the spring of 1789, it was perfectly clear for all to see that Britain was the country most likely to secure the first victory for the anti-slavery campaigners. It seemed certain that the parliamentary struggles and the campaign by the British abolitionists to win over public opinion would quickly be successful.[10] But it was not to be; the various colonial interests put up much stronger resistance than had been expected and were able to contain the onslaught of the 'philanthropists'. Thus, at the time that the Estates-General were meeting in France, and especially when the revolution of the spring and summer of 1789 was radically altering the nature of the French political regime, the ground favourable to an initiative to obtain a first abolition of the slave trade seemed to have shifted from the banks of the Thames to those of the Seine. In this area, as in so many others, Paris had become the focus of the hopes of European reformers. Thomas Clarkson and the English abolitionists saw this clearly. By August 1789 Clarkson was in Paris to observe events close-up as they occurred and help prepare an intervention in the Constituent Assembly to secure rapid promulgation of a decree against the French slave trade, which would inevitably have an immediate influence on the British Parliament. Thus, in 1789 the English abolitionist was counting on an impetus from France to advance his cause. Compared to the period when the Société des Amis des Noirs had been founded, barely a year earlier, the roles had been reversed, and so had the sources of impetus.

But the task of French abolitionists was not as straightforward as the almost unanimous vote of the Declaration of the Rights of Man and the Citizen might lead one to expect. For while the Declaration of the Rights of Man included an unconditional condemnation of slavery, it still remained to get its principles applied in the colonies. The resistance of colonial interests was much more effective than might have been believed in the heady days of the votes of 4 and 26 August 1789. It rapidly became apparent that the deputies favourable to the colonists and the merchants in the ports were far more numerous, better organized and more prestigious than those supporting the cause of the blacks. Barnave, Moreau de Saint-Méry, Bégouen and Malouet, among many others, enjoyed great influence. On the other side, the Amis des Noirs, whether members of the society or not, were much less well represented and, above all, had not succeeded in getting their most prestigious members elected to the Estates-General. Neither Brissot nor Clavière nor Condorcet had a seat, and the reinforcement provided by newcomers such as Grégoire or Pétion de Villeneuve – or even Robespierre, not a member of the society, but with definite anti-slavery views – could not make up for this undeniable shortage of well-known and influential parliamentary figures to speak for the Amis des Noirs in the Assembly. Clarkson quickly realized this when he arrived in Paris. In order to act in the Assembly, a powerful spokesman was needed and the only possible one was the Count de Mirabeau, who appeared to be the big political winner of the summer of 1789. He was the only patriotic tribune of any standing comparable to the spokesmen of the colonists solidly installed in the Assembly, who went onto monopolize almost all the seats on its Colonial Committee after 2 March 1790.[11] Thus, it was Mirabeau, acting both on his own personal account and on that of his closest friends,[12] who made contact with the most famous representative of the London abolitionists. The two men entered at once into a close collaboration, and it is easy to reconstruct how it operated. First, the correspondence between Étienne Dumont and Mirabeau already gives us confirmation of the work that brought the two men together. On 11 or perhaps 12 November 1789, Mirabeau sent this note to Étienne Dumont: 'It's for today, my dear Dumont, I shall not move or receive anyone at all, if you want to come, so that we can finish examining this speech, and it is all the more convenient as we shall get out the facts to ask Mr Clarkson for.'[13] This note confirms that at that date Mirabeau was preparing a speech on the slave trade, but the documentation used by Jean Bénétruy did not allow him to get to the bottom of the nature of the relations between Mirabeau and Clarkson in the work of drafting the great speech on the slave trade that the tribune hoped to make very soon to the Constituent Assembly, at a time when Mirabeau's influence was at its peak.[14] This is how Bénétruy concludes his analysis of this question:

> The three months that followed have left us no information about the paper on the slave trade. It was during that period that a variety of contributions increased its volume. It was almost ready to be presented with honour to the Constituent Assembly when the question of the slave trade came on the agenda at the beginning of March 1790.[15]

The absence of sources on the subsequent preparations for this famous memorial on the slave trade leads Jean Bénétruy to assign a probably highly exaggerated role to Étienne Dumont in the drafting of the document. In fact, it seems most likely that the paper in question was essentially the fruit of the collaboration between Mirabeau and Clarkson.[16] There is a large number of letters between the two men, preserved in the Musée Paul Arbaud in Aix-en-Provence, among the papers of the Fonds Mirabeau.[17] Between 13 November and the end of the following December, Mirabeau received a series of letters from Clarkson, some of them very long, providing him with all the details he requested on the modalities of the slave trade, in England, on the coast of Africa and the arrival in the islands, including the most concrete details on the conditions of the middle passage and the punishments inflicted on captives who revolted or who simply did not take kindly to blind obedience.[18] Spread out over more than 200 pages of correspondence, of which we unfortunately only have the part emanating from Clarkson, here was the reality of the slave trade set out in all its horror before Mirabeau's very eyes. From the very first letter, dated at the Hôtel d'York, Paris, 13 November 1789, it is quite clear that Mirabeau was the one who initiated the approach and that Étienne Dumont acted as intermediary from the outset:

> Monsieur Dumont having asked me for some clarifications on the situation of blacks in slavery I am writing this letter of which the one I have the honour to send you is a translation given me by a French friend who came to see me. I am taking the liberty of forwarding it to M. Dumont by your hands, because it includes a number of facts of which I have the best proofs. I propose, Sir, to send you tomorrow the clauses that I felt necessary for the abolition of the slave trade and on the days following to communicate to you the information that you have done me the honour of asking of me so that without wasting your time you can give it the attention you deem suitable.

The most salient fact in this correspondence, which we cannot go into in detail here, is the 'consultant' role played by Clarkson in relation to the tribune of the Constituent Assembly. Day after day, the letters sent to Mirabeau brought him a mass of facts about the slave trade and above all numerous considerations on the tactics to be adopted to win victory for the blacks' cause in an Assembly that knew little about the subject and was very sensitive to the pressures from the interests of the ports and colonial circles. In accordance with what had, from the very beginning of the society, been the political project of the Amis des Noirs, Clarkson wanted to show Mirabeau that a good strategy, must, if it were to have any chance of success, limit its demands to the abolition of the slave trade alone:

> My opinion, like that of all those who have looked closely at the subject, is *that one ought to demand only the abolition of the slave trade.*[19] It is the source of all evils, and if the axe is applied to it, slavery in the islands will fall after it, and will fall advantageously for the planters and for the slaves without any need to touch it.... This reasoning compels us to put aside any idea of emancipation.[20]

Clarkson's stand on this point was, of course, quite in accordance with the 'programme' of the Amis des Noirs, but the long succession of 'pieces of advice' to Mirabeau had the result of markedly distorting this 'programme'. For the question asked by Mirabeau, which can be reconstructed from the way the original letter of 14 November is worded, did not bear directly on the abolition of the slave trade, but rather raised the general question of the means of destroying the *system* of slavery: 'You have honoured me by asking my opinion on the motion that it would be suitable to make for the destruction of the system of slavery of negroes, and I do not lose a moment in writing to you on that point.'[21] Mirabeau had in fact asked Clarkson about the most politic modalities of working up to the destruction of the system of slavery, and the response obstinately stuck to proposing one single way: to abolish the slave trade and allow slavery to wither away, slowly, with no upheaval. I have no intention here of maintaining that the ambitions of the Amis des Noirs were bolder or that their project was more radical than the one hinted at by Clarkson to Mirabeau; that would be going too far and would give the French abolitionists an audacity that they assuredly did not have. But yet it remains the case that another key point of their 'programme' envisaged several plans for the gradual abolition of slavery without any compensation to slave-owners. In the advice that Clarkson was giving Mirabeau, there was no mention of a gradual abolition imposed by law. It is thus likely that just when it was finally possible to glimpse the emergence in France of a first great debate on the colonial question, the 'minimalist' focus that was adopted – limiting the debate to the slave trade – was in part the fruit of the long exchange of letters in the autumn of 1789 between Mirabeau and Clarkson. For, unlike the gradual abolition plans imagined by many authors, the abolition of the slave trade proposed by Clarkson was not a first step that would be followed by others bearing directly on slavery; on the contrary, the whole economy of the plan proposed to Mirabeau rested on the abolition of the slave trade alone:

> It is not difficult to prove that we should begin with this demand, and that, having obtained it, we should go no farther. If we ask for emancipation as well as abolition

at the same time,[22] the planters will say that we are taking their property – property that the laws of France itself encouraged them to acquire. We would necessarily call down on ourselves the opposition of the planters and all their adherents … not only would the question of emancipation be lost, but that of abolition would be exposed to the same danger. Added to that, among other arguments, it might be argued that emancipation is not at present desirable. The slaves would not benefit from it, the planters in several instances would face ruin and the revenue would be the loser for a considerable time.[23]

Abolishing the slave trade was thus not a means but an end. The slow disintegration of slavery – as it were, by some sort of internal decay – would be the inevitable consequence, without the need for any further legislative action in future. This meant introducing into the French abolitionist movement a reductive dimension that it did not have when it was founded, in particular by taking into account the accusation that the planters would surely not fail to make against any idea of emancipation of slaves by law, that it would be an attack on property. On this point, the Paris Amis des Noirs were in agreement with Condorcet,[24] who had explicitly refused to consider slaves as legitimate property:

> We have shown that the master has no right over his slave; that the action of detaining him in servitude is not enjoyment of property but a crime; that by freeing the slave the law is not attacking property but ceasing to tolerate an action which it ought to have sanctioned with capital punishment. The ruler therefore owes no damages to the master of slaves, just as he owes none to a thief deprived by a judgement of possession of the thing stolen.[25]

Such reasoning makes no appearance in the advice given by Clarkson to Mirabeau and designed to develop a political strategy to be implemented in the very near future. The projects of the Société des Amis des Noirs made abolition of the slave trade one of the lines of attack against the system of slavery, but just because it was the first element to be put into effect, it was not the sole element. However, with the intervention of what might be described as the 'pragmatism' of the British abolitionists, abolition of the slave trade became the sole measure envisaged. Mirabeau was certainly strongly influenced by this long correspondence with Clarkson; it does not appear that he opposed his arguments, and he limited his parliamentary action to the fight against the slave trade. Furthermore, it is likely that Étienne Dumont, one of his other advisers on this subject, did not think otherwise. It is significant that the Société des Amis des Noirs itself, at the beginning of 1790, actively contributed to the publication of a French translation of Clarkson's book, *Essai sur les désavantages de la traite des nègres* (Essay on the Impolicy of the Slave Trade), with a preface by Gramagnac, then Secretary of the Société des Amis des Noirs.

We know that in fact the great debate on the slave trade, so minutely prepared by Mirabeau and the Amis des Noirs, never took place in the Constituent Assembly. The formation of a Colonial Committee, almost wholly dominated by colonial interests, made it possible to sidestep this subject and limit the intrusion of the Constituent Assembly to the creation of the notorious Colonial

Assemblies, which by the decree of 8 March 1790 became the sole bodies empowered to alter the status quo in the islands. In this Assembly, the parliamentary initiative had definitely slipped away from the Amis des Noirs, and they had to restrict their actions to the question of 'free people of colour', first to have inserted into the Instruction of 28 March their right to participate in the formation of electoral assemblies, and then, in May 1791, to extract from a hesitant Assembly a start towards equality between whites and 'free people of colour'. The debates on this question contributed to the abandonment of the demand for abolition of the slave trade, despite the fact that it had been the centrepiece of the project of the Amis des Noirs before becoming, in late 1789, under the influence of Mirabeau and Clarkson, the sole prospect of immediate action.

The failure of the parliamentary offensive of late 1789 and early 1790 did not put an end to Mirabeau's plans to use the materials on the slave trade so painstakingly accumulated, in particular thanks to the correspondence with Clarkson. Since the Assembly was incapable of listening to these harsh truths, a more hospitable platform would have to be found for them to be heard. Mirabeau turned to the Société des Amis de la Constitution, where his popularity was still intact in early 1790. The great speech which the Constituent Assembly had not heard was therefore made to the Jacobins. For reasons that are unclear, this speech to the Jacobins was not printed after its delivery, on 26 February 1790, and it remained unpublished until 1835, that is until the publication of Mirabeau's *Mémoires* by his adopted son, Lucas de Montigny.[26] The text published by Lucas de Montigny occupies almost a hundred pages of the seventh volume of the *Mémoires*, even after certain cuts in the text, for reasons not explained by the publisher.

This long memorial on the slave trade in fact constitutes the synthesis of the position at which the Amis des Noirs had arrived after the confrontation of their initial 'programme' with the constraints of political debate in a framework radically transformed by the Revolution. The different layers, lying one on top of the other to form this long text, are detectable, despite the work of 'tidying up' done by Mirabeau and his various collaborators.[27] The broad outlines of Mirabeau's approach to radically transforming the system of slavery in the colonies can be summed up in a few points.

First, there was a vigorous condemnation of the principle of slavery, but one which took good care not to conclude that what was needed was immediate abolition. Then, contrary to immediate abolition, Mirabeau took up and explicated the thesis of gradual abolition, and in that we cannot but observe that he had remained faithful to the ideals that had presided over the foundation of the Société des Amis des Noirs. Clarkson's strategic argument had not been accepted in this 'anti-slave testament' of Mirabeau. But the fact that the speech was not published immediately reduced its impact considerably. Third, Mirabeau took up the idea that immediate abolition of the slave trade was possible and that there had to be action without delay. Here, Mirabeau's words drew heavily on the massive body of arguments supplied by Clarkson, without, however, accepting the latter's minimalist logic. Finally, and this was an important innovation, Mirabeau made himself the spokesman for a vast project to redirect French colonization towards Africa, without any form of slavery.[28] The key points of Mirabeau's argument were taken up in Clavière's work published in the spring of 1791, but with an obvious weakening of the political dimension of the text, in order to highlight the commercial aspects.

Thus, at the end of this brief survey it is possible to offer an overall appreciation of Mirabeau's role in the Société des Amis des Noirs' scheme of things. First, Mirabeau was the person who was able to make available to the society a means of propaganda, at a time when control of the press limited possibilities of action. Next, he was a loyal advocate of the political line laid down by the Amis des Noirs, giving extensive coverage to British activities and enabling links between the Paris and London abolitionist societies. With the beginning of the Revolution and the emergence in France of a representative regime, Mirabeau became an ideal spokesman within an Assembly where the majority of members were rather hostile to the Amis des Noirs. It was this strategic position of Mirabeau's that Clarkson grasped at once when he sought a means of getting abolition of the slave trade in France adopted, in order to speed up the process already engaged in England. Yet the correspondence between the two men highlights the difference between the two approaches: for the Paris Amis des Noirs, abolition of the slave trade would precede the adoption of a plan for the gradual abolition of slavery, whereas for Clarkson, the abolition of the slave trade would be enough on its own – the wasting away of slavery would follow it as night follows day. The failure of the French parliamentary attempt to secure the immediate abolition of the slave trade, apart from the fact that it irreversibly directed the action of the Amis des Noirs towards the defence of the 'free people of colour' alone, precipitated a global reformulation of the 'programme', which may have found its final form in Mirabeau's long speech. We have no means of knowing the underlying reasons for its non-publication. Thus, Mirabeau, founding member of the Société des Amis des Noirs, was one of its most faithful proponents, even if his parliamentary role in this area was, in the last analysis, rather limited.

Notes

1. On the Société des Amis des Noirs, see the following studies inter alia: C. Perroud, 'La Société française des Amis des Noirs', *La Révolution Française* (1916), pp. 122–47; M. Dorigny, 'Amis des Noirs', article in *Dictionnaire historique de la Révolution Française*, ed. A. Soboul, Paris, P.U.F., 1989; M. Dorigny, 'La Société des Amis des Noirs, les Girondins et la question coloniale', in *Actes du Colloque Esclavage, colonisation, libérations nationales*, Université de Paris VIII, February 1989, Paris, Éditions L'Harmattan, 1990; M. Dorigny, 'La Société des Amis des Noirs et les projets de colonisation en Afrique', *Annales Historiques de la Révolution Française*, 4, 1993. *La Révolution française et l'abolition de l'esclavage*, 12 Vols, Paris, Éditions EDHIS, 1968, has published many of the documents emerging from the Société des Amis des Noirs, especially in Vols 6–9.

2. The first issue of the *Analyse des papiers anglais* was published on 14 November 1787; after that it appeared very regularly, with one issue every five days, or seven a month.
3. *Analyse des papiers anglais*, Vol. 1, p. 416.
4. *Analyse des papiers anglais*, Vol. 19, p. 474.
5. Ibid., p. 488 [Eng. original in British Library Add Mss 21,255].
6. *Analyse des papiers anglais*, Vol. 2, No. 28, p. 102.
7. On the role of Anglophobia in colonial and pro-slavery circles under the Restoration and especially the July Monarchy, see Philippe Vigier's essay in this volume, which brings out Guizot's hesitations and his eventual retreat in the face of pressure from Anglophobe colonists over abolitionist demands, despite his own convictions.
8. At the end of the debate in the Constituent Assembly in May 1791, the colonists' supporters had a list printed of the deputies who had voted in favour of the free men of colour. In order to discredit those deputies, the list was published with this explicit heading: 'List of deputies who voted for England against France on the question whether the National Assembly should sacrifice its colonies: yes or no, 12 May 1791' (List published in *Archives parlementaires*, Vol. 26, pp. 25–6).
9. This offensive by the Amis des Noirs aimed at the new Assembly involved the despatch of the following addresses: 'Lettre à MM. les députés des trois Ordres, pour les engager à faire nommer par les États généraux, à l'exemple des Anglais, une Commission chargée d'examiner la cause des Noirs', Paris, May 1789; 'Lettre de la Société des Amis des Noirs à M. Necker', Paris, June 1789; 'Adresse à l'Assemblée nationale, pour l'abolition de la traite des Noirs. Par la Société des Amis des Noirs', Paris, February 1790; 'Seconde adresse à l'Assemblée nationale, par la Société des Amis des Noirs, établie à Paris', Paris, Imprimerie du Patriote français, 9 April 1790, 7. In addition to these documents explicitly drafted by the Société des Amis des Noirs itself, there was the document by Jean-Louis de Viefville des Essars, 'Discours et projet de loi pour l'affranchissement des nègres, ou l'adoucissement de leur régime, et réponse aux objections des colons', Paris, Imprimerie nationale, 1790, 40. This last document was submitted to the Société des Amis des Noirs and received its approval, but the author took responsibility for its contents himself. The reason for this is that at that time the Société des Amis des Noirs was basing its strategy on abolition of the slave trade alone and not on that of slavery itself – even of gradual abolition, as Viefville des Essars was calling for.
10. On the British abolitionist movement in the late 1780s, see James Walvin's essay in this volume.
11. The Colonial Committee, officially established on 2 March 1790, comprised the following members: Bégouen, a leading merchant in Le Havre; de Champagny, a naval officer; Thouret, Deputy for Rouen; Gérard, proprietor in Saint-Domingue; Le Chapelier, Deputy for Rennes; Gareshé, Deputy for Saintes, slave trader in La Rochelle and estate owner in Saint-Domingue; Count de Reynaud de Villevert, former Governor of Saint-Domingue and owner of an estate; Pellerin de la Buxière, proprietor in Saint-Domingue; Alexandre Lameth, whose brother, Charles Lameth owned a plantation in Saint-Domingue and was also a deputy; and, finally, Antoine Barnave, immediately elected rapporteur of the Committee, whose links with the Club Massiac were notorious.
12. In order to understand the complex relations between Mirabeau and his 'political workshop', it is vital to turn to the magisterial study by Jean Bénétruy, *L'Atelier de Mirabeau, quatre proscrits genevois dans la tourmente révolutionnaire*, Paris, Éditions Picard, 1962. For Étienne Dumont's collaboration in the common work with Clarkson and Mirabeau, in the autumn of 1789, see, in particular, pp. 345–52.
13. Cited by J. Bénétruy, op. cit., p. 349.
14. It was on 20 November 1789 that Mirabeau made his famous speech lambasting Necker's financial policy, leading the Assembly to reject the Minister's plan which proposed to convert the Caisse d'Escompte into a state bank. Although wholly drafted by Clavière, which everyone knew at the time, the glory of it redounded on Mirabeau, who counted on using this prestige to advance the cause of the abolition of the slave trade. More than ever, Mirabeau was the right man at the right time.
15. J. Bénétruy, op. cit., p. 349.

16. In order to understand the genesis of this long labour, we would need to be able to know precisely what belongs in Mirabeau's memorial and what in the long *Adresse* published by Clavière in 1791, after Mirabeau's death, under the title *Adresse de la Société des Amis des Noirs à l'Assemblée nationale, à toutes les villes de commerce, à toutes les manufactures, aux colonies, à toutes les Sociétés des Amis de la Constitution; Adresse dans laquelle on approfondit les relations politiques et commerciales entre la métropole et les colonies, etc*, ed. E. Clavière, member of that society, 2nd edn, rev. and corrected, Paris, Desenne and at the office of the *Patriote français*. The first edition of this *Adresse* had been published in the *Courrier de Provence*, No. 287, 25 April 1791, pp. 291–445. There is a striking similarity between numerous passages in the two texts. It is highly likely that Clavière contributed significantly to the preparation of Mirabeau's *Mémoire*, in 1789–90, and later reused the same materials for the *Adresse* of 1791, which was couched in much more general terms than Mirabeau's speech.

17. Fonds Mirabeau, dossier 102. I should like to thank Henri Aureille to whom I am grateful for sending me a complete copy of this correspondence.

18. This correspondence between Thomas Clarkson and Mirabeau has been presented by F. Thésée in the three articles: 'Autour de la Société des Amis des Noirs: Clarkson, Mirabeau et l'abolition de la traite (août 1789–mars 1790)', *Présence africaine*, No. 125, 1983, 125.

19. Emphasis by Clarkson.

20. Fonds Arbaud, dossier 102, letter of 14 November 1789.

21. Ibid.

22. By emancipation, Clarkson always meant that of the slaves, and by abolition, that of the slave trade alone.

23. Letter of 14 November 1789.

24. Ibid.

25. M.-J. Condorcet, *Réflexions sur l'esclavage colonial des nègres, par M. Schwarz, pasteur du Saint Évangile à Bienne, membre de la Société économique de B****, Vol. 7, new edition revised and corrected, Neufchâtel and Paris. Text published in *La Révolution française et l'abolition de l'esclavage*, op. cit., Vol. 6.

26. *Mémoires biographiques, littéraires et politiques de Mirabeau, écrits par lui-même, par son père, son oncle et son fils adoptif*, 8 Vols, Paris, 1834–35. The speech on the slave trade and slavery is to be found in Vol. 7, pp. 121–209.

27. On the 'confection' of the text, see J. Bénétruy, op. cit., pp. 346–51.

28. For this aspect, may we refer the reader to our article in *Annales Historiques de la Révolution française*, No. 4, 1993, cited in note 1.

Chapter 11

Slavery and French Economists, 1750–1830

Philippe Steiner

> We hope, before we die, to see slavery eliminated from the countries subject
> to European rule. But at least we are certain of showing, with an abundance
> of evidence, that its abolition will be an operation that is as useful as
> it is just and much easier than is generally believed.
> (Dupont de Nemours, 1771b)

THE SECOND HALF of the eighteenth century on which we shall focus initially paid little attention to the economic problems raised by slavery. Yet it provided the occasion for an initial economic formulation of those problems that revealed the difficult position of political economy. Subsequently, French economists in the early nineteenth century found it uphill work to adjust their economic arguments to their philosophical choices.

Reasons for the Relative Lack of Interest of Economists in Questions Raised by Slavery

In the eighteenth century, economic thought took little interest in the question of slavery.[1] It is not that the subject was completely absent from economic discussions – far from it – but it was dealt with only in passing.

'Familiarity' with slavery meant that economists quite often behaved just like anyone else: they did not question what was everyday common sense. Thus, to take one author who wrote before the period we are looking at, but whose work became widely known after 1775, R. Cantillon (Part I, Chapter 11) states as a self-evident truth that a landowner organizes his estate employing either free labour or slave labour. Things changed only slowly. In his *Inquiry into the Principles of Political Oeconomy* (1767), Steuart considered it necessary to examine servile labour in Europe. It is true that he feels it no longer possible to treat the subject without some discussion of the difficulties that can arise from the use of slave labour,[2] although in his case he is thinking of the conditions in which such labour is preferable to free labour.

There are two possible reasons for this relative lack of interest. First, the political economy of the period was, overwhelmingly, massively preoccupied with the impact and consequences of the self-interested behaviour of agents in the operation of the economy and society. With such an approach, it is easy to understand that slave labour would hardly come into the discussion and, at best, would serve as a basis for comparison to illustrate the major argument. The example of Turgot (1766) is revealing on this point. He, too, envisaged the alternative of employing free cultivators or slaves, but how little interested he is in this question comes out in two ways. First, what he writes shows that the distinctions that concern him are those between proprietors, cultivators (the productive class) and artificers (the stipendiary class); the distinction between freemen and slaves is negligible and of no importance for his argument. Second, while he does have a little to say about slave labour,[3] confining his comments to a purely 'historic' register by relegating slavery to the origin of policed societies, he seems to see in it no more than the traces of a past without a future.

Second, if we leave these high spheres of economic speculation and look either at more practical economic questions or at a different way of constituting political economy which asks about the 'political' use of trade, we easily observe that, in this period, sustained attention is focused on the economic disparity between France and England. Usually, the discussion is essentially on the situation of these two countries in the context of Europe alone, with the question of slavery being neglected. When the framework is enlarged to take account of the colonies, slavery may take a place in economic thought. But there again, it is a very small place. For example, in 1754 de Gournay translated and annotated Josiah Child's *A New Discourse of Trade*, but found nothing to say about slavery when dealing with the colonies (Chapter 10). All his attention is focused on the manner in which colonial trade can be organized so as to accelerate the development of the metropole. Similarly, when Quesnay discusses Montesquieu's opinion on the colonies, he does not have a single word to say about slavery (Quesnay, 1766); Boesnier de l'Orme (1775) did the same in his chapter on the colonies. In his very influential *Éléments du commerce*, Forbonnais (1754) devotes only two pages to the question of slavery, and then only to say how important the low cost of Negroes is for the health of agriculture and by what means this low price might be maintained. There is no point in giving more examples since this sort of argument became a ritual that satisfied people even when the question of slavery began to heat up.[4]

The Economic Analysis of Slavery

Having set out the general background so as to avoid giving the false impression that French economists in the late eighteenth century took a great deal of interest in the issue of slavery, it now remains to see what they said when they did look into it.

After being converted to Quesnay's doctrine, Mirabeau Sr. dealt with the question of colonial slavery in *L'Ami des hommes*. He saw the colonial system as the monstrous resultant of three principles not made to combine: the spirit of domination, the spirit of trade and the spirit of population. Taking his stand on the last of these, Mirabeau felt that the first two principles hindered the development of population as, while the spirit of population 'attracted strangers to the cultivation of land, these slaves became commodities, their misfortune makes their masters lazier and every man endowed by nature with a white colour believes himself privileged for idleness' (Mirabeau, 1758, III, 262). This slavery, worse than that of antiquity because it was based on skin colour, had detestable economic consequences. By forcing slaves to cultivate the land, the labour that ought to have had the highest priority was degraded (ibid., p. 283), and the farming of land by slaves 'worn out by labour for their masters' (ibid., p. 285) gave a mediocre yield. This hampered the growth of population since each year those whom this sad fate caused to disappear had to be replaced by others drawn from Africa.

Subsequently, the physiocrats paid little attention to the colonies and slavery, with two notable exceptions. *Les Éphémerides*, the school's important journal, dealt with the question several times, and an eminent member of the school of thought, Le Mercier de la Rivière, named intendant of Martinique from 1759 to 1764, could not ignore the economic reality of slavery.

Le Mercier de la Rivière, who was knowledgeable about physiocratic economic theory and anxious for the proper administration, especially the proper financial administration, of Martinique, came back again and again to the economic aspect of slavery. From the writings – associated with or intended for the local or metropolitan administration – devoted to this subject, three themes emerge: first, the labour of the slave is more costly than that of a freeman; second, the slave is capital; and third, the slave is the means of ensuring a proper basis for taxation. This last point he developed at length.

Le Mercier set out the first theme only once in a short account in 1763. In the memorial written up for Choiseul in 1762, he took up the theme of the agricultural difficulties arising from the excessively high price of slaves due to the scarcity of this commodity and the high transport costs of the French slave trade relative to the British (Le Mercier, 1762, pp. 108–9). He therefore proposed a set of measures designed to promote the entry of slaves into the islands. A year later, he took another tack, explaining that it was in France's interest (militarily and economically) to increase the island's white population. To achieve that, slaves would have to be kept to farming and removed from arts and crafts to make way for white workers. Le Mercier went on to make an economic calculation to justify his assertion:

> Given that the price of the labour of blacks must serve to feed them and to maintain their masters, who are bigger consumers than ordinary white workers, and also produce a product which serves as the interest on the principal purchase price of Negroes at the rate at which that interest should be vis-à-vis capital subject to change, depreciation and total loss, it must necessarily be much dearer than that of work done by whites. (Le Mercier, 1763, p. 161)[5]

Such thoughts necessarily led to the second theme developed by Le Mercier: the slave as capital. The quotation above says so expressly, but it also emerges from other passages in which Le Mercier, good physiocrat that he was, considers that the slave is an essential part of agricultural capital. Even more precisely, Le Mercier quite systematically establishes a link between the number of slaves and the gross product (in cash) of an estate (Le Mercier, 1762, p. 113; 1763a, pp. 157–8; 1763b, pp. 207–11).

Finally, there is the third theme linking taxation and slavery. Given the connection established by Le Mercier between the number of slaves and the gross product of estates, it was tempting to base the tax on the number of slaves employed. At first, Le Mercier was little inclined to go down that path. He recalled, as did the physiocrats, that to tax the gross product or, what amounted to the same thing, the advances that the slave represents, is to overlook the difference between gross product and net product arising, for example, from the different qualities of the land. Subsequently, Le Mercier got round the difficulty by classifying estates by the number of slaves and took into account the differences in the relationship between the gross product and the number of slaves by means of a regressive tax system. Le Mercier adopted this solution to the extent that it made it possible to lighten (by half) the burden of 'cultivators' by taxing masters who were employing their slaves in the towns. This led Le Mercier to diverge from strict physiocratic doctrine by bringing out a net product of slave labour, whereas the physiocrats usually recognized only the net product of the soil.[6]

The question of slavery rebounded among the physiocrats when the *Éphémérides* published a letter forwarded by a subscriber regarding the emancipation of slaves by the Quakers in Pennsylvania. The editor of the journal, Dupont, simply added a short note indicating that such an example was of a sort that could be tried elsewhere.

The question once again found its place in the journal with the appearance of Turgot's 'Réflexions sur la formation et de la distribution des richesses' (Reflections on the Formation and Distribution of Wealth). The faithless publisher Dupont altered his friend's text chiefly on three points: advances, interest rate formation and slavery. The alteration on this last topic shows that Dupont's purpose was to make the text a diatribe against slavery, which the original was not. That does not mean that Turgot was only lukewarm in his opposition to that 'abominable custom' (Turgot, 1766, p. 547 [1793, p. 22]), but it introduced two differences. First, Turgot was here giving a succinct overview of the essential principles of political economy, and he objected to Dupont altering his text so as to slip in a 'piece of eloquence' (letter to Dupont, 2 February 1770). Second, contrary to Dupont, Turgot did not believe that slavery was unprofitable to the master and that what was unjust was economically not profitable. He agreed with Benjamin Franklin when it came to showing that slave labour was more expensive than generally believed, but anyone in the islands who was out to make a quick fortune would find benefit in employing such labour (letter to Dupont, 6 February 1770). This exchange, which on Turgot's side was both sharp and well argued, did not stop the impetuous Dupont who produced his major contribution on the question the following year.

In the long article that he devoted to this question in 1771, Dupont made a calculation designed to estimate the cost of slave labour to the person employing it. His calculation can be summarized as follows:

Capital cost of slave	120 livres
(purchase price 1,200 livres, interest rate 10 per cent)	
Cost of replacing capital	120 livres
(average life of slave estimated at 10 years)	
Cost of policing slave labour	18 livres
(purchase of slave serving as foreman)	
Cost of replacing foremen	12 livres
(average life of foremen estimated at 15 years)	
Feeding of slave	100 livres
Feeding foreman.	12 livres
Expenses incurred through marronnage	38 livres
Total	420 livres

This calculation satisfied Dupont. He felt that he had not only demonstrated that the cost of slave labour[7] was markedly higher than the cost of the food given the slave, but also that there was no difficulty in getting white wage-earn-ers to come from the metropole who were paid not much more than 30 livres per annum for their subsistence (Dupont 1771a, p. 235). And Dupont tri-umphantly concluded: 'Humanity and philosophy have long and loudly been declaring that it is abominable to have [slaves]. Political arithmetic is beginning to prove that [slavery] is absurd, that free workers would not cost more, would be happier, would not be open to the same dangers and would do double the work' (ibid., p. 246). But his enthusiasm at the 'results' of his political arith-metic did not convince Turgot, who pointed out to him that the annual wage of a white worker in the colonies was as high as 1,500 livres (letter of 6 February 1770). Dupont was thus demonstrating the opposite of what he intended.

A Controversial Question at the Beginning of the Nineteenth Century

The economic debate about slavery took on a new dimension with the resur-gence of political economy at the beginning of the nineteenth century. After the first abolition in 1794, with the debates occasioned by the possible restoration of the institution,[8] French economists began to pay more attention to slavery.

Jean-Baptiste Say attempted a synthesis of the economic contributions in a discussion of the arguments of Smith, Steuart and Turgot, but he was unable to escape the difficulty that appeared in the correspondence between Dupont and Turgot. The annual cost of a slave, he said, amounted to 300 francs for food, to which had to be added the interest on the capital necessary for buying the slave, 200 francs annually. Here Say followed Steuart, and, against Smith and Dupont, took no account of the expense of maintaining the slave though he did take account of the cost of capital laid out. This total of 500 francs was decidedly less than the cost of the most unskilled free labour in the colonies, since wages were high there, at 1,800 francs a day (Say, 1803, I, p. 218). But Say seeks to go even further: 'I think then that I can affirm that the labour of the slave is less costly than that of a free man; I even think it possible to affirm that it is more productive provided that it is managed by free men' (ibid., p. 224). Against the arguments of Dupont, Steuart, Smith and Turgot, who all refer to the low productivity to be expected from slave labour wherein the motive of self-interest is lacking, he advances the following arguments. First, the labour that is needed in the plantations is not skilled labour, so that slave labour may be suitable for unskilled work[9] performed under the supervision of free workers. Say disputes the argument based on self-interest by stressing that while the slave's work is limited by the abilities of the individual, it is not so by a will or needs, which are not involved because they are replaced by those of the master. On the other hand, the free worker is limited not simply by his abilities, but also by his will, in particular because he feels few needs and is incapable of providence. Second, the self-interest of the planters makes them not overwork the slaves so as not to reduce their capacities and to make the best use of them. Third, Say considers that the defence of this system by the colonists shows that they find their advantage in it and that for them it is a profitable operation. He passes over differences in the quality of land rather lightly, but he adds a quantitative element to this last argument: in Saint-Domingue, the annual net product of a plantation amounts to 16 per cent, whereas it usually reaches only 3–4 per cent in the metropole (ibid., p. 223). At the Restoration, C. Ganilh's calculations produced the same sort of result. The net product rate (net product over fixed capital) and the gross product rate (gross product over total capital) are higher in the slave-grown crops of the islands than they are in the metropole: 7 and 12 per cent respectively in the islands as against 3 and 8 per cent in the metropole (C. Ganilh, 1815, I, p. 288).

The acknowledgement that slavery was profitable for the planter does not make Say a defender of that institution;[10] he saw it as odious and immoral, and so distinguished between the interest of the colonist and the interest of society. It is true that without slavery there would be no more plantations, but while such a situation would obviously be harmful to the planter, would it also be so for society? No! he replies, since there would still be sugar which can be produced in Africa – in Egypt in particular – or even in southern Europe. Would such sugar cost more? No! replies Say again, since the saving made on the slave's wages profits the planter and not the consumer (Say, 1803, I, p. 226). The abolition of slavery would simply amount to the sugar islands' shifting from the status of modern colonies to the status of old colonies (that is, colonies of settlement) for the welfare of the blacks and the metropole and cancelling the rents[11] obtained by violence against the facts of economics.

Say would subsequently moderate and then alter his position as he showed himself to be less and less convinced of the profitability of slave labour. In the second edition, he distanced himself from the calculation made in 1803, but in 1826, in the fifth edition of his *Traité*, he shifted his opinion sharply. Now he no longer felt that the plantation system was profitable:

> Whatever the case, everything has changed; and to take the French Antilles only, either the institutions and the method of farming there are bad, or the system of slavery there has depraved, in two different senses, both the master and the slave and degrades the qualities that constitute true industry – intelligence, activity and economy. The fact is that it is no longer possible, in Martinique and Guadeloupe, to withstand the competition from several other countries which can supply Europe with sugar much more cheaply. (Say, 1826, p. 225)

In a way, experience had spoken. It was no longer possible to believe that slave labour was more productive than free labour, even if it was less costly, and it no longer required an explanation of the anomaly of a particularly high rate of return to capital invested in the plantations.

At the same time, C. Comte was treating slavery at length and giving the question great prominence by devoting to it the fourth volume of his *Traité de législation* (1827). He thought that this subject was the means by which he could show that the most advanced nations were far from having made all the progress necessary in the area of social and moral science (1827, IV, pp. 6 and 11) and that here was an institution that required reform. Comte's approach, in line with the social science of the period, was particularly broad, but the chapter entitled 'Of the Influence of Domestic Slavery on the Production, Growth and Distribution of Wealth', almost copied from Say, is more directly relevant to our purpose. In it, Comte criticizes the narrowness with which economists had posed the question of slavery, that is the comparative evaluation of free and slave labour (ibid., pp. 237–8). The role of violence in economic relationships makes such a question wholly pointless: it is equivalent to asking whether a blow with a stick is enough to cover the legitimate price of a good (ibid., p. 240). However, with this reservation made, Comte takes up the problem bequeathed by political economy to pronounce himself firmly in favour of free labour. He advances a series of arguments of which the following are the most important. First, the effects of slavery are disastrous on the human faculties that contribute to production, both for the slaves, who derive no benefit from their work, and for the masters, who are dazzled by the 'vices and prejudices that slavery gives them' (ibid., p. 247). Second, as regards the effect of slavery on wealth production, there are numerous indicators of its economic inefficiency: masters are far from living in opulence since 90 per cent of them are indebted and at the mercy of their creditors; the Southern states of the United States show that manufactured goods cannot be produced there and have to be imported or made by foreign labour (ibid., pp. 262–3). Third, the distribution of wealth in the slave areas highlights its inadequate character since everything is consumed there unproductively and nothing is accumulated (ibid., p. 281). His conclusion is unambiguous:

[F]rom what has been said, it follows, first, that slavery is an invincible obstacle to the formation and accumulation of wealth ..., second, that, in the countries worked by slaves, labour is infinitely less productive for the worker and above all for the master, than it is in countries where work is performed by free men; finally, it follows that, in the state of slavery, the small quantity of wealth that can be produced is distributed in the way most contrary to equality, morality and justice. (1827, IV, pp. 281–2)

Comte's arguments had a strong impact on economists, and Say and Sismondi followed him explicitly. In his *Cours complet*, Say finally abandoned the 1803 calculation and altered the manner of calculating the maintenance costs of slave labour by returning to the position of Dupont and Smith: such expenses were high and fell on the master (Say, 1828–9, I, p. 248).[12] The chapter that he devotes to this subject brings out Say's embarrassment, caught as he was between the lessons of experience and his own past positions. On the one hand, experience shows that the slave system is no longer profitable, despite all the sacrifices made by the mother country (ibid., 247); the ruin and growing indebtedness of colonists are sure indicators of that. On the other hand, this situation clearly worries him when he tries to explain it: 'Wherein lie these costs of production higher than the natural value of the product? Is it in the fact that slaves are used for cultivation? Does it lie in the inability of the planters, or in greater difficulties to be overcome than are to be met with elsewhere? I admit that I find these different questions difficult to answer' (ibid., pp. 247–8). Say then refers to those in Europe who have used the argument from experience, and hence from the prosperity of the sugar islands under slavery, to reject that position: 'Gentlemen, in political economy, the causes are so numerous, and act in such a complicated way, that demi-savants, superficial observers are often deceived' (ibid., p. 249). And Say goes on:

I should believe in their prosperity if, abandoned to their own resources, without the help and expenditure of European governments, without the capital that the speculators from their metropoles bring there every day and without the monopoly that the duties imposed on products similar to theirs ensures them, I had seen their population double every twenty years, as we have seen in the colonies that have become independent. (Ibid.)

In his *Études sur l'économie politique*, Sismondi follows Comte even more explicitly than does Say (Sismondi, 1837, I, pp. 265, 291). Like Say, he relies on recent experience and indicates how growing sugar with slave labour ruins planters in the islands, whereas growing sugar beet using free labour enriches the French farmer (ibid., p. 295). The planters are in a state of economic weightlessness since it is only the customs duties that maintain the semblance of wealth from which they profit. The salient point in Sismondi's approach, however, lies in the assertion that slavery must be eliminated without compensation for the owners (ibid., p. 291). The slave is not capital that has to be repaid at emancipation, since, just like the capitalist in the case of free labour, the planter buys a right to dispose of the surplus (gross production less consumption) created by the labour of the slave. If care were taken – unlike what had actually happened in the British colonies – to emancipate the slave and make him a sharecropper, then a harvest made more abundant by the free and self-interested work of the sharecopper would make it possible to pay a higher rent to the owner (the former slave-owning planter) than what he had previously obtained as a surplus, while considerably increasing the share that would go to the worker (ibid., p. 309).[13]

* * *

When all is said and done, what emerges from this survey is rather disappointing. The new science introduced by the physiocrats and the economic science of the French classics were both very hesitant indeed in their economic arguments when they turned to the question of slavery. It seems that 'philosophical' prejudices dictated a good many calculations seeking to 'demonstrate' what one wanted to see demonstrated, and the changes, real or assumed, of the colonists' situation led them to revise drastically the economic arguments in a way that seems highly suspect. Has much changed after more than two centuries of intense thought in political economy?

Notes

1. An analysis of the thirty-eight references appearing in the index under *esclavage* (slavery) of the INED (1956), where the date of publication is known, shows how late an awareness of the problem developed: 75 per cent of these references date from 1780–1799, and 20 per cent from the period 1770–1779. That leaves little for the period 1750–1770, when the great thoughts on economic theory were being published.
2. According to him, 'policy profits from slavery when it is [economically] possible without worrying about the spirit of liberty in Europe' (Steuart, 1766, I, p. 227).
3. The terms that Turgot employs (1766, pp. 546–7 [pp. 21–2] – 'violating all the laws of humanity', 'abominable custom' – demonstrate how repugnant he finds the institution.
4. Tolosan is a good illustration of this: 'This is not the place to examine whether the slave trade is compatible with sentiments of humanity. The reasons for or against this trade are developed in the various memoirs written on this question, today much debated in France and England. We shall simply observe that so long as the European nations continue to have their colonies cultivated by slaves, a nation whose possessions require many hands must avoid, so far as is possible, being dependent on others for the supply of the Negroes that it needs' (1789, p. 61).
5. Starting from there he proposed a plan for the differential taxation of slaves depending on whether they were employed in cultivating the land or in arts and trades such that gradually the slaves would be brought back to cultivation.
6. In all Le Mercier's writings discussed here, he demonstrates a subtlety and an originality in argument lacking in his other physiocratic writings (notably Le Mercier, 1767). Taking slavery into account thus plays a key role in marking the limits of Quesnay's theory, but that is an idea that we cannot develop in detail in this essay.

7. For the three points relating to expenditure incurred by overseers, Dupont calculated on the basis that there was one overseer for every ten slaves. It is therefore expenditure per slave.
8. The position of Micoud d'Umons is revealing on this point. In a work published in 1802, he took up the idea developed in the eighteenth century that trade could not exist without agriculture and hence without slavery (Micoud d'Umons, 1802, II, p. 67). The slave is the productive force without which land is worthless, and therefore there is everything to be gained by allowing the British to sell slaves to the French islands: 'By selling us their Negroes, [the British] are actually selling us the raw material of the American trade, they are selling their own soil' (ibid., p. 69). The starkness of his position endorsing the inequality of the slave leads him to suggest cynically that religion should serve as a balm for the Negroes (ibid., p. 96).
9. In fact, that does not contradict the ideas advanced by Steuart and runs only very partially counter to Smith, who felt that slavery was profitable in the colonies for sugar and tobacco growing but not in the United States for wheat growing (Smith 1776, I, pp. 388–9).
10. But, for all that, his argument did arouse controversy. C. Ganilh (1809, I, pp. 215 et seq.) waxes indignant about Say's particular position and reminds him of Smith's letter. Later, Charles Comte (1826–7, IV, p. 253, note 1) mentions a little work by Adam Hodgson entitled, 'A Letter to Mr. J. B. Say on the Comparative Expense of Free and Slave Labour'.
11. The term 'rent' here is taken in the meaning that with the help of the law, some individuals make gains at the expense of society as a whole. This is what Frédéric Bastiat and Vilfredo Pareto would later call 'spoliation'.
12. Say (1828–9, I, Chapter 13) takes up the arguments developed by Comte on the costs taking into account of the costs of policing – the cost of whip lashes – and the costs occasioned by domestic slaves.
13. Sismondi's reasoning is sometimes a little superficial. He admits, moreover, that he does not want to study the responses of the planters, who 'stuff your head with the details of a sugar cane plantation' (1837, I, p. 292). Sismondi does not indicate from where the funds with which the owners (ex-planters) are to establish their sharecroppers (ex-slaves) are to come, and he gives no relevant argument on the highly disputed point of the labour of sharecroppers, assuming, without saying more, that they will want to produce as French peasants would marketing their product.

Bibliography

ANONYMOUS. 'Lettre sur l'affranchissement des nègres en Pennsylvanie'. *Éphémérides du citoyen.* Vol. 9. 1769, pp. 172–5.
ANONYMOUS. 'Lettre sur l'esclavage des nègres'. *Éphémérides du citoyen.* Vol. 12. 1771, pp. 51–77.
BOESNIER DE L'ORME. *De l'esprit du gouvernement économique* (1775). Kraus Reprint, 1980.
CANTILLON, R. *Essay de la nature du commerce en général,* 1728–50. T. Tsuda (ed.). Kinokuniya, 1979.
CHILD, J. *Traité sur le commerce,* 1669. Fr. trans. T. Tsuda (ed.). Kinokuniya, 1983 [Eng. orig., *A New Discourse of Trade* (1693); the translation uses later amendments].
COMTE, C. *Traité de législation.* Paris, A. Sautelet et Cie, 1826–7.
———. *Décade Philosophique, Littéraire et Politque* (Year II–XII).
DUPONT DE NEMOURS, P. S. 'De l'esclavage des nègres'. *Éphémérides du citoyen,* VI, 1771a, pp. 178–246.
———. 'Compte rendu de Mr. Buttini "Lettres africaines"'. *Éphémérides du citoyen,* IX, 1771b, pp. 68–118.
FORBONNAIS, F. VÉRON DE. *Éléments du commerce.* Leyden, 1754.
GANILH, C. *Des systèmes d'économie politique.* Xhrouet, 1809.
———. *La Théorie de l'économie politique.* Déterville, 1815.

GOURNAY, J. VINCENT DE. *Remarques sur le 'Traité sur le commerce' de J. Child* (1754). T. Tsuda (ed.). Kinokuniya, 1983.

INED. *Économie et population: les doctrines françaises avant 1800.* P.U.F., 1956.

MAY, L.-P. *Le Mercier de la Rivière (1719–1801): Mémoires et textes inédits.* CNRS, 1978.

MERCIER DE LA RIVIÈRE, P.-P. LE. 'Mémoire sur la Martinique' (1762). In: L.-P. May, *Le Mercier de la Rivière (1719–1801): Mémoires et textes inédits*, pp. 102–54. CNRS, 1978.

———. 'Procès-verbal de l'Assemblée concernant l'imposition de la Martinique' (1763a). In: L.-P. May, *Le Mercier de la Rivière (1719–1801): Mémoires et textes inédits*, pp. 155–65. CNRS, 1978.

———. 'Observation sur l'imposition ordonnée par le Roi et particulièrement sur les droits d'entrée et de sortie' (1763b). In: L.-P. May, *Le Mercier de la Rivière (1719–1801): Mémoires et textes inédits*, pp. 175–226. CNRS, 1978.

———. *L'Ordre naturel et essentiel des sociétés politiques* (1767). P. Guethner, 1910.

MICOUD D'UMONS, C. E. *Sur les finances, le commerce, la marine et les colonies.* Agasse, 1802.

MIRABEAU, V. RIQUETI MARQUIS DE. *L'Ami des hommes ou traité de la population.* 4th edn. C. Herold, 1758.

QUESNAY, F. M. 'Remarques sur l'opinion de l'auteur de "Esprit des lois" concernant les colonies' (1766). In: INED, F. *Quesnay et la physiocratie.* Vol. 2, pp. 781–90. P.U.F., 1969.

SAY, J.-B. *Traité d'économie politique.* 1st edn. Crapelet, 1803.

———. *Traité d'économie politique.* 2nd edn. Déterville, 1814.

———. *Traité d'économie politique* (1826). 5th edn. Calmann-Lévy, 1972.

———. *Cours complet d'économie politique pratique* (1828–9). Guillaumin, 1852.

SISMONDI, J. C. L. *Études sur l'économie politique* (1837). Vol. I. Slatkine, 1980.

SMITH, A. *An Enquiry into the Nature and Causes of the Wealth of the Nations* (1776). Indianapolis, Liberty Press, 1979.

STEUART, J. *An Inquiry into the Principles of Political Oeconomy* (1767). Kelley, 1967.

TOLOSAN. *Mémoire sur le commerce de la France et de ses colonies* (1789). Kraus Reprint, 1980.

TURGOT, A. R. J. 'Réflexions sur la formation et la distribution des richesses'. In: G. Schelle (ed.), *Oeuvres de Turgot et documents le concernant, 1766,* Vol. 2. Alcan, 1914 [Eng. trans., 'Reflections on the Formation and Distribution of Wealth'. London, 1793]; also in P. D. Groenewegen, *The Economics of A.R.J. Turgot.* The Hague, Martinus Nijhoff, 1977].

———. 'Correspondance avec Dupont'. In: G. Schelle (ed.), *Oeuvres de Turgot et documents le concernant,* 1764–81. Vols 2–5. Alcan, 1914–23.

Further Reading

BÉNOT, Y. *La Révolution française et la fin des colonies.* Paris, La Découverte, 1987.

———. *La Démence coloniale sous Napoléon* Paris, La Découverte, 1992.

ENGERMAN, S. L. 'Slavery'. In: J. Eatwell, M. Milgate and P. Newman (eds), *The New Palgrave: A Dictionary of Economics.* Vol. 4, pp. 350–5. London, Macmillan, 1987.

MAY, L. P. *Le Mercier de la Rivière (1719–1801): Aux origines de la pensée économique.* CNRS, 1975.

MELON, J. F. *Essai politique sur le commerce.* 2nd edn (1736).

PAGE, P. F. *Principes d'économie politque et de commerce des colonies.* Brochot, 1801.

STEINER, P. J.-B. 'Say et les colonies ou comment se débarrasser d'un héritage intempestif?' In: F. Demier and D. Diatkine (eds), *Smith et l'économie coloniale.* Cambridge, Cambridge University Press/Maison des Sciences de l'Homme, 1995.

Part III

The Revolution and the First Abolition: Insurrections in the Islands, Debates in the Revolutionary Assemblies, Abolitions (1789–1802)

Chapter 12

The Chain of Slave Insurrections in the Caribbean, 1789–1791

Yves Bénot

WHILE IT IS TRUE that the various slave insurrections that occurred in the French colonies in the Caribbean from the summer of 1789 onward all failed, unlike the one that erupted in Saint-Domingue in August 1791, they still merit attention and above all an examination of their common features. These men who, to take an expression used of resistance elsewhere, rose before the dawn deserve not to remain anonymous, or certainly not to remain so when we know something of them.

First, let us recall the principal dates of these movements. On 30–31 August 1789 there was the attempt in Saint-Pierre de la Martinique, and at the beginning of October, another in the south of Saint-Domingue. In November, major disturbances occurred in Martinique, where an overseer was killed in the south of the island. On 4–6 December 1790, there was an attempted insurrection in French Guyana on the upper Approuague, and on 11–12 April, another attempted uprising in Guadeloupe, in the Capesterre-Petit-Bourg region. In late October to early November, several parishes in Martinique experienced the beginnings of an uprising. Furthermore, all through the civil war between whites, from September 1790 to March 1791, many slaves deserted their plantations. In St Lucia, there may have been an attempt in December 1790, as a letter suggests. At the end of January 1791, movements for three free days for slaves broke out in southern Saint-Domingue around Port-Salut. On 11 May in Martinique, near Saint-Pierre, an insurrection was nipped in the bud. On 16 May, in Guadeloupe, there was an attempt around Sainte-Anne. At the beginning of July, there were reports of insurrections on several plantations around Port-au-Prince in Saint-Domingue. At the end of the year, that is, after the insurrection in Saint-Domingue, which had got bogged down in a prolonged struggle, there was the attempt by Noël Bonhomme at Marie-Galante. In Saint-Domingue, other insurrections broke out around Léogane in March 1792, and then around Cayes from June 1792 onwards, which lasted until 21 September 1793 and the proclamation of the abolition of slavery. Under the Republic, there were reports of movements for the 'three days' in Martinique in the summer, which were immediately put down, while in Guadeloupe, two insurrections occurred, one at Trois Rivières in April, the other around Sainte-Anne in August. Finally, in St Lucia, slaves participated in the insurrectionary movement led by Genty in late December 1793. One of the insurgents was probably Palème, who would later play an active role in the guerrilla war against the British occupation in 1794–5 and ensure the bridgehead that would allow the disembarkation of the troops despatched by Victor Hugues in 1795. And that listing takes no account of less spectacular episodes. It will of course be said that there had been slave insurrections before the French Revolution. That is surely true, but the ones we have mentioned themselves signified their relationship to the events unfolding in France in their own discourse, whenever that discourse has come down to us in a reasonably reliable form. And that relationship deserves all the more attention because in this period, the Revolution in France was not overly concerned with slaves.

The first movement in date order, the one at Saint-Pierre de la Martinique, has, of course, been studied in detail by Léo Elisabeth. It occurred before news of the taking of the Bastille could have reached the Antilles, but still at a time when it was known that things were stirring in France, if only the Estates-General. The news that did spread was that the King had already granted general freedom to slaves, a claim that would reappear just two years later in Saint-Domingue. It is worth remarking that this remarkable extrapolation may have originally appeared in a credible form, at least in France, for at least two freemen of colour, who had had some contact with the slaves, Alexis René and J.-L. Genty, had lived in France before 1789, as indeed had one of the men behind the insurrection in Saint-Domingue, the future colonel, Paul Lafrance, who had been taken there for a while, but as a slave. And in certain circles in Paris there were those who saw in a number of initiatives by the Minister of the Colonies, de Castries; in the government's tolerant attitude towards the Société des Amis des Noirs, founded at the beginning of 1788; or in the abolitionist campaign by Mirabeau's journal *L'Analyse des papiers anglais*, which was also tolerated, signs of a more or less pro-black tendency in the royal government. Louis XVI's refusal to ban the Société des Amis des Noirs as he was asked to do by Gouy d'Arsy in April 1789 could only have strengthened that impression – which nothing later confirmed, until the King came down decidedly in favour of the colonists following the insurrection in Saint-Domingue in November 1791. Of course, what was simply impression and rumour was amplified to the point where it became an active myth, only this time in support of a clear-cut demand that had its origins in the plantations.

Whatever the case, the plan for an insurrection, which was indeed a plan for a general uprising, was leaked by the investigative zeal of a mixed-race overseer, a certain Louis Ducoudray, at some date before 25 August 1789. Whether preparation for the insurrection had also been spied upon by the free black Alexis René, as the pro-slave magistrate Dessalles asserted, is difficult to confirm or deny. The letters sent to the Commandant of Saint-Pierre and the Governor on 26 and 29 August signed 'We the Negroes' are in any case the work of an author who clearly drew his inspiration from the great tirades of Diderot in Raynal's *Histoire*. There were other letters until about 10 and 11 September, after the failure of the insurrection but before the great wave of arrests. It must at least be observed that these threatening letters specified that the insurgents would not harm members of the clergy; in Saint-Domingue, where of course there were no warning letters, it is a fact that the insurgents spared the priests.

So, on 25 August, St Louis's Day, which was still celebrated, military forces gathered in Saint-Pierre, and nothing happened. It was during the evening of 30 August that the attempt began, and the army intervened swiftly. The next day, however, according to the available official reports, two gangs went on strike and took to the bush. But they returned to work on 1 September, according to a report from the correspondent of the Bordeaux house of Gradis because the parish priest of Basse-Pointe had managed to convince them to go back to their plantations in return for a guarantee that they would not be punished. But the Justice Department did not feel bound by this promise: there were two executions on 10 September, those of the slaves Jean-Dominque known as Foutard and Honoré, whom an anonymous letter the following day hailed as 'martyrs of liberty'. But the main leader, who was only arrested on 20 September some distance from the town, seems to have been one Marc, 'driver of the gaol, belonging to *sieur* Jacquier, concierge', and hence a town slave, who had participated in (or perhaps presided over) secret meetings, in rue d'Orange, and whose strong personality can only be guessed at from the very brief references there are to him. He was executed – broken on the wheel – on 13 October along with five others.

But the decree by the governing council on 12 October indicates that one of the leaders, named Fayance, had escaped, and that the investigation into him was to continue. He was a very different personality, and we shall meet him again.

Although Governor Vioménil had ordered an island-wide hunt for maroons at the beginning of September, Fayance had escaped, while 200 maroons had been retaken. The mulatto militias – and also militias made up of blacks 'serving for their freedom' – had shown themselves to be disciplined throughout this affair, although a small group of mixed-race and free blacks were concerned about problems of equality and liberty. In any case, there is no doubt that the objective of Marc and his comrades was indeed a general and not a localized movement, and that he sought immediate unconditional general freedom.

In October, in the south of Saint-Domingue, as we have seen, there was a first movement, but so far as we can tell, this one did not refer to the myth about the King. Rather, it had to do with the news that arrived from France right at the beginning of the month: the taking of the Bastille, the tricolour cockade, in which the slaves saw a sign of freedom, which they called on to be implemented. Several were executed at once, while again, the mulatto militias remained disciplined and in the service of order. But in Martinique, the August attempt continued to resonate in the plantations throughout the colony, notably in the southern parishes. Various reports addressed to the Governor mention as much in early November, and an insurrection was feared. A planter who used his mixed-race son as a spy reported comments about the freedom granted by the King and refused by the colonists in early November. Nevertheless, Vioménil indicated a nuance, which is not surprising since the events of 14 July had been known in the colony since mid-September. According to him, the slaves 'believed that the sovereign *and the nation* [emphasis added] had agreed to assimilate them to the whites'. The murder of the overseer Alleron on 9 November – which may have been a premature initiative, such as the Chabaud fire on 14 August 1791 in Saint-Domingue – provided the excuse to unleash repression. Six slaves – Claude, Paul, Gabriel, Gille, Gidéon and Robert – were executed, with their heads put on display on the main roads 'at the end of long pikes'. For some months afterwards, order seemed to reign over the plantations, and the towns were disturbed by other conflicts.

In December 1790, it was the turn of French Guyana to see a serious attempted uprising, which was thwarted, perhaps, only by a defection or, more likely, action by spies for the colonists. But it was preceded by 'rumblings', as Governor Bourgon wrote at the end of 1789. He reported a gang in which 'all the blacks came to tell their master that they knew that they had been declared free in France and that they wanted to enjoy that blessing'. The Governor had therefore armed all the colonists. In November, an overseer was wounded on a plantation, and a slave was arrested after attempting to flee into the woods. After which, 'the investigation was taking too long and the people loudly demanded the punishment that he deserved and he was executed', 'the people' obviously being the whites. The Aprouague insurrection on 4 December started off much like the one in Saint-Domingue, only on a smaller scale. One gang, that of *sieur* Saint-Marcel, rose up one night, killed the colonist and then his partner, went off to neighbouring plantations, executed the colonists, gathered reinforcements and weapons on the way, and took two soldiers who were getting water as prisoners. The returned to the plantation from which they had set out, and sent an emissary to raise the plantation of a municipal official, Néron de Morangiès. But this envoy, 'whether seeing the error of his ways or something else', says a report, alerted the official himself, who at once organized the response. The insurgents found themselves facing an armed detachment, and battle was joined – the first case, it seems, of such a confrontation. Only after the arrival of reinforcements for the whites were the rebels dispersed. There followed a hunt for the blacks who had taken refuge in the woods. In February 1791 there were seven executions for which the executioner was paid 105 livres. In the fighting, Néron was wounded and died a week later. An eyewitness account by the widow of Saint-Marcel has the slave Basile, whom she describes as 'the leader of the plot', saying: 'Have you not heard tell of our freedom; we know that the priest has a big packet of papers which has come from France, that it was something the good Lord had promised him since long ago, and even that he had heard it from the mouth of whites, and that the assembly meeting that took place on 19 November was to prevent them being given their freedom....' Thus, the alleged abolition was now being directly related to the Revolutionary events in Paris, and no longer to a gesture by the King. In that respect, it can be accepted that the slave-owners and planters who drew up a petition against the Colonial Assembly in August 1790 and referred to these events were doubtless not wrong to blame 'the word "freedom" repeated unthinkingly all over in a land of slavery'. But that means, too, that the slaves, who were more logical on this point than the Constituent Assembly, saw at once the profound import of the new slogans that had come from France.

The same was true in Guadeloupe for the attempted insurrection which was allegedly planned for the night of 11–12 April 1790 in the districts of Capesterre, Goyave and Petit-Bourg, but which was part of a plan for a general insurrection, the first fires being intended to give the signal to many other districts. If we are to believe the report of Governor de Clugny – a man of the Ancien Régime – 'wretched domestics who had so often heard the word "freedom" spoken in the meetings, believed themselves free and had persuaded the negroes in the gangs that they were too, but that the whites were carefully concealing the news that they had received from France in this connection'. These same reports also reveal that a link had been established with the maroons in the interior highlands of Guadeloupe. In addition, and without further detail, de Clugny mentions 'two deserters who were at the head of the maroon negroes' of whom one had been arrested.

Another document, cited by Anne Pérotin-Dumont, adds the further detail that the domestics were asserting that 'since the French had dethroned their king, they were allowed to shake off the yoke and get rid of their masters …'. The discourse of the insurrection was already taking a republican form, but the content remained the same.

In Martinique, it was the freemen of colour, rather than the slaves, who were the target of the anger of the so-called 'patriots' of Saint-Pierre in the lynchings of 3 June 1790; of the fourteen mulattoes lynched, only one was a slave. This day of horrors was the starting point of a whole series of developments that led to the outbreak of a civil war between whites starting in September 1790. It was a civil war between the 'patriot' merchants in the towns and the planters, but the former had the support of virtually all the troops of the line, except for a company of grenadiers that had gone over to the planters. To provide themselves with an army, these latter then had to turn to the men of colour and free blacks, who certainly had no reason to support the party of those who had had no compunction about lynching them. The slaves, especially those of Saint-Pierre, also had nothing to expect from the people in the towns. Thus, an army of the country party that was essentially made up of mulattoes officering black slaves came into being. It is at this point that we find Fayance again, having emerged from hiding to command before the besieged town of Saint-Pierre a sort of black army that was constantly being reinforced by all the town slaves who were able to make their escape. The planters were highly appreciative of the military effectiveness of Fayance and his army.

But not all slaves took the side of the plantation owners. In October and November, insurrections broke out in many parishes, more particularly in the region of south Marin. Governor Damas, who had thrown in his lot with the planters, wrote on 6 November 1790 to his colleague Clugny:

> Serious disorders have broken out, the sad effect of the wretched example given by the insurrection of the troops, the forgetting of all duties and the violation of all laws.... Detachments had to be sent into almost every parish to put down the slaves and they were obliged to make a number of examples. I have the satisfaction of learning that order is being restored everywhere.

Given the blockade established before the two main towns of the colony, which required significant forces, it must be thought that Damas had sent mainly white detachments against the slaves while his coloured army held the front in the civil war. The messages of congratulations addressed to the Governor on his departure for France in March 1791 frequently refer to the repression of the slave revolts by his actions. The details are lacking everywhere, but it seems that while the attempted insurrections failed, a number of slaves took advantage of this situation to abandon the estates and wander about the countryside.

When the civil war ended in March 1791 with the arrival of a new governor, Béhague, accompanied by civil commissioners and troops to replace the mutinous units which were sent back to France, the fact remains that there were thousands of slaves who were armed and militarily organized. For several weeks, the new authorities trod very warily and skilfully. As for Fayance, he was hurriedly given his freedom, with many congratulations. Now he had become a royalist, and so he would remain, except that he later shifted his allegiance from the King of France to the King of England. He left Martinique with the royalist colonists at the beginning of 1793 and went to Trinidad, which was then Spanish but became English in 1795. According to Dauxion-Lavaysse, who knew him there, Fayance served, with a sidekick, as an agent in underground operations for the British Governor until one day, after some excess, the said Governor got rid of him by having him assassinated by the sidekick. A singular fate – but one that was quite atypical.

The civil commissioners would later explain to Paris how they had had to proceed:

> We also felt it prudent to mollify the principal leaders whose domination over the minds of their comrades could serve our views, just as it could harm them if we had not taken good care to bind them to us; gifts carefully handed out, a few liberties granted to the most intelligent among them, to those who had shown themselves most loyal produced the best effect.

Naturally, the Governor's proclamation guaranteed that slaves who returned to their masters would risk no punishment from these latter. It seems from the documents that it was more difficult to secure respect for that undertaking from the so-called 'patriots' than it was in the countryside. Béhague ought to have intervened personally in the streets of Saint-Pierre to oppose the violence of these bourgeois self-proclaimed revolutionaries, obviously for political rather than philosophical reasons. In any case, the opportunity was lost, and the brief revolt of 11 May near Saint-Pierre – leaving one dead – could not bring it back. It was a unique moment, one that might, *mutatis mutandis*, be compared with the circumstances of 1919, when 4 million men under arms in France laid down their weapons rather than turn them against those who had sent them to the slaughter.

In Guadeloupe, at about the same time, an attempted revolt broke out in the region of Sainte-Anne, in Grande-Terre, with a novel set of arguments. According to Clugny's report, it was a mulatto slave who

> had convinced many negroes in the countryside to enter into his plan, saying that I had received a decree from the National Assembly, which granted freedom to blacks, but that I did not want to publish it until I had sold my property, and given that that might take some time, they ought, since they were the stronger, to get it for themselves.

The insurrection had been planned for the night of 15–16 May 1791, but a 'negro slave' denounced it on 15 May to the municipality of Sainte-Anne, and the gathering was dispersed, with eighteen arrests.

In French Guyana, two informers, Pierre and Barthélemey, slaves belonging to *dame* Mangeot and *dame* Morin, were freed by the Colonial Assembly on 25 January 1791, for their information at the time of the Aprouague insurrection. Was the insurgent sent to the Néron de Morangiès plantation and who turned informer one of these two? The above-quoted report is remarkably elusive on the reason for his attitude ('… or something else'). However that may be, such facts are evidence of the constant efforts made by the colonists to find stool pigeons among the slaves themselves, in addition, naturally to the usual *grands moyens*. Both colonizations – the more recent one that was not founded on institutionalized slavery and that of the Ancien Régime – sought to protect themselves by encouraging informers. The archives reveal the role of these stoolies only on exceptional occasions, but they give an indication of the sort of pressure such a dangerous presence must have caused. If the insurrection in northern Saint-Domingue escaped it, it is doubtless a sign of careful preparation which, likewise, can only be guessed at.

To return to Guadeloupe, with the attempt at Sainte-Anne we have moved from the theme of the 'beneficent King' to that of an 'abolitionist Constituent Assembly'; however, the same logic contained in the proclamation of liberty must still be applied to all, failing which it would not be liberty. At bottom, whether the argument invoked was the King, freedom in general, or the Constituent Assembly, it was the same sort of story, despite the apparent dissymmetry of the first, for the myth of the King was that of the King who summoned the Estates-General and who called for reform and the expression of ideas. That is how it could be combined without contradiction in the letters of August 1789 to the inspiration drawn from the call for revolt in the *Histoire des Deux Indes*.

In Saint-Domingue, in late January 1789, in the south, an apparently more modest demand than general liberty was heard – the demand for three free days for the slaves, to enable them to spend those days working for their own subsistence and perhaps also to sell their produce on the market. Of course, nothing was granted them, but this idea reappeared in the insurrections of July 1791 in the plain of Cul-de-Sac, and later in Martinique, in the summer of 1793.

These last insurrections in which actual fighting occurred, and which were only put down after countless summary executions, appear to us today as the prelude to the great insurrection in the north. Yet they seem to have broken out on different plantations, at different times: in short, they lacked coordination. If we are to believe the colonist Guiton, soldiers who had come from France the previous year had had contact with slaves on certain plantations and had spoken to them about the Declaration of the Rights of Man. And we must observe that while in the insurrection in the north the leaders adopted the theme of the King and stayed with it until 1794, slaves taken separately or certain groups among them also referred in the earliest days to the Rights of Man, while others referred to the 'three days'. While the insurrection had a reasonably united leadership capable of taking the lead in a prolonged struggle (possibly the lesson of the previous attempts, or the consequence of the impossibility of getting it over and done with at once by taking Le Cap), the whole was not monolithic, and a variety of inspirations could coexist around the common desire for freedom.

Apart from the launching of the armed struggle in Saint-Domingue – news of which Béhague, for example, ensured that censorship would prevent from getting through to Martinique (even in Paris, where there was ample information available, it was often too confused and contradictory for the public to be able to grasp it clearly) – there would be other attempts in the Windward Islands. Yet none would triumph.

These failures doubtless have to do with one fundamental difference from the situation in Saint-Domingue: nowhere else had the traditional system of controlling slave labour with mulatto militias and blacks serving for their freedom (still unattained after twelve years) ceased to function. In Saint-Domingue, following the whites' refusal to implement the decree of 15 May 1791, the mulattoes had ceased to give service everywhere by July. No such breach was opened up anywhere else. It might also be thought that at least in Martinique, the execution of those who might have been leaders of stature, Marc, for example, was a severe blow. Finally, the position of the islands did not allow them to find logistical support on their border, a factor that was very important in the Saint-Domingue insurrection, as it was for Vietnam after 1949 or for the Algerians especially after 1956.

It remains that in everything that they could glean of the Revolutionary events in France, slaves everywhere read a demand for freedom and universal equality that resonated with what had always been their own demand. What the Revolution did not do could only be attributed to the well-known perfidy of the white slave authorities on the spot. Their logic read, over and beyond the circumstances, the hesitations and double-thinking of the parliamentarians of the Revolution that so often failed to live up to its innermost wellspring.

Chapter 14

The Role of the Saint-Domingue Deputation in the Abolition of Slavery

Florence Gauthier

> It must be clearly understood: there was no 'French Revolution' in the French colonies. There was in each French colony a specific revolution, that occurred on the occasion of the French Revolution, in tune with it, but unfolding according to its own laws and with its own goals.
>
> However, there was one point common to the two phenomena: the rhythm.
>
> A. Césaire, *Toussaint Louverture, la Révolution*
> *française et le problème colonial*

THE ABOLITION OF SLAVERY in the colonies by the Convention, voted on 16 Pluviôse Year II (4 February 1794), was undoubtedly one of the most important acts of the revolutions of the Rights of Man and the Citizen. Yet the history of this act and its words has been little studied, and it is only very recently that there has been research into it. There are abundant sources, and we therefore need to ask ourselves about the lack of curiosity that can be observed in French historiography over the last two centuries, despite the importance of the event.[1]

What we intend to do here is to use the evidence currently available to reconstruct the story of the encounter between the revolution in France and the Caribbean revolution. Our subject is limited to the role of the Saint-Domingue deputation in the abolition of slavery on 16 Pluviôse Year II (4 February 1794), and in the preservation of this abolition during the Thermidorian reaction, which, as we shall see, stirred fears that this great conquest of liberty might be called into question.

Formation of the Société des citoyens de couleur in Paris

> As for the slave trade and black slavery, let the governments of Europe resist as they will the cries of philosophy and the principles of universal liberty which are

growing and spreading among the nations. Let them learn that it is not in vain that the peoples are shown the truth.... Yes, we dare to predict confidently that a time will come, and that day is not far off, when we shall see an African, with his curly hair, and with no other recommendation but his common sense and his virtues, come and take part in law-making within our national assemblies.

Sonthonax, *Les Révolutions de Paris*,
25 September 1790

This philosophical prediction by Sonthonax, who was an actor in abolition, deserved to be recalled in a study devoted to the Saint-Domingue deputation.[2] We shall begin the story of the encounter of the two revolutions in 1793, being unable, in the framework given here, to go further back.

One of the lessons of this encounter is to reveal that, contrary to what has been generally accepted, the abolition of 16 Pluviôse was the end-product of a long preparation.

A few days after the revolution of 10 August 1792, which overthrew the property-based, slave-holding, monarchical Constitution of 1791, Julien Raimond, at the head of a large delegation of citizens of colour, was received at the bar of the Assembly on 7 September 1792. He called for the formation of a legion of soldiers of colour to defend the revolution. Raimond's proposal was accepted, and thus the Legion of Americans came into being.[3]

It is to be noted that the people of colour identified themselves both as French citizens and as a specific group, wishing to organize themselves into a specific military corps, when they could have simply blended into the regiments of national volunteers.

In the spring of 1793, these soldiers received orders to return to the colonies. This they objected to, refusing to take the risk of being returned to slavery. On 15 May 1793, the Convention adopted a decree rescinding the order.[4]

On 17 May 1793, the Legion of Americans published an 'Adresse à la Convention nationale, à tous les clubs et sociétés patriotiques, pour les Nègres détenus en esclavage dans les colonies françaises d'Amérique' (Address to the National Convention, and to All Patriotic Clubs and Societies, for the Negroes Held in Slavery in the French Colonies in America).[5]

The Address spoke for a million slaves and called on lawmakers to adopt a decree abolishing slavery in the colonies: 'We demand our freedom; our rights are imprescriptible, natural and based on humanity.' It linked the right of blacks to own property, engage in business and enter any job to abolition, and concluded by pointing out to lawmakers what they must do:

Thus, a confirmatory decree, backing those already issued, will restore everything to a proper and indispensable equality; from which we conclude that the present address be drafted as a motion by your committee on legislation, and on that a decree be issued declaring free every inhabitant of the French colonies subject to the republic, and under the protection of its laws, as well as those absent from them and who so remain; finally, that slavery is abolished for all blacks in the French colonies: that henceforth no master shall have any right over those men, except as may be agreed between them for their wages and their labour; and so that no one should be unaware of it, that a copy of the present be printed and sent immediately to the civil commissioners representing the republic in America, to every community and canton, so as to encourage on all sides that friendly disposition that ought henceforth to reign among all.

By this means you will cover yourselves with immortal glory and restore peace and prosperity to the colonies, which already send you their blessings.

It is worth pointing out that a few months later, the Convention would abolish slavery in a manner very similar to the one indicated in the Address, in response to a demand previously formulated. This group of citizens of colour went on to wage a campaign for abolition directed at the Jacobin Club, the Convention and the Commune of Paris, as we shall see.

On 3 June, the very morrow of the revolution of 31 May–2 June 1793, the Société des Amis de la Liberté et de l'Égalité, known as the Jacobin Club, received a deputation of citizens of colour headed by 114-year-old Jeanne Odo, who presented their demand for the abolition of slavery. The Jacobins took an oath to free the blacks.[6]

The next day, 4 June, the Convention received this same deputation, which presented the Address of 17 May and then offered, 'in the name of its fellow-citizens a tricolour flag: a white, a mulatto and a black were depicted standing, armed with a pike crowned with a liberty cap. On the flag this inscription can be read: Our union shall be our strength'. The president of the Convention accepted the flag and gave the fraternal kiss to Jeanne Odo. The whole assembly stood before her as a sign of respect. Grégoire took the floor to support the Address and asked the Convention to eliminate pigmentational aristocracy and declare the blacks free.[7]

The tricolour flag presented by the deputation of citizens of colour does not have the same significance as the tricolour of the revolution in France. On the blue background is a black, on the white is a white, and on the red is a mulatto. The union of the three colours is summoned up to overthrow the pigmentational aristocracy and found a new social contract on the unity of the human species and equality of rights.

The Address of 17 May and the flag of pigmentational equality were an expression, at that date, of what the content of the revolution in the colonies was: general liberty for blacks, pigmentational equality, destruction of colonial society.

In inventing the specific flag of the colonial revolution, the deputation of citizens of colour was translating into the language of that revolution the tricolour of France, which had a different specificity. This doubling of a universal into two singular expressions was expressing the quest for an alliance. The language of universal rights was becoming more refined, by being capable of expressing this dialectic internal to the universal, since the two revolutions were based on the postulate of the unity of the human species, whose common purpose was beginning hesitantly to express itself.

The different content given to the tricolour gave concrete form to the encounter between these two revolutions in the spring and summer of 1793.

And we have seen that the Convention received and accepted the flag of the colonial revolution.

We should note, finally, that this flag of pigmentational equality was taken up again by the Saint-Domingue deputation and then by Toussaint Louverture when he went over to the anti-slavery republic in May 1794. This invention corroborates Aimé Césaire's analysis, which we quoted at beginning of this essay.

To return to the campaign waged by the deputation of citizens of colour. On 8 June, it was received with its banner – 'Rights of man and the citizen of colour. Live free or die' – by the Conseil général of the commune of Paris, which organized a demonstration on the Champ-de-Mars and was also presented with the flag of pigmentational equality.

On 11 June, the commune of Paris offered the deputation, in exchange for its flag, a pennant bearing on one side 'a white, a black and a mulatto with this inscription: "Men of colour you shall be free", and on the other, freedom and equality supporting a globe with these words: "Universal freedom and equality."' This pennant was later handed to the citizens of colour for civic festivals and 'when they march united'. The Société des gens de couleur was born.[8]

On 12 June, the commune of Paris proceeded to a 'baptism of liberty'. Chaumette presented a child of colour and asked for him to be jointly adopted by himself and the commune of Paris. The President of the Conseil général baptized him free, renewing the promise that slavery would be abolished.[9]

As these events were unfolding, the Convention was drawing up the new Declaration of the Rights of Man and the Citizen and the Constitution, which were adopted on 24 June 1793. The Declaration of the Rights of Man expressly banned slavery in its preamble, Article 3 and Article 18, which also specified that the human person is not property that can be bought and sold.

The Constitution of 1793 is the only French constitution not to be colonialist, and that fact alone deserves mention. Although it did not meet the call for the abolition of slavery, it did open the way, let it not be forgotten, to a questioning of a *politique de puissance* and a quest for new relations among peoples.[10]

Formation of the Saint-Domingue Deputation

The Convention had not replied to the Address of the Société des citoyens de couleur. Other events converged with this campaign being waged in France to lead to the vote of 16 Pluviôse. Those events happened in Saint-Domingue, and need to be recalled.

In June 1793, the new Governor of Saint-Domingue, Galbaud, who had just arrived at Le Cap, rebelled against the civilian commissioners Polverel and Sonthonax. Galbaud was backed by the pro-slavery colonists. However, rebel slaves came from the surrounding hills to take part in the battle for Le Cap, and with their support Galbaud was defeated and obliged to flee, soon followed by some ten thousand colonists.

Following this important victory, the rebel slaves called for general freedom. In the summer of 1793 there was a genuine movement of citizens coming together, deliberating and drawing up petitions. On 24 August, the commune of Le Cap voted for general freedom in North Province. This is how Jacques Garnier described it:

> They [the slaves] had become the defenders of the soil of freedom: it was at last time for them to recover their natural rights. The commune of Le Cap Français met on 24 August 1793. The free men who composed it, the liberty cap in their midst, had the honour to be the first to vote unanimously for the general freedom of Africans and their descendants who were on the soil of North Province. The deed was drafted and carried for his provisional endorsement amid cries of 'Long live the French Republic', taken up by fifteen thousand souls, to commissioner Sonthonax, who received the address from the commune as an expression of justice and humanity, which had been calling out for two centuries for the abolition of slavery.[11]

Sonthonax did not take the decision on abolition all on his own; he was responding, as we can see, to the movement of these new citizens who fought from June to August for general freedom. Sonthonax published a proclamation, on 29 August following, which abolished slavery and, for the first time in Saint-Domingue, made the Declaration of the Rights of Man and the Citizen part of the Constitution.[12] Sonthonax extended general freedom from Le Cap Province to the whole of Saint-Domingue, entrusting Polverel with the task of proclaiming it in West and South Provinces. This he did on the following 21 September.

Sonthonax then proceeded to organize the election of deputies from North Province to cross the Atlantic and sit in the Convention. West and South Provinces, in the throes of civil war, were in no position to organize elections. On 23 September, six deputies – three blacks, three whites and three mulattoes – were elected on the principle of pigmentational equality, reflecting in real life the flag of this new equality brought into being by the Saint-Domingue revolution. Those elected were Jean-Baptiste Belley, Louis Dufay, Joseph Boisson, Pierre Garnot, Jean-Baptiste Mills, Réchin and three substitutes.[13]

While all this was happening, the British were landing in Saint-Domingue in response to a call from the slave-owning colonists.

Part of the deputation sailed for France by way of the United States: Belley, Mills, Dufay, Garnot and Joseph Georges (a substitute) reached Philadelphia on 6 November, not without difficulty.

Let us imagine for a moment what the Saint-Domingue deputation represented. The living reflection of the flag of general freedom and pigmentational equality was crossing the Atlantic, en route for the Convention. Included were the first deputies of colour in history, elected by former slaves who had become citizens. For the pro-slavery lobby, powerfully organized by the colonists who had emigrated to the United States, England and France itself, the Saint-Domingue deputation ought not to arrive alive. In fact, it took four months for the deputation to reach Paris, suffering attacks all along the way. To protect itself, it split up in New York: Belley, Mills and Dufay embarked for France, leaving Garnot and Georges to take over, if necessary.

In France, the pro-slavery lobby immediately attacked the deputation, denying the legality of its election, and even succeeding in having its members briefly imprisoned.[14]

However, on 15 Pluviôse Year II (3 February 1794), the Convention confirmed the election and admitted the Saint-Domingue deputation to sit. From that moment, the general freedom of blacks who had become citizens had been recognized by the Republic, along with Sonthonax and Polverel's decision, so far as concerned Saint-Domingue.

On 16 Pluviôse (4 February), Dufay set out at length the deputation's mandate to the Convention. What was that mandate? Was it to ask the Convention to abolish slavery in Saint-Domingue? That is what has been generally believed. But we have just recalled that the Convention had already recognized it the evening before by admitting the deputation to sit. So the mandate must have been something else. Dufay was mandated, with Belley and Mills, to propose a contract of association between the new people of Saint-Domingue, who had won freedom themselves, and the people of France, who were also waging their struggle for freedom. Dufay was proposing to the French Republic a common policy of war against French slave-owning colonists and their British and Spanish allies.

Were the two revolutions going to combine to conduct a common policy against the pro-slavery colonial system? Was the France of freedom going to commit itself to a policy of decolonization? That is what was at stake in the encounter.[15]

The Convention accepted this offer, and then decided to widen the freedom won in Saint-Domingue to general freedom throughout the French colonies. It adopted a Declaration of the abolition of slavery in the colonies, the basis for a new contract of association between these peoples, followed by a decree extending citizenship to those affected:

> The National Convention declares slavery abolished in all the colonies. In consequence it declares that all men, without distinction of colour, domiciled in the colonies, are French citizens and enjoy all the rights assured under the Constitution. Refers back to the Committee of Public Safety to make an urgent report to it on the measures to be taken to bring this decree into force.

That same evening, the Saint-Domingue deputation was received at the Jacobin Club to which it presented the flag of pigmentational equality, the same as that of the Paris Société des citoyens de couleur.[16]

The Committee of Public Safety and the Minister of the Navy set about forming a civilian commission to accompany the troops charged with carrying the decree of 16 Pluviôse to the Windward Islands, which the British were in the process of occupying, and French Guyana.

Furthermore, the Saint-Domingue deputation provided a series of proofs that gradually revealed the network of the pro-slavery lobby active in France, whose members were infiltrating clubs, municipal institutions, ministries and the committees of the Convention.

The decree of 19 Ventôse (9 March 1794) allowed the arrest of members of the Massiac Club and of all the colonial assemblies who were in France, as well as a check of the papers of all colonists residing in Paris.

In April 1794, a major expedition of seven ships, with nearly 1,500 soldiers set sail for the Windward Islands, two months after the vote of 16 Pluviôse. One ship was going to find Polverel and Sonthonax so that they could give a report to the Convention on their long mission.

The second part of the Saint-Domingue deputation reached Paris in July 1794, made up of Étienne Laforest, substituting for Réchin, Joseph Boisson and Pierre Garnot.[17]

The Saint-Domingue Deputation, Target of the Pro-Slavery Lobby during Thermidor

The effect of the episode of 9 Thermidor Year II (27 July 1794) and its aftermath was initially to interrupt the policy pursued since 16 Pluviôse, and then to reverse it, culminating in the restoration of slavery in 1802. The pro-slavery lobby responded at once, seeking to regain lost ground, but was temporarily restrained by the Constitution of 1795, as we shall see.

Initially, the pro-slavery lobby's offensive was directed against the Saint-Domingue deputation, challenging the legality of its election, and waging a campaign of calumnies against it, lumping its members with Polverel and Sonthonax by accusing them all of 'Robespierrism', a serious charge at the time.[18]

The campaign of calumnies began on 19 August 1794 and was launched by Page and Brulley, colonists who had been imprisoned since 7 March. Their tactic was to obtain the release of the colonists arrested under the decree of 9 March, and to secure the creation of a joint accusers/accused commission, bringing themselves face to face with Polverel and Sonthonax.

They found support among the pro-slavery colonists, who took up this campaign with the slogan 'Africans are strangers, only white colonists are French'. This slogan was accompanied by one about the 'inferiority of Africans'. A small group of deputies took part in this campaign, principally Gouly, Defrance, Creuzé-Pascal, Littey, Lassalle and Serres.

Despite warnings from the Saint-Domingue deputation, Sonthonax and a number of deputies, the Convention rescinded the decree of 9 March 1794 and released the colonists who had been arrested, except for members of the Massiac Club, and then set up the accusers/accused commission.[19]

After these initial victories won between August and November 1794, the pro-slavery lobby embarked on a new campaign by openly attacking the abolition of slavery: they were preparing for the anniversary of 16 Pluviôse.

Gouly, deputy for the Île-de-France, played a key role. A covert supporter of slavery in Year II, he had protected himself by joining the Jacobin Club. Under the Thermidorian Convention, he vigorously attacked the deputies on the Left and the anti-slavers in the Convention. In particular, he secured the arrest of Levasseur de la Sarthe, who had played a major role in the session of 16 Pluviôse.

In November 1794, Gouly went public with his pro-slavery opinions, and presented the Committee on Colonies with a modification of the decree of 16 Pluviôse by proposing the umpteenth 'specific constitution' for the colonies. Since the colonial 'specificity' was slavery, it was an attempt to exempt the colonies where abolition had not taken effect from its application.[20] Gouly was thus following up the various proposals for a specific constitution for the colonies made by the pro-slavery colonists during the Constituent Assembly.

Belley, too, was preparing the anniversary of 16 Pluviôse, and proposed to bring abolition into effect wherever it had not yet been effected, accompanied by a land settlement to enable the new freedmen to provide for their own existence. Finally, he called for resources to prevent the pro-slavers from causing trouble.[21] Belley's proposals were a continuation of the policy pursued following 16 Pluviôse Year II by the *montagnard* Convention.

On the anniversary of 16 Pluviôse, there was an important debate in the Convention. The sitting began with the welcoming of a deputation of citizens of colour, who backed the measures proposed by Belley. Then there was a debate prepared by the Committee on the Colonies.

This debate deserves lengthy study, but here we shall focus on the following points. Gouly spoke at length to propose a forward colonialist policy towards the Mediterranean and India, with the aim of sharing the empire with England. He asked that the abolition of slavery not be implemented in the Indian Ocean islands, so as not to disturb them, since he saw them as the springboard for the conquest of India. But his proposal was not adopted.

As the debate continued, Gouly supported a curious measure: as regards the Indian Ocean islands, deputies should be sent bearing the Declaration of abolition, with the power to discuss it with the representatives of those islands. He insisted that these envoys act as 'conciliation commissioners', and not have effective means to enforce abolition, in order, he said, not to clash with prejudices.

The debate resumed on 12 February. The discussion got to the basic issue: Should the declaration of 16 Pluviôse be brought into force or not? If it was to be brought into force, then there was no point in sending 'conciliators', who might abandon abolition. Instead, responsible commissioners, with the task of supervising effective implementation of the decree, should be sent.

Finally, the Convention voted on three articles, the first two of which read:

Article 1. In accordance with the instructions which shall be given to the commissioners sent by the National Convention to the colonies, these commissioners shall not diverge from the principles which make the colonies an integral part of the one, indivisible and democratic French Republic.

Article 2. They shall not be able to change anything in the status of persons as fixed by the law of 16 Pluviôse in the colonies.

It will have been noted that Article 1 made the colonies an integral part of the Republic, which was new: this decree returned to a colonialist *politique de puissance* which was not envisaged by the Constitution of 1793. A page of the

Revolution was turned, and the concept of the one and indivisible republic here ceased to have the same content as in the previous period.

Furthermore, Article 2, adopted along with the others, made the Declaration of 16 Pluviôse subject to a new vote. But that Declaration formed part of the Constitution and thus had no need to be voted on again.

Voting was by roll call: of 482 voting, there were 304 ayes and 178 nays.[22]

Gouly's proposals were thus rejected. Yet this vote allowed the pro-slavers to express themselves 'freely' within the Convention, and that was serious. Despite the results of this vote, the Thermidorian Convention took no concrete action to pursue enforcement of the abolition of slavery.

* * *

This volume contains the essay by C. Wanquet on the despatch of two civil commissioners to carry the abolition decree to the Mascarenes, under the Directory in 1796. We cannot avoid commenting that this attempt, which failed, was offered as the application of Gouly's proposal to send 'negotiating' commissioners, that is ones who might decide to withdraw, rather than commissioners charged with bringing abolition into effect. The negotiators negotiated not with the interested parties – and with good reason, since slaves had neither civil nor political rights – nor a spokesman, but with the representatives of the colony, and they were the slave-owners. The negotiators did not press their point and slavery was maintained in the Mascarenes.

Gouly stands out as a politician skilful at proposing means of avoiding implementation of principles and laws. If the Directory did not insist on implementing the abolition decree, and was content with sending the two commissioners to take a trip in the Mascarenes, it was because by then the political will had changed, thereby laying the ground for the ultimate step of restoring slavery taken by Bonaparte in 1802.

Finally, let us note that it was under the Directory that the Saint-Domingue deputation saw its election annulled; the campaign by the pro-slavery lobby had succeeded on this point. (See the essay by B. Gainot in this volume for more on this point.)

The Colonialist Constitution of 1795: The Rights of Man in the North Overthrow Universal Rights

It is well known that after some hesitation, the Thermidorian Convention decided, following the popular uprisings of May 1795, to suppress the lawful Constitution of 1793, carrying out a parliamentary coup d'état. This operation involved the suppression of the Declaration of the Universal Rights of Man and the Citizen and universal suffrage and the return to an aggressive and colonialist *politique de puissance*.

In his report on the colonies presented on 4 July 1795, Boissy d'Anglas, the theoretician of this new Constitution, justified the restoration of a *politique de puissance* at length. This speech deserves a long analysis but here we shall highlight the following points. Boissy legitimized a policy of commercial domination and unequal exchange in the framework of the competitive system among European powers for world mastery.

He put forward the idea that freedom is not a universal right, but depended on the climate, and that the climate of the north is favoured: 'Nature had promised liberty to the north of this hemisphere, and it kept its word.'[23]

The north, according to Boissy, comprised Europe and the United States: their industry and needs required the subjection of colonies. Those colonies situated outside of the north were not fit for freedom or sovereignty because of the climate, and must therefore limit their ambitions to being wisely and peacefully governed by fair and humane men from the north:

> No people that is not essentially agricultural and warlike can retain its independence; but, if we consider the agreeable climate and the rich crops of our colonies, it will be judged that the men who live in them can be neither the one nor the other. They have been softened by the influence of a constant mild temperature; everything that might flatter the senses is abandoned by nature to their varied desires; almost without farming they harvest the richest gifts of the earth, and, far from aspiring to a liberty that it would cost them too much effort to retain, as it would to conquer, they sleep amid opulence and the pleasures that it procures them.... Such a people must therefore limit its wishes to being governed by humane and fair men, enemies of tyranny.

And as, according to Boissy, the French government is fair and humane, it will not restore slavery. The colonies will be subject to the same laws as the metropole. They will send deputies to sit in the metropolitan assembly. They will be divided into several departments, but will be provisionally administered on the spot by administrators appointed by the metropole: 'Thus you will give those parts of the French empire the certainty that they have never had, of being essentially assimilated to every other part of the Republic.'

We can see that Boissy was a major theoretician of the French colonialist national interest and assimilation,[24] which makes him a modern theoretician of assimilationist colonialism.

Boissy had thus replaced universal rights with a hierarchy among peoples and swept aside the postulate of the unity of the human species, in order to justify the return to a *politique de puissance*.

It will have been noted that the justification of inequality among peoples based on climate is at most a prejudice – or rather a vulgarity – and constitutes a regression when compared to what was demanded intellectually in Enlightenment thought.

For Boissy, the new hierarchy of the human species still stands in terms of the rights of man. But these new rights of man are reserved for the self-proclaimed fair and free part of governments in the north. Boissy replaces the pigmentational aristocracy of the colonial Ancien Régime with the aristocracy of the civilization of the north, charged with dominating and civilizing the rest of the world.

Boissy reveals to us here an interesting avatar in the history of the Rights of Man. Boissy counters the concept of universal rights not with the rights of the white man, but with the rights of the man of the north. He had thus territorialized – placed a geographical limit – on the concept of the rights of man, whereas in the philosophy of modern universal rights, at work in the Declarations of 1789 and 1793, rights are a property of the individual and the human race, not of a thing and not of a place.

* * *

These avatars of the history of the rights of man and the citizen enable us to ask questions about what we mean by modernity. What precisely is it?

The revolutions of the eighteenth century offer a wide range of different and contradictory experiences. Can we then speak of a single modernity?

Is it universal and mutual rights and the postulate of the unity of the human species?

Is it a matter of the rights of man of the north self-proclaimed by men of the north?

Is it a matter of suppressing the very words 'Rights of Man', as Bonaparte tried to do after 1802, and restoring slavery and colour prejudice in French constitutional law and the public law of Europe?

To what thoughts and what experiences is reference being made when we use this term 'modernity' in the singular? Modernity is not one, nor is history. And what is true of the single model of modernity is equally true of the single so-called French model.

This wide range of conflicting experiences once again poses a problem: they are all, equally, still happening today.

What is to be done?

Notes

1. On this subject, see C. L. R. James, *Les Jacobins noirs. Toussaint Louverture et la révolution de Saint-Domingue* (1938), rev. Fr. trans., 1983 [*The Black Jacobins* (1938), 2d rev. ed., New York, Vintage Books, 1963]; A. Césaire, *Toussaint Louverture. La Révolution française et le problème colonial*, Paris, Présence africaine, 1961; Y. Bénot, *La Révolution et la fin des colonies*, Paris, La Découverte, 1988.
2. On the power of anti-slavery philosophy, see A. Césaire, *Toussaint Louverture*; Y. Bénot, *La Révolution*, 'Introduction'.
3. *Le Moniteur*, 9 September 1792, session of the Legislative Assembly of 7 September. This Legion was raised on 6 December 1792, *Le Moniteur*, 8 December 1792.
4. *Le Moniteur*, 17 May 1793.
5. 'Adresse à la Convention', dated 17 May 1793 and published in Paris by Galletti, 15 pp., reprinted in *La Révolution française et l'abolition de l'esclavage*, Vol. 5, No. 3, Paris, E.D.H.I.S., 1968.
6. A. Aulard, *La Société des Jacobins*, No. 5, Paris, 1895, p. 227. The Jacobins' journal records that Marat and Robespierre were present at that session.

7. *Journal des débats*, No. 260, p. 51, reproduced in *Archives parlementaires*, Vol. 66, p. 56; *Le Moniteur*, 7 June 1793, gives a less complete version. This episode is mentioned in A. Césaire, *Toussaint Louverture*, p. 187, which was the first to use it. See also Y. Bénot, *La Révolution*, p. 171; L. Abénon, J. Cauna and L. Chauleau, *La Révolution aux Caraïbes*, Paris, Nathan, 1989, p. 115. On these episodes, see F. Gauthier, *Triomphe et mort du droit naturel en révolution*, Paris, P.U.F., 1992, pp. 228 et seq.

8. *Le Moniteur*, 12 and 14 June 1793. On the same day, 11 June, one of the signatories of the Address of 17 May, Labuissonière, was arrested, and Julien Raimond was denounced. The pro-slavery lobby was reacting to the anti-slavery campaign, which, as can be seen, was not easy to wage.

9. *Le Moniteur*, 15 June 1793. Commune of Paris. The Société des gens de couleur is present at the festival of 10 August 1793.

10. On this, see F. Gauthier, *Triomphe et mort*, Part 3, 'Une cosmopolitique de la liberté'.

11. A.N. DXXV 82, dossier 804, *Mémoire de J. Garnier, commissaire du pouvoir exécutif au siège du tribunal du Cap*, 7 November 1794, 34 pp. ms. See also the speech by Dufay, *Archives parlementaires*, Vol. 84, 'Convention, séance du 16 pluviôse an II (4 février 1794)', p. 277.

12. Since 1789, using means including violence, the pro-slavery colonists in Saint-Domingue had prohibited publication of the Declaration of the Rights of Man and the Citizen. The Address of 17 May mentioned this, as did J. Garnier. See also the proceedings of the colonial assemblies in Saint-Domingue.

13. Verbatim report of the election published in *Archives parlementaires*, Vol. 84, p. 265. See also J. Price Mars, 'Les origines et le destin d'un nom J. B. Belley Mars l'ancêtre', *Société haïtienne d'histoire* (Port-au-Prince), No. 36, 1940.

14. See F. Gauthier, *Triomphe et mort*, p. 228. See Y. Bénot, 'Comment la Convention a-t-elle voté l'abolition de l'esclavage en l'an II', and F. Gauthier, 'Inédits de Dufay, Santerre et L. Leblois au sujet de l'arrivée de la députation de Saint-Domingue à Paris', *Annales historiques de la Révolution française*, special issue on the colonies, 1993, pp. 349–61 and 514–18, respectively.

15. The deputation had clearly expressed as much even before 16 Pluviôse, in its letter to the Convention drafted at the time of its members' arrest the previous 31 January: 'For the rest, either the National Convention wants to admit the deputies from the colony of Saint-Domingue or it does not. If it does want to, we are in order. If it does not, it is not our fault if were appointed; let it leave us free and masters of our fate to go away, or rather let it have us taken home, since we only came for it', A.N. DXXV 57, dossier 563, published by F. Gauthier, 'Inédits de Dufay, Santerre et L. Leblois'.

16. *Archives parlementaires*, Vol. 84, 'Convention', pp. 276–83. A. Aulard, *La Société des Jacobins*, No. 5, p. 638: 'They presented the three-coloured flag on which were painted a black, a white and a mulatto.'

17. F. Gauthier, *Triomphe et mort*, pp. 239 et seq. It is therefore no longer possible to say that the *montagnard* Convention did nothing to implement the Declaration of 16 Pluviôse Year II. The most active members of the pro-slavery lobby in Paris were Page, Brulley, Larchevesque Thibaud, Verneuil, Millet, Clausson and Duny.

18. This same lobby had slandered Polverel and Sonthonax at the time of the *montagnard* Convention, accusing them of being linked to Brissot. Under the Thermidorian Convention, now that Robespierre had become the adversary, it adapted its accusations to this new situation. On all this section, see F. Gauthier, *Triomphe et mort*, Part 4, pp. 260–80.

19. Those who took part in this libellous campaign were the Saint-Domingue colonists Verneuil, Clausson, Millet, Duny and Larchevesque Thibaud. See A.N. ADXVIIIC 336, and the replies of Dufay, Belley and Leborgne. Voting for the accusers/accused commission took place on 30 September, and for the repeal of the decree of 9 March, on 17 November 1794.

20. A.N. ADXVIIIC 336, where are to be found Gouly's proposal and his 'Vues générales sur l'importance du commerce des colonies …', Belley's response, 'Le bout d'oreille des colons ou le système de l'hôtel de Massiac mis à jour par Gouly, par Belley député noir de Saint-Domingue'; DXXV 57, dossier 965, Dufay's response to Gouly, 'Encore une petite calomnie de Bazile Gouly'; and Dufay's response to the calumnies of Defrance and Gouly, 'Un représentant du peuple calomnié par un représentant du peuple calomniateur'. See also C. Wanquet, 'Un

'Jacobin' esclavagiste, Benoît Gouly', *Annales historiques de la Révolution française*, special issue on the colonies, 1993.

21. Belley, 'Le bout d'oreille des colons ou le système de l'hôtel Massiac mis à jour par Gouly', p. 8, which can be dated to late November 1794.

22. *Le Moniteur*, 139, pp. 385–90; 140, pp. 455–60; 141, p. 471.

23. *Le Moniteur*, 322, session of the Convention of 4 August 1795. Boissy's climate theory must not be confused with Montesquieu's. Without going into detail, it will be remembered that Montesquieu refers to a universal natural right attaching to the person, unlike Boissy, and that he does not justify European *politiques de puissance*, nor commercial domination, nor unequal exchange. See V. Bertand, 'La conception du commerce dans l'esprit des lois de Montesquieu', *Annales Historiques de la Révolution française*, No. 3, 1987, pp. 266–90.

24. Father Maury, a leading light on the Right in the Constituent Assembly, was also a theoretician of assimilation in the framework of a pro-slavery colonialist policy. Boissy, although not pro-slavery, had a hierarchical view of peoples in 1795, and denied freedom, economic independence and sovereignty except to those in the north. The thought of the Rights of Man opened a breach in these justifications of European *politiques de puissance*, by preparing the concepts of the universal natural right of individuals, the right of peoples to sovereignty and the law of nations. It seems to us that the interest of the revolutions of the Rights of Man and the Citizen lies precisely in their attempts to widen that breach, and realize those rights. But Boissy opposed universal rights, although his conception of a non-slave assimilation created such an illusion. This is what Aimé Césaire says on this point: 'Assimilationism is an outdated doctrine to be locked away in the property-room. There is no left assimilationism, since no doctrine or practice which removes whole peoples from history and returns them to anonymity could be a left doctrine or practice. Our age is the age of identity rediscovered, the age of difference acknowledged, of difference mutually agreed, and because it has been agreed, one that can be overcome in complementarity, which, I hope, makes possible solidarity and a new fraternity.' Speech to the French National Assembly, 29 September 1982.

Chapter 15

The Constitutionalization of General Freedom under the Directory

Bernard Gainot

The Laborious Materialization of a Principle

The evolution of the colonies 'retained' by France after 1793–4 (essentially Saint-Domingue and Guadeloupe, the Mascarenes and Cayenne, with which we shall not deal in this essay) had a dynamic of its own that had very little to do with what was happening in the metropole. Yet this latter was to attempt to seize back the initiative through centralized management of the colonial bureau in the Ministry of the Navy and the Colonies, and also by gradually shifting the monitoring of information and operations from the Executive to the Legislative Body, a shift which, once completed, was supposed to ensure constitutional normality.

In this gap between what was happening in the colonies and central decision-making, the fate was played out of the universalist project of the Republic under the Directory, an integrative and voluntarist project that denied all differences, whether 'pigmentational aristocracies' or sociocultural particularisms. This project was not something just dreamed up for the occasion, but rather the concrete manifestation of the objectives of a whole political culture deriving largely, but not only, from the Enlightenment; we shall not deal here with that problematic.[1]

For knowledge of this period we are largely dependent on the sources constituted by the Ministry of the Navy and the Colonies, and reports from the committees of legislative bodies.[2] These series must be treated with caution; they give information on the opposing pressure groups seeking to influence official colonial policy. They do not provide us with first-hand information about the local situation; knowledge of that can be gained only through studies based on fieldwork, such as those of Anne Pérotin-Dumon on Guadeloupe[3] and Claude Wanquet on the Mascarenes,[4] or the article by Sabine Manigat on the concrete content of general freedom under the regime of Toussaint Louverture.[5] All of these viewpoints open up wholly novel perspectives on what was actually happening in the de facto self-governing areas which grew in strength in the colonies under the Directory, and constitute, as it were, the backcloth that explains the contradictions of official policy. The problems that they raise will not be dealt with as such.

Rather, in this essay, we shall limit ourselves to stressing the close inter-relationship between the debate over the colonies and the course of general policy. Far from being marginal, the debate over the colonies was highly relevant to the central workings of the republican state. It also played a key role in defining the values and arguments employed by the cultural intermediaries who shaped public opinion.

In order to fuel this debate and improve its decision-making, the government's first priority was to obtain information. But it was also very hesitant as to the best action to take to ensure post-Revolutionary stability.

A Disputed Heritage (1795–1797)

The National Convention bequeathed to the Directory several broad guidelines for determining a line of conduct in colonial affairs. These were universal principles, such as equality of political rights with no regard to pigmentation, and the decree of 16 Pluviôse Year II on general freedom, which was declared to apply to the whole territory of the Republic. This declaration of universal principles was regarded as inseparable from the military victories that had made it possible, at least in part, to hold on to the colonies. And that alone meant that the action of commissioners Sonthonax and Polverel in 1793 was justified. Garran-Coulon's major report, presented in the name of the Committees of Public Safety, the Navy and the Colonies combined, portrayed the commissioners and the 'regenerated' republican army as the real defenders of the Declaration of the Rights of Man and the Citizen, whereas hitherto they had been accused of having deliberately spread ruin and massacres.[6]

In the name of the Committee of Public Safety, Defermon, speaking before the Convention, lauded the 'men who were friends of freedom', who had succeeded in restoring the situation in the island. His eulogy embraced Laveaux, the acting Governor General; his chief mulatto assistants, Vilatte, military commander at Le Cap, Beauvais, military commander in the south-west and André Rigaud, military commander in the southern peninsula; and the black General Toussaint Louverture, military commander of the centre-west. Laveaux had ensured the promotion of all his military assistants; these promotions were confirmed by the Committee of Public Safety. The action taken by the commissioners was also justified, while the colonists were treated like the former feudal lords:

> If we are asked what is the public spirit of the colony, we would reply: where your decree on the freedom of blacks is not carried into effect, the republic is unappreciated, and the British or the Spanish predominate; and the colonists have preferred to throw themselves under a foreign tyranny rather than give up possession of slaves.[7]

According to Defermon, the justification for the proclamation of general freedom by the commissioners lay far beyond mere military necessities. Far from ruining the economy of the Antilles, the economy had been 'regenerated' by the introduction of free labour:

> Let there be no more talk of the necessity of slavery for agriculture. Several estates have continued or resumed their work under the law of freedom, with no other difference than in how what they produce is shared, with cultivators now receiving a quarter, whereas before their master took no account of their toil.[8]

This version of the facts angered the defenders of the colonists, who did not accept the decree of 16 Pluviôse. Their spokesmen were essentially two deputies from the Île-de-France, Serres and Gouly,[9] who were key members of the colonial committee of the Convention in Year II. They used the tactic that had once been used by Page and Brulley; those ardent pro-slavers had not scrupled to pass themselves off as equally ardent Jacobins, in order to secure the condemnation of Brissot and other abolitionists, such as Milscent, Leborgne and Sonthonax, in the spring of 1794.[10] Now that Jacobinism was no longer the official rhetoric, Gouly, who was also an active agent of Thermidorian reaction in the Ain, applied this official rhetoric to the particular cause of the white planters. According to him, Laveaux and his henchmen were no more than 'zealous agents of tyranny'; as for Serres, much less self-controlled, he could not envisage 'Africans' being French citizens.[11]

For the time being, Serres's and Gouly's protests remained isolated. The Defermon report served as a reference point in the years that followed; blacks and men of colour deserved well of the fatherland, which, in addition, had a 'debt of humanity' towards them. To restore the previous prosperity, free labour was the solution that reconciled principles and efficiency; complete fusion, the assimilation of the metropole and its colonies was the ultimate aim of 'regeneration'. This programme was to be found in the Constitution of Year III: unity of the Republic,[12] the guarantor of general freedom.[13]

The largest and most influential colonial deputation, the one from Saint-Domingue, was itself living evidence and the repository of such principles. By its presence since Pluviôse Year II, it symbolized the integration of the 'regenerated people' into the Republic; in its three-coloured composition – whites, mulattoes and blacks – it represented equality of rights.

A first warning shot shook this harmonious structure: on 30 Ventôse Year IV (20 March 1796), at Le Cap, the mulatto General Vilatte rebelled against Laveaux's authority. The governor restored the situation with the help of the black troops of Toussaint Louverture, whom he rewarded by making him his immediate military assistant.[14]

The commissioners delegated by the Directory, on the recommendation of Truguet, the Minister of the Navy[15] (Sonthonax, Leblanc, Giraud and Julien Raimond), arrived shortly after and approved Laveaux's conduct and Toussaint's promotion, thereby alienating the mulatto generals, and especially André Rigaud.[16]

The Directory transmitted the documents relating to the Le Cap affair to the Council of Five Hundred. A commission with Marec as rapporteur accepted that Sonthonax and his colleagues had been right to approve the conduct of Laveaux, the representative of legitimate metropolitan authority, of which Toussaint was, as it were, the 'protector'.[17]

The Marec commission presented its report on 11 Ventôse Year V (1 March 1797). A few months later, the new Legislative Body that emerged from the elections of Year V again threatened to upset the balance of official policy, which had been so laboriously restored.

The majority of the Legislative Body were advocates of the reactionary theses of the Clichy Club.[18] Among its main leaders, Viénot-Vaublanc, Barbé-Marbois, Villaret de Joyeuse and Bourdon de l'Oise were advocates of ending the official colonial policy laid down in 1795. These leading figures of the constitutional right made absolutely no distinction between their offensive against Revolutionary legislation and their determination to restore the colonies to their pre-Revolutionary order and prosperity. Most historians have not sufficiently stressed this fact, and have neglected the colonial dimension, which was fundamental to the crisis of 1797.[19]

The Clichy Club's attack focused on the following points. The main target was the Minister of the Navy and the Colonies, Truguet, who was a staunch advocate of implementing the official programme in the colonies. The members of the Clichy Club accused him of withholding information and of allowing only the Legislative Body and public opinion to know about the reports from the commissioners and Laveaux, which gave a falsely optimistic picture of the situation in Saint-Domingue. The secondary targets were thus those same commissioners, who they insisted be recalled to France. Such was the intent of the major speech made by Vaublanc on 10 Prairial Year V (29 May 1797).[20] The commissioners were 'insolent satraps' (Doulcet had described them as 'plagues on the colony'):

> By these features you will have no difficulty in recognizing those patriots of the moment, those philanthropists, those advocates of public happiness....[21] Wretched people athirst for pillage, and equally avid for murder, they have made the Revolution a game of chance; of the Republic, a woman for sale; of the property of others, a prey on which they fall from all sides, in all shapes.

Laveaux was not spared; he had handed the colony over to 'military anarchy', where the 'white race was outlawed'. Laveaux was 'one of those who has most contributed to giving the Negroes the spirit of insubordination and licence'. Toussaint, on the other hand, was not attacked directly, but that is because the whole of Vaublanc's speech was shot through with deep racial contempt,[22] which denied that 'Negroes' (*nègres,* as he called them) had any autonomy of thought or action ('the Negroes must be wrenched from their own furies' by disarming them and returning them to the estates). The time had not yet come in 1797 to call for the repeal of the decree of 16 Pluviôse; rather, it was the time for indirect attacks, for tactical undermining.

This meant justifying the 'rebel' colonial assemblies in the Mascarenes which had expelled Baco and Burnel, the agents of the Directory, who had come to ensure application there of the 'fatal decree' of 16 Pluviôse.[23] This expulsion occurred on 3 Messidor Year IV (21 June 1796), but the distance meant that full information came to the knowledge of the Legislative Body only at the time of the debate in the spring of 1797. It was an affair that hugely embarrassed many members of the Clichy Club, especially Villaret-Joyeuse, who had pleaded for a policy of intimidating the black 'rebels' in Saint-Domingue. But he was closely linked by bonds of interest and conviction to the white 'rebels' in the Indian Ocean, and, of course, did not advocate any forceful action against them. The context was not yet ripe for the brutal admission that the only way out of the contradiction was to abrogate the troublesome decree of 16 Pluviôse and restore a strict racial hierarchy.

Tactically, then, since the moment had not yet come for a radical redirection of colonial strategy, the members of the Clichy Club would support the group of mulatto officers who had rebelled against the civil commissioners and against Laveaux. Vilatte, whose release they called for; and André Rigaud, whose emissaries they warmly welcomed, prominent among them being Pierre Pinchinat.[24]

On 24 Germinal Year V (13 April 1797), the report of the commission of enquiry into the disturbances at Le Cap the previous year, of which Blad was rapporteur, concluded that those disturbances were the result of a 'popular riot', and not of a 'conspiracy', which marked a shift in Vilatte's direction compared to the conclusions of the Marec report. The individuals arrested and detained at Rochefort for their involvement in this affair now therefore came under the civil tribunals, and not the military commissions.[25]

But, still indirectly related to the support for the demands of the mulattoes, it was above all the problem of the representation of Saint-Domingue in the Legislative Body that polarized debates. It was a very complex problem, which is the subject of a separate study that I shall not repeat here.[26]

Several rival deputations claimed the right to be seated. Two deputations had been elected at Le Cap for the North Province of Saint-Domingue, one in Year IV, around Laveaux, Sonthonax and Brothier,[27] the other in Year V, which included people close to Sonthonax (Mentor, Leborgne, Vergniaud and Tonnelier).[28] Each of these two deputations claimed to represent the whole colony alone, something which other deputies elected in South and West Provinces, notably Pierre Pinchinat and Rey-Delmas, contested.[29]

The main aim of the members of the Clichy Club was to secure the rejection of the credentials of the deputies from North Province of Saint-Domingue, either by stressing the unconstitutionality of the vote,[30] or by taking up the arguments of other deputations to the effect that the votes at Le Cap were the result of terrorism by both black troops and Sonthonax's men.[31] They got what they wanted on 8 Ventôse Year V (26 February 1797), when Doulcet de Pontécoulant, in the name of a special commission, secured the adoption by the Council of Five Hundred of a resolution which 'declared null and void all the nominations made by an alleged electoral assembly held in Saint-Domingue on

21 Fructidor Year IV'. This resolution was confirmed by the Council of Ancients on 11 Germinal Year V (31 March 1797).

Very few representatives tried to block this attack, which threatened to have serious consequences for the fate of the colonies. Joseph Eschassériaux pleaded for a sweeping amnesty and rapid implementation of the constitution of Year III.[32] Garran-Coulon recalled that the Convention had already discussed the same topics, and that it had approved Sonthonax. As for Quirot, he complained that in the speeches by members of the Clichy Club, all he could hear were echoes of the grievances of the white colonists, in whom he had absolutely no confidence, and he would very much like to hear 'other arguments'.[33]

Did the debate of May–June 1797 have any impact on public opinion, outside the Legislative Body and individuals who had – or had had – material interests in the colonies?

The press was not indifferent to colonial questions. A paper as representative of the Clichy school as the *Journal de Perlet* gave wide coverage to colonial debates, waged an active campaign for the recall of the civilian commissioners, vigorously and deliberately backed Villaret-Joyeuse, and was pleased by the departure of Minister Truguet at the end of Messidor Year V.[34] Those opposed to the Clichy Club were represented by *Le Républicain des Colonies*, belonging to Bottu, of whom we have made a special study.[35] This paper specialized in colonial questions, but it did not shrink from taking a stand on significant questions that were engaging the public at the same time; for example, it defended political clubs, which, under the name of 'constitutional circles', were endeavouring to resist the right-wing offensive. But, in the current state of our research, we have not been able to find any allusions to the maintenance of general freedom in the addresses from these circles, which would make it possible to link them to the messages of congratulations sent to the Convention by the people's clubs after the decree of 16 Pluviôse, studied by Jean-Claude Halpern.[36] Support for Bottu's positions came essentially from Truguet, who took out 600 subscriptions to the *Républicain des Colonies*, if we are to believe Vaublanc, who denounced the fact vehemently at a sitting of the Council of Five Hundred.[37]

Shortly afterward, on 30 Messidor Year V, Truguet was replaced by Pléville-Lepelley, a minister fully in favour of restoring the pre-Revolutionary status quo in the colonies, who took as head of the colonial bureau Lescallier, former Civil Commissioner in Réunion. The latter drafted the ministerial report which completely exonerated the colonial assemblies responsible for the expulsion of Baco and Burnel.[38] Moreover, in the course of the summer of 1797, the supporters of restoring the pre-1793 colonial order seemed to have won all along the line. Laveaux, who had arrived in France and was endeavouring to justify his conduct,[39] resigned himself to the fact that his conduct would not be endorsed: he asked for a command in a home division.[40]

On 3 Messidor Year V (21 June 1797), on a proposal by Bourdon de l'Oise, a new government agency was appointed for Saint-Domingue, headed by a single commissioner, General Hédouville, a compromise candidate between the Directors and the majority of the Councils. Bourdon urged that Hédouville should be accompanied by an impressive military armed force 'in order to restore order and tranquillity there'.[41] Meanwhile, implementation of the constitution was suspended, which was in accordance with the views expressed by Villaret-Joyeuse.

The departure of Truguet, hostile to such a compromise, was predictable. Bottu protested against this underhand way of subjecting Saint-Domingue to 'military despotism' in the last issue of his paper.[42] Everything was now in place that would lead to the forced departure of Sonthonax, to Toussaint's and Rigaud's increasing mistrust of everything that came from the metropole, to the consolidation of autonomous rule.

In all this, the coup d'état of 18 Fructidor Year V thus appears as a quite unforeseeable twist in a crisis that had seemed resolved for two months to the advantage of the supporters of a colonial restoration and the opponents of general freedom. These latter, led by Vaublanc and Villaret-Joyeuse, were included in the outlawing of the deputies belonging to the Clichy Club. One of the very first series of measures adopted by those who had defeated them was to convene a colonial commission which reversed the course of events: admitting the deputies from northern Saint-Domingue, first and foremost Laveaux and Sonthonax (who was by then at sea, in complete ignorance of the outlawing of his enemies); implementing as speedily as possible the constitutional order in the colonies; rejecting the military solution for Saint-Domingue. Joseph Eschassériaux was made rapporteur of this commission on 25 Fructidor Year V (11 September 1797), just a week after the coup d'état.[43]

General Freedom and National Autonomies: Law and Reality (1797–1799)

Étienne Laveaux was now the voice of the official colonial line, which simply took up the principles that were set out in 1795 and then implemented by Truguet: the colonies were 'integral parts' of the Republic; they were subject to the same laws; this 'integration' was the best possible guarantee that general freedom would be maintained.

Laveaux set out this doctrine at the tribune of the Council of Ancients, on his admission to the Legislative Body, on the third complementary day of Year V (19 September 1797). It was a speech suited to the occasion, in which Vaublanc, the head of the 'royal faction', was sharply denounced, and the day of 18 Fructidor was deemed to ensure that the decree of 16 Pluviôse would remain in force. But it was also a policy speech; Laveaux once again justified the work of 'regeneration' that had been accomplished, by violent methods ('the colony will only know peace when all those who detest freedom and equality have been removed from it', he had written in 1795).[44] But it was time now to set up the representative system in Saint-Domingue, that is establish institutions that reflected the new realities and gave the new freedmen the possibility of becoming full citizens. Finally, Laveaux sought to justify the conduct of Toussaint Louverture, to whom he paid warm tribute and whose loyalty to the Republic he guaranteed, but he also justified the conduct of Sonthonax, of whose expulsion by Toussaint Laveaux was at that time unaware.

In the months that followed, the legislative programme proceeded as Laveaux had set it out. At the end of 1797, organic articles provided for both the 'departmentalization' of the colonies and the irreversibility of the abolition of slavery throughout the territory of the Republic.[45] The adoption of these organic articles, and especially of Title III ('Of the state and the rights of citizens'), owed much to the opinions of Laveaux, such as they emerge from his speech that accompanied the presentation of this bill. It involved spelling out the implications of Article 9 of Title II of the Constitution on 'the political state of citizens', which granted the right of citizenship to those who had defended the fatherland.[46] Until then, the army had been the sole path to social advancement for blacks. It is significant in this respect that the three blacks who sat in the assemblies of the Republic should all have been soldiers.[47] But Laveaux advocated a significant extension of the right of citizenship to include 'cultivators':

> This Article 9 cited is only in favour of those who have fought in one or more campaigns for the establishment of freedom; that might suggest that all blacks who are cultivators are not citizens.
>
> Let there be no more uncertainty, citizen representatives, if you wish to establish peace and domestic tranquillity; no more uncertainty as to the political status of black citizens. Has not the cultivator rendered himself as useful as the black who has borne arms? With what would the army have been fed if no one had wanted to cultivate the land? France sent nothing to the colony of Saint-Domingue: if we agree that the status of cultivator is harmful for Europeans, let us honour this status to encourage blacks to continue it.[48]

To support his arguments, Laveaux was here putting himself on the same ground as those who suggested that France's commercial interest assumed that the status of 'cultivator' (the agricultural labourer in the plantation system) was incompatible with the granting of political rights to those same workers. But he was also taking a stand in terms of justice and the moral contract binding the 'new freedmen' to the people of the metropole. After advancing arguments designed to appeal to metropolitan merchants, Laveaux spoke in the name of the 'new people', whom he also saw himself as representing:

> Today now that the laws give us back control over ourselves, today now that, like the French in Europe, we have conquered our freedom, we ask you for payment for all the time that we have worked for you, we claim compensation for all the ill-treatment that we have experienced.[49]

But there were divergences. To establish his authority more firmly and to ensure the realization of the programme that he deemed he had been mandated to apply on his election in Saint-Domingue, Laveaux presented himself as the spokesman of a united parliamentary group, and the privileged link with the colony. He was less successful in this than he was in his legislative achievement, yet the one was the condition of the success of the other.

The parliamentary group had been elected solely by the electoral assemblies in the north of Saint-Domingue, and was made up of twelve representatives following the admission of Étienne Mentor to the Council of Five Hundred, which occurred only on 12 Prairial Year VI.[50] It was thus only in May 1798 that the situation was fully regularized; several legislative commissions had worked on the electoral files. Among the members of these commissions were Garran-Coulon, Joseph Eschassériaux, Quirot, Dabray, Cholet (but also Monmayou, Blad, Chamborre, Guillemardet, Oudot, Humbert of the Meuse, Leclerc of Maine-et-Loire and Duport). Cholet presented a summary report in the name of these commissions, 'on the elections held in Year IV in the two divisions of the south and west of Saint-Domingue, and on the elections in the colony for Year V' (BN, Conseil des Cinq-Cents, Floréal Year VI Lc(43)1929-990). Its symbolic unity was reflected in its three-coloured composition: five whites (Laveaux, Sonthonax, Vergniaud, Brothier, Leborgne), four mulattoes (Boisrond, Tonnelier, Thomany, Petitniaud) and two blacks (Mentor and Annecy). But this symbolic unity was profoundly undermined by divergences arising from the clash between Toussaint and Sonthonax in the summer of 1797.

The deputation stubbornly continued to defend general freedom, but the existence of a group hostile to Toussaint Louverture around Sonthonax, Leborgne, Mentor, Vergniaud and Thomany became more and more apparent. The attacks were allusive but convergent. 'However strongly I may repudiate the calumnies directed against black republicans and republicans of colour, I am far from excusing the serious errors that some of us have committed',[51] warned Mentor. And Thomany was even stronger a little later:

> It pains me to admit that there are men among the freed caste who have shown themselves little worthy of their new estate; there are some who, in positions of command, have shown contempt for national authority and have abused it unceremoniously.[52]

Sonthonax was much more direct in his denunciations. He portrayed himself as the victim of 'a plot hatched by priests and émigrés, of whom Toussaint Louverture was the instrument', more manipulated than instigator of the revolt against the national government: 'Made to be governed, his fate is to be subject to an external control. His superstitious and unenlightened conscience has made him dependent on counter-revolutionary priests who, in Saint-Domingue, as in France, are using every means to overthrow freedom.'[53]

Such stands led to friction with the other group that had remained loyal to Toussaint. Brothier even sought to oppose Mentor's admission to the Council of Five Hundred, which earned him an accusation of racism from Mentor: '[F]rom the way in which citizen Brothier spoke to the Council of Ancients, on the 15th of this month, against the admission of black deputies to the Legislative Body, one might believe that Vaublanc and his faction still reigned over the two Councils, in order to keep republicans from the Antilles out of it and "black men" in particular.'[54]

Laveaux (and Annecy, to a lesser extent) was still trying to arbitrate between the two 'factions'; his peers still continued to regard him as the essential link between Saint-Domingue and Paris. In Pluviôse Year VII, symbolically, when Jean-Louis Annecy was secretary of the Council of Ancients, he made the speech for the anniversary of the decree of 16 Pluviôse.[55] It was a plea for the total integration of the colonies into the Republic, and it was also a ringing eulogy of Toussaint Louverture.

Yet Laveaux's stock was falling. Toussaint was distancing himself since he would have liked Laveaux to cut himself off completely from Sonthonax and his group, and marginalize his influence, making up for having failed to obtain his removal as he had hoped by having him embark in Fructidor Year V.[56] Toussaint sought to diversify his contacts, either by establishing direct relations with the Ministry of the Navy through his secretary, Guybre, or the director of artillery of Saint-Domingue, Colonel Vincent, or by opening up politically. His concern was not to present a 'partisan' image in order to avoid once again being surprised and destabilized by an attack such as the one launched by the Clichy Club in 1797. Thus, he was happy to accept the deputy of Ille-et-Vilaine, Rallier, a conservative republican closely associated with commercial interests in the Atlantic ports, as his relay in the Legislative Body. Was this reorientation a consequence of the opinions in his entourage made up of counter-revolutionary whites, as Sonthonax thought? Whether or not that is true, Toussaint did not hesitate to revive against the former civil commissioner the accusations and stratagems used by the Clichy Club against the 'Robespierre of the Antilles'.[57]

Was the colonial question once again a political issue at the end of the Directory? It seems not; at least, the positions were less clear-cut than they had been in the spring of 1797. The cleavages had more to do with persons than principles. And yet these personal rivalries were to have considerable consequences, in the medium term, for the maintenance of general freedom.

Now that the institutional framework seemed to be established, the serious debates of the period 1797–9 are altogether fascinating, because they lay the bases for a long-term reorientation of colonial policy,[58] whether in the entourage of Minister of Foreign Affairs Talleyrand, in the intellectual circles of the 'Décade philosophique' and the Institut, or with the project that was taking shape in the winter of 1799 for establishing a Société des Amis des Noirs et des Colonies.[59] At two meetings, this society brought together about forty individuals in the office of Granet, head of the colonial division of the Navy Bureau, with figures representing very different schools of thought: Father Grégoire, Sonthonax, Jean-Baptiste Say and, above all, Wadstrom, who seems indeed to have the been the figure who was holding the group together.[60] But it was above all the presence of Sonthonax at the second meeting that precipitated the crisis, provoking the expulsion of the society from the Ministry buildings and engendering the very bitter resentment that Toussaint was to show towards Father Grégoire.[61]

Sonthonax was by then a leading figure in the democratic opposition to the second Directory. He was even the most influential figure in it, if we are to believe the reports of British secret agents, which mention Mentor and the 'Swede' Arkstrom (*sic*, for Wadstrom) among the members of a club number-ing four hundred members and led by Antonelle and Félix Le Peletier in the winter of 1799.[62] During the summer of 1799, Mentor was writing in the *Jour-nal des Hommes Libres de tous les pays*, the organ of the neo-Jacobin movement. In it, he denounced Toussaint in particular for having signed a commercial agreement with the British Major Maitland, which Mentor saw as treason.[63]

The *Journal des Hommes libres* sometimes reported colonial problems but these were not really a key issue, since the situation was very confused and nothing was clear-cut. Of course, there would be ritual reaffirmations that blacks and men of colour were French citizens, and the 'rebel' colonists of the Île-de-France would be lambasted, but major questions were raised by the arrival of news from Saint-Domingue: the agreements with the British and the Americans, and the growing tensions between Rigaud and Toussaint.

Victor Hugues was suggested for the Ministry of the Navy at one point, but the paper did not insist on it. Conversely, it expressed satisfaction at Bottu's appointment to the post of assistant to Granet, evidence that the bat-tles fought by the *Républicain des Colonies* in 1797 were known to and shared by the democrats.[64]

Laveaux linked up with Sonthonax, Mentor and Leborgne in the Club du Manège in July 1799. When the existence of this club was threatened by the revisionists, he firmly stood by the political clubs in the Council of Ancients.[65] A certain form of political solidarity had been preserved down to this time between the two great currents inside the deputation, although the differences over how to assess developments in Saint-Domingue (and also in Guadeloupe, where Laveaux distanced himself from the stewardship of Victor Hugues, who was recalled to France in 1798) were getting deeper and deeper. The heirs of the Clichy Club of 1797 took no account of such divergences and continued to treat with the same contempt all those advocating the colonial policy of integration through maintaining general freedom. Also, the *Dictionnaire des jacobins vivans,* which appeared in Hamburg in September 1799 lumped together Laveaux, Sonthonax and Mentor among the 'fierce tigers' and the 'cannibals' who had laid waste the colonies.[66]

During the summer of 1799, the authorities undeniably moved closer to the positions of Sonthonax and his group. Proof of that is the report of the Min-ister of the Navy of 1 Fructidor Year VII (18 August 1799).[67] This report was the work of Granet, the head of the colonial division, as Minister Bourdon-Vatry had only just taken office. It admitted that 'anarchy' had been spreading more and more widely since Sonthonax's departure:

> Among not the least active causes of General Hédouville's departure was the sort of triumph that those who boasted of having forced citizen Sonthonax to flee the colony himself had been allowed to enjoy. Party spirit, ever blind in its vengeance, saw in this former agent only the man, the constant object of its hatred and its calumnies; it closed its eyes to the insult done in his person to the legal repre-sentative of the French government; it did not see, or did not want to see, that its

ill-considered applause encouraged others to give any of his successors who sought to free themselves from the yoke and passions of those in dominant positions the same treatment as Sonthonax had received.[68]

The report went on to be more moderate in its appreciation of the Toussaint-Maitland agreements. It refused to speak of treason, and noted that 'several honourable citizens' (Laveaux's reputation with the ministry was still wholly intact, but this may also refer to Rallier) had defended Sonthonax's conduct. But, as regards the looming confrontation between Rigaud and Toussaint, the choice was clear, and wholly reflected the parallel evolution of the Sonthonax-Leborgne-Mentor group in favour of the mulattoes. Rigaud was assuredly the man in the colony on whom the Executive Directory could at this point count most surely and most effectively.[69]

And it was just now that Laveaux decided to distance himself, literally as well as figuratively, from official policy. He had asked to be one of the 'three agents known for their attachment to general freedom' sent to the Antilles in accordance with the law of 12 Nivôse Year VI. He published yet another justification of Toussaint Louverture's conduct before his departure; significantly, he did not choose the democratic *Journal des Hommes Libres*, then being targeted by the police, but the very conservative *Publiciste*.[70]

Yet Laveaux would not see Toussaint again; the destination of his mission was changed and in the end he headed for Guadeloupe.[71] What was the reason for this change? Was it due to interventions by Toussaint, who could not face the prospect of having to face a man for whom he had felt (and perhaps still felt) real affection? Was it due to a shift of opinion in the Ministry, which, in the context of a clear choice in favour of Rigaud, did not look kindly on its chief agent's sympathies for his opponent?

Conclusion

From now on, division and mistrust gripped the supporters of general freedom. Through the breaches thus opened, the protagonists in the 1797 debate rushed, now assured that time was on their side, the coup d'état of Brumaire having removed all doubts about unitary constitutionalism. (The Constitution of Year VIII made the colonies separate territories to be governed by 'special laws'.) This marked the victory of those who had long advocated the restoration of the pre-Revolutionary colonial order.

Conscious of the fragility of the new colonial order that had emerged from the decree of 16 Pluviôse, the abolitionists could not but see it as fitting into metropolitan attempts at stabilization; they were therefore assimilationists, because, according to them, only a single path for access to a higher stage of development existed for all the peoples on earth.

Thus, the metropolitan political debate was enriched by what was happening in the colonies with such an intensity that in 1797 what was at stake was as vital as in the first years of the Revolution. But the supporters of general freedom posed the problem at the level of general principles, without fully taking account of changes in the relations of force on the ground, or in the means of applying those principles.

The revelation of such a gap first caused concern and then paralysis and allowed the restoration of slavery in 1802. Far from being a logical conclusion, marked out since 1795, that restoration cannot be understood in isolation from the confrontation between parties, the clash between egalitarian expectations and the nostalgia of lost interests.

Notes

1. This problematic is developed at length in Yves Bénot's *La Révolution française et la fin des colonies*, Paris, Éditions La Découverte, 1988, which gives the period of the Directory its due place, in which many 'Revolutionary' historians skip lightly from 1794 or 1795 to 1802 or 1804. Those who argue that the metropolitan positions were opportunistic draw in varying degrees on the argument advanced by Louis Sala-Molins in *Le Code Noir*, Paris, P.U.F., 1987: '[S]word in hand, the blacks braved the Republic, which had not planned anything for them except for maintaining under inherited shackles the tyranny of the Capets' (p. 262).

2. In the French Archives Nationales, AFIII 207–10; papers of the Colonial Bureau of the Ministry – fonds 'colonies', series CC/9/A/10–27; correspondence between the colonial authorities, between the executive Directory and its local agents. memorials and petitions, etc. Série C (papers of the Revolutionary assemblies) was also consulted; the files of the rapporteurs of the committees of the Council of Five Hundred on colonial affairs (Marec, Eschassériaux, Viénot-Vaublanc, Sonthonax, Laveaux, Villaret-Joyeuse, etc.) were consulted in the Rondonneau collection [AD XVIII(a) – opinions and speeches of deputies]. The Ministry of War also contains important sources for the period of the Directory; in the archives at Vincennes, we particularly consulted the personal files of senior officers such as Desfourneaux, Laveaux or Pageot; the papers of the expedition to Saint-Domingue [B 7(1)], and a number of memorials which present proposals for recovering the colony of Saint-Domingue in the 'Mémoires et reconnaissances' collection.

3. Anne Pérotin-Dumon, 'La Convention et le Directoire à la Guadeloupe, 1793–1799); la rencontre du fait révolutionnaire et du fait colonial', *Bulletin de la Société d'Histoire de la Guadeloupe*, 1970.

4. Claude Wanquet, *Histoire d'une révolution: la Réunion; 1789–1803*, 3 Vols, Marseilles, Jeanne Laffitte, 1984; and idem, 'Révolution et 'créolité': l'exemple des Mascareignes', paper for the world colloquy for the bicentenary (Paris, 1989), *L'image de la Révolution française*, ed. M. Vovelle, Vol. 2, pp. 952–62, Paris, Pergamon Press, 1989.

5. Sabine Manigat, 'Les fondements sociaux de l'État louverturien', paper for the international colloquy at Port-au-Prince, *La Révolution française et Haïti* (September 1989); and idem, 'Qu'est-ce que la liberté générale en 1793?' *Annales historiques de la Révolution française*, special issue, 'Révolution et colonies', July–December 1993, pp. 363–72.

6. 'Rapport officiel sur les troubles de Saint-Domingue fait au nom de la commission des colonies, des Comités de salut public, de législation and de marine réunies' by Garran de Coulon (Imprimerie Nationale, Years V–VII, 1797–8), 4 Vols [BN, Le (38) 1729].

7. *Le Moniteur*; report of the settings of the National Convention of 5 Thermidor Year III (Reprint, Vol. 25, p. 316).

8. Ibid.

9. On Benoît Gouly, see Claude Wanquet, 'Un 'jacobin esclavagiste, Benoît Gouly' *Annales historiques de la Révolution française*, special issue, 'Révolution et colonies', July–December 1993, pp. 445–68.

10. Yves Bénot, *La Révolution française et la fin des colonies*, Patis, Éditions la Découverte, 1988, Chapter 7; Florence Gauthier, *Triomphe et mort du droit naturel en révolution: 1789, 1795, 1802*, Paris, P.U.F., 1992.
11. *Le Moniteur*, op. cit.
12. Title I, Article 6: 'The French colonies are an integral part of the Republican, and are subject to the same constitutional law.'
13. Title III, Article 18 of the organic law of 12 Nivôse Year VI on the constitutional arrangements for the colonies: 'Every black individual, whether born in Africa or in foreign colonies, transferred into the French islands, shall be free from the moment he sets foot on the territory of the Republic; in order to acquire right of citizenship, he shall for the future, be subject to the conditions laid down by Article 10 of the constitutional act.'
14. Victor Schœlcher, *Vie de Toussaint Louverture*, Paris, Ollendorff, 1889; reprinted, Karthala, 1982.
15. AN, AF III 209, dossier 956. Particularly interesting for our purposes is the letter of recommendation from Fourcroy in favour of Julien Raimond: 'French principles have triumphed … the status of persons, the laws and the constitution are the same for France in Europe and for the American departments; this state of affairs is based on the abolition of slavery and the political equality now established between colonists of all colours …' (14 Brumaire Year IV–5 November 1795).
16. AN, Col. CC/9/A/12.
17. AN, AD/XVIII(a)/49, dossier 'Marec': 'Rapport au nom de la commission des colonies occidentales sur la situation de l'île Saint-Domingue.' This commission, with Marec as rapporteur, also included Bergoeing, Villers, Garran-Coulon, Lecointre, Joseph Eschassériaux and Riou.
18. *Dictionnaire Historique de la Révolution Française*, Paris, P.U.F., 1989: article 'Clichy, Clichyens', pp. 231–2, by J.-R. Suratteau; and article 'Viénot de Vaublanc', p. 1089, by E. Ducoudray.
19. A few examples: neither A. Soboul (*Histoire de la Révolution Française*, Paris, Gallimard, 1962, Vol. 2, pp. 238–42) nor D. Woronoff (*La République bourgeoise de thermidor à brumaire*, Nouvelle histoire de la France contemporaine, Paris, Éditions du Seuil, 1972, pp. 65–75) mentions this aspect. Conversely, G. Lefebvre (*La France sous le Directoire*, new edition, Paris, Éditions sociales, 1978, edited by J.-R. Suratteau) mentions the colonial question in Chapter 9 of Part I, 'Le conflit entre le Directoire et les Conseils'.
20. *Le Moniteur*, Vol. 28; sitting of the Council of Five Hundred of 10 Prairial Year V; and AN, AD XVIII(a)/66, dossier 'Vaublanc'.
21. The members of the Clichy Club used the same tactics as Page and Brulley and Serres and Gouly: lumping everything together. The commissioners were thus successively the agents first of Brissot, then of Robespierre. They were now the agents of Babeuf, whose trial was taking place at this very time in Vendôme.
22. Toussaint was particularly sensitive to such contempt in his memorial dated at Le Cap, 8 Brumaire Year VI: 'Réfutation de quelques assertions d'un discours prononcé au Corps législatif le 10 prairial an 5, par Viénot-Vaublanc' [B.N. 8o Lk (12) 536].
23. AN, AFIII 209, dossier 959, piece 48 et seq.; expulsion of Baco and Burnel. AN AFIII 208, dossier 947, piece 38: 'Motifs de l'arrêté de l'assemblée coloniale du 24 ventôse qui déclare que le décret de la Convention, du 16 pluviôse, relatif à la liberté des Noirs esclaves, est inadmissible dans la colonie, quant à présent' [Grounds for the order of the Colonial Assembly of 24 Ventôse, which declares that the decree of the Convention of 16 Pluviôse, on the freedom of black slaves, is inadmissible in the colony, for the time being].
24. *Le Moniteur*, Vol. 28; report of proceedings of the sitting of the Council of Five Hundred of 10 Prairial Year V, opinion of Tarbé; he attacked Sonthonax, portrayed as the 'executioner of whites', which was classic, but also as the 'relentless enemy of mulattoes'. Bourdon de l'Oise said a great deal along the same lines.
25. *Le Moniteur*, Vol. 28 (24 Germinal Year V–13 April 1797). The report was presented to the sitting of the Council of Five Hundred on 27 Ventôse Year V.
26. B. Gainot, 'La députation de Saint-Domingue aux corps législatif du Directoire', in *Léger-Félicité Sonthonax*, Paris, Société française d'histoire d'outre-mer and Association pour l'étude de la colonisation européenne, 1997, pp. 95–110.

27. The report on the election can be found at AN, C483, piece 123.
28. AN, C513, piece 99; verbatim report of the electoral assembly of Saint-Domingue held at Le Cap, 20 Germinal Year V.
29. AN, C527, piece 283; file on the electoral assembly of West Department, Saint-Domingue, held at Léogane, 20 Germinal Year V. There were even other electoral assemblies, such as the one held at Cayes-de-fond for the south, in Fructidor Year IV, which elected Brulley and Yon Paullian as representatives.
30. Doulcet report on the elections in Saint-Domingue, presented at the sitting of the Council of Five Hundred, 5 Ventôse Year V.
31. See the very violent article in the *Journal de Pellet*, No. 420, 16 Nivôse Year V (5 January 1797) entitled 'Reflections on the elections in the colonies'. The elections were conducted by men engaged in 'sedition'; these 'seditionists' had had proprietors' throats cut, and then had the properties distributed to the murderers. In return, they expected recognition of the 'brigands' who were demonstrating a 'slavish devotion' and a 'stupid ignorance'; this 'handful of Africans' so stigmatized had chosen 'every henchman of the anarchist faction' to come and sit in the Legislative Body. The deputies from northern Saint-Domingue were therefore no more than 'the alleged deputies of the negroes of Saint-Domingue' (issue of 15 Nivôse).
32. *Le Moniteur*, Vol. 28; report of the sitting of the Council of Five Hundred of 16 Prairial Year V (4 June 1797).
33. Ibid., sitting of 13 Prairial Year V (1 June 1797); the reminder of the 1795 debate in the National Convention naturally enraged the Council in the spring of 1797.
34. *Journal de Pellet*, BN; issues from No. 416 (12 Nivôse Year V–1 January 1797) to No. 660 (16 Fructidor Year V–2 September 1797). This paper was banned after 18 Fructidor. *Le journal historique et politique de la Marine et des colonies*, belonging to Chotard Senior and Deaubonneau, was the mouthpiece of pro-slavery colonial groups. In 1797 it campaigned to invalidate Laveaux's election and to have Sonthonax put on trial. At pressmark Lc(2)2649, there is only a single issue at the BN, No. 69, of 29 Vendémiaire Year V (20 October 1796).
35. B. Gainot, 'Bottu, le républicain des colonies', *Annales Historiques de la Révolution française*, special issue 'Révolutions aux colonies', July–December 1793, pp. 431–44.
36. J.-C. Halpern, 'Sans-culottes et ci-devant esclaves', paper presented to the Saint-Denis colloquy 'Esclavage, colonisation, libérations nationales, de 1789 à nos jours', Paris, Harmattan, 1989, pp. 136–43.
37. *Le Moniteur*, Vol. 38; report of the sitting of 13 Messidor Year V (1 July 1797).
38. AN, AFIII 209, dossier 959, piece 52; covering letter to report of Minister Pléville Le Pelley, of 4 Brumaire Year VI (25 October 1797).
39. 'Compte-rendu par le général Laveaux à ses concitoyens, à l'opinion publique, aux autorités constituées' [Report by General Laveaux to his fellow citizens, public opinion and the constituted authorities], 1 Floréal Year V (B.N.).
40. Archives de la guerre, Vincennes, dossier 'Laveaux' (gd/137 (2)); letter from Laveaux to Truguet: 'I will not conceal from you that I would find it very agreeable to command a military division inside the Republic. The one that is within my department of Saône-et-Loire would be infinitely flattering to me' (Germinal Year V). Truguet warmly recommended Laveaux for a command in a home division, or a post as government agent in the Windward Islands (1 Thermidor Year V).
41. *Journal de Perlet*, No. 587, 3 Messidor Year V.
42. *Le Républicain des Colonies*, Vol. 19, 15 Messidor Year V (3 July 1797).
43. AN, AD XVIII(a)/29, dossier 'Eschassériaux'; in addition to Joseph Eschassériaux, the commission appointed to verify the validity of the elections in Saint-Domingue was made up of Dabray, Garran-Coulon, Cholet and Quirot. We have seen that the representatives, almost single-handedly, had endeavoured to counter the arguments of the members of the Clichy Club in Prairial. Eschassériaux could now condemn 'the system of ruling everything by military force, a system that was impolitic and doomed', which was bound to lose the colonies for France permanently. He asked that the Constitution be applied to the colonies at once.
44. AN, Col. CC/9A/9; report to the National Convention (1 Vendémiaire Year III); 'réflexions et observations sur la colonie' [report and observations on the colony].

45. Law on the constitutional organization of the colonies, of 12 Nivôse Year VI (1 January 1798) (*Bulletin des lois*).

46. J. Godechot, *Les constitutions de la France depuis 1789*, Paris, Flammarion, 1970, p. 104: 'Frenchmen who have fought in one or more campaigns for the establishment of the Republic shall be citizens unconditionally.'

47. Belley was commander of the gendarmerie, Mentor adjutant-general, and Annecy captain in the First Regiment of freebooters at Le Cap (AN, C527).

48. AN, AD/XVIII(a)/43, dossier 'Laveaux': 'Opinion de Laveaux sur les colonies', sitting of the Council of Ancients of 12 Nivôse Year VI (1 January, 1798), pp. 6–7.

49. Ibid., p. 8.

50. The report presented on 11 Brumaire Year VI (1 November 1797) by Cholet, in the name of a commission composed of Joseph Eschassériaux, Dabray, Garran-Coulon, Quirot and himself, concluded that the elections that had been held at Le Cap in both Year IV and Year V (AN, C 527) were valid. This resolution thus completed the reversal that had occurred in the regime's colonial policy after Fructidor Year V, with the Eschassériaux report, and the adoption of the organic articles. The operations of the electoral assembly that was held at Le Cap on 20 Germinal Year V were examined by a special commission, and validated on 26 Pluviôse Year VI (14 February 1798). Étienne Mentor posed a problem because of the age limit (he was twenty-eight when he was elected); his case was examined by a special commission, of which the rapporteur was Pierre Guyomard [A.N. AD/XVIII(a)37]; speech to the Council of Ancients on the elections in Saint-Domingue, 8 Prairial Year VI). In the end Mentor was admitted to take his seat, and swore the oath on 12 Prairial Year VI (31 May 1798) [AN, AD/XVIII(a)/50, dossier 'Mentor'; 'speech of 12 Prairial Year VI, on the oath of hatred of the kingship, and the attachment of blacks and men of colour to the Republic'].

51. AN, AD/XVIII(9a)/50, dossier 'Mentor'; speech of 12 Prairial Year VI (see previous note).

52. BN, speech by Pierre Thomany to the Council of Five Hundred, 16 Pluviôse Year VII [Lb(43)2755/2802].

53. AN, AD/XVIII(a)/64 dossier 'Sonthonax': speech of 16 Pluviôse Year VI to the Council of Five Hundred. This speech repeated the main points of a report that Sonthonax had submitted to the Minister of the Navy, Bruix, on 11 Pluviôse Year VI (30 January 1798) (AN, AFIII 210, dossier 962).

54. AN, AD/XVIII(a)/50, dossier 'Mentor'; pamphlet to assert his right to sit in the Legislative Body.

55. AN AD/XVIII(a)/43, dossier 'Laveaux'.

56. BN, NAF, ms.12 104; see in particular Toussaint's letter to Laveaux of 13 Prairial Year VI (22 May 1798). Toussaint expresses his surprise that Laveaux 'should be one of the representatives of the people of Saint-Domingue who was most anxious to welcome Sonthonax', the latter being moreover described as a 'monster', whose sole concern during his second mission had been 'to stir up passions, the desire for vengeance, to destroy the little order that you had had so much trouble to restore....'

57. Ibid., letter from Toussaint to Laveaux, 17 Prairial Year VI: 'Robespierre also seemed to like freedom, but where would the republic be without 9 Thermidor?'

58. On these projects, see Y. Bénot, op. cit.; on the transitions between two colonial periods, see Francis Arzalier, 'Le colonialisme et le messianisme des droits de l'homme en France', paper presented to the Saint-Denis colloquy 'Esclavage, colonisation, libérations nationales' (February 1989), Paris, L'Harmattan, pp. 203–11.

59. AN, AFIII 206, dossier 943, pieces 58–64; months of Nivôse–Pluviôse Year VII (January 1799).

60. This attempt to resurrect the Société des Amis under the second Directory was the subject of a separate paper presented to the meetings in commemoration of the decree of 16 Pluviôse at Épinay-sur-Seine, in February 1994.

61. P. Pluchon, *Toussaint Louverture, un révolutionnaire noir d'Ancien Régime*, Paris, Fayard, 1989, pp. 394–5. Right up until Leclerc's expedition, he continued to be very suspicious of the envoys of the constitutional Church.

62. J. Godechot, 'Le Directoire vu de Londres', *Annales Historiques de la Révolution française* (1949).

63. 'L'ennemi des oppresseurs de tous les temps' AN, AD/XX(a)/197 (continuation of the *Journal des Hommes libres*), issue of 23 Fructidor Year VII (9 September 1799).

64. *Le Journal des Hommes libres de tous les pays* commented favourably on the appointment of Bottu on 12 Thermidor Year VII (30 July 1799).

65. On this whole debate, see B. Gainot, *Le mouvement néo-jacobin à la fin du Directoire: structure et pratiques politiques*, Part I (thesis for doctorate, Paris I, January 1993).

66. *Dictionnaire des jacobins vivans, dans lequel on verra les hauts faits de ces messieurs, dédié aux frères et amis*, Hamburg, 1799, by 'Quelqu'un, citoyen français'. A list of 207 names follows, including those of Victor Hugues, a 'cannibal'; Laveaux, 'a wild animal'; Mentor, 'an escapee from the scaffold'; Leborgne; Sonthonax, who 'represents the wild beasts of the colonies'; and Eschassériaux, who protects them all.

67. AN, Col. CC/9A/23.

68. Ibid.

69. Ibid.

70. 'L'ennemi des oppresseurs de tous les temps', No. 12, 29 Fructidor Year VII (15 September 1799); in the *Publiciste*, Laveaux persisted in vouching for Toussaint's loyalty. Such devotion was in blatant contradiction with the paper's line: at this time it was reprinting Rigaud's proclamations denouncing Toussaint's 'treason'.

71. AN, col. C7A/51; order appointing Baco, Jeannet and Laveaux to Guadeloupe and also war archives (Vincennes) dossier 'Laveaux' (g.d.137/2); 'mémoire justificatif sur la Guadeloupe'. Laveaux sailed with Baco and Jeannet from the island of Aix on 23 Brumaire Year VIII (17 November 1799) and reached Basse-Terre on 11 December 1799.

Chapter 16

Baco and Burnel's Attempt to Implement Abolition in the Mascarenes in 1796: Analysis of a Failure and Its Consequences

Claude Wanquet

THE ATTEMPT IN 1796 to implement the decree of 16 Pluviôse Year II in the eastern colonies of the Île-de-France (now Mauritius) and Réunion and its failure represent the most spectacular and, in terms of its consequences, the most important episode in the history of abolition in the Mascarenes.[1] After lengthy debates, the Council of Five Hundred passed a law of 5 Pluviôse Year IV (25 January 1796) empowering two agents, appointed by the Directory for a term of two years and given very wide powers, to implement the Constitution of Year III, and hence abolition, in the Mascarenes. The agents, named the very next day, were René-Gaston Baco de la Chapelle and Étienne-Laurent-Pierre Burnel.

Baco, a former lawyer with the *parlement* of Brittany, had been deputy for Nantes, his native town, in the Constituent Assembly. He was elected mayor of the city at the end of 1792, and the following year organized energetic and victorious resistance against the Vendéans. Accused by the Montagnards of federalist sympathies, he was then imprisoned and most probably owed his release solely to the fall of Robespierre. At the time of his appointment, he was a deputy in the Council of Five Hundred. Burnel's appointment is probably to be explained by his knowledge of the Île-de-France, where he had lived between November 1790 and March 1794. There he had been a journalist, lawyer, secretary of the Colonial Assembly and a member of the local Directory. In 1794, he launched an unsuccessful commercial venture with the United States, where he lived for several months before returning to Europe in 1795. His appointment provoked a chorus of protests from the deputies from the Mascarenes in Paris, who accused him of dissolute habits, improprieties in his professional life and political hypocrisy. All of these accusations would be repeated later.

After a few weeks of hurried preparation in Rochefort, the expedition set sail for the Indian Ocean in March 1796 and reached Port-Louis without incident on 30 Prairial Year IV (18 June 1796). Several days of crisis followed that were written up at length in numerous reports and commented on by those involved. I shall briefly summarize the facts, but will be mainly concerned with their possible interpretations. Ignoring the island regulation that disembarkation on the island could take place only with the agreement of the Colonial Assembly, the agents intended to visit the local authorities immediately on their arrival. That decision aroused sharp tension but, in the end, the day of 30 Prairial ended in an atmosphere of apparent fraternization between the new arrivals, the authorities and the town's population. As soon as they first appeared in the Colonial Assembly, the agents asked it to appoint a commission of nine members to discuss with them the means of carrying out the task entrusted to them.

Apart from a few procedural disagreements, the following two days went by without any serious incidents, with the agents inspecting the local national guard and engaging in the first discussions with the Commission of Nine. We do not have the text of the instructions given by Truguet, the Navy Minister, to Baco and Burnel before their departure, but according to their respective testimony, it is clear that the agents were hoping to win over the local political leadership by spreading abolition over twelve months. There would be a sort of probationary period in which an authoritarian labour regime on the estates would be introduced, rather like the system followed by Victor Hugues in Guadeloupe or Toussaint Louverture in Saint-Domingue.

However, Baco and Burnel's appeal seems to have alternated between issuing calming declarations and threats to use force, or even military terror, in the event of resistance. While the negotiations were proceeding, a large number of colonists living in the countryside flocked into the town. On 3 Messidor (21 June 1796), there was an abrupt denouement of the crisis. One final meeting was held between the agents and the Commission of Nine who, if we are to believe Baco,[2] were ready to accept the programme drawn up by the representatives of the Directory. But a crowd movement occurred, and the colonists invaded the room where the meetings were being held. After a few minutes, the colonists accompanied the agents back to the port, demanding their immediate departure on the corvette *Le Moineau,* which set sail at once for the Philippines.

Then it was time for explanations, interpretations and, inevitably, the search for excuses. On their return to France, which they had easily secured from the crew and officers of Le *Moineau,* the agents asserted that it would have been 'easy for them during 72 hours to proclaim the decree'.[3] How can we explain their failure? Their republicanism and the exalted idea that they had of their mission do not seem to be in doubt. Burnel was particularly eloquent in condemning slavery, and his subsequent career in French Guyana confirms his ideological choices. Baco's energy, already shown by his earlier behaviour in Nantes, is attested to by every eyewitness account.

If we are to believe Magallon, the general commanding the newly arrived troops, gradual measures taken to implement the decree would have won if not the support, at least the acquiescence of the colonists.[4] The correspondence of Hyrne and Gillot,[5] sent by the Assembly of Réunion to that of the Île-de-France a few months earlier, does indeed show that there were considerable divisions in Port Louis over what attitude to adopt towards abolition. This was particularly true among the merchants who dominated political life and for whom the decree of 16 Pluviôse obviously did not have the same significance as it did for the landed proprietors in the countryside and in Réunion.

According to the version given by the Colonial Assembly of the Île-de-France in its addresses to the Legislative Body of 3 and 21 Thermidor Year IV (21 July and 8 August 1796),[6] it was solely the 'terrorist' behaviour of the agents that was alone responsible for the decision taken to expel them. These addresses dwell at length on all of the vices attributed to Burnel and present his attitude in the island as dictated by a desire for personal revenge motivated by hatred. The Assembly acknowledged that Baco was 'preceded by a reputation as an honourable man which ought to win him public respect' but that 'his imperious tone and his threatening strong language soon revealed him as an apostle of terrorism'. In fact, the Assembly was here taking up a theme that had been extensively used in 1794–5 by the islands' deputies in Paris and above all Gouly,[7] to the effect that the most ardent promoters of immediate and total abolition belonged in fact to 'the poisonous tail of Robespierrism'. To that, the Assembly added an equally traditional argument – that Baco and Burnel were actually disguised agents of Britain, which flattered itself that it could seize the islands without having to resort to a military expedition and one of whose ships had been seen, 'at a given spot', near the Île-de-France when they had landed.

For its justification, the Assembly again asserted that it had been itself carefully preparing a programme for gradual abolition of which the suspension of the slave trade since 1794, the stepping up of manumissions and the granting of political equality to free men of colour were early signs.[8] It presented the decision to expel Baco and Burnel as the result of a 'sudden and spontaneous popular explosion'; the decision to expel the agents prevented the event from turning into a massacre. But while exonerating itself over the final episode, the Assembly accepted responsibility for the overall operation as one more proof of the island's unbreakable loyalty to the French Republic, already shown by its resistance to the British squadrons and the exploits of its pirates. The expulsion of Baco and Burnel is thus portrayed as being inspired by the desire to keep valuable colonies safe for France, as an essential key to the Indian Ocean and an indispensable base for an eventual attack against the British in India, something that the islands' deputies in Paris were ardently promoting.

In reality, it is impossible not to place full responsibility for the dismissal of the Directory's envoys on political decision-makers in the Île-de-France. Several orders prior to their arrival and, in particular, a long memorial of 14 Floréal (3 May 1796), also adopted unanimously by the Assembly of Réunion on 17 Prairial (5 June 1796),[9] assert in unambiguous terms the determination of the islands to refuse for the time being any implementation of abolition. The similarities between these documents and Gouly's most violently racist writings are obvious. Even as the colonial leaders were emphasizing their philanthropic and liberal intent, they were asserting that blacks were fundamentally incapable of using properly the freedom that others were seeking to grant them. Abolition would be a return to their natural idleness, their natural violence, their 'lack of civilization'. The example of the disasters experienced by the American colonies was held up, and the rejection of abolition was justified in the name of humanity – not only for the whites, who would inevitably be massacred, but also for the blacks, whom it would inevitably lead to famine and chaos. These documents also rejected all of the 'organic laws' dreamed up by the government in Paris and finally proposed, as a last resort, by the islands' deputies in Paris after the adoption of the Constitution of Year III,[10] to allow an authoritarian transitional regime before complete abolition.

In fact, it was the Assembly itself that organized the mass demonstration through couriers despatched to the countryside and through careful and discreet preparations by the National Guard. The choice of the Philippines as the place of deportation was not a matter of chance either, the aim being, as the agents stressed, to gain as much time as possible before eventual reprisals from the metropole by sending them as far away as possible.

Yet Baco and Burnel had held one major trump card – a large armed force. There were probably some 1,000 sailors and 700 soldiers in the force that arrived with them, in addition to which there were almost 900 men already in garrison and the crews of a few ships of the Republic which had gone before them. According to d'Unienville, a particularly important participant-observer, Baco and Burnel at one point envisaged 'lodging in the barracks', which might have changed the course of things. They are said to have given up the idea for fear 'of seeming to make a rather inglorious retreat'.[11] The explanation is not without merit, but it is possible also to see in the behaviour of the agents their determination to give the colonial authorities a further guarantee of their moderation, as well perhaps as an expression of their optimism and the conviction, which they shared with many French politicians full of praise for the Constitution of Year III, that the persuasive power of the principles of that Constitution was such that it would win over all the colonists.

However, Baco and Burnel's main explanation for their failure is their betrayal by the military chiefs who ought normally to have helped them in their task[12] – a betrayal, first and foremost, by Governor General Malartic. In his report on the events,[13] Malartic explains that he was 'seized' by the crowd and carried to the Assembly and that his sole concern was to avoid bloodshed and to protect the agents from popular violence. That version is confirmed by the colonial authorities but takes no account whatsoever of the governor's responsibility in the affair. Threatened by the agents with very serious sanctions, even going as far as hanging for having seen fit to oppose their early landing the first day, Malartic had in fact become a sort of symbol in the eyes of the colonists. But he had already taken their side much earlier by ratifying, on

30 Nivôse (20 January 1796), their declaration, concluding that implementation of the decree of 16 Pluviôse in the island was unacceptable.[14] Malartic, the agents asserted, lied to them when he claimed to have the situation well in hand, whereas in reality he was a plaything in the hands of the colonists. Effectively, 'not in good health, infirm and weakened by age', according to Truguet,[15] the elderly Governor General, who had several times requested to be recalled, was a political weathercock, always on the side of the strongest. 'He would have hanged us if he had been instructed to do so', said Baco and Burnel, 'and would have done the same to the colonists if we had not warned them.'[16] There was also the fact that Malartic's deep-seated royalist sympathies were well known and that he had even most likely aided the insurgents by his decision to confine the troops to the barracks.

The position of the senior officers who had come with the agents is similar on many points. Vice-Admiral Sercey and General Magallon, long time friends, were both erstwhile aristocrats, the former a marquis and the latter a count. They both appear to have suffered during the voyage from Burnel's caustic comments and the agents' abuses of authority. However, their behaviour on 3 Messidor shows distinct nuances.

Sercey, a brilliant naval officer in the American War of Independence, was the admiral who, at the time of the burning of Cap Français, had organized the transfer to the United States of Saint-Domingue colonists who had escaped the massacre. Arrested on his return to France, he, too, owed his life to the death of Robespierre. His royalist beliefs seem to be undeniable, and even though he asserted that he had yielded to 'the general will'[17] and taken no direct part in the removal of Baco and Burnel, there is no sign that he attempted to oppose it or disavow it in his subsequent correspondence.[18]

Magallon belonged to a family of soldiers and had served with distinction as an assistant to Hoche in the Army of the West; he seems to have been a much more sincere republican. As early as 1794, he had been encouraging the despatch of an expedition to the East Indies in which he clearly hoped to play a glorious role. But he was a man who was bitter at having been placed by the French authorities under the orders of Malartic when he arrived in the colony.[19] While personally favourable to abolition, with some reservations, he explained his attitude above all by his overriding concern to obey the orders of the Governor General, his immediate superior. He is, however, said to have asked the agents for a written order on precisely how he was to behave. Baco is said to have drafted this order to resist and then put it, unsigned, into his pocket. Magallon, too, was carried along by the crowd to the Assembly, and is said to have protested against 'the violence done to him' and asked to suffer the same fate as the agents, which he was refused.[20]

In the last analysis, and whatever may have been the innermost sympathies of all those involved, it seems that from now on the military chiefs were endorsing the policy of the colonial authorities and giving a veneer of legality to decisions, the end-product of which was, in the name of the higher interests of France, to reject its constitutional principles. However, this responsibility was amply shared by decision-makers in Paris. It was they who, on 11 Fructidor

Year III (28 August 1795), had confirmed Malartic in his authority,[21] deliberately closing their eyes to the republicanism, energy and efficiency of a man whom it had decided to replace as early as 1793 (a replacement that failed to take place at that time for reasons of domestic politics, the new Governor General envisaged, Choderlos de Laclos, having been, rightly, accused of being a friend of the traitor Dumouriez). Yet with the senior officers gone over to the side of the colonists, these latter still had to ensure that the rank and file, the *petits blancs* and the slaves would not move.

According to several witnesses, the soldiers did nothing to defend the agents in any real sense when the popular riot erupted, but ran and took cover in the barracks, where their apparent determination to resist appeared formidable. But they were quickly appeased by a mixture of threats from the National Guard and promises of exceptional gratuities by the Colonial Assembly. Moreover, they were not 'the dregs of republican troops' who, according to Villèle, had committed 'a thousand atrocities' in the Vendée,[22] but rather, for the most part, young and inexperienced recruits.[23]

According to d'Unienville, on their arrival, the agents enjoyed the sympathy of 'malicious individuals' among the ordinary people of Port-Louis.[24] Baco and Burnel subsequently asserted that the *petits blancs*, the majority of the population of Port-Louis, supported the abolitionist cause, and it is true that many of them were expelled from the island in the years that followed on that pretext. But they did nothing at the time of the crisis, and their gatherings were 'promptly dispersed' on 3 Messidor. Maure even asserts that 'shared dangers and interests had brought the most diametrically opposed views together' and that 'large numbers of sans-culottes marched in agreement with the rest of the population'.[25]

As for the slaves – and this perhaps is what is most astonishing – they played absolutely no role in the affair. Were they, as island propaganda had it, less desperate than those in the Antilles? Or were they taken by surprise, like everyone else, at the speed with which the denouement occurred? One thing, though, is certain: at no point did Baco and Burnel, unlike Sonthonax or Victor Hugues, consider appealing to them.

We come back always to the same question: Could the agents have resisted more energetically, more effectively? Doubtless, they lacked cohesion. The memoirs of colonists lay great stress on the agents' disagreement during the voyage and even on the actual fisticuffs alleged to have occurred between them when the belongings of a Dutch administrator, a passenger on an American vessel, captured by the British and retaken by Sercey's division, were ransacked. It is not clear whether the incident actually happened, but there seems to be no denying that Burnel's biting humour grated on his colleague's nerves. More seriously, Burnel, 'a smaller version of Victor Hugues', in the words of a historian of French Guyana, did lack energy. In any case, he easily gave way to popular pressure, and Maure even hints that he had been gradually won over to the colonists' arguments.[26] Baco, on the other hand, as we have seen, envisaged resisting and explains that he had abandoned the idea to avoid bloodshed. Perhaps, in fact, it would have taken very little to alter the outcome, even simply a different layout of the area. '[F]ortunately for us', noted Villèle, 'the barracks were at the other end of town.'[27]

The most important thing about the affair are the comments that followed. In order to avoid the accusation of having lacked political sense and energy, the agents asserted, in effect, not only that they had been within an inch of success, but, above all, that the colonist's decision to expel them was paradoxically a guarantee that a subsequent expedition would meet with easy success.[28] This astonishing reasoning rests on the argument that the colonists' decision would inevitably lead to a very grave internal crisis that would have several ramifications: a withering away of the slave trade, with no one wanting to buy slaves, who would soon be freed; an upsurge by the *petits blancs*, who were very attached to the authority of the French Republic; the emigration of a few principal colonists, who as traitors to that Republic would flee their inevitable punishment by going abroad; and an accentuation of the collapse of the value of the local paper currency, as all hope of seeing it guaranteed by the National Treasury evaporated. In addition to these speculations, Burnel added a long section on how easy it would be to secure acceptance of abolition in the islands of France and Réunion by offering to retain on the spot only those new freedmen who were well disposed and to use the rest as an army for the conquest and colonization of Madagascar, also presented as an important possible bastion for fighting against Britain in the Indian Ocean. This was an idea, we would stress, that was also dear to Gouly and was regularly brought up throughout the Revolutionary period.

In late 1796 and the spring of 1797, these hypotheses were stated on the occasion of a very important debate, dominated, as Bernard Gainot stresses in his essay, by the counter-revolutionary offensive of members of the Clichy Club. The colonists had found strong defenders of their cause in Paris, in particular Admiral Villaret-Joyeuse and Barbé-Marbois, both brothers of residents of the Île-de-France, and Viénot Vaublanc, a well-known royalist and the man behind a violent polemic against Truguet. During the first months of 1797, this tendency seemed to be winning the upper hand, and the leaders of the Mascarenes were even openly congratulated by some in the Council of Five Hundred for the patriotic conduct they had displayed by driving out the envoys of the Directory. But the coup d'état of 18 Fructidor Year V (4 September 1797) turned the political situation on its head, resulting in the arrest or exile of all the royalist sympathizers, who happened to be at the same time the protectors of the colonists in Paris.

Nevertheless, this political shift did not alter what had become somewhat the official version of the affair, fully developed in a long report to the Directory by the new Minister of the Navy, Pléville-Lepelley.[29] This version fully corroborated Burnel's account and encouraged illusions as to the easy success of a future attempt to implement abolition. One individual now played an essential role in supporting this policy – Daniel Lescallier. A former commissioner of the Constituent Assembly in the eastern colonies, Lescallier was reputed to be a steadfast abolitionist, with a thorough knowledge of the problems of the Indian Ocean. A skilful politician, he became an essential figure in the Ministry of the Navy and the Colonies.

After 1798, there was a succession of projects entailing an expedition to the East Indies. First, a project was entrusted to Pierre Monneron, a member of a trading family strongly implanted in the Île-de-France and in India, who, with a single frigate, his republican good faith and his positive reputation among the inhabitants of the Mascarenes, could succeed, it was thought, where Sercey's division had failed.[30] In the end, Monneron's mission, which was closely tied up with the dreams nourished by Bonaparte's expedition to Egypt, was countermanded, probably following the disaster at Aboukir Bay on 1 August 1798.

The idea was taken up again the following year, and a project was put in place whose realization – significantly – was entrusted to Admiral Villaret-Joyeuse. While the secret instructions given him included implementation of abolition, this was to be done tactfully and with not simply the agreement but also the active participation of the colonists in the Mascarenes. However, the mission entrusted to Villaret was above all diplomatic and military, foreseeing territorial or ideological expansion by France into East Africa, the Indian Ocean and even the Far East.[31] That mission was also countermanded.

But in 1800, there was an actual, if rather experimental, attempt at emancipation entrusted to Joseph-François Charpentier de Cossigny, who had been unofficial deputy of the Île-de-France at the end of the Constituent Assembly and under the Legislative Assembly. The intention was to make the slaves in the powder mill in the Île-de-France wage-earners before finally emancipating them. Cossigny, an engineer by profession, was appointed manager of the mill. This experiment was to be a trial run before a general emancipation of the island's slaves. But Cossigny, whose previous writings amply demonstrated the reservations he felt about abolition, had hardly arrived than he was easily got at by the colonists and quickly returned to the metropole.[32]

By way of conclusion, we may wonder, above all, about the determination and will of the French Republic to ensure implementation of the abolition decree of 16 Pluviôse Year II in the eastern colonies.

The whole affair throughout comes over as a confrontation between, on the one hand, the defenders of a principle that was supposed to be untouchable and universal and, on the other, those who claimed to speak in the name of pragmatism and experience when they proposed postponing and/or adapting this principle to local realities.

In analysing all of the twists and turns of this confrontation over fundamentals, one cannot but first be struck by the delay – almost two years – between the vote for abolition and the decision to implement it in the eastern colonies, and then be surprised by the lack of discernment and even the blindness of the French authorities, perhaps in the choice of their representatives and certainly in their analysis of their failure and of their future imagined success. Cossigny clearly revealed the truth about Lescallier when he wrote to him: 'You believed or perhaps you pretended to believe, as I did, that the sending back of the agents Baco and Burnel was the work of just a few individuals, because you wanted to calm the insane rage of a few fanatical directors.'[33] But the description could, it seems to me, be applied to the majority of those responsible for the colonial policy of the time. Was it an error of appreciation that can be blamed on the generosity of their illusions? Or should we not rather attribute it, first, to a willingness, maybe subconscious, possibly deliberate, to choose an interpretation that was comfortable, and, second, to what today we would call 'a soft consensus' to the deterioration of a situation, thus avoided having to assume actual responsibilities while making it possible to retain a clear conscience.

Notes

1. The main points of this essay are dealt with at length in C. Wanquet, *La France et la première abolition de l'esclavage (1794–1804): le cas des colonies orientales, îles de France (Maurice) et la Réunion*, Paris, Karthala, 1998.
2. Letter of 14 Frimaire Year V (4 December 1796), printed in *Le Moniteur* and published by Saint-Elme Leduc in *Île de France. Documents pour son histoire civile et militaire*, Port-Louis, 1925, pp. 289–90.
3. È.-L.-P. Burnel, *Essai sur les colonies orientales*, n.p., 1798, p. 13.
4. Letter to the Minister of the Navy and the Colonies of 10 Fructidor Year IV (27 August 1796), A.N. Col C4/111.
5. A.D.R. (Archives départementales de la Réunion), L 331.
6. A.N. Col C4/110.
7. See C. Wanquet, 'Un "Jacobin" esclavagiste, Benoît Gouly', *Annales Historiques de la Révolution Française*, Nos 293–4, July–December 1993, pp. 445–68.
8. On this policy and its limits, see C. Wanquet, 'La suspension de la traite négrière par les Mascareignes durant la Révolution française, anticipation ou leurre', paper presented to the Saint Louis/Dakar colloquy 'La Révolution et l'Afrique', April 1989 (28 pp., ts.); and idem, 'La perception des problèmes de couleur dans les Mascareignes pendant la Révolution et le syndrome dominguois', paper presented to the Port-au-Prince colloquy 'Haïti et la Révolution française', December 1989, Port-au-Prince, Editions Henri Deschamps, 1995.
9. N.A.M. (National Archives of Mauritius), B 23/B and A.D.R. L 30.
10. Letters from the deputies from the Mascarenes to the National Assembly, Besnard, Serres and Gouly, 'to the colonial assemblies and constituted authorities of the islands', of August or September 1795, A.D.R. L307.
11. *Statistique de l'île Maurice et ses dépendances*, Vol. 2, p. 209.
12. Letter from R.-G. Baco of 14 Frimaire Year V cited above (note 2) and È.-L.-P. Burnel, op. cit., pp. 14 and 21.
13. Letter to the Minister of the Navy and the Colonies, No. 138, n.d., A.N. Col C4/111.
14. A.D.R. L 65.
15. Rapport au Directoire sur les événements des colonies orientales de la fin de 1796 [Report to the Directory on events in the eastern colonies at the end of 1796], A.N. Col C4/110.
16. È.-L.-P. Burnel, op. cit., p. 14, note 2.
17. Letter to Truguet of 27 Messidor Year IV (15 July 1796), A.N. Col C4/111, p. 121.
18. See his letter dated 28 October 1802, cited by Adrien d'Épinay, *Renseignements pour servir à l'histoire de l'Île de France. Jusqu'à l'année 1810, inclusivement*, Île Maurice, Imprimerie Dupuy, 1890, p. 451.
19. See, for example, his letters to Truguet of 3 Nivôse and 7 Pluviôse Year IV (24 December 1795 and 27 January 1796), A.N. Col C4/110.
20. 'Précis des évènements' addressed to the Minister, 26 Messidor Year IV (14 July 1796), A.N. Col C4/111.
21. A.N. Col C4/110, p. 223.
22. J. de Villèle, *Mémoires*, Vol. 1, Paris, Perrin, 1888–90, p. 143.

206 | *Claude Wanquet*

23. Letter from the commissioners of Réunion to the Colonial Assembly of the Île-de-France of 18 Fructidor Year IV (4 September 1796), A.D.R.L.331.
24. *Statistique de l'île Maurice et ses dépendances*, Vol. 2, p. 212.
25. *Souvenirs d'un vieux colon de l'île Maurice*, p. 154.
26. Ibid., p. 156.
27. J. de Villèle, op. cit., p. 144.
28. Burnel's *Essai sur les colonies orientales* provides the best example of this theory.
29. Report of 6 Brumaire Year VI (27 October 1797), A.N. Col C4/111.
30. Instructions from Bruix, Minister of the Navy, to Monneron of 5 Brumaire Year VII (26 October 1798); and Monneron's comments on the project of 21 Thermidor Year VI (5 August 1798), A.N. Col C4/112.
31. Instructions of Ventôse Year VIII (March 1800), A.N. Col C4/113.
32. See C. Wanquet, *Histoire d'une Révolution. La Réunion (1789–1803)*, Vol. 3, Marseilles, Jeanne Laffitte, 1984, pp. 425–7.
33. Letter of 11 Brumaire Year IX (2 November 1800), A.N. Col C4/114.

Chapter 17

Port-la-Liberté, Year III: Demographic Approach to New Citizens

Lucien René Abénon

ON 4 FEBRUARY 1794, the Convention abolished slavery. Among the colonial populations of the French empire, it was those of Guadeloupe who were the chief beneficiaries of this decision. In Saint-Domingue, to deal with the black revolt, Sonthonax had already made the first move in August 1793. British-occupied Martinique did not benefit from abolition. In the Mascarenes, the colonists and the freedmen saw to it that it was not implemented. Consequently, the measure took effect only in French Guyana and Guadeloupe. And of these two territories, the latter was, far and away, the more populous and economically wealthier.

It is well known that it was Victor Hugues, landing at Gosier and gradually conquering the island back from the British, who truly implemented the Convention's decision. What do we know of this newly freed population? So far as I know, to date there has been no overall study of this subject. And yet the documents are there, including the 1797 census[1] and the registers of births, marriages and deaths of the new citizens.

Such a demographic study is hampered by the shortness of the period in which the population of Guadeloupe was free: those eight years, from 1794 to 1802, do not even cover a single generation. Moreover, the earliest registers have a major drawback in that the entries are often what might be called 'catching-up' entries: the population was registering with a delay of several months, and sometimes several years, births, marriages and deaths that had occurred some time before. The Catholic registers, which would be of great help in such a study of the period envisaged, do not exist, most of the parish priests having fled before the advance of Victor Hugues.

What we intend to do here is to make a study of the newly liberated populations of Port-la-Liberté, the new name given to the city of Pointe-à-Pitre, using as our main source the new registers of births, marriages and deaths.

The town had been created in the early 1760s at the time of the British occupation. Its marshy site, cut through with many hills, made development difficult, and the town owed its survival to its excellent harbour, which provided a perfect shelter to boats in bad weather, and to its central location between the two islands that make up Guadeloupe. There had been a catastrophic fire in 1780, which left only 20 of its 132 houses standing. It was thus a new town that Victor Hugues had taken in June 1794, a town that was far from the size it is today, since it extended only around the Place de la Victoire, the scene of the recent siege. Port-la-Liberté was chiefly composed of wooden houses. The town bordered on the communes of Petit-Bourg, Gosier and Abymes. That means that it included large areas of countryside, and cultivators from the neighbouring sugar plantations would come to town to be registered. Some inhabitants of the neighbouring communes appear to have done the same, some because they were temporarily resident in town, others even though they were not resident at all.

The census of 1 Messidor Year V (20 June 1797) shows a population of 4,305. It may be surmised that the town must have undergone rapid growth following the arrival of Victor Hugues, since, on the one hand, many inhabitants had fled the disturbances and repression and had later come back to resettle and, on the other, the arrival of the proconsul, with his troops recruited from the metropole or other islands in the Antilles or locally recruited, profoundly altered the demographic make-up of the town.

Port-la-Liberté was not a very large town in population terms, although its economic role was growing by the day. The population of the town can be broken down as follows:

	Whites	*Rouges* (Coloureds)	Blacks
Men over 21	445	178	409
Women over 21	239	435	788
Young men, 14–21	42	60	93
Young women, 14–21	82	155	233
Male children	128	242	230
Female children	98	267	181
Total	1,034	1,337	1,934

As can be seen, the population of European origin accounts for almost one-quarter of the total. That is a high figure, if we remember that in 1789 the island had 13,712 whites for 92,881 slaves, or only about 12 per cent of the population. We also know that during the troubles many of the Europeans emigrated. It seems evident that by 1797 many of them had returned. Victor Hugues's soldiers added to their numbers, which explains the high proportion of men among the white population. It may well be that some whites had fled their estates and taken refuge in the town where they felt risks were lower. It is evident that, overall, Port-la-Liberté seems much more 'white' than the rest of the colony, which might be explained by its role as a trading port and as the place where people arriving from France landed. It is worth pointing out that about one-third of the whites were under 21. The population of European descent was thus not very young, which is not surprising in this type of population marked by a low or at least relatively low birth rate.

There were 1,337 *rouges* (coloureds, or people of mixed race), a little over a quarter of the population. The term is equivocal since it can apply to all the degrees of mixing, which in the Antilles are extremely numerous. It can equally well describe octoroons, quadroons, mulattoes or câpres. In any case, it can never be synonymous with the old description 'freedmen' (*libres*). In 1789, there were 3,058 such individuals in Guadeloupe, less than 3 per cent of the population. The label *rouge* thus includes a not insignificant proportion of former slaves. It may be supposed that mixing was more marked in a port town than in the sugar estates in the rural areas.

Contrary to what we observe for the whites, here there are far more women than men (435 women over 21 for 178 men over 21). Perhaps, but this is only a supposition, the coloureds had paid a heavy price in the recent events. For example, it will be recalled that several hundred free men were executed after the surrender of Berville's camp. Perhaps too those who had signed up with Victor Hugues were garrisoned in different parts of the island. In any case this imbalance between the sexes is very marked among the coloureds. It is also noteworthy that this group is young: 724 young men and women under 21 as against 613 adults, which again marks the extent of mixing since the group includes both the children of coloured parents and the offspring of unions between blacks and whites.

There are 1,934 blacks, a little less than half the total. Here, again, there are more women than men, either because the men were usually under arms or because the women had more freedom to leave the plantation and settle in town. The proportion of the population that is young is similar to what we find for whites (737 young people under 21 compared to 1,197 adults). We know that slaves have a rather low birth rate. In sum, what stands out about the population of Port-la-Liberté is the extent of mixing, something which it is moreover not always easy to appreciate in detail.

As regards the socio-professional distribution, we can be certain that the population counted is almost wholly urban. The census of 1797 states clearly that it covers the town of Port-la-Liberté and not the district. No cultivators or plantation residents are listed. Conversely, traders are particularly numerous. There are 514 of them, including 227 whites, 152 coloureds and 135 blacks. The term clearly covers a wide variety of realities, from the petty trader to the shopkeeper. It appears that one of the essential functions of the town is trade at every level. Domestic servants are almost wholly people of colour. In this area, the Revolution had changed nothing. Children, particularly black children, have a typical role. Of 1,076 domestics, 451 are coloured, of whom 181 are under 14 years old, while of the 625 black domestics, 346 are under 14 years old.

Leadership positions are almost wholly occupied by whites. They work as notaries, lawyers, tax collectors, commander of the National Guard, engineers and teachers. Women generally have no activity. People of colour in the broad sense of the term are artisans, petty traders and, as we have already indicated, domestic servants. The men are masons, coopers, wheelwrights and so forth. The women are seamstresses, hawkers, washerwomen, or women of confidence. In this world, *petits blancs* often find themselves competing with the population of colour: ten white carpenters, twenty-seven coloured, twenty-one black; three white fishermen, nine coloured, twelve black. Among soldiers, this mixture is particularly striking. The battalion of sans-culottes contains every racial component of the population.

To get a more complete picture of the demographic situation of Port-la-Liberté, we looked at the town's registers of births, marriages and deaths. As is well known, unlike in the Catholic registers, births, deaths and marriages are listed separately. We therefore had three registers to consult thanks to the kindness of Mr Hervieu, the director of the Guadeloupian *Archives départementales*, and Miss Chauleau, director of the *Archives* of Martinique.

These registers are microfilmed. For births,[2] there are fifty-six entries from 30 Nivôse Year III to 30 Vendémiaire Year IV (21 January–21 October 1795). For marriages,[3] there are fifty-eight entries from 13 Floréal Year III to 5 Pluviôse Year IV (2 May 1795–21 January 1796). For deaths,[4] there are eighty-six entries from 21 Fructidor Year II to 2 Floréal Year III (17 September 1794–2 April 1795).

Since our study relates to men of colour, we focus on that part of the population. It seems easy to distinguish between the population of European origin and the rest of the population, since the former always have a family name. Whites almost always sign, while people of colour practically never do so. Of fifty-eight marriages, thirteen are between white Creoles or Europeans; four are mixed marriages; the others involve people of colour. There is hardly ever room for doubt. Thus, when on 26 Nivôse, Jacques Asseline, captain of infantry in the 41st battalion, aged 30, native of Villevallier in the Yonne, married Marie Joseph, aged 21, native of the commune of Fraternité, formerly Sainte-Anne, daughter of citizen Jean and citizeness Marie-Thérèse Dupré, it is quite obviously a mixed marriage. It is true that the mother has a surname, but we know that that was quite a common custom among the free people of colour.

It is sometimes difficult to identify a particular individual racially. Thus, who is Jean-Baptiste du Saillant, aged 33, native of Saint-Pierre de la Martinique, the bearer of an old name among the Creole aristocracy? He is described as the son of Toussaint Dusaillant, mariner, and Marie Magdaleine. On 30 Prairial he marries Marie Julienne, daughter of citizen Étienne and citizeness Désirée. There can be no doubt that we are dealing here with people of colour.

At what age did people marry? In this area, given that the ages of people of colour are only roughly known, we have to be satisfied with approximations. Very often the registers mention X, aged about 30. Again, the mention of age at first marriage does not have the same significance as it does in the metropole. Formerly, slaves had virtually never married, and so such unions simply formalized a long-standing situation. Thus, in the case of six marriages, children born previously were recognized. It sometimes involved very long-established households, since when Mathieu and Victoire were married on 15 Floréal Year III, they acknowledged four children aged between 8 and 14, and when Jean-François married Nanette on 17 Thermidor Year III, two sons and three daughters were acknowledged, the youngest, Ambrose, being 13 months old and the oldest, Marie-Catherine, aged 12.

Marriages of People of Colour at Port-la-Liberté

Date of Marriage	Name of Groom	Age	Occupation	Origin	Name of Bride	Age	Occupation	Origin
13 Floréal Year III	Étienne Montfleury	25	Soldier	St-François	Régine Hilaire	18	–	Sainte-Anne
14 Floréal	Augustin Christophe	40	?	Capesterre	Marie Bibiane Béguet	18	–	Morne-à-l'Eau
15 Floréal	Mathieu	35	Sergeant	Anse-Bertrand	Victoire	36	–	–
1 Prairial	J.-B. Lacroix	30	Wigmaker	Le Moule	Anne Marie	16	–	Port-la-Liberté
3 Floréal	Louis	25	Soldier	Coast of Africa	Marthe	26	Washerwoman	Sainte-Anne
6 Floréal	Pierre Louis	33	Soldier	Robert (M.)*	Marie Claire	28	–	Trou-au-Chat (M.)*
16 Prairial	J.-B. Honoré	22	Corporal	Fort-Royal (M.)*	Sabine	26	Seamstress	Port-la-Liberté
30 Prairial	J.-B. du Saillant	33	Corporal	St-Pierre (M.)*	Marie Julienne	20	–	Port-la-Liberté
1 Messidor	Joseph dit Chazeau	45	Soldier	Rivière-Salée (M.)*	Marie Catherine	30	–	–
11 Messidor	Sylvestre	25	Soldier	Petit-Bourg	Luce	22	–	Sainte-Rose
15 Messidor	Pierre Léon	25	Halberdier at the prison	Puerto Rico	Catherine	40	–	Port-la-Liberté
10 Messidor	Magloire	28	Mariner	Coast of Africa	Françoise	30	Washerwoman	Coast of Africa
18 Messidor	Augustin	30	Soldier	Port-Louis	Elisabeth	28	Seamstress	Gros Ilet (St Lucia)
18 Messidor	Maurice	28	Worker in lime-kiln	Coast of Africa	Felicité	30	–	–
27 Messidor	Augustin	30	Carpenter	Marie-Galante	Marie Christine	30	Washerwoman	Le Moule
1 Thermidor	Séraphin	36	Carpenter	Les Abymes	Marie Cécile	30	Seamstress	Port-la-Liberté
18 Thermidor	Aubin	33	Cultivator	?	Zabeth	?	Cultivator	Port-la-Liberté
20 Thermidor	Marcel Marquet	26	Sergeant	St-François	Marie Nicolas	30	–	Capesterre
18 Thermidor	Nievy	55	Cultivator	–	Célestine	40	Cultivator	Coast of Africa
27 Thermidor	Annicet	40	Lieutenant	St Lucia	Marie Thérèse	23	Seamstress	Port-au-Prince (St-Domingue)
9 Fructidor	Bernard	36	Steward	Port-la-Liberté	Toinette	30	–	Coast of Africa
11 Fructidor	Pierre Prudent	28	Soldier	Robert (M.)*	Émilie	24	Washerwoman	Coast of Africa
6th sans-culotide	Pierre	35	Carpenter	?	Constance	30	Washerwoman	Coast of Africa
24 Vendémiaire Year IV	J.-B. dit Darluc	38	Captain	La Dominique	Magdelaine	37	Trader	?

Marriages of People of Colour at Port-la-Liberté (*cont.*)

Date of Marriage	Name of Groom	Age	Occupation	Origin	Name of Bride	Age	Occupation	Origin
24 Vendémiaire	Louis dit Ibo	45	Soldier	Coast of Africa	Adélaïde	28	Washerwoman	Coast of Africa
13 Brumaire	Jean Pierre	22	Soldier	Sainte-Rose	Florence	22	Seamstress	Port-la-Liberté
13 Brumaire	Jean	25	Soldier	Morne-à-l'Eau	Simone	25	Cultivator	?
9 Frimaire	Pierre	45	Cooper	Port-la-Liberté	Eugénie	28	Washerwoman	Coast of Africa
28 Frimaire	Fabien Varreaux	29	Soldier	Fort-Royal (M.)*	Ursule	30	Seamstress	Gosier
11 Nivôse	Louis Castelneau	34	?	St-Pierre (M.)*	Jeannette	30	–	Basse-Terre
16 Nivôse	Faustin	28	Soldier	Petit-Goyave (St-Domingue)	Félicité	25	Seamstress	Petit-Canal
21 Nivôse	Tham	30	Mariner	Coast of Africa	Magdelaine	30	Trader	Coast of Africa
26 Nivôse (1)	Jacques Asseline	30	Captain	Villevallier (Yonne)	Marie Joseph	21	–	Sainte-Anne
5 Pluviôse	Isaac Olivier	25	Soldier	Baie Mahault	Geneviève	24	Seamstress	Basse-Terre

(1) = Mixed marriage
(M.)* = Martinique

Note: Some people of colour had a family name. Mere reference to their parentage indicates their origin.

Overall, these marriages appear to be well balanced in terms of the ages of the spouses; where there are disparities they are not excessive. The average age at marriage is 32.6 for men and 27.1 for women. It is rather curious to note that the new citizens conform quite well to what can be observed in France at the same time, which comes as a surprise, given what were obviously very different social conditions.

A look at the origins of the grooms indicates that the population is largely from abroad. Of thirty-one men, only three are natives of Port-la-Liberté; seven come from Grande-Terre (two from Saint-François, one from Port-Louis, one from Anse-Bertrand, one from Morne-à-l'Eau, one from Les Abymes); four come from Guadeloupe proper (from Capesterre, Petit-Bourg, Sainte-Rose and Baie Mahault). Over half come from outside the island (five are said to come from Africa), and are therefore *bossales* brought into the colony as children. Only one apparently can establish who his parents were. He gives the names of his father and mother as Opradize and Ognongily, a rough rendering of African names. For the rest, it is noted that they cannot remember the names of their parents 'being taken from their country at a very tender age'. One bears the African name of Tham, the others have French names.

One of the grooms comes from Marie-Galante, one from La Dominique, seven from Martinique (one from Robert, one from Rivière-Salée, one from Fort-Royal, three from Saint-Pierre and one not specified). Almost all are soldiers in the 1st Sans-culotte Battalion that had come to fight alongside Victor Hugues. The presence of these Martinican soldiers must be noted, since it shows that men of colour from the sister-island did not stand aside from the combat under way to win freedom. Mention should be made, too, of one man from Puerto Rico and another from Saint-Domingue (Petit-Goyave).

The origins of the women differ from those of the men. Seven are natives of Port-la-Liberté, proving that there was indeed a population settled in the town; seven come from Grande-Terre (three from Sainte-Anne, one from Gosier, one from Morne-à-l'Eau, one from Le Moule, one from Petit-Canal); four come from Guadeloupe proper (two from Basse-Terre, one from Capesterre, one from Sainte-Rose); eight brides came from the coast of Africa, which confirms the importance of *bossales*. There are also one woman from Martinique, one from Saint-Domingue and one from St Lucia. The female population thus appears to be much more settled than the male. In general, however, creolization would appear to be well advanced, and we are far from the situation in Saint-Domingue where in 1789 the majority of blacks was made up of *bossales*.

Overall, at Port-la-Liberté, at least for the period with which we are concerned, the racial barriers appear to be a little less strong than they used to be. It seems that, and this is particularly the case when we are looking at military marriages, both black and white witnesses were present together. General Pélardy, Commander-in-Chief of the armed force of Guadeloupe, signs as witness at the marriage of Augustin Christophe and Marie Bibiane Béguet on 14 Floréal (a marriage between people of colour) as he does on 22 Prairial at the wedding of Pierre Daniau, captain in the engineers, and Marie-Anne Martin, who are Europeans. At the marriage of Magloire, mariner, and Françoise (people of colour), the witnesses are Mercure Boulanger Papillon of the 2nd Sansculotte Battalion (a European), Charles René (a man of colour) and Louis Guérin (a white). As we have already said, the witnesses of European origin almost always sign, whereas the men of colour almost never do.

The five divorces that appear in the register of marriages at Port-la-Liberté all involve the population of European origin. Overwhelmingly, they involve wives whose husbands have been absent for several years and who are anxious to remarry. People of colour did not resort to divorce simply because for them marriage was a recent institution, and there was no reason to break it so soon.

What can the birth register tell us? It contains fifty-six entries in total: eight entries of civil baptism and forty-eight birth entries. The civil baptism entries consist in giving a name to young African slaves who have not been baptized. They are sponsored by two adults who act as godfather and godmother, and the civil registration officer gives a baptismal name.

Overall these citizens are young and include: Elisabeth, aged about 13; Michel, about 11; Henriette, about 14; Anne, about 15; Élise, about 14; Justine, about 18; Jean, about 15; Marie-Françoise, about 14; and Gertrude, about 20.

These are most likely adolescents anxious to become more closely integrated into Creole society. Their presence confirms the numerical significance of *bossales*. It may indeed be wondered whether these are young children seized in raids at a very early age, or rather simply children who had lost their mothers when still babies so that no one can say from where they come.

One feature of the birth entries that is particularly interesting is that some refer to births that had occurred long before. The widest gap between a birth and registration is three years, but differences of two or three months are not infrequent, which obviously makes it difficult to use this document for demographic analysis. Overall, the children of colour are all born out of wedlock. Most of the time the father is named, but it is rare for him to be present at the registration. Out of forty-five births, the father is present twelve times, which suggests almost conjugal relations with the mother; thirty-seven times the father is named; in seven cases he is a soldier; one is stated to be deceased, 'having come to join the volunteers arrived from France in Prairial'; one has been wounded in the attack on Berville's camp; one died from head injuries caused by a bomb; another was killed in the attack on the camp at Saint-Jean. Among the fathers, many are cultivators described as working on estates in the region: that is true of nineteen cases. One is described as a labourer, and Mathurin is recorded as a gang boss on the Belle-Plaine plantation.

Some stories stand out. Such, for example, is the case of Victor Hugues's opponents. Lalanne is stated to be an émigré, while Roch has been sentenced to the chain gang without it being possible to say if he has been sentenced as a common criminal or if his sentence is for political reasons.

A number of individual problems occur. Thus, Laurent, who has a child by Marianne of Morne-à-l'Eau, is said to be 'resident at citizeness Nénette's'. As for Bernard, a carpenter on the Double plantation, he comes to declare two children the same day: Saint-Éloi, a month and a half, born of citizeness Félicienne, and Augustin, three and a half months, born of citizeness Bibias, which is a rather rare case of sentimental bigamy, unless this is simply a survival of African habits of polygamy among the slaves in the Caribbean. Overall, the register of births shows that there were close contacts between the urban area and the adjoining rural areas. The register of births can provide a little information on the population of Port-la-Liberté, but it is not enough to allow us to study the birth rate and fertility of any particular racial group. The delay in registering births makes such registration a very rough-and-ready affair, while the absence of surnames makes family reconstitution almost impossible, the period covered by the experience of registration (1794–1802) being too short for the study of a generation.

As for the death register, it can do no more than confirm what we have seen elsewhere. We must note from the outset that this register is the one least rich in information about people of colour. That may be because they were unwilling to have their dead registered, or perhaps they saw no point in it. Of the eighty-six death entries, only seventeen relate to individuals of colour. Not much can be gleaned from them, except perhaps the extent of infant mortality: five died under age 5, and five died between the ages of 5 and 20. The other deaths are between 20 and 33. Only one woman died as old as 45. Overall, it seems that life was not long among the new citizens.

Although the sample studied is too small to allow any certainties being extracted from it, it would seem that death struck quickly and early among the population of colour, and there must have been few older people among them.

What we can conclude from this study is that at Port-la-Liberté at this time, a large population of European origin was living, probably a quarter of the population. People of colour were engaged in trade, crafts and domestic service. The military was also much sought after as a vocation. The new citizens largely came from outside the town, chiefly from Grande-Terre and the windward side of Guadeloupe proper. There were many people from Martinique who had come to fight on behalf of freedom. Many Guadeloupians did the same, which put a military stamp on the town. There seem to have been some interracial unions, which becomes apparent at births, marriages or deaths, when it is common to see white citizens act as witnesses for people of colour. This fraternization seems above all to occur among men from metropolitan France who had come to fight alongside Victor Hugues, whereas in this area the colonists holed up on their plantations seem much more unforthcoming.

Overall, this population of colour seems to be young. It is marked by the fighting that had just occurred and which caused many deaths. There seem to have been many African elements, and these newcomers had no hesitation in joining the fight against slavery. Note, too, the large numbers of young Africans with no father or mother who found godparents in the town.

We thus have a population of colour that is quite diverse socially, relatively mobilized to defend a hard-won freedom, a population that has retained traits of its previous condition, a predominance of illegitimate births, a high level of concubinage and a high level of child mortality. It is this population that, overall, will mobilize when the straitjacket of slavery is forced on it again.

Notes

1. Guadeloupian *Archives départementales*, Microfilm I Mi 37.
2. Microfilm 5 Mi 20 R 3.
3. Microfilm 5 Mi 20 R 4.
4. Microfilm 5 Mi 20 R 5.

Bibliography

ABÉNON, L. 'Aux origines d'une ville antillaise, Pointe-à-Pitre'. Schœlcher Colloquy of the C.A.R.D.H., 1986.
ADELAÏDE-MERLANDE, J. *Delgrès, la Guadeloupe en 1802*. Paris, Karthala, 1986.
LACOUR, A. *Histoire de la Guadeloupe*. Vols 1 and 3. Basse-Terre, n.p., 1857 and 1858.

Chapter 18

Saint-Domingue: From French Colony to Independent Haiti – a Numismatic Iconography

Jean-Charles Benzaken

Colonial Currency under the Ancien Régime

We take the following lines from Robert Lacombe, author of the *Histoire moné-taire de Saint-Domingue et de la République d'Haïti jusqu'en 1874*:[1]

> The constant doctrine of the monarchy on currency circulation in the colonies is clearly expressed in this circular of 4 March 1699: 'His Majesty being informed that, for some time, those doing business in America have been sending gold and silver coins there instead of goods, and knowing how harmful the consequences of such trade would be to the Kingdom through the outflow of silver' ... prohibits the transport of gold and silver coins to America.

Thus, the only French currency, and even then scarce and clipped, or even counterfeit, to circulate in the colonies was billon coin. The silver currency was the Spanish piece of eight or *gorda*, whence the French name *gourde* and its divisions: the *demi-gourde* (a half-piastre coin), the *gourdin* (quarter of a *gourde* coin) and the *escalin*, represented by the old Spanish one-real coin. The gold currency was also Spanish currency and even more often Portuguese currency.

Currency in Saint-Domingue: From the War of Independence to the French Revolution

Let us turn once again to the words of Robert Lacombe:

> Commerce and the slave trade were considerably hampered by the hostilities [War of American Independence, 1775–83]. Therefore the colonists in Saint-Domingue were granted permission to fit out ships themselves to go and purchase slaves on the coast of Africa. In this way they could continue to sell blacks

to the Spaniards.... Finally, the interloper trade with the Spanish colonies came to be regarded as a matter of course. The result of this state of affairs is that cash became unusually plentiful in Saint-Domingue.[2]

But he continued:

Yet in Saint-Domingue the shortage of cash returned with a vengeance after the end of the American war. This could be explained in 1783, since in addition to the resumption of trade there were the purchases by colonists, deprived of French products for five years: it was explained later by the fact that the Spaniards stayed away and went and purchased fabrics and slaves from the English and thus carried their silver currency elsewhere. Calonne and Vergennes provided England with the long-awaited opportunity to replace France in the Antilles and to collect for itself the piastres needed for the Madras mint, while they allowed English manufactured goods to flood the metropole and dangerously threaten its industry.[3]

The Revolutionary Period

The uprising in Saint-Domingue (1791) permanently aggravated the shortage of cash by precipitating the repatriation of coin by colonists. Currency issues in Saint-Domingue and later in Haiti during this dramatic period were inspired by Gresham's law but a sadly ironical Gresham's law: 'Since good currency is irretrievably leaving the country, we need to create bad currency in order to be able to have any.' Silver coins were therefore debased, either by cutting them into pieces or by reducing the amount of silver in silver currency.[4]

We know of a counterfeit, minted in brass, of the French one-sol, so-called 'scales' coin dated 1793, Year II, engraved by Dupré (Figure 1). It was minted in a makeshift workshop, which explains its extremely crude appearance.[5] The decision to counterfeit this particular coin seems not to have been wholly fortuitous, since on 29 August 1793, Civil Commissioner Louis-Félicité Sonthonax proclaimed the general freedom of black slaves in the north – his colleague Polverel did so in the south and west on 31 October – and the obverse of this coin shows a tablet inscribed LES HOMMES SONT ÉGAUX DEVANT LA LOI (Men Are Equal before the Law). Well before 16 Pluviôse Year II, then, this coin – if it is accepted that it was indeed minted in 1793 – seems to endorse the new state of affairs. It is equally symptomatic that this coin was again minted, this time with the date 1801, at a time when these coins had been replaced in France by five-centime and one-décime coins with the head of the French Republic as early as Year IV. Coins counterfeiting the one-décime coin

Figure 1

dated Year VIII were also minted, but in far smaller numbers, it seems, than the one-sol coins with scales dated 1801.

Coins of Toussaint Louverture

Let us briefly recall the career of Toussaint Louverture up to the period with which we are concerned here. The Convention appointed him brigadier general on 22 July 1795, and major general on 17 August 1796. On 25 December 1798, the government promoted him to the rank of commander-in-chief of the army. The Constitution proclaimed at Le Cap on 8 July 1801 appointed him Governor for Life, by the terms of Article 28.[6] Article 19 gave him the power to propose laws.[7]

Toussaint Louverture was so concerned about the shortage of low-denomination coins – doubtless also so anxious to assert the political authority of the French Republic, and his own,[8] over the Spanish part of the island that had been assigned to France by the Treaty of Bâle, signed on 27 July 1795 – that as soon as he entered Saint-Domingue, on 27 January 1801, he decided to have small coins minted there. On 15 Nivôse Year X (5 January 1802), while he was actually still in Saint-Domingue, he ordered the emission and doubtless put into circulation the series of coins of which we shall speak below.

> Having long felt the need to procure for the colony of Saint-Domingue a currency which might replace the currently existing one, the scarcity of which is felt every day, I caused to be struck at Saint-Domingue double *escalins*, *escalins* and half-*escalins* with on one side the effigy of the Republic with the legend 'République française' and on the other the inscription of the denomination of the coin with the legend 'Colonie de Saint-Domingue'.[9] (Figures 2 and 3)

Let us linger for a moment on the legality of the emission and the types and legends of the coins. All is perfectly in accord with Article 1 of the Constitution of 1801: 'Saint-Domingue forms the territory of a single *colony* which is part of the French empire but which is subject to *special laws*' (emphasis added).

Figure 2 Figure 3

Although the text of the law providing for the creation of this currency, decided on by Toussaint Louverture, laid down that the central type is LA RÉPUBLIQUE FRANÇAISE, here more than ever we need to look closely at the stages and meaning of the formation of the allegory of the French Republic, the Goddess of Liberty. This allegory of the Republic is first that of freedom, freedom for which the French had been fighting since 14 July 1789, and, as we shall endeavour to show, it seems to us here to refer above all to the freedom so desired by the slaves.

Chronologically, it is clear that in France the allegory of freedom, Liberty, appeared in 1789. The allegory of the Republic, created on 21 September 1792, simply took up Liberty's representations, adding sometimes the fasces, sometimes the tablets of the law and sometimes the scales. But let us return to Louverture's coins.

The commander-in-chief did not describe this Republic in detail, and it is almost certainly the engraver – a French goldsmith named Tixier, or more probably Tessier, who was in any case extremely maladroit and about whom we unfortunately know nothing – who saw to the details as he engraved the coins.[10] But we can be sure that he must have worked closely with Toussaint.

Let us look at how writers on numismatics have described these coins. Zay writes that the Republic (see Figure 2) is clothed in a long robe with a belt; a girdle attached to her shoulders hangs down on both sides of the robe. In her right hand she is holding a fasces bundle pierced by an axe, and in her left, a pike surmounted by a Phrygian cap.[11]

Victor Guilloteau, apparently upset by this 'girdle', completely omits it from his description.[12] So, too, does Mazard.[13] Lacombe also errs when he writes: 'These coins … represent on the obverse the French Republic upright, wearing a Phrygian cap and leaning on a pike.'[14]

It is quite possible that what we have represented are the chains, here broken, that were attached to the collar placed round the neck of slaves punished by their masters.[15] Among the links, it looks as if there are hearts – an impression reinforced by an examination of the obverse of the one-*escalin* coin – which would give this Liberty-Republic an attribute of fraternity.[16]

Let us now look at the position of this French Republic. In 1801, as in 1792, the seal of the French Republic (Figure 4) is still the Republic upright resting one hand on the pike and the other on the fasces pierced by an axe. A small difference, perhaps due to the lesser competence of the engraver Tixier, is that the pike and the fasces are reversed in the hands of the Republic. Bonaparte, First Consul, had not yet changed anything, but what we have here is a rather terminal sort of image on the cuts and headings, which are more revealing than the

Figure 4

official seal of the Republic of the changes that were occurring. The Directory had already given the Republic a seat and a Phrygian cap. And, whatever Zay says, the cap here is not a Phrygian cap, since it has neither ear flaps nor neck cover. Under the Consulate, the heading of the letters was deliberately reduced to a double concentric circle inscribed with the words LA LOI and where there is a pike surmounted by a cap to which are affixed two oak sprigs. Toussaint Louverture thus chose a Liberty that apparently had much more of the 'mountain' about it.

As regards the features of this Republic, it is indeed difficult to judge because of the thinness of the planchet and the fact that the coin is so worn. Is it a black slave woman? Whether that is so or not, Louverture's Liberty seems to be wearing on her head a headdress, a sort of madras handkerchief that was widespread among the slaves[17] and identified by Lacombe as a Phrygian cap.

Finally, there is the dress that this Liberty is wearing. Its key feature is of course the antique drape, but the numerous vertical folds may evoke those stripes that Pastoreau indicates were so fashionable at the time of the Revolution and are to be found on many cotton prints.[18]

The allegorical female figure of the French Republic engraved on these coins by Toussaint Louverture's order may thus very well be that of a black Liberty who has broken her chains, a Liberty of which the general saw himself as the guarantor.

We know what happened to him: Bonaparte's anger; the expedition of general Leclerc; the arrest (7 June 1802), deportation and death of Toussaint Louverture in the Fort of Joux (1803); the victorious resumption of the struggle by the black inhabitants of Saint-Domingue, who feared the restoration of slavery decreed on 30 Floréal Year X for all the colonies except Saint-Domingue, French Guyana and Guadeloupe;[19] and finally the proclamation of the independence of the island by the name of Haiti on 1 January 1804. But faithfulness to French Revolutionary iconographic representations did not come to an end. Haiti's currency will show that.

Haiti's Currency up to 1848

After the departure of the French, the western part of Saint-Domingue – that is, Haiti – rapidly split into two states. The northern state, which was quite wealthy and over which Britain exercised a firm economic hold, was the land of King Christophe. The other state, in the poorer south, was a republic with Pétion as president.

In the early years of independence, the monetary features peculiar to colonial Saint-Domingue survived. The French colonial monetary unit, the livre, was maintained until 1815. Spanish and Portuguese coins also continued to circulate. Above all, the shortage of coins continued everywhere, especially in the south and west.

King Christophe had superb silver coins struck in London, which remained uncirculated; only brass coins of 7 sols 6 deniers and 15 sols circulated

Figure 5

(Figure 5), which on the obverse continue the type of coins of Toussaint Louverture described above. The sole difference is that the Republic is holding the pike and the fasces in the same manner as the French Republic, with the legend MONNOIE D'HAÏTI, replacing RÉPUBLIQUE FRANÇAISE, the date 1808, and the value. On the reverse and in the centre there is a shield, adorned with a laurel wreath and crowned with oak, bearing the monogram of Henri Christophe with the Latin legend LIBERTAS RELIGIO MORES. The adoption of the monarchy must have favoured the use of Latin, but as regards ideas, it is the heritage of Toussaint that predominates: the liberty of blacks; the importance of the Catholic religion, which he had declared the state religion; and the morality on which he laid repeated stress.[20]

As for Pétion, whose republic had serious financial problems, he also had brass coins struck. On the obverse of these coins there are the arms of Haiti, which have come down to the present day, and which derive directly from French Revolutionary iconography. It involves a trophy of arms, cannon, shot and flags, in the middle of which rises a palm tree crowned by a freedom cap (Figure 6). Of course, the palm tree was the island tree that had been chosen to be the Tree of Liberty,[21] but in Europe in the seventeenth and eighteenth centuries it was often represented on medals[22] and is to be found in France during the Revolution (Figure 7). The obverse contains no epigraph. The reverse bears the legend RÉPUBLIQUE D'HAÏTI, and the year of independence, AN X to XIII, which is undeniably reminiscent of the French Revolutionary calendar. In the centre, the denomination (6, 12 or 25 hundredths of a *gourde*) is encircled by a snake which is swallowing its tail (Figure 8). European iconography was very

Figure 6

Figure 7

familiar with this type, which it called uroboros (Figure 9). This type was also known to Africans, as Lacombe points out,[23] though the shape of the head is slightly different. Is it a rattle-snake? In that case, it would be more American than European. In Europe, the snake that is swallowing its tail signifies survival, continuity, eternity; otherwise, the snake signifies prudence, something that appealed to the Haitian lawmaker, according to Lacombe.[24]

On the obverse of Haitian copper coins after 1828 there is the fasces bound with the axe and pierced by the pike with the liberty cap on it, framed by the value expressed in hundredths, the legend LIBERTÉ ÉGALITÉ and the year of

Figure 8

Figure 9

independence (Figure 10). As described by Linstant-Pradine: 'Article 4: the type of the said coins of 1 and 2 centimes is determined as follows: On one of the sides, the value in letters of the coin and the year of the Christian era in Arabic numerals, interlaced with two palm fronds bound at their feet to two trunks by a knot, and separated at the top by a star; for legend these two words RÉPUBLIQUE D'HAÏTI. On the other side, a fasces of arms resting on a base and in the middle of which rises up an axe surmounted by the liberty cap; to the [left] of the fasces the value of the coin in Arabic

Figure 10

numerals and to the [right] the letter C; for legend these two words LIBERTÉ, ÉGALITÉ. And at the bottom, the thousandth of the year of independence expressed in Arabic numerals.'[25]

To conclude, it is easy to demonstrate the specificity of Haitian monetary iconography in a direct line from the iconography of Liberty introduced by the French Revolution.

Notes

1. R. Lacombe, *Histoire monétaire de Saint-Domingue et de la République d'Haïti jusqu'en 1874*, Paris, 1958, pp. 15–16.
2. Ibid., pp. 33–4.
3. Ibid., pp. 38–9.
4. Ibid., pp. 39–40.
5. J. Mazard, in *Histoire monétaire et numismatique des colonies et de l'Union française*, Paris, Bourgey, 1953, p. 57, and Lacombe following him think that the workshop was situated at Jacmel. We rather take the view that it was at Port-au-Prince, according to the following document: 'A mint *like the one at Port Républicain* [emphasis added] has been established in Santo Domingo....' Letter from Pons, justice of the peace at Saint-Domingue correspondent of the French government, to the citizen Minister of the Navy and the Colonies, 29 Floréal Year IX. A.N. Colonies CC 9 B 18.
6. 'In consideration of the important services that the general has rendered to the colony in the most critical circumstances of the evolution and in accordance with the wishes of the grateful inhabitants, the reins shall be entrusted to him for the rest of his glorious life.'
7. 'The regime of the colony shall be determined by laws proposed by the governor and made by an assembly of inhabitants who meet at fixed times in the capital of this colony, and named the Central Assembly of Saint-Domingue.'
8. The French general Kerverseau, who had been sent with General Chanlatte to the president of the Spanish *audiencia* of Saint-Domingue and who did not like Toussaint, saw it quite clearly. He wrote in his 'Rapport sur la partie espagnole de Saint-Domingue depuis sa cession à la République française par le traité de Bâle, jusqu'à son invasion par Toussaint Louverture, présenté à Paris, au ministre de la Marine le 13 fructidor an IX': 'Once master of the whole island, so that there should remain no attribute of sovereignty that he had not usurped, he conceived the idea of minting coins and established at Saint-Domingue a mint of *gourdins* and *escalins*.' A.N. Colonies CC 9 B23. When Toussaint Louverture occupied the Spanish part of the island (and it was no doubt one reason for his impatience to do so), he hurried to secure possession of the contents of the public treasury, in order to finance his projects and notably to procure the metal necessary for minting the coins that he was planning. Unfortunately for him, he found less that 400,000 *gourdes*, whereas he had expected at least a million: 'Thus after having seized from the republic, under cover of alleged decrees of the most important agency of its colonies, he went on to steal 400,000 *gourdes* from the king of Spain, in the name of the republic, and in order to make the very heavens complicit in his crimes, he ordered public prayers and the exposition of the Holy Sacrament for the whole time of his stay in Santo Domingo' (ibid.). Toussaint took these coins with him to prison in Joux Fort. Thus, the chief military officer of the castle reported to the Minister of the Navy on 26 Vendémiaire, year XI, that Toussaint was carrying two small coins which he said were worth 15 sols and 7 sols 6 deniers. These correspond exactly to the two- and one-secalin coins. A.N. Colonies CC9 B19.
9. These silver coins have a fineness of 780 thousandths and weigh 3.600 gr., 1.710 gr. and 0.810 gr. There were no *gourdins*, as Kerverseau claims. The colonists did not like copper currency, which is why the lower denomination coins are made of brass. Another important fact

is that Kerverseau was trying to damage Toussaint Louverture. Although he could not have seen these coins before they were put into circulation – since he was writing the report cited in the previous note on 13 Fructidor Year IX, whereas the coins are later than 15 Nivôse Year X – he had no hesitation in writing: '[F]ollowing his habit of always cloaking his usurpations and covering himself with a sacred shield, he wanted these new coins to declare on one side the words République française and on the other the name of Toussaint Louverture. That was a monstrous and sacrilegious vision which, impressing on the scene of the crime itself the name of the criminal and that of the sovereign authority that he was making a mockery of, condemns him rather than justifies him and makes each of those coins so many pieces of evidence that accuse him of treason and call down national vengeance on his head.'

10. '… a French goldsmith named Tessier is the director and fabricator of the coins. It is said that it is only for small coins which however are all the more plentiful in the Spanish part because the 8 *escalins* that make up the *gourde* being underweight, export offered losses that kept them in the island….' Letter from Pons, cited in note 5.

11. E. Zay, *Histoire monétaire des colonies françaises*, Paris, 1892.

12. V. Guilloteau, *Monnaies françaises, colonies 1670–1942, métropole 1774–1942*, Versailles, 1937–42.

13. J. Mazard, op. cit.

14. R. Lacombe, op. cit., p. 41.

15. In France it has been common to see broken chains accompany the allegory of Liberty, but they were on the ground: 'Vitalis, aged between 18 and 20 "who voluntarily attended the office of the gendarmerie, having around his neck an enormous iron collar and a heavy chain a metre long weighing together 4–5 kg."' Report from the commandant of France gendarmerie, cited by Arlette Gautier, *Les Soeurs de 'Solitude', histoire des femmes esclaves aux Antilles françaises 1635–1848*, Mémoire de 3e cycle, Paris, 1981, p. 32.

In a letter written by one Lafont and received by the Minister of the Colonies on 3 Thermidor Year IX, it is stated that Toussaint's flag 'is white with three black heads. The last packets that he had sent to Jamaica were sealed with his seal which is *a long rectangle in which there is a broken chain* [emphasis added] and three black heads'. A.N. Colonies CC 9 C 2.

In Year XI, Kerverseau, who was by then the general commanding the former Spanish part of the island, which had become the department of the Ingane, had Tixier or Tessier make the stamp with which he sealed official documents (Figure 11). The 'République française' is identical to that on the one-*escalin* coins of Toussaint Louverture. In particular, the broken chains are still there. After all, Kerverseau was not a slave-owner, since he writes in a report to the Minister of the Colonies, dated 24 Prairial Year VIII: 'I have seen with no less satisfaction the assurance given by the First Consul of the Republic that there would be no infringement of the sacred principles of liberty. That is a homage paid to the dignity of human nature…. No portion of French territory can any longer be stained with the opprobrium of slavery.' And when he speaks of the former slaves,

Figure 11

Kerverseau describes them as 'cultivators [*cultivateurs*]'. A.N. Colonies CC 9 B 23.

16. See Illustrations 15, 16 and 18 in Marcel David's book, *Fraternité et révolution française 1789–1799*, Paris, Aubier, 1987. See also the engravings by Bonneville, who shows two black women with as a legend, respectively: 'In freedom like you the French Republic, in agreement with nature, would have wished it: Am I not your sister?' and 'Me equal to you. Colour is nothing; heart is everything: Are you not my brother?'

17. M. Vovelle, *La Révolution française: Images et récit 1789–1799*, Paris, Éditions Messidor/Livre Club Diderot, 1986, Vol. 2, p. 243. Or Illustration 3 in David's book cited above.

18. M. Pastoreau, *L'étoffe du diable. Une histoire des rayures et des tissus rayés*, Paris, 1991: 'The origin of this fashion lies in the craze for things American in France and those countries hostile to England in the late 1770s. The American revolution was also the child of the Enlightenment, and the flag with the thirteen red and white stripes of the thirteen American colonies in rebellion against the British Crown appears as the image of freedom and the symbol of new ideas.' And he adds in a note: 'It is possible that the American revolutionaries may have chosen a striped fabric, the symbol of slavery (the striped dress was already by 1770 that of prisoners in the penitential colonies of Pennsylvania and Maryland) to express the idea of the serf breaking his chains and, by the same token, reversing the code of the stripe: from being a sign of the deprivation of liberty it becomes with the American revolution, the sign of liberty won.' There is no need to stress the close links, especially commercial ones, between Saint-Domingue and the United States.

19. Slavery was restored there on 16 July 1802, which made the former slaves in Saint-Domingue think that their turn would not be long in coming and drove them to rebel.

20. Odette Roy Fombrun thinks that the medals for valour and virtue created by the comte d'Estaing by the ordinance of 15 January 1765 to reward the 'mulattoes, griffs and free blacks who distinguish themselves by their merit, loyalty or bravery' influenced Christophe, who was said to have been decorated with it for taking part, under the orders of the Governor of Saint-Domingue, in the attack on Savannah. O. R. Fombrun, *Le drapeau et les armes de la République d'Haïti*, Port-au-Prince, Éditions Deschamps, 1987.

21. It was at the foot of such a tree, at Le Cap, on 29 August 1793, that Sonthonax had proclaimed general freedom. 'For the Haitian revolutionaries', writes Odette Roy Fombrun, 'the summit of the palm tree – the symbol of liberty for the slaves of Saint-Domingue – ought to be bearing this freedom cap. In fact, the palm tree and the cap could not fail to accentuate the desire for union of the already freed and the newly freed, a union already represented by the colours blue and red (in the flag).' O. R. Fombrun, op. cit., p. 43.

22. For example, on the reverse of the medal of Louis XIV celebrating the capture of Landau on 17 November 1703, in G. Van Loon, *Histoire métallique des XVII provinces des Pays-Bas*, The Hague, 1732, Vol. 4, p. 415.

23. R. Lacombe, op. cit., p. 54, note 2: 'This emblem appears on a French medal struck in honour of the Council of Five Hundred under the Directory, but it is also an African emblem, symbolizing the eternal return; it has been found on old buildings in Timbuktu and on the walls of the palace of the kings of Dahomey.' David Geggus further observes that the Daballa-Wedo snake is a divinity of the voodoo cult; D. Geggus 'Haitian Voodoo in the Eighteenth Century: Language, Culture, Resistance', *Jahrbuch für Geschichten,* Cologne, 1991.

24. D. Geggus, op. cit., p. 54.

25. Baron Linstant-Pradine, *Recueil général des lois et actes du gouvernement d'Haïti depuis la proclamation de son indépendance jusqu'à nos jours*, 6 Vols, Paris, 1866–86.

Part IV

The Restoration of Slavery and the Reconstruction of the Abolitionist Movements (1802–1848)

Chapter 19

30 Floréal Year X: The Restoration of Slavery by Bonaparte

Jean-Marcel Champion

TWO FATEFUL DATES are 16 Pluviôse Year II (4 February 1794) and 30 Floréal Year X (20 May 1802). The first marks the abolition of slavery by the National Convention, a belated measure when Article I of the Declaration of the Rights of Man and the Citizen had proclaimed, as long ago as 26 August 1789, that 'men are born and remain free and equal in rights'. The second, 30 Floréal Year X, marks the partial restoration of slavery by the First Consul of the Republic, Napoleon Bonaparte.

The text of the law of 30 Floréal Year X is short, comprising four articles:

Article 1 – 'In the colonies restored to France by the terms of the Treaty of Amiens of 6 Germinal Year X, slavery shall be maintained in conformity with the laws and regulations in force prior to 1789.'

Article 2 – 'It shall be the same in the other French colonies beyond the Cape of Good Hope.'

Article 3 – 'The trade in slaves and their importation into the said colonies shall be conducted in conformity with the laws and regulations in force before the said period of 1789.'

Article 4 – 'Notwithstanding all earlier laws, the regime in the colonies shall be subject for ten years to regulations which shall be issued by the government.'[1]

The text of this law calls for five observations:

First observation – the law of 30 Floréal Year X applies only to two groups of colonies: Martinique and its dependencies, on the one hand, and the two islands in the Indian Ocean, Réunion and Île-de-France, on the other. The colonies in these two groupings had in common that in none of them had the decree of 16 Pluviôse been implemented.

Second observation – no mention is made in the law of 30 Floréal of the other colonies, Saint-Domingue, Guadeloupe and French Guyana, that is those where the abolition of slavery had been implemented, or had even preceded the law of 16 Pluviôse Year II.[2]

Third observation – it must be stressed that the text of the 1802 law does not contain the expression 'restoration of slavery'. Article 1 simply states that slavery shall be maintained.

Fourth observation – in four sentences there is twice the mention of laws and regulations in force prior to 1789, that is to a colonial situation in which slavery was the dominant social and economic reality.

Fifth observation – the slave trade is fully maintained.

In reality, the law made a de facto situation official: slavery was maintained where it had never been abolished; it was not restored, or not yet restored, where it had been abolished. By Article 4, the First Consul also reserved to himself the right to take decisions by way of regulation, without going through the Assemblies, on everything to do with the regime of the colonies, that is essentially on the status of individuals. Article 91 of the Constitution of Year VIII already stipulated that the regime of the French colonies was determined by special laws. Thus, the law of 30 Floréal Year X violated one of the fundamental principles of the Revolution, but it cannot be denied that it was constitutional.

How and why had a decision been reached which, while only partial in its application, was nevertheless a total denial of the achievement of the Revolution? Let us first note that the date of the promulgation of this law, 30 Floréal Year X, is not fortuitous: it was the day when the peace of Amiens was itself declared. Moreover, Article 1 of the law referred directly to that peace.[3] At the time of the signature of the preliminaries of peace in London, on 1 October 1801, the colonial question had been one of Bonaparte's overriding concerns. Now that the seas were becoming free again, he could act. His objectives for the colonies were threefold:

- to restore order and France's authority in all its colonies, including those that had experienced slave uprisings and general emancipation;
- to restore economic prosperity there; and
- to use the Antilles, and particularly Saint-Domingue, as a platform for an active policy directed at the American continent.

Bonaparte's position on slavery was thus tied up with the achievement of those three objectives: it was above all a pragmatic position, which was to harden as circumstances changed. The fundamental objective was to maintain the colonial status quo. In the proclamation of the Consuls of 24 Frimaire, two days after the promulgation of the Constitution of Year VIII, it was stated that the French Constitution was based on 'the true principles of representative government, on the sacred rights of property, liberty and equality'.[4] Even before the end of hostilities with Britain, Bonaparte had already drafted his doctrine in place, as evidenced by the secret instructions that he sent on 14 January 1801 to his two representatives in Saint-Domingue, Rear Admiral Combis, for the Spanish part annexed to France, and the colonial prefect Lequoy-Montgiraud, for the French part, of which Toussaint Louverture had just been appointed captain general. Bonaparte gave orders to Rear Admiral Combis to reassure the white population as to the 'views of the French government which, learning from the tragedies of the French part, will not give unlimited freedom to men unlikely to be able to make good use of it'.[5] He instructed him to remind the Spaniards that the principles of the French government sought 'to govern peoples according to their customs and usages'. To the colonial prefect, the First Consul wrote that the metropole 'can wish nothing that might harm the freedom won, but seeks only to regularize the enjoyment of it so as to make it both lasting and useful for the colonists and the mother country'.[6] These instructions are thus clear and perfectly reveal Bonaparte's pragmatism. He was moving towards simultaneously maintaining slavery where it still existed and maintaining freedom where slavery had been suppressed, while introducing compulsory paid labour for all. This last was not original, since Victor Hugues had done it in Guadeloupe and Toussaint Louverture in Saint-Domingue.

On 7 October 1801, seven days after the signing of the preliminaries of peace in London, Bonaparte spelt out his views. In a letter to Decrès he wrote:

> A frigate must set sail on 24 Vendémiaire from our ports to carry to Guadeloupe the news of the peace and the order to General Lacrosse to inform the inhabitants of Martinique and St Lucia, in the name of the government, that they have nothing to fear for the freedom of the Negroes, that they will be kept in their present state, that is in slavery. A fast-sailing sloop must leave at the same time to carry the same news to the Île-de-France; you will inform General Magallon of the government's intention of keeping the Negroes in the position where they are now.[7]

Conversely, for Saint-Domingue, it was stated on 8 November 1801: 'Inhabitants of Saint-Domingue, whatever your origin and your colour, you are all French, you are all free and all equal before God and before the Republic.'[8] Thus, at that point, there was no ambiguity. Another significant and very official document is the 'Exposé sur la situation de la République' (State of the Republic), which Bonaparte delivered before the Legislative Body on 1 Frimaire Year VIII, 22 November 1801:

> In Saint-Domingue and Guadeloupe there are no more slaves, everyone is free, everyone will remain free. Wisdom and time will bring order back, and restore culture and work there. In Martinique the principles will be different: Martinique has retained slavery and slavery will be retained there. It has cost mankind too much to attempt again in this part a new revolution.

He then went on to spell out that for the Île-de-France and Réunion, the status quo would be maintained, that is slavery.[9] Bonaparte's ideas were clear: there would be no going back on abolition where it had taken effect; everywhere else slavery would be maintained. Principles would give way to practice.

We need now to look at the legislative aspect. The essential document here is the note of Floréal Year X, 27 April 1802, addressed to Consul Cambacérès. In this note, Bonaparte asked Cambacérès to prepare a bill on the status of slaves in the islands:

> It seems to me that in regard to the regulations to be made for the blacks, the colonies should be divided into two groups: those where the laws on the emancipation of the blacks were published and have been more or less perfectly put into execution, and those where the old order has been maintained.

The First Consul then went on to suggest to Cambacérès different regulations for each group: maintaining freedom where it existed, maintaining slavery where it had never been abolished. But in this draft there is specific mention of the continuation of the slave trade, in both groups of colonies already defined, and subject to the regulations in force under the Ancien Régime.[10] According to this plan, there would thus be slaves in both categories of colonies: in the colonies where slavery had never been abolished, new captives imported via the slave trade would be added to those already there; in the colonies where slavery had been abolished, slaves could be imported and they would live and work alongside the 'new freedmen', including in Saint-Domingue, but the blacks freed by the decree of 16 Pluviôse, along with those who had rendered services to the state, in particular in the army, would remain free. That amounts to a very complex set of arrangements whose implementation on the ground, particularly in the colonies where slavery had been abolished, would have raised a whole hornet's nest.

To put this law into proper form, Cambacérès turned to a number of members of the Council of State: Admiral Bruix, Regnault de Saint-Jean-d'Angély and Dupuy. There were a few difficulties, but they did not come from the Assemblies: only the Tribunate would have been able to stand in the way, and that had been carefully purged. But the Senate pointed out, correctly, that it was not very constitutional to have two different regimes, in a single law, for French colonies. This led to a shift towards a single regime de facto, implicitly contained in what was omitted in the law of 30 Floréal Year X: it refers only to slavery being maintained, and is completely silent about the new freedmen whose status was thus made exceedingly precarious, especially as the government could make regulations by simple ordinance. Thus, Bonaparte had restored slavery where it had never been abolished, and kept silent about actual abolition and what would become of it. This was worse than the original proposal.

Why did Bonaparte accept this much harsher and ambiguous drafting? We must straightaway rule out any active role by Josephine; she did not intervene in this affair. Bonaparte's political entourage, on the other hand, was strongly attached to the old colonial system and could not imagine the colonies being prosperous without slave labour. As colonial administrators or sailors who had made their career under the Ancien Régime, they could not advise Bonaparte any differently. For example, the head of the colonies desk in the Ministry of the Navy was Guillemin de Vaivre who had held this post under the Ancien

Régime; similarly, the members of the Council of State, navy and war section, were imbued with the traditional principles of the navy on colonial matters. The successive Ministers of the Navy – first Forfait and then Decrès – were well-known supporters of slavery; in addition, Barbé-Marbois, who had been last but one of Saint-Domingue's intendants before the Revolution, was director and then Minister of the Treasury.

In fact, Bonaparte was wrong to follow such self-interested advice. In 1802, everyone was reasoning according to the administrative, economic and social systems of pre-1789, beginning with the many colonists driven out of Saint-Domingue by the troubles, whose only dream was of reconquest and the restoration of slavery.

One question arises. How sincere was Bonaparte about abiding by implementing what was left unsaid in the law of 30 Floréal in regard to Guadeloupe and, above all, Saint-Domingue? In Guadeloupe, the response was unequivocal: in July 1802, Richepanse restored slavery, even though the island had experienced the regime of abolition. As for Saint-Domingue, a coded letter from Captain General Leclerc, addressed to Admiral Decrès, is equally enlightening:

> Do not think of restoring slavery for some time. I think I can arrange everything so that my successor has no more to do than to put the government's decree into effect, but after the endless proclamations that I have issued here to ensure the blacks their freedom, I do not want to contradict myself, but assure the First Consul that my successor will find everything ready.[11]

It is quite clear that Bonaparte, perhaps out of a concern for uniformization, intended to restore slavery where it had been abolished.

Several decrees that accompanied the law of 30 Floréal Year X strengthened the trend towards a return to the colonial Ancien Régime, with explicit references to the pre-1789 situation. Three examples illustrate this reverse evolution: on 29 Prairial (18 June 1802), the tribunals of the Ancien Régime that were maintained in the colonies returned to France by the Treaty of Amiens, dressed up in new names, Tribunal de première instance or Tribunal d'appel;[12] on 4 Messidor (23 June), the *Exclusif mitigé* of 1783 was restored in commercial matters;[13] on 13 Messidor (30 June), blacks and people of colour were forbidden to enter metropolitan France without an explicit authorization.[14]

The consequences of this freedom-destroying legislation are well known. On 16 July 1802, the restoration of slavery in Guadeloupe became effective, contradicting repeated promises. In Saint-Domingue, the measure, which was known about at once, was universally seen as the prelude to the restoration of slavery. When the whites celebrated imprudently, the blacks saw it as proof that their worries in that area had been justified.

The restoration of slavery in Guadeloupe sealed the fate – already deeply compromised – of the Leclerc expedition. Having landed at Le Cap on 4 February 1802, Bonaparte's brother-in-law initially succeeded in defeating Toussaint Louverture's army, despite the strong resistance that he encountered. Alternating force and negotiation, he skilfully took advantage of the divisions and jealousies among the black generals to force Toussaint Louverture to capitulate (1 May 1802), before arresting him (7 June) and sending him to France. He temporarily won over the black generals whom he had no hesitation in employing to combat the remaining resistance.[15]

The military situation swung the other way at the beginning of August, under the influence of three factors:

- yellow fever, which struck a metropolitan army unused to the climatic and epidemiological conditions of the island;
- the refusal of the blacks – particularly in the north – to allow themselves to be disarmed, since they saw possession of their weapons as the ultimate guarantee of their freedom; and
- the news of the restoration of slavery in Guadeloupe, which literally lit the fuse.[16]

One after another black generals, officers and men defected. The insurrection was general and widespread. Leclerc resisted with what troops remained. Struck down with yellow fever himself, he died at age 30, on 11 Brumaire Year XI (2 November 1802). His successor, Rochambeau, continued a ferocious war which proved hopeless because of the disproportion of forces and the rupture of the peace of Amiens. His capitulation on 19 November 1803 marked the end of the second war of independence on the American continent. On 1 January 1804, at Les Gonaïves, General Jacques Dessalines proclaimed the Republic of Haiti.

The betrayal of Revolutionary principles had served no purpose, except to precipitate the final disaster for the French expeditionary force in Saint-Domingue. In this tragedy, Bonaparte bears the principal responsibility. Two major errors of assessment were made:

- militarily, Bonaparte repeatedly reasoned in function of his Egyptian experience which was not transposable to Saint-Domingue; and
- socially, he was wrong to follow the unsuitable advice of an entourage of experts in colonial affairs, trained under the Ancien Régime and incapable of understanding the situation created by the Revolution in Saint-Domingue after 1791.

In France, no one saw that the events in Saint-Domingue were not a mere slave revolt, but rather an irreversible political and social revolution. Bonaparte, who owed everything to the Revolution, did not understand that another revolution was unfolding thousands of kilometres away from the metropole.[17] In the last analysis, it is Toussaint Louverture who won.

Notes

1. J.-B. Duverger, *Collection complète des lois, décrets, ordonnances, réglemens et avis du Conseil d'État*, Paris, 1826, Vol. 13, p. 446.
2. In Saint-Domingue, the civil commissioners Sonthonax and Polverel abolished slavery on 29 August and 21 September 1793.
3. The day before, 29 Floréal, the Legislative Body passed the decree instituting the Legion of Honour. It was also working on the Civil Code. Does this indicate the restructuring of society in a conservative direction? Undoubtedly it does, but with two reservations: first, in the metropole, Bonaparte took account of the Revolutionary heritage, particularly in social matters; second, in the colonies, the reconstruction of society could be conceived without restoring slavery where it had been abolished. In this area, Bonaparte seems not to have had any preconceived ideas. He was not a theoretician; he was an authoritarian pragmatist who, at this time, was still attentive both to the advice that he was given and the advice that he sought.
4. J. Godechot, *Les constitutions de la France depuis 1789*, Paris, Flammarion, 1970, p. 162.
5. *Correspondance de Napoléon Ier*, No. 5293.
6. Ibid., No. 5294.
7. Ibid., No. 5786.
8. Ibid., No. 5859.
9. Ibid., No. 5874.
10. Ibid., No. 6053. The continuance of the slave trade is envisaged 'until the French government has been able to agree with the British government and the other governments for suppressing the slave trade by common agreement'. It is specified that blacks brought in by the slave trade will be treated as they are in the other European colonies and as they were in 1789.
11. Paul Roussier, *Lettres du général Leclerc, commandant en chef de l'armée de Saint-Domingue en 1802*, Paris, 1937, letter CXXI, dated by Roussier to 7 Fructidor Year X (25 August 1802); in fact, the correct date is 5 Thermidor (24 July), the date which appears on the register of Leclerc's register of correspondence preserved in the Davout archives (Bloqueville collection) at Auxerre.
12. J.-B. Duverger, op. cit., p. 470. Article 1 states: '… the tribunals existing in 1789 shall continue to dispense justice, both civil and criminal, following the forms of procedure, the laws, regulations and scale of punishments then in force, and without any change to the organization, jurisdiction and competence of the said tribunals.'
13. Ibid., p. 472. Article 1: 'The decree of Council of 30 August 1783, concerning foreign trade in the French islands in America, shall be enforced, according to its form and tenor, in Martinique, Guadeloupe, St Lucia and Tobago, both for the opening and location of entrepot ports and for the nature of import and export merchandise permitted, formalities to be completed, and duties to be levied.' While the *Exclusif mitigé* was indeed restored in 1783, following the end of the American war, the decree of 30 August dates from 1784. It is worth noting that this important document was prepared by marshal de Castries with the help of Guillemin de Vaivre, then intendant-général of the colonies. On this question see Jean Tarrade's thesis, *Le commerce colonial de la France à la fin de l'Ancien Régime. L'évolution du régime de 'l'Exclusif' de 1763 à 1789*, Paris, 1972, 2 Vols, Vol. 2, especially Chapter 15, entitled 'The Decree of 20 August 1784, an Attempt to Stabilize the *Exclusif mitigé*', pp. 531–89.
14. J.-B. Duverger, op. cit., p. 485.
15. On Leclerc, see in particular P. Roussier, op. cit.; J.-M. Champion, 'Le général de division Victoire-Emmanuel Leclerc', *Mémoires de la Société historique et archéologique de Pontoise, de Val-d'Oise et du Vexin*, Actes du Centenaire, 67, Pontoise, 1979, pp. 59–105; and Henri Mézière, *Le général Leclerc et l'expédition de Saint-Domingue*, Paris, 1990.
16. In his correspondence, Leclerc stresses this point: 'All the blacks are convinced by the letters from France, by the law restoring the slave trade and by the decrees of general Richepanse restoring slavery in Guadeloupe, that we want to make them slaves again, and I can only secure disarmament through long and stubborn fighting' (P. Roussier, op. cit., letter CIX of 18 Thermidor Year X, 6 August 1802). Leclerc also states: 'immediately news arrived of the

restoration of slavery in Guadeloupe, the insurrection which had until then been only partial, became general' (ibid., letter CXXVIII of 29 Fructidor, 16 September 1802). And again, in a letter to Davout, dated 5 Vendémiaire Year XI, 27 September 1802: 'The men that I am fighting are brave and fanatical. General Richepanse's decree restoring slavery in Guadeloupe has made them all insurgents. They let themselves be killed rather than surrender and they kill those of my men who have been spared illness' (Claude Hohl, 'Les papiers du général Leclerc au musée d'Eckmühl', *Bulletin de la société des sciences historiques et naturelles de l'Yonne*, Vol. 107, 1975, p. 181).

17. See Article 1 of the Constitution of Haiti of 27 December 1806: 'Slavery cannot exist on the territory of the republic; slavery is abolished there forever' (Baron Linstant-Pradine, *Recueil général des lois et actes du gouvernement d'Haïti depuis la proclamation de son indépendance jusqu'à nos jours*, Vol. 1, 1804–8, Paris, 1866–86, p. 169).

Chapter 20

Slavery, Colonial Economy and French Development Choices during the First Industrialization (1802–1840)

Francis Démier

THE QUESTION OF slavery was not some marginal element in the economic thinking that accompanied the industrialization of France as it emerged from the Napoleonic age. Restoration of a colonial economy was symbolic of a return to the prosperity of the late eighteenth century, a component of the economic nostalgia for 'La France atlantique'. But reconstructing an efficient colonial economy also appeared as a necessity for a whole textile industry – cotton textiles, in particular – which was at the heart of the manufacturing development of France in the first half of the nineteenth century. The problem was, however, a considerable one in so far as the very bases of colonial prosperity had been profoundly undermined by the revolutionary episode and as the cost of reconstructing a colonial empire threatened to be at the expense of the industrialization and financial recovery required of France if it was to remain a great power.

The Need to Reconstruct a Colonial Economy

From the era of the Revolution to the episode of Napoleon, the collapse of the French colonial system and trading networks can be seen in the stark figures often mentioned in parliamentary debates at the Restoration, and accepted by the vast majority of deputies and peers. The trade of the French colonial empire had fallen from 100,000 tonnes of goods on the eve of the Revolution, to 7,000 tonnes in what remained of it in 1813. In the spring of 1814, after the defeat of Napoleon, the leaders of the new government were convinced that there would be no recovery of France without the restoration of colonial prosperity. They all still had in their minds the figures of a prosperous trade which gave France a positive overall balance and, at the end of the day, brought a net inflow of precious metal – 70 million francs' worth, it was thought. Despite official rejection of mercantilism, this lost profit remained one of the most reliable measures of the amount by which France was being enriched. On the eve of the Revolution, 165 million francs' worth of colonial produce was imported through French ports, of which 120 million came from Saint-Domingue alone. Of these imports, 108 million was re-exported to the 'northern countries' – of which almost half was coffee – which made it possible to supply France with iron, copper, timber, tars and, above all, precious metal. The colonies also constituted a very favourable market for French manufacturers, who sold there 80 millions francs' worth of goods which came from all over France.[1]

But the approach of French economists was not free of ambiguities or even contradictions. A majority in the Atlantic ports called for a return to the most strict *Exclusif mitigé*, purely and simply. Conversely, quite a few voices were raised to express scepticism as to a possible quick return to the networks of the *Exclusif mitigé* – it had been forgotten that they had been facing growing difficulties since the 1760s. For these 'sceptics', there was of course the major problem of colonial indebtedness, and the considerable burden on port circles, heavily committed to financing the plantations, of refloating the whole economic system of the sugar islands. But there was also the pressing manpower problem posed by the abolition of the slave trade by the terms of the peace treaties. To put the economy of the Antilles back on its feet and develop that of Bourbon, it was thought that there would be a need to import 36,000 blacks in a relatively short time. The cost estimated by the shipowners of Nantes amounted to 29 million francs. There were widely shared doubts as to whether the ports could still mobilize such a sum.

There were also worries from an analysis of the colonial market itself. The European market in which the French were more or less the equals of the British on the eve of the Revolution was now, because of the decayed state of colonial networks, firmly in the hands of London. After the defeat of Napoleon, the whole textile and food industry owed its salvation only to selling off stocks cheaply in the wake of the British armies, and these stocks were the ruin of many a manufacturer trapped in the rock-bottom prices at the end of the blockade and the enormous duties imposed on colonial produce.

Finally, many shipowners doubted whether they could make slavery really economically efficient again. That is what explains the development in colonial circles of thinking about slavery itself. Some thought in terms of a reform, or at least an evolution of the social system with space for an intermediate status, achieved on merit and inspired by the second serfdom, 'a serfdom [it was said at the Nantes chamber of commerce] rather like the state in which the peasants of Poland and Russia still are today, except [for] making this new serf *un homme de pointe*, and then a free farmer'.[2]

After a period of hesitation, largely due to political uncertainties, the French made their choices between 1814 and 1816. A determined core of shipowner-merchants, including Admiral and Dufort de la Rochelle and Lezurier de la Martel, played a very active role, backed up by army men who were attentively listened to in Parliament and anxious for a return to the colonial system for strategic and political reasons. This movement won a high level of protection for the French colonial economy against its foreign competitors, a protection which appeared to herald the promise of a more or less rapid return to colonial prosperity. The Nantes Chamber of Commerce declared:

> For France, the return of our colonies and the recovery of Saint-Domingue are for France goals of the highest importance, and it is desirable that the government should concern itself with the matter at the earliest possible moment. It is the means of restoring our naval power, enabling French manufacturing, whose products once found a vast outlet in the trade of the Antilles, to flourish and thereby procure work for our workers and port workers and, finally, restoring to the unhappy colonists the remains of their old fortunes.[3]

It proved impossible to do as some would have wanted and extract a ban on foreign equivalents, since the market did not allow it. The weakness of colonial production necessitated recourse to foreign products and the London market. That being so, it was only possible to consider protection seen as a sufficient stimulus to investment in the large-scale Atlantic trade and in the plantations themselves. French manufacturers, refiners and textile factory owners remained very much on the alert and intended to avoid any stifling of their own industrial effort, especially after the period of very high prices at the time of the blockade.

Nevertheless, the choice of protection for the colonies, which was also a choice for reconstructing the 'colonial system', was the fruit not of some marginal intrigue, but rather of a genuine, carefully considered and calculated alliance, reached after skilful parliamentary manoeuvres and a precise weighing of the political stakes. Port interests benefited in parliamentary debates from the determined support of metropolitan big property interests and also from that of manufacturers, particularly a cotton lobby in the Chamber of Deputies that manoeuvred skilfully and with an acute awareness of its strength, which it acquired during the Napoleonic era. The cotton manufacturers were very clear:

> The colonies are part of France ... the colonies have only ever been able to trade directly with France, it is in the ports of France that their produce must be landed and it is from them that the colonies must necessarily receive their supplies and the manufactured goods needed for their consumption....[4]

The system of laws put in place to reconstruct a colonial economy based on slavery was not simply the fruit of some intrigue, but the consequence of an agreement worked out among the various protectionist groups in the two houses of Parliament – above all landowners and manufacturers – and it was one of the most important components of the new 'economy-nation' constructed following the empire. This economy was to be agricultural, manufacturing, mercantile and also colonial, since the colonies were then regarded as an indispensable dimension of the economy-nation. Slavery was one component of that, and the constitutional liberals who were to take power in government, while remaining discreet on the question of slavery, yet accepted the ideological and moral constraints of it, since that was the price of the political consensus between the France of the Ancien Régime and the France that emerged from the Revolution.

A Partial Recovery of the French Colonial System

In the years following the Napoleonic period, the colonial economy, although reduced to modest dimensions after the loss and then the independence of Saint-Domingue, nevertheless partly lived up to the expectations of economic circles in the metropole. There was quite a steady recovery of imports from the colonies: 16.9 million francs in 1816; 27.6 million francs in 1817, 27.3 million francs in 1818, 25.3 million francs in 1819 and 30.6 million francs in 1820.

Yet this marked recovery in landings represented no more than half the imports of 1789, which amounted to 65.6 million francs. But these results were obtained in very different conditions from those that prevailed before the Revolution. The recovery was based on a very strong increase in the production of the Lesser Antilles and Bourbon. Imports into France from these two producing areas rose from 19.2 to 30 million francs between 1816 and 1820. The progress was striking but quite insufficient to keep France supplied with colonial produce. The development of production went hand in hand with a profound shift in the French colonies towards the production of sugar, at the expense of other products such as coffee and cocoa in particular, but also of dyes, which were essential for the French textile industry.

The bulk of those products being gradually abandoned in the French colonies came from the London entrepot but also from India, and, for raw sugar, from Brazil and Cuba. These imports, in particular those from India, were paid for in cash since France was not yet capable of re-establishing these long-distance export networks. The reconstruction of the colonial system thus proceeded without the positive flows of cash that had previously enriched France, and the gaps in supply and the essential imports even led to precious metal deficit at a time when mercantilist ideas were far from having been abandoned in French ruling circles.

These difficulties were soon noted by manufacturers, most of whom were favourable to the agreement reached in 1814 among the various components of the French economy, but were disappointed at not rediscovering, as many had expected, the favourable export networks that had once made them rich. Exports of manufactured goods to the colonial empire amounted to 80 million francs in 1789, but around 1820 they were stagnating at 30 million francs, and many manufacturers were concerned about the complacency of colonists in regard to the smuggling of British and American goods into the islands. Ternaux, the most high-profile individual in Parisian manufacturing was explicit:

> Since the peace of 1814, none of the advantages which ought to result from having colonies have been obtained, while their staple goods have been constantly favoured by the metropole. The markets in the islands constantly supplied with British manufactured items have offered only a difficult and often disastrous outlet

for our manufactured goods. Recoveries have generally been difficult and often impossible, through lack of adequate laws to protect creditors....[5]

As the 1820s began, the first balance sheet of the reconstruction of a colonial empire, articulated closely on the needs of the industrialization and economic recovery of France, remained patchy. The immediate success of sugar production that enabled French refineries to resume their rank in Europe cannot conceal the gaps and imbalances of a colonial economy that was unable to meet all the needs of the metropole. This economy, although protected, thus remained partly subject to the pressure of the international market, and was caught up in an economic logic that then affected raw materials required by industry. Protective duties on colonial produce remained moderate and taxes hit colonial sugars reaching the French market at a time when the Restoration had to face up to serious financial problems.

Crisis of the Colonial Economy and Division of Economic Interests

The whole French colonial system was shaken by a great turning-point in the business cycle, which affected not only France but the whole international market. That turning-point was the collapse of prices in the 1820s. In London, where sugars from India, Brazil and Cuba poured in, the prices of raw sugar fell by half, affecting the whole international market.

At the same time, it became apparent that in the French colonial empire the recovery of the plantations had been achieved with rising costs. The expenses of plantations in the Lesser Antilles had almost doubled since 1815. Salt beef costing 40 francs had risen to 100 francs, despite American imports. French shipowner-merchants were managing to circumvent the abolition of the slave trade quite satisfactorily, but the price of slaves had risen sharply, from 1,400 francs in 1816 to 1,800. On all sides, complaints poured in and many were already thinking of turning to new sources of labour, possibly free workers drawn from India and China.

Not only had the rise in costs made it impossible to resolve the festering problem of French colonial indebtedness but that debt had increased. By the early 1820s, it had risen to 180 million francs. Credit conditions had become so risky that the cost of borrowing money had risen to 25 per cent. Before the House of Peers, Chaptal cited the example of an estate in Martinique with expenses of 25,200 francs in 1789 that had risen to 41,700 francs by 1822. Several testimonies, including that of the Count of Sesmaisons, mentioned the collapse in the profitability of plantations, a fall which raised questions about the investment and modernization that was under way. According to him, a sugar mill in Martinique that produced 180,000 quintals of raw sugar and had a turnover of 900,000 francs yielded an income of only 7,650 francs, which reduced the return on capital to 1.2 per cent per annum at a time when credit was disappearing.

It was in this very difficult context that a highly organized colonial lobby was formed around a core of planters in the Antilles. These latter sent a delegation of fifty-two planters to Bordeaux: it stayed there several months and had available to it a large sum of gold raised from a collection among planters.[6] This lobby had a political head. Its spokesmen in Parliament were the Duke de Fitzjames, peer of France, the Marquis de Lally Tollendal, the Count de Sesmaisons and Révellière, and deputies and soldiers who had been directly associated with colonial circles, such as Lieutenant General Ambert.

The aim of this colonial group was to join with those calling, at a moment when the Restoration government was swinging to the Right, for a change of direction in protectionist policy. Until then, only manufactured products enjoyed the benefits of prohibition, since through them it was national labour that was being protected. Now, producers of grains, wool, livestock, coal and iron were calling for prohibition to combat falling prices that were reducing property rents, undermining profits and compromising investments. Sugar producers, too, wanted to secure a monopoly of the national market, hoping it would lead to higher prices by driving out foreign equivalents; for them above all this meant sugars from India and Brazil, which were being landed at ever lower prices. These foreign sugars represented only one-fifth of French consumption, but they were blamed entirely for the global fall in prices. Beyond that, the sugar producers also wanted to obtain a revision of the tax system and a big cut in the duty on colonial sugars entering France. They hoped, too, to push the government into securing an official restoration of the slave trade, the only way of ensuring any marked fall in labour costs.

The offensive by colonial circles was accompanied by a change of tone, style and arguments, which clearly identified the planters' movement with the ultra right. The discourse became tinged with a touchy nationalism: 'Sugar is the wheat of the colonies', the colonies are an integral part of the protected national economy and they are owed the same respect. The most public face of this alliance between the ultras and the colonial lobby was Count Vaublanc,[7] deputy from the Calvados, a former ardent supporter of Napoleon who had become an apologist for prohibition and an ardent defender of ultra views. He was supported by a powerful body in the house, which drew most of its members from the military. The colonies meant the survival of a powerful fleet, and beyond it was a navy; hence, restoring the country's power was a vital strategic issue for France at a time when the ultras had no intention of being outdone by the supporters of Napoleon. This line of argument, the different strands of which were skilfully co-ordinated by Villèle, secured higher protective tariffs in 1822, which kept out most foreign sugars. The law of 17 December 1814 had set the surtax on foreign sugars at 10 francs for 50 kg, and that of 27 July 1822 raised it to 25 francs.

This outcome was obtained after a very hard-fought battle with the liberal opposition, which increasingly made the colonial question a major economic and political issue. This liberal group was organized around a core of wealthy merchants-bankers who considered that the restoration of the colonial *Exclusif mitigé* with a strictness that it had never had under the Ancien Régime was exceedingly dangerous. By limiting the ambitions of French trade to the narrow space of the colonies, much reduced in the course of the revolutionary upheaval, French business was depriving itself of the new routes of the recently independent Spanish America and was reducing its ambitions in the direction of India and Asia. Eventually, such a choice would prevent it from facing Britain on an equal footing. This was the language used by Odier and Pillet-Will in the Paris Chamber of Commerce and by Larréguy, a big Paris merchant-broker, and it was that of the majority of the Conseil général du commerce. In the ports it was also the language of a new generation of more adventurous shipowners who had believed in government by the constitutionalists: Balguerie-Stuttenberg in Bordeaux, Thomas Dobrée in Nantes, Delaroche in Le Havre. Dobrée, who believed in the new markets in Spanish America, declared:

> The present colonial system crushes manufacturers everywhere. Using my system, consumers will be open to them worldwide.... The level of civilization that society has reached and the luxury that results from it mean that the peoples need to communicate with one another.... Would not the prosperity of everything to do with our fleet be better assured by opening up to it every possible route....[8]

Their action found political support in Benjamin Constant and Jacques Antoine Manuel, who spoke out in the Assembly, wrote in the left-wing press and were active in liberal Paris salons where merchants rubbed shoulders with young, politically committed intellectuals. Economists such as Jean-Baptiste Say and Adolphe Blanqui, at the Athénée in Paris, the Conservatoire des arts et métiers and the École spéciale de commerce de Paris, contested the colonial economy based on the *Exclusif mitigé*, quoted Smith and attacked a system of labour built around slavery. In the press, the *Commerce*, the *Producteur* and *Le Constitutionnel* reported their ideas. The efforts of the liberal world were brought together in the Société de morale chrétienne, which was organized on the model of the Liverpool Evangelical Society. La Rochefoucauld-Liancourt and Alexandre Delaborde, a liberal deputy for the capital, set its tone. In 1822, it set up a Comité pour l'abolition de la traite des Noirs.

The Limits of the Liberal Movement on the Problem of Slavery

We need to have a clear appreciation of the scope of the work and criticisms of this movement on the question of slavery. Originally, it was a movement that emerged from business, but also from some cotton manufacturers who considered that the colonial system had now become a hindrance to the expansion and modernization of the economy and that it cost the metropole too much by overloading it with ever-rising costs. Humblot-Conté, a liberal deputy in the Chamber of Deputies, estimated the cost of the *Exclusif mitigé* at 20 million francs. He took into account the surcharge imposed on foreign sugars and other colonial products, and the high costs of the colonial 'system' itself. The movement was thus initially a movement of notables, principally concerned with their money and their production costs, and not terribly sensitive to the question of blacks.

It is a short step from the economic to the social. In the furious debate between interests over the sugar question there were, on the one side, the plantation owners in the islands and the shipowners whose credit kept the plantations alive, and on the other, the refiners in the ports and Paris, whose chief concern was to find cheap raw sugar. The planters and their media, associated with the ultras, were convinced that sugar must be sold dear, that it must pay a genuine rent to plantation owners, that it was still an item of luxury consumption and that it could belong in only a highly hierarchical society. On the other side, the refiners were those who had made an investment, who wanted to reduce the cost of raw materials, who were determined to make sugar an object of mass consumption, who thought in terms of the market, who quoted Say and who were liberals.

The economic issue quickly became politicized, since every debate saw the planters and the ultras and the government – all supporters of the Spanish Bourbons, whom they had consolidated on their throne through the military intervention of 1823 – pitted against the liberals, very hostile to the Spanish monarchy and passionate advocates of the independence of South America. For all the merchants and economists, Spanish America constituted both an economic prospect that drew a line under the colonial past, and a new area of prosperity that could not be abandoned to the British; it was a symbol of the fight for freedom and independence.

On the problem of slavery itself, what the two sides had to say was more complex, more nuanced. What was at issue here was the fight against the slave trade. The question constantly recurred in Constant's speeches. It marginalized France in a progressive Europe. The ultra government was in cahoots with the slave traders, and its position was contrasted with that of the British, better from every angle, including on the question of the slave trade. The parliamentary debates conversely are very allusive on the question of the abolition of slavery. Most calls were for reform. The condition of blacks must be made less harsh, and the critical but also moralizing discourse that the philanthropists were developing on the labour question was extended to the question of slavery. In a small pamphlet published in 1830, P.-A. Dufau, a well-known philanthropist, attempted to persuade the planters that their deepest interest lay in initiating a reform of slavery, which, he argued, was the condition for a modernization of the plantations.[9]

There were very few clear-cut stands against slavery at this time. Adolphe Blanqui, professor at the École spéciale de commerce, condemned slavery on both economic and moral grounds, while Louis de Tollenare, a Nantes economist and merchant, but also a philanthropist, declared that 'slavery is an injustice, that it is in the highest degree an outrage to justice, the basis of all civilization …'.

Overall, the movement remained moderate, dominated by economic considerations rather than by any moral and political concern. But it was a powerful movement which rejected out of hand the path adopted by the Right to solve the economic difficulties that had appeared with the British crisis of 1823. In the 1827 elections, this movement won the departure of Villèle, and the monarchy under Charles X was unable to win again in Parliament. In 1828, it secured agreement for the appointment of a commission of enquiry into the colonial system, with the aim of reducing the prohibitive duties on foreign sugars and beginning a reform of the colonial regime himself.

Yet this liberal movement, which was to sweep away the Restoration politically, secured only very modest results on the colonial question, so much so that one might speak of an actual failure of the opposition challenge. There are several explanations for this stubborn resistance put up by an economic system that might well have been thought to be very much undermined, or even fatally condemned, as the 1820s began.

The Colonial System Protected by French Economic Conservatism

Contrary to first impressions, the economic system of the French colonies proved in fact to be more efficient than it was thought in overcoming the crisis precipitated by the fall in prices, which began in 1820. The virtual prohibitions granted to colonial products succeeded in halting the decline in prices. In the sugar islands, now granted a monopoly on the national market, investments had been made: there were more modern ploughs, more mules and more steam engines. New investment is estimated to have amounted to 15 million francs. There was a steep rise in the price of slaves: figures around 1,800 or even 2,500 francs are often mentioned in Cayenne, but the rise was countered by looking for productivity gains.

The enquiries conducted by Mr de Beilac, the director of customs in the Antilles, found a marked transformation in the way slaves were treated.[10] Slaves were better fed, but Saturdays, which had often been set aside for working on private plots in former days, were now devoted to the plantation. Sunday rest was granted, but the working day was extended. The hospitals were improved, and there was a trend towards rising numbers of slaves due to a high birth rate, which required increased attention to maternity units. The price of half a quintal of raw sugar had risen by the late 1820s from 18–20 francs to 28 or even 32 francs. Plantation profits had also bounced back by 9 or 10 per cent, according to the local administration. A third of the planters had succeeded in liquidating their debts by 1830 – a significant result, although it varied considerably from region to region.

Overall, these advances were enough to delay the critical choices and basic reforms. They also limited the impact of the harshest criticisms of the rationality of the slave system. By integrating itself closely into the French system of prohibition, the colonial system, and also slavery, were protected. They were part of a whole, which was the economy-nation, and which, despite its increasingly conservative features, unlike in the days following the fall of Napoleon, remained the basis of the economic policy of the first industrialization.

After 1830, manufacturers hesitated to attack a colonial system for fear of having to extend the debate to the protection afforded by France. The military men were a standing reminder that the navy could not live without the colonies, which alone represented half the ship movements of the merchant navy. The bureaux argued that it was still the solution for preserving the French trade balance. Protected throughout a socio-economic structure in which the parts held together, the colonial system and slavery, which had been threatened in the 1820s, obtained a respite as the 1830s began. Count d'Argout, rapporteur of the great survey launched on the government's initiative in 1829, gives the key to the behaviour of those responsible for economic policy:

> The monopoly exercised by the colonies is harmful to France but none of those who spoke to us has suggested eliminating it entirely, either so as not to upset the interest of colonists too much or because it is thought that since current legislation has encouraged them to expand their crops considerably, there would be a sort of injustice in suddenly depriving them of all protection, but we are agreed to demand some moderation of that protection....

*   *   *

The problem of slavery thus appears in the first phase of the industrialization of France as a rather modest part of a wider and mainly economic colonial problem. The first requirement was for the colonial empire to recover, that empire being, in the minds of the majority of those in leadership positions, an indispensable component of the power and wealth of France. The difficulties of the slave trade, the cost of slavery and the need for international agreement with victorious Britain were all obstacles standing in the way of that recovery. Sensitive to the political campaign being waged by the British against the slave trade and, anxious, too, not to weaken the constraints of the *Exclusif mitigé*, many pragmatic notables would have liked an evolution, a reform, an alleviation of the costs of a colonial system which could no longer play the essential role that it had played under the Ancien Régime due to the prosperity of Saint-Domingue.

This aspiration to change, however, was prudent: it remained narrowly restricted to economic matters and to the slave trade, concerning which British pressure was strong. It was not sufficiently determined to attack the roots of the system, especially as this latter, once again buttressed by rising customs duties, credit and national consumption, gradually recovered its lost profitability. The problem seemed to have been overcome by 1830, especially as indigenous beet sugar and sugar from the colonies worked together and both needed high prices and a protected national market. Things changed with the dispute over the two sugars that erupted in the 1840s. The challenge to cane sugar, which had become the pillar of the colonial economy, by a metropolitan, modern, aggressive and cheaper sugar capitalism would make the system of the *Exclusif mitigé* vulnerable once again, and beyond that would repose the problem of slavery in new terms.

Notes

1. See Saint-Cricq, Director of Customs, *Archives parlementaires*, 19 January 1822.
2. 'Mémoire de la chambre de commerce de Nantes', 1 July 1814, Archives Nationales F 12/637.
3. 'Mémoire adressé par la chambre de commerce de Nantes à Monsieur le directeur général du Commerce', 27 July 1814, Archives Nationales F 12/637.
4. Extract from 'Mémoire adressé à Monsieur le Directeur général du commerce par la Chambre de commerce de Rouen', July 1814, Archives Nationales, F 12/637.
5. See Ternaux to the Conseil général du commerce, 23 April 1822, Archives Nationales F12/2492.
6. *Pétition des colons propriétaires-planteurs des colonies françaises, des négociants et armateurs, des manufacturiers raffineurs de la ville de Bordeaux*, Bordeaux, Pinard, 1822.
7. Comte de Vaublanc, *Du commerce de la France en 1820 et 1821*, Paris, 1823.
8. T. Dobrée, *Pétition adressée à la Chambre des Députés*, Nantes, Mélisset, October 1821, p. 6.
9. P.-A. Dufau, *De l'abolition graduelle de l'esclavage dans les colonies européennes et notamment dans les colonies françaises considérée à la fois dans l'intérêt des esclaves, des maîtres, des colonies et des métropoles*, Paris, 1830.
10. See *Conseil supérieur du commerce, de l'agriculture et de l'industrie. Enquête sur le régime des sucres*, Paris, Imprimerie royale, 1829.

Chapter 21

The Reconstruction of the French Abolitionist Movement under the July Monarchy

Philippe Vigier

THIS ESSAY IS intended to highlight three main points.

Before getting into the discussion, we need to remind ourselves how much, in this area as in many others, the 1830 Revolution prepared the ground for the 1848 Revolution – even though the 'quarante-huitards' (men of '48), and first and foremost Victor Schœlcher, went much further, especially as regards the abolitionist movement, than most liberals under the July Monarchy. But it was not because the 'Resistance Party' and the centre-right won control of the government in 1831 over the party of 'Movement' – the rightward drift of the Orleanist monarchy becoming more apparent after 1840 – that the majority of liberal leaders forgot an infringement of the Rights of Man – albeit a black man! – that many of them had been denouncing before 1830 when they were in opposition.[1] It was in fact '1830' that made possible a reconstruction of the French abolitionist movement, and it would be wrong to believe that that movement was in a minority among French notables and its representatives in parliament (slight though the immediate results of this action may have been), and that it did not influence subsequent developments. The best proof of this, in my view, is that the radical decisions taken in February–May 1848 by a republican-democratic government were not reversed (at least in principle) by a 'party of order' and that Louis Napoleon Bonaparte did not want, or dare ,to go back on the decision to abolish slavery, something which his predecessors at the beginning of the century had not hesitated to do.

It is this renewal and expansion of the French abolitionist movement that I shall discuss first, stressing above all the leading role played in it by the Société française pour l'abolition de l'esclavage. Founded in 1833, it saw itself as a pressure group, endeavouring to influence both public opinion and the two chambers and through them successive governments. Knowing the social and political make-up of this society is valuable, and we have a reliable guide in A.-J. Tudesq, whose *Les grands notables en France de 1840 à 1849*, though now already dated, remains a mine of information and relevant commentary.[2] Virtually all of the key members of this society, at a time when there was a property-based franchise, were great notables with otherwise widely differing political and religious opinions, from the conservative Orleanist Protestant François Guizot to the republican ('radical' was the word used then) freemason Victor Schœlcher – who, as we shall see, was an active member of the Society.

But it remains the case that Protestants played an essential role in the Society, stimulated, of course, by the vital part played by their British co-religionists in the abolition of slavery enacted and realized on the other side of the Channel between 1833 and 1838. Members of the French Reformed Church had already been influential, in 1822, in creating a committee for the abolition of the slave trade within the Société de morale chrétienne, in which the prime movers were Guizot and the count de Laborde. But according to Tudesq, 'the most representative of the Protestant notables waging the campaign against slavery under the July Monarchy was count Agénor de Gasparin regarded by the slave interests as one of their most formidable adversaries'.[3] In the 1840s, he was very active in persuading the consistories of Paris and, above all, of the provinces to get signatures on petitions addressed to parliament.[4]

However, the role played by Protestant notables – and through them the British example – must not obscure the fact that Catholic circles (considered here in the broadest sense of the word, to include both the practising and the non-practising) also provided the anti-slavery movement with some of its leading figures. Alexis de Tocqueville, rapporteur of the 1839 parliamentary committee, endeavoured to 'defuse' the arguments of the colonial lobby – to which we shall come later – by proposing that the colonists be compensated. The fact that his proposal failed to withstand the pressures of the colonial lobby did not prevent him from remaining a committed supporter of abolition in his subsequent parliamentary activities.[5] As for Charles de Rémusat, the 'prince of youth' in the mid-1820s, Minister of the Interior in 1840, he describes himself in his *Mémoires* as an 'old negrophile' – which is certainly not unrelated to the fact that he was a passionate admirer of 'English liberalism'.[6] For Hippolyte Passy, another member of the anti-slavery 'networks', this liberalism was much more a matter of economics: he was a member of several governments under Louis-Philippe, and, above all, was the first to raise the question of slavery on the floor of the chamber, in 1837.[7] But it was only in 1840–1 that the man who, in Tudesq's opinion, was to patronize the abolitionist campaign at the end of the July Monarchy came out clearly: duke Achille Victor de Broglie (1785–1870).[8] He chaired the committee formed on 26 May 1840 'to examine questions related to slavery and the political constitution of the colonies'. This committee, established by the Thiers-Rémusat ministry (February–October 1840), doubtless at the instigation of the latter, enabled the abolitionists (despite modest results in elections, for reasons which will be set out below) to draw the attention of enlightened opinion to the urgency of the problem, especially as the de Broglie report, laid before the chamber in 1843, reached much the same conclusion as the Tocqueville report of 1839.[9]

Furthermore, the work being undertaken by parliamentarians was extended and disseminated by the action of a large section of the press, which, of course, expanded enormously in size and influence under the July Monarchy.[10] How can we not be sensitive to the fact that the *Journal des débats* – the semi-official paper of an Orleanist regime that was moving steadily to the right – 'approves the formation of the de Broglie committee and criticizes the colonists in the Antilles for seeking to maintain slavery', in an article dated 5 July 1840? It is true that, like de Tocqueville, and the majority of the de Broglie committee, it hoped for a compromise solution – one that would harm neither the interests of the colonists nor the economic future of the islands.[11] The Fourierist Victor Considérant's *Démocracie pacifique* was also abolitionist, but much more radical, situated as it was at the other end of the political spectrum. The Guadeloupian lawyer Charles Dain waged the same anti-slavery campaign in it[12] as another 'Antillean immigrant' into the metropole, Cyrille Bissette, did in the *Revue des colonies* – the man and the publication deserving a few lines here, especially as we now know much more abut them, thanks to the thesis by Stella Pâme.[13]

Bissette, an astonishing and disconcerting individual, belonged to that group of free people of colour who, for the most part, says Pâme, were looked down on by whites and detested by blacks, while they themselves detested whites and looked down on blacks. In fact, I think the reality was more complex. It reminds me, *mutatis mutandis*, of the status of the French petits bourgeois that I have studied closely. In this precise case, everything depends not only on the particular combination of black and white, from the mulatto to the quadroon and beyond,[14] but also, and especially, it seems (this explains my continental reference), on the socio-political circumstances. Those circumstances might drive free people of colour either to the side of the whites or to the side of the blacks – just as, in France, depending on the time, the petit bourgeois (artisan, shopkeeper, clerk) feels sometimes petit, sometimes bourgeois. That, to come back to the point, is what explains the astonishing political trajectory of Bissette, who, in his early days, when there was strong hostility between 'Creoles' and free people of colour, made himself the ardent defender of black slaves against 'white colonists' in the columns of the *Revue des colonies*, a monthly that appeared irregularly between 1834 and 1842, which Pâme has analysed convincingly.[15]

So, under the July Monarchy, Bissette fought the same radical fight as Victor Schœlcher – who, after 1848, would become his sworn enemy in the politics of the Antilles, dominated for several years by the confrontation between followers of Schœlcher and those of Bissette. By then, Cyrille Bissette had become the spokesman of the Creoles and the Martinican Party of Order. However, I refer readers to Nelly Schmidt and her writings on this matter,[16] which falls outside the chronological framework I have set myself. Here, I shall simply add to the names that I have just mentioned that of Victor Schœlcher. It was under the July Monarchy that the liberator of the slaves began his battle, after two journeys in 1829–30 and 1840–1 in the southern United States and, above all, the Caribbean – Cuba, Jamaica and the French and British West

Indies.[17] The wretched plight of the black slaves that he observed with his own eyes impelled him to come out, in 1833, for the abolition of slavery. Following his second journey, made after the 'gradual abolition' enacted for the British colonies (which was not achieved without difficulty), the bourgeois-rentier argued in 1842 for 'the immediate abolition of slavery'.[18] Such a 'radical' stand naturally did not fit in with the solutions advocated by virtually every other notable of the time any more than did the tone of the numerous articles that he wrote for the *Réforme* – the 'left republican' newspaper that he had helped to establish in 1843 with Ledru-Rollin, Louis Blanc and others.[19] Yet it remains the case that, while, as a republican, he rejected the narrowly property-based regime which most of the leaders of the Société pour l'abolition de l'esclavage supported, he nevertheless agreed to work with them 'for the good cause', just as other leading Orleanist notables asked, even ordered, him to do their writing when drafting one or other of their petitions (an example is provided at the end of the chapter).[20]

Just as they had done so before under the July Monarchy, 'abolitionists' faced a powerful anti-abolitionist 'colonial party'. This continued to bring together in Paris the representatives of most of the prominent slave-owning planters who refused to give up their slaves and the spokesmen of the merchants in the Atlantic coast ports – Bordeaux, Nantes and Le Havre. The former had an official body, representing the 'colonists of the islands (Martinique, Guadeloupe and Bourbon)' and French Guyana: the Conseil des délégués des colonies, which, in addition to the influential planters, included members of both chambers. According to A.-J. Tudesq,[21]

> the two most active members were Jollivet, deputy for Rennes and advocate at the Royal Court in Paris, and above all baron Charles Dupin, delegate from Martinique and president of the Conseil des délégués for many years. He was the principal spokesman for the opponents of emancipation, and he was remarkably skilful at using his influence, his membership of many other committees and his overvalued scientific reputation[22] to transform the defence of slavery into a defence of the colonies, and to interest in the defence of the colonies many interests represented in parliament and cabinets.[23]

Defence of the colonies also meant, of course, defence of the interests of the Atlantic trade. Already stunned, and rightly so, by the loss of Saint-Domingue, the 'pearl of the Antilles' (the serious difficulties in which 'free Haiti' was embroiled were moreover a valuable argument for the anti-abolitionists), the merchants of Normandy or the Gironde refused to contemplate an abolition which, in their eyes, would ruin what remained of the colonial economy and trade, an argument repeated over and over by the chambers of commerce of Bordeaux, Nantes and Le Havre.[24]

All this helps to throw light – and this will be the third and last point of what I have to say – on the limited impact of abolitionist activity that was supported *in principle* by the majority of those who, in this ultra-property-based regime, held political power. This observation, well brought out in particular by A.-J. Tudesq, became especially apparent after 1840, with the explicit adhesion of Guizot to the views of the de Broglie committee, set up, as we have seen, under the previous administration. But the man who, as we know, was to be Louis-Philippe's principal minister until his fall had to take account of the wave of Anglophobia that was sweeping the parliamentary majority (including some of those who were, like him, abolitionists). Guizot did not realize, in particular, that by granting British warships, of which there were many more than there were French warships, the right to search both French and British ships to confirm that they were not carrying victims of a slave trade condemned by both countries, he risked being accused of harming national interests. That is what he was criticized for by accusers on all sides in the parliamentary session of 1841–2, after which Guizot was forced practically to abandon enforcing that right.[25]

He at least appeased his conscience, like that of his abolitionist friends, by securing the passage in 1845–6 of several measures that went a little further than the mere *theoretical* improvements made during the previous decade to the condition of slaves in French colonies.[26] The law of 18 July 1845, in particular, aimed to encourage the manumission of slaves by providing the freed slave with a small amount of money and allowing him to own property. The state set the example by collectively freeing the black slaves on its domain in the colonies of Martinique, Guadeloupe, French Guyana and Bourbon.[27] Tudesq regards these legal provisions as 'a first step towards abolition', and he adds: 'When abolition was proclaimed under the Second Republic, the debates in the Chambers of the property-based monarchy had prepared and won round metropolitan opinion; the measure adopted was irreversible.'[28]

But it remains true, as the same author says, that 'the effect of the laws of 1845 had been modest in the extreme', in so far as, like earlier half measures, they were poorly enforced locally by the colonists and all supporters of the status quo.[29] The latter were especially skilful at exploiting the divergences that had appeared within the anti-slavery movement, in particular during debates in the de Broglie committee and the parliamentary debates that had followed: Would slave emancipation be immediate and radical, or partial and gradual, with or without a transitional period of apprenticeship after the British example? Despite a clear anti-slavery majority, especially in the Chamber of Deputies, the Orleanist monarchy in its last years was here, as in many other areas, incapable of taking a decision.

We can thus understand the exasperation of a man like Victor Schœlcher, who in August 1847 drew up – on Société pour l'abolition de l'esclavage letterhead – a *Pétition aux Chambres pour demander l'abolition de l'esclavage dans les colonies françaises* (Petition to the Chambers to ask for the abolition of slavery in the French colonies). In it, he denounced the inadequacy and, above all, the non-implementation of the partial measures adopted hitherto by a government which 'has several times declared that its formal desire was to destroy forever this institution, a shameful vestige of barbarous times'. France 'had not demonstrated its wishes with enough unity'. So, following the British example, he suggested to parliamentarians that they set up and lead, in the principal towns of the kingdom, committees working for 'the *total* and *immediate* abolition of slavery', in particular through 'petitions designed to gather the maximum possible number of signatures'.[30]

In fact, only the 'Éclairs de février' would enable him, a few months later, to bring about the triumph of this radical solution. Decidedly, whatever Solzhenitsyn may say in his old age, revolutions do not only have perverse effects.

Notes

1. See the previous essay by Francis Démier, who, moreover, is one of those, along with M. Agulhon and a few others, who have done most to give the importance and significance of 'Les Trois Glorieuses' of July 1830 their proper place in the history of the nineteenth century. See also the special issue of *Romantisme*, to mark the 150th anniversary of the Revolution of 1830.
2. A.-J. Tudesq, *Les grands notables en France de 1840 à 1849*, Paris, P.U.F., 1964, 2 Vols, Vol. 1.
3. A.-J. Tudesq, op. cit., Vol. 2, pp. 835 and note 367: 'In addition to his action in a number of societies, see his publications, in particular *Esclavage et traite* (1838) and *De l'affranchissement des esclaves et son rapport avec la politique actuelle* (1839).' Agénor-Étienne de Gasparin (1810–71) must not be confused with his father, Adrien de Gasparin (1783–1862), who was Minister of the Interior in 1836 and, above all, one of the greatest agronomists of his time, who is dealt with extensively in my thesis on *La Seconde République dans la région alpine*, Paris, P.U.F., 1963, Vol. 1, pp. 28, 32–4, 38–41; Vol. 2, pp. 52–4, 64–6, etc.
4. A.-J. Tudesq, op. cit., cites many of these petitions, which are in the petition files (C2.209–2.225) of the archives of the assemblies now preserved in the Archives Nationales.
5. On the parliamentary debates and positions on the problem that concerns us here, further details will be found in the section devoted to 'a humanitarian crusade for the abolition of slavery' in *L'Histoire de la France coloniale* by J. Meyer, J. Tarrade, A. Rey-Goldzeiguer and J. Thobie, Paris, A. Colin, 1991, Vol. 1, pp. 383–7. One should also, of course, consult what there is about the problem of slavery in the *Oeuvres complètes* of Alexis de Tocqueville, in particular Vol. 3, *Écrits et discours politique*, Paris, Gallimard, 1962, pp. 48, 124–5.
6. C. de Rémusat, *Mémoires de ma vie*, Paris, Plon, 1962, Vol. 4, p. 8.
7. J. Meyer et al., op. cit., 384.
8. He also was several times a member of Orleanist governments, and a firm supporter of the Anglo-French Entente Cordiale; he was the father of Albert de Broglie (1821–1901), the man of moral order in the 1870s, with whom he must not be confused. It is true that the genealogy of this family, originally from Piedmont, is not easy to remember – and yet it is important for an understanding of our national history, in every area (see *Dictionnaire de biographie française* by P.-R d'Amat, Vol. 38, p. 402).
9. A.-J. Tudesq, op. cit., p. 837; J. Meyer et al., op. cit., p. 384 et seq.
10. See C. Bellanger, J. Godechot, P. Guiral and F. Terrou, *Histoire générale de la presse française*, Paris, P.U.F., 1969, Vol. 2, pp. 91–143, and general histories of the July Monarchy.
11. A.-J. Tudesq, op. cit., p. 850.
12. See the note devoted to Charles Dain, lawyer for Adolphe Blanqui, at the Tours/Blois trial in 1847, in A. Blanqui, *Oeuvres*, Nancy, Presses universitaires de Nancy, 1993, Vol. 1, p. 508.
13. Thèse de troisième cycle devoted to Cyrille Bissette (1795–1858), prepared under the supervision of F. Mauro, and defended at Université de Paris X-Nanterre.
14. S. Pame, *Cyrille Bissette, un martyr de la liberté*, Fort-de-France, Desormeaux, pp. 16–17. Bissette, described as 'mulatto', was probably rather a 'quadroon'.
15. Ibid., pp. 240–76.

16. See her thèse de troisième cycle defended at Université de Paris X-Nanterre, in December 1978, under my supervision: 'La vie politique en Guadeloupe au début de la période post-esclavagiste (1848–1871).'

17. For all this, see N. Schmidt's recently published *Victor Schœlcher*, Paris, Fayard, 1990, 440 pp., pp. 22–95, and, for more details, her thesis for the doctorat d'État on 'Victor Schœlcher et le processus de destruction du système esclavagiste aux Caraïbes au XIXe siècle', defended in March 1991, under the supervision of F. Caron, at the Université de Paris IV.

18. The expression 'for the immediate abolition of slavery' is to be found in several pamphlets published by Schœlcher between 1842 and 1848: see N. Schmidt, op. cit., pp. 339–40. Schmidt also asserts that 'this second Caribbean journey shook Schœlcher's ideas in favour of gradual emancipation of the slaves. While in 1833 he had envisaged a package of reforms designed to transform the laws "without danger", as he said, for the prosperity and public order of the colonies, the failures of British apprenticeship precipitated his decision to militate for immediate suppression' (ibid., p. 30). In all her works, Schmidt insists on the need to replace the history of the French Antilles in the 'Caribbean world', following directly in the footsteps of Schœlcher who 'was the pioneer in France of writings on the history of the Caribbean in a comparative perspective' (ibid., p. 46).

19. N. Schmidt, op. cit., pp. 281–2, provides a list of the articles that appeared in this paper where he wrote a 'colonial column'. On Schœlcher, the *Réforme* and the Republican Party, see Schmidt, op. cit., pp. 60–3, as well as the classic work by G. Weill, *Histoire du parti républicain en France (1814–1870)*, Paris, 1928, 2nd edn, pp. 146–8.

20. For the present, I shall simply refer to Schmidt, op. cit., pp. 60–71.

21. From whom I borrow most of what I say here, referring for more details to the pages devoted in A.-J. Tudesq, op. cit., pp. 838–46, to 'the defence of the colonies and the opponents of immediate abolition'.

22. For once, I am not in agreement with Tudesq: among other contributions to French science Charles Dupin was the true founder of statistical studies. That being so, like his elder brother, André Marie, known as Dupin the elder, he must not have been unaware of the financial advantages that this or that responsibility or intervention might bring about.

23. A.-J. Tudesq, op. cit., p. 839. On the countless anti-abolitionist publications of the period, which 'fuelled' the discourse of the colonial lobby, there is a good account in a long note in Schmidt, op. cit., pp. 287–8.

24. Numerous quotations in A.-J. Tudesq, op. cit., pp. 841–6.

25. This famous affair of the 'right of search' is reported, at greater or lesser length, in every history of the July Monarchy. I shall therefore say no more about it, especially as it is important not to confuse the question of the slave trade with that of the legal status of the victims of that trade, although undoubtedly the two problems overlapped in many ways.

26. J. Meyer et al., op. cit., pp. 283–384, provide a detailed description of what the authors call a 'one step at a time policy'.

27. S. Charlety, Vol. 5 of *L'Histoire de la France contemporaine* (ed. E. Lavisse), pp. 286–8.

28. A.-J. Tudesq, op. cit., p. 851.

29. See J. Meyer et al., op. cit., pp. 383–4.

30. The text of this petition is in the Bibliothèque Nationale, shelfmark LK9-751.

Chapter 22

Resistance Movements in the French Colonies: The Bissette Affair (1823–1827)

Éric Mesnard

ON 12 JANUARY 1824, the Royal Tribunal in Martinique sentenced three 'free men of colour', Bissette, Fabien and Volny, to the galleys for life. They were accused of having taken part in a conspiracy designed to 'overthrow the civil and political order in the French colonies'.

In France, their lawyers, with the support of leading liberals, waged a campaign to win public opinion over to their side and obtained a new trial in 1827, which ended in the acquittal of Fabien and Volny and the sentencing of Bissette to ten years' banishment.

The sole alleged 'crime' of Bissette and his companions was to have disseminated in Martinique a pamphlet entitled *De la situation des gens de couleur libres aux Antilles françaises* (On the situation of free people of colour in the French Antilles). This document did no more than denounce the unfair treatment meted out to 'free people of colour' and claim equal rights for them, and them only.

The Bissette affair reflected a hardening of the conflict between whites and 'free people of colour' and, in France, breathed new life into the debate on the situation of the colonies. The liberals took up the cause of the 'free people of colour', while the plantocracy brandished the 'spectre of Haiti'. The old slave-owning colonial order was trying to make history stumble.

The political and legal twists and turns of the Bissette affair have been described in detail by several historians, notably by Stella Pâme in her thesis entitled *Cyrille Bissette* (Paris X, 1978). I shall here set out the main points.

At the beginning of December 1823, a 32-page pamphlet with a red cover was brought into Martinique. This lampoon, entitled *De la situation des gens de couleur libres aux Antilles françaises*, had been published legally in France and had been presented to the Minister of the Colonies without there being any question of banning it. At most, the Director of the Colonial Bureau, Bayardelle de Loreinty, envisaged preparing a refutation of it.

This document, later attributed to Bissette, was most likely written by figures in the metropole friendly to free men of colour (the marquis de Sainte-Croix or Lainé de Villevêque).

The pamphlet denounces the injustices suffered by 'free men of colour' and calls on the government to remove discriminatory measures which, according to the author, run counter to the *Code Noir* and 'the present state of civilization'.

'Free men of colour' are presented in it as 'a class as useful as it is hardworking', whose conduct 'defies censure'. They are victims of 'birth or colour prejudice' and are 'both excluded from honourable occupations, and exposed to all the whims and all the snubs of the privileged caste which fears their industry and their intelligence' (text of the pamphlet published by P. Baudé in *L'affranchissement des esclaves aux Antilles françaises* [Fort-de-France, 1948], p. 129 [a copy of the original is in the British Library; see p. 10]).

The closing sentences of the document (ibid., pp. 137–8 [pp. 32–3]) highlight the legalism of the 'free men of colour' and stress their determination to maintain the slave-based colonial order.

> An attempt is being made, we know, to frighten the government, and to convince it that we shall lose our colonies the moment that free people of colour, having won the rights that they are demanding, will glorify in the title of Frenchmen and be able, in both hemispheres, to bless the name of the monarch who has freed them from the demeaning distinctions to which they are condemned! We shall not reply to those counsellors who claim to see the future, what is absurd is its own refutation.
>
> They would have liked to present to the king a supplication signed by all of them, but fearing that the meetings that such an approach would have necessitated might be wrongly interpreted, and provide new weapons for malevolence or calumny, they have contented themselves with publishing this exposé, convinced that, however supplications reach the foot of the throne, they will win the attention of an enlightened, just and magnanimous prince.

As this quotation shows, the pamphlet was in no way a subversive onslaught. It was rather a call, for the 'free men of colour' alone, for the benevolent arbitration of the metropolitan government. I shall return to this point.

The Bissette affair, properly so called, began on 12 December 1823. After Cyrille Bissette was denounced to Governor Donzelot, who initially attempted to play down the incident, his house was searched. Two copies of the red pamphlet were found there. On 13 December, Bissette was arrested.

On 21 December, a slave, who was later freed, 'revealed' a plot put together by the free men of colour to incite the slave gangs to revolt. The next day, two 'free men of colour', Fabien and Volny, joined Bissette in prison. Then, in the following days, a full-scale round-up was conducted, which hit the social élite of the 'free men of colour'.

On 2 January 1824, at his first arraignment, the procurator, Deslandes, alleged without proof that a secret organization existed, charged with leading an insurrection against the whites. He accused Bissette of being the leader of a plot designed 'to overthrow the established order with the help of pamphlets tending to stir people up'.

On 12 January 1824, making its judgement on appeal, the Royal Tribunal in Martinique sentenced Bissette, Fabien and Volny to be branded in public with the letters G.A.L. and then to be sent to the galleys for life.

As regards the other 'free men of colour' arrested at the end of 1823, 141 were sentenced to be deported for life, and 60 others were expelled without trial. In total, taking into account the families, 700 individuals were driven out of the colony.

The governor had the companies of colour of the militias of Saint-Pierre and Fort-Royal disarmed, and asked for the despatch of troops 'to calm the white class'.

After the Martinican phase of the affair, which ended with the triumph of the colonists, the metropolitan phase began with the liberals to the fore.

Bissette and his companions arrived in Brest and took their case to the Court of Cassation (Appeal Court). They were defended by the lawyers Isambert and Chauveau-Lagarde (who had been Brissot's defender).

After a campaign to win over public opinion waged in the press and in the chamber by the liberal leaders (Chateaubriand, Casimir Périer, Benjamin Constant, the duke de Broglie, etc.), the case was referred to the Royal Tribunal in Guadeloupe.

On 28 March 1827, Fabien and Volny were acquitted, and Bissette was sentenced to ten years' banishment. Bissette then settled in Paris, where he embarked on a new career.

What Were the Lessons of the Bissette Affair?

The immediate effect, in the metropole, was a revival of interest in colonial questions, and 'enlightened' public opinion proclaimed its sympathy for 'free people of colour'.

As regards Martinican society, the Bissette affair laid bare the exacerbation of the conflict between whites and 'men of colour' (for Guadeloupe, see Josette Fallope, *Esclaves et citoyens – Les Noirs à la Guadeloupe au XIXᵉ siècle* [Basse-Terre, 1992]).

The white population of the islands came from a variety of backgrounds but contempt for 'men of colour' was, in a crisis, a binding force. The determination to maintain the 'colour bar' was hammered in. The 'flaw' of African origin was declared to be 'indelible'. Added to this for the mixed race, who formed the largest group among the 'free men', was the accusation of 'licentiousness' and 'bastardy'.

E. Hayot has noted the apparent contradiction between the individual attitude of Creole whites, who were generally concerned about what happened to their natural children and their free men, and the collective attitude of the group, which was worried about the increasing numbers and economic

importance of 'men of colour', and opposed even the most limited emancipation of 'free men of colour'.

An ecclesiastic, wondering about this, wrote: '[W]hy do people spend the
day constructing with great resort to legal texts barriers that they are quite
decided to breach at night?'

The stories of the colonists from Saint-Domingue who had taken refuge
in the Lesser Antilles exacerbated whites' concern. For example, one of the
judges of the Martinican tribunal that sentenced Bissette and his companions
in 1824 (Amboise Gouin) was a Creole from Saint-Domingue.

This fear of an 'anti-white' plot was heightened by the economic slow-
down confronting the plantocracy, as it faced up to competition from the metropolitan sugar beet industry and liberals' mistrust.

The Bissette affair reflected a hardening of the conflict between whites and
'free men'. Some colonists regretted that there had not been a capital execution and proposed to tighten discriminatory measures even further. The most
radical talked of exiling 'men of colour' en masse and deporting them to Senegal or French Guyana.

The group of 'free men of colour' was diverse both socially and in terms
of skin colour.

As regards numbers, this group had grown rapidly. In 1816, the number
of Martinican 'free people' for the first time overtook the number of whites.
When the Bissette affair erupted, there were about 11,000 'free people' and
10,000 whites.

Economically, the group of 'free people' was chiefly in competition with
the *petits blancs* in the towns. About a third of 'free people' lived in towns and
were engaged mainly in construction and trade.

The Bissette family was an illustration of this economic and social rise of
some 'free people'. Charles Bissette, Cyrille's father, had become a master mason
in Fort-Royal. He married a free mixed-race woman, the natural daughter of
Joseph Tascher de la Pagerie. He owned slaves, whom he used in his business.
When he died in 1810, he left his widow a house and savings that enabled
her to start a business.

Cyrille Bissette, the oldest of their six children, also succeeded. He married a mulatto woman, Marie-Rose Séverin, daughter of a master blacksmith.
Bissette's writings testify to a solid education, and his defenders insisted on
how 'organized' Bissette's life was before his arrest. He saw himself as a man of
order who had every interest in not questioning the slave-based colonial order.
At his interrogation in 1823, he stated:

> I never had the idea of stirring up free men of colour against whites; those to
> whom I read it [the lampoon] had as much interest as I did, being all property
> owners, in maintaining order and tranquillity in the colony and stood only to lose
> if it was disturbed.

In October 1822, Cyrille Bissette helped to put down the slave revolt at Le Carbet, and his lawyer, *maître* Isambert, stressed in pleading his client's case that he had left his dying mother's bedside to help do so.

Following that repression, Governor Donzelot noted in the report he sent to the ministry: 'The militiamen who have been mobilized, both white and coloured, tried to outdo one another in zeal and devotion to put down the revolt and hunt down the criminals.'

Until the 1830s, the 'free people of colour' were seeking to have discriminatory measures removed, based on Article 59 of the *Code Noir*. To achieve that, they were counting on the support of liberals and the hesitations of the government over the application of segregationist measures. The 1823 pamphlet challenged the 'colour bar' in the sole interests of the 'free people' (*libres*).

In a document of 12 December 1830, entitled *Lettres à un colon*, Bissette did not question metropolitan policy, including when it accepted the slave trade, but asked that colonists be subject to the laws of the metropole.

He contrasted the hard-working class of 'free people' to the 'privileged caste' descended from the 'scum of France ... from filibusters, buccaneers, beggars, fugitives from gaol and men condemned by public opinion' (pp. 7–8).

According to him, it was the colonists' attitude that was the cause of disorder. The whites were accused not only of ingratitude but of lacking patriotic feeling:

> The soul of the colonists ... closed to humanity is also closed to love of country [p. 23]. As the foremost example of this, I put the cowardly behaviour that they exhibited at various times in delivering Martinique and Guadeloupe to the British.... Of course, if men of colour had enjoyed civil and political rights, they would have been opposed to that high treason; proof of that is to be found in the patriotism that they displayed in Guadeloupe, in 1794, in keeping the colony for the mother country. It is true that at that time they participated in public responsibilities.... These facts show that the sole means not only of saving the colonies but of retaining them lies in complete and absolute emancipation ... [p. 23].

Here, he was referring to the emancipation 'of the free people', of course.

The Policy Advocated by Bissette

The policy advocated by Bissette was coherent. Against the maintenance of the 'colour bar', he asserted the existence of two 'classes' in colonial society: the 'free men' (whatever the colour of their skin) and the slaves.

He appealed to the arbitration, which he hoped would be benevolent, of the metropolitan authorities to ensure the application of 'good French legislation', which had been distorted by the 'privileged caste' in the colonies.

The absent slaves are, in fact, always present in this debate. It was not until 1834 that Bissette took a stand in favour of their emancipation. This slow evolution was essentially due to the disappointment caused by the application of the law of April 1833. While it granted political rights to 'free men of colour', it did not allow them, given the increase in the poll tax and the way it was calculated for the colonies, effectively to exercise those rights. It was not until 1845 that the mulatto Clavier became the first 'man of colour' to be elected to the Colonial Council.

Chapter 23

Changes in Colonial Ideology in France before 1848: From Slavery to Abolitionism

Francis Arzalier

FROM THE COMPLEX-FREE pro-slavery sentiment of the majority in eighteenth-century France, colonial ideology gradually evolved through to outright anti-slavery: militant abolitionism would be one of its favourite arguments at the end of this change, under the Third Republic.

This reversal of attitudes to slavery developed – gropingly and with all its contradictions – notably between 1815 and 1848. The conquest of Algiers in 1830 and of Algeria that followed played an important role in this shift. This essay is intended to throw light on this evolution, using both well-known and less well-known novels and political or historical discourses of this period, which are such a good expression of mentalities.

Contradictions of Colonial Ideology under the Restoration (1815–1830)

The reactions of the political leaders of the Restoration, including the most 'liberal' such as Richelieu, were still unthinkingly pro-slavery. The facts, British pressure and slave uprisings might force them to imagine that slavery might be coming to an end, but that did not mean they became abolitionists: they were too attached to the colonial status quo.[1]

Benoît Lacombe, a bourgeois from Bordeaux, magisterially portrayed in J. Cornette's thesis,[2] a Revolutionary in Year II, made rich by the colonial trade and national assets, a notable of the empire and the Restoration, dreamed in his declining years of a return to the slave-based order, the golden age of trade: 'I am interested in establishing a flour-mill at Gaillac, if our colonies offer outlets and security: I have seen with pleasure that Saint-Domingue was returning to France, I should very much like the same to be true of Cap Français (!) all will be for the best and each will then make his industry flour-ish' (6 March 1815).

In 1820, Gaspard Théodore Mollien's *Voyage en Sénégambie*, one of the first and best French accounts of exploration in West Africa, was published The work was a success, and a reprint appeared in 1822. It reported a journey financed by the traders of Saint-Louis du Sénégal with the avowed intent of promoting the slave trade. Along the way, Mollien justifies the enslavement of Africans with an argument that was already widespread and was to become even more so:

> The sight of this village demonstrated to me how fruitless for mankind was the generous principle which, in Europe, impels philanthropists to press for the abolition of the slave trade. Can blacks enjoy any happiness in their country, under the yoke of princes who can, at any moment, take them from their families or their country or have their throat cut, as their whim takes them?

Between 1827 and 1831, the same Mollien, who helped negotiate Haiti's independence and debt, wrote hundreds of manuscript pages on the history of the lost colony and its state; they exude an obvious nostalgia for the golden age before 1789. He accepted, of course, that slavery had in fact disappeared, but saw it as very regrettable.[3]

But, at the same time, the Restoration witnessed the development of a diffuse set of anti-slavery sentiments. They appeared first, and this was nothing new, in a number of ideologists, who saw themselves as the heirs of the Enlightenment or the Revolution.[4,5,6,7]

But the survivors of those days were now being largely overtaken by a new generation of writers and politicians who made no reference to Year II, were often rather straight-laced monarchists and based their rejection of slavery on a religious humanitarianism not at all unlike the one widespread in Britain in the eighteenth century. In the Société de la morale chrétienne, which fought for abolitionism from its foundation in 1822, were to be found the duke de Broglie, his friend Benjamin Constant, Guizot, d'Argout and Auguste de Staël who, while certainly opposed to the ultras, were very moderate on political and social issues.[8]

When Count Molé, Minister of the Navy and the Colonies, declared in 1822 that 'nothing could save the colonial system based on slavery from its coming collapse', that did not imply condemnation of the ownership of man by man, but was rather a realistic observation by a statesman. The law of April 1827, strengthening anti-slave trade measures, which S. Daget calls the second French abolitionist law,[9] approved by 220 deputies against 64, reveals a shift in mentalities among the political and social leaders of Restoration France.

There is confirmation of this in literary works, symptomatic of the ideological choices of both authors and readers. *Bug-Jargal* – about a tragic black rebel, pure and generous, even though cruel – justifies slave revolts. Written in 1819, it was taken up and enriched in 1826 by the young Victor Hugo, who politically was far removed from the heritage of Year II.[10] In 1825 Charles de Rémusat, a member of the Société de la morale chrétienne, wrote a play, which was never performed, telling the story of the Haitian revolt and justifying it by detailing the odious treatment inflicted by the colonists. Rémusat, though a moderate notable, went overboard in the play, stigmatizing a member of the Assembly who comes from Paris to the islands with his bloody sectarianism, his bombastic language and his bloodthirstiness.[11]

Chateaubriand was certainly no abolitionist at the time of the parliamentary debate on compensation for the colonists of Saint-Domingue, but in him the politician was as contradictory as the writer was talented. His *Itinéraire de Paris à Jérusalem*, which appeared in 1811 and was more read under the Restoration, was symptomatic of the shift under way in mentalities in France.[12] In it, condemnation of slavery becomes part of both counter-revolutionary ideology and colonial discourse. This semantic reversal developed from the image of Islam and the Ottoman Empire, which underwent a profound transformation in the French imaginary in the space of a generation. In the eighteenth century, Enlightenment writers liberally praised the tolerance of Islam in contrast to the Catholic intolerance that they were fighting and 'saw the Muslim East through fraternal and understanding eyes'.[13] This friendly gaze on the Ottoman Empire was still a constant feature of the French attitude during the Revolution. Between 1793 and 1796, the French government formed what was effectively an anti-Austrian alliance with the Turkish empire, which was broken only by Bonaparte's landing in Egypt in 1798.[14]

After the Egyptian adventure, slowly but surely the image shifted: the lands under Turkish rule became targets of colonial conquest, and the Muslim Turk became the enemy to be fought. In the *Itinéraire*, Chateaubriand, a monarchist and a Catholic, justifies the crusades not only from a religious viewpoint, but also in terms of an anti-slavery philanthropy:

> The point in question was not merely the deliverance of that sacred tomb, but likewise to decide which of the two should predominate in the world, a religion hostile to civilization, systematically favourable to ignorance, despotism, and slavery, or a religion that has revived among the moderns the spirit of learned antiquity and abolished servitude.... The spirit of Islamism is persecution and conquest; the Gospel, on the contrary, inculcates only toleration and peace.

It is in this logic of a crusade for the deliverance of the Christian slaves that Chateaubriand proposed in 1816 an expedition against the pirates of Algiers, in a sort of 'reverse' abolitionist perspective: 'The British Parliament, by abolishing the slave trade, seems to have indicated to our emulation the object of an even finer triumph: let us put an end to the slavery of whites!'

In 1826, in the preface to the new edition of the *Itinéraire*, Chateaubriand openly advocated a war of conquest against Turkish Islam, and denounced the supply of French warships to the pasha of Egypt with a virulence that he had never applied to the Atlantic slave trade, real indeed though it was: 'Did warships built in Marseilles, for the pasha of Egypt, contrary to the true principles of neutrality, escort those convoys of living human flesh or those cargoes of triumphal mutilations that go to decorate the gates of the seraglio?'

The 'Romantics' popularized such images of an Islam to be brought down – as being a vector of slavery for men and peoples – and created a veritable fashion replete with literary works and paintings: Vigny, in 1822, with *Héléna*; Delacroix in 1824 and 1827 (*Massacre of Chios, Greece Expiring on the Ruins of Missolonghi*); Hugo with the *Orientales* and *L'enfant grec*, which topped them all, in June 1828. Together, they called for European intervention, which would inevitably herald the carving up of the Ottoman Empire into colonies.[15,16]

The Société de la morale chrétienne was also an active participant in this change before 1830. Its committee against the slave trade was the most active, but it was also waging a campaign to liberate the Greeks from what it called Turkish 'slavery'. In 1830, some of its members achieved political power, with d'Argout, Minister of the Navy, Guizot and the banker Lafitte. But *realpolitik* commanded, and slavery persisted for eighteen more years in the French colonies.

The Capture of Algiers in 1830

The genesis of the event has been widely analysed, sufficiently to refute the myth, constructed in the nineteenth century, of a France forced into the expedition by a fly-whisk.[17,18] The justification of the conquest of Algiers in terms of the desire to eradicate piracy and the enslavement of Christians, endlessly replayed in France before and after 1830, rests for the most part on falsehoods. Of course, in the seventeenth century, Algiers had thousands of slaves and thousands of Christian renegades, who sometimes played a leading role there.[19] Father Dan, a priest who lived in Algiers, wrote of 25,000 captives in 1637:[20] only 800 remained in 1788 and a hundred or so in 1830 when the French occupied the city. By then, there was nothing remotely comparable to the hordes of slaves who, at that very moment, were working the sugar cane fields in Guadeloupe and Martinique. Algerian piracy had in fact practically disappeared in the eighteenth century, and now served only as a pretext for France's 'African temptations'.[21,22]

However far removed it was from reality, this moralizing discourse designed for Frenchmen spread as the conquest broadened after 1830, to the point where, in the course of the following generation, it became one of the 'founding myths of French Algeria', in the words of J.-F. Guilhaume,[23] at a time when French expeditions into the interior of the country, described in the correspondence of military officers, revealed not only an unheard-of brutality but also behaviour that came very close to slavery. Was Colonel de Montagnac so far removed from the slave trader when he described this exploit as a pacifier in 1840? 'You ask me what we do with the women we take. We keep a few as hostages, others are exchanged for horses, and the rest are sold, at auction, like beasts of burden.... Among these women, there are often some very beautiful ones....'[24]

1830–1848: Pro-slavery Mentalities on Borrowed Time?

Approval of slavery as a social system in the colonies was still being proclaimed loud and clear by some authors. In *Réflexions sur les colonies*, a certain Foignet describes a sort of slave Eden in the French Antilles with such a wealth of details that the picture merits citation:

> I call on all impartial individuals who have visited our Antilles in the last ten or twenty years. They will say as I do that the blacks are better clothed, better fed, better housed; that the working day is shorter than in Europe; that their hours of rest, plus one whole day a week, are granted them precisely, to enable them to cultivate the garden that each is given and to tend to the animals that they are allowed to rear; that on Saturdays, market days and Sundays, they are free to go and sell their petty wares and indulge in their usual pleasures, dancing above all which normally goes on until the following morning. The slightest service provided on those days is generously paid for by the master. They almost always buy what their slaves have been unable to sell in the market. So, except in working hours when, by ancient custom, they wear hardly anything, you see the blacks dressed so cleanly and so neatly and one might say with such a luxury of jewellery that proclaim their affluence, just as their health and their joy contradict all the absurdities that are parroted about them.[25]

A polemical piece of writing and an extreme case it may be, but this unadorned apology is not an isolated example.[26,27,28]

Apart from these ringing endorsements of slavery, the dominant discourse on the institution, which remained a reality, often involved tacit or suggested acceptance.

Pro-slavery mentalities were not simply residual in France between 1830 and 1848. These eighteen years of 'borrowed time', almost a generation, were in that sense hardly different from the Restoration.

1830–1848: Abolitionism and Colonial Mentalities

The strictly abolitionist trend is sufficiently well known for me not to linger over it. In order to illuminate the political context, we shall highlight the prime role in this battle of the republican press (Ledru-Rollin's *La Réforme*, *Le Siècle* and Buchez and Roux's *L'Atelier*, etc.) and, of course, the place of Schœlcher, an indefatigable and prolific militant, between 1830 and 1848.[29]

In a similar vein, Lamartine, confused centrist that he was in terms of general policy, made repeated, outspoken statements of his anti-slavery convictions.[30]

But abolitionism during the July monarchy also drew inspiration from Christianity, including Catholicism. Abolitionism brought together men of the left such as Ledru Rollin and Béranger, 'centrists' such as Lamartine and Tocqueville, Orleanist moderates such as Barrot, La Fayette, Molé and Achille de Broglie, and the ultramontane Montalembert.

Montalembert, who was in no way a liberal in politics and religion, clearly asserted as early as April 1831 his condemnation of slavery, from which, he argued, Christianity had delivered the Roman world.[31] The most damning condemnation in the name of religious imperatives came from the Christian reformer and journalist F. R. de Lamennais. While the 'modern slavery' that he denounced was first and foremost that of French proletarians, he clearly anathematized this insult to the dignity of man made in the image of God:

> the essence of slavery is the destruction of the human personality ... we call him a thing, *res*: that is what the noblest of God's creatures has become....[32] If then someone should come and say, You are mine; reply, No, we belong to God, who is our father, and to Christ, who is our master....[33] At certain times, and in certain countries, man has become the property of man; he has become an article of traffic; he has been sold and bought, like a beast of burden.... Brethren have said to brethren: We are not of the same race as you; our blood is purer. You and your offspring are destined to serve us for ever.[34]

Abolitionism was more a moral than a political demand, and as such, it could align with all sorts of ideological positions, including conservative ones. It was even sometimes backed by economic interests whose prime concern was not altruism. Thus, the rural bourgeoisie in Picardy, though far from progressive in its social and political choices, defended tooth and nail the beet sugar that it produced against colonial sugar. In 1836, a merchant from Saint-Quentin, an eminent member of the Société des Sciences, Arts, Lettres et Agriculture of the town, read a long 'epistle on sugar' that he had written. Celebrating the local version and virtues of this product in a few dozen bombastic verses, he denounced

> this negro dungeon that carries the sugar-making slave to the planter. There, marked by the whip, the black child of Africa refines with his blood the sugary vat. As he crushes the cane, the wheel carries off the black's limbs strip by strip....With a public stigma, our century pursues this monstrous traffic, the slave sees his freedom looming not far off; in a few more years, the accursed sons of Ham, risen up to the level of the other sons of Adam, carrying back to the deserts our manners, our industries, will go and civilize their barbarous homelands. The last slavery will be gone, mankind will triumph and Christ will have won.[35]

This curious 'Liberian' vision of the disappearance of slavery, which bestows on the sugar beet interests the blessing of religious philanthropy, was also the beginning of a colonial project in Africa.

The 'sugar beet lobby' was a reality, and it weighed in the direction of abolitionism. But we should not exaggerate its strength: in 1837, it failed to prevent the deputies from voting a law taxing beet sugar. In 1836, the Aisne had 44 sugar mills, producing 57,00 tonnes of sugar. By 1840, there were only 36, producing 2,800 tonnes. And only after that did growth resume, vigorously: 4,018 tonnes in 1845, 6,700 tonnes in 1851, after abolition (and 500,000 tonnes in 1985!).[36]

In Louis-Philippe's France, slavery remained a reality. Abolitionism was, therefore, a political combat for some. But apart from that, many novels, plays and paintings vilified slavery, whether in a clause in a speech, as part of the story and the characters, or in a phrase.[37,38,39]

This 'inclusive' anti-slavery and its ambiguities are to be found in the works of Alexandre Dumas, a successful and prolific author. Despite, or because of, his Haitian ancestry, Dumas was not a militant abolitionist. But his work is full of incidents associated with colonial questions. In 1838, he published the travel notes of the painter Dauzats in Egypt, filled out with real or imaginary memories of his father, the general in the Egyptian campaign. In it, Dumas, like Chateaubriand, presents slavery associated with Islam in a negative light.[40] He produced a historical drama, *Charles VII chez ses grands vassaux*, with his customary bit of violence thrown in. In this 'romantic' story, Yacoub, one of the central figures, is reduced to slavery by Muslim clericalism. He rebels and is freed, and returns to the desert.[41] Here again, the denunciation of slavery is associated with a denunciation of Islam. Dumas states even more clearly his opposition to the slave trade and slavery in 1838 in *Capitaine Pamphile*,[42] and in 1843 in *Georges*, which reveals the circumstances of his mulatto heritage.[43] But he always couples this ill-fitting abolitionism with an absolute rejection of Islam, which justifies his approval of the colonization of Algeria. It was in this light that in 1846 he made a journey to North Africa at the expense of the French state, on the ship the *Véloce*, and acted as a propagandist for the French conquest.[44]

It was not only Dumas. The majority of Romantics combined opposition to slavery with denunciation of Islam, which was portrayed as the carrier of slavery, and that led more or less directly to colonial projects that involved carving up the Ottoman Empire, of which the conquest of Algeria was part. Until 1830, the anti-Muslim discourse was almost exclusively anti-Turkish. Greece was now independent; the first peril was in Mitidja, inside Abd el Kader's tents. Muslim fanaticism was denounced in the most general way as the enemy to be brought down, even allusively.

The Crusaders Entering Constantinople, painted by Delacroix in 1840, and hung by King Louis-Philippe in the museum at Versailles, which he had just established in 1845, played on these feelings among the public, although the actual event had set Christian against Christian. But here there is something snide about the evocation of the crusades by the favourite painter of the duke d'Aumâle, shortly after the defeat of Abd el Kader.

In the same concern to portray an Africa where Islam went hand in hand with religious fanaticism, political despotism, slavery and barbarism, many 'geographical' accounts, some written long before, were published, having been chosen to correspond to the image of the continent that the French public had. Thus, *Voyage dans les régences de Tunis et Alger*, written by Peyssonel a century earlier, was published in part in Paris in 1830 and in full in 1838. A revealing fact is that many sections of the manuscript, preserved in the municipal library at Avignon, were suppressed in the 1838 book, such as this one:

> The Turks of this country are very humane towards their slaves. I who have been in America and in the Levant, I can attest that it is a certain confusion for Christians, that I have witnessed many cruelties and even inhumanity by Christians

towards their negro slaves, and much affability and good manners by the Turks towards the Christian slaves.[45]

Everything that failed to support the negative image of Islam was censured. The 'same skill' presided at the publication of works translated by the Tunisian scholar El Tounsy, who described the slave trade and slavery in Central Africa in about 1820, presented as a consequence of Muslim proselytism.[46]

Lamartine, an isolated case, rejected this negative image of Islam, and saw himself, unlike Dumas, as a traveller very understanding of oriental customs.[47] But this respect for the other, one that acknowledged the tolerance and moral values of Islam, did not prevent him from dreaming up a plan for the conquest of the Arab lands as early as 1833:

> A European adventurer with five or six thousand soldiers from Europe could easily overthrow Ibrahim and conquer Asia, from Smyrna to Bassora, and from Cairo to Baghdad, advancing step by step; by taking the Maronites of Lebanon as the pivot of their operations; by organizing behind it, as it advanced, and by making the eastern Christians its means of action, administration and recruitment; even the desert Arabs will be on his side, the day he can pay them: those people worship nothing except money, their god will always be the sword and gold.

This curious colonial project – for that indeed is what it was, a sort of premonition of Napoleon III's 'Arab kingdom' – rested on acceptance of Islam by the European conqueror, but foreign intervention would, according to Lamartine, eradicate polygamy and slavery. Justification of expansion overseas by anti-slavery is also present in Lamartine's plan.

The same connection is to be found in Schœlcher. Describing, without indulgence, Egypt in 1845[48] after his journey to the banks of the Nile, the indefatigable abolitionist denounced Mohammed Ali ('the alleged civilizer is but a vulgar slave trader') and condemned Islam because it justified slavery. It was largely at his instigation that on 7 May 1846 the Société pour l'abolition launched a petition for the freeing of the slaves in Algeria, at a time when the conquest was still in full swing. The approach reveals all his ambiguity: the humanist concern is also in this case an incitement to further entrench the colonial conquest.

Such an observation has nothing surprising about it, since the same ambiguity was present in the very reality of the colonial occupation of Algeria, associated from the beginning with a civilizing messianism, which saw itself and thought of itself as an emancipating force. That helps us to understand the important role played by freemasonry in the conquest, well studied by Yacono.[49] In 1831, the capture of Algiers was celebrated ecstatically by the 'La Persévérance couronnée' lodge of Rouen, because it 'laid low a tyrant, broke the chains of a people, assured the tranquillity of the Mediterranean, and wiped away for ever the shameful vassalage of Europe'. The first lodge established in 1834 at Oran, L'Union africaine, within the army itself, set as its objective 'to enlighten and instruct the Arabs' and 'replace ignorance and slavery with science and freedom' (1847). Established in 1845, the lodge in Constantine, by taking the name Saint Vincent-de-Paul, was not claiming allegiance to any sort of clericalism, but rather to the myth of the liberator of the Christian slaves.

* * *

Using abolition to justify colonization, already present in the essential book of the Saint-Simonian Enfantin in 1843,[50] would flourish even more in France, from the time of the Second Empire to the point where it became one of the founding myths of the colonial mentality. This is the legitimist Louis Veuillot describing Africa in 1862:

> The father sells the son and if he does not sell him, it is the son himself who sells his father, or cuts his throat and sometimes eats him. That is how inner Africa is, the Africa of the black children of Ham the accursed; and something of their tragic fate falls on anyone who comes to touch this land of slaves.[51]

Father Godard, former parish priest of Laghouat, went one better in 1871, with his *Soirées algériennes, corsaires, esclaves et martyrs de barbarie,* and ensured himself popular success when he wrote 'this tissue of contradictions and nonsense which is known as the Quran'.[52] The myth grew after 1900, with the image of de Brazza appearing in every school textbook of the Third Republic right up until the middle of the twentieth century.

Notes

1. *Lettres du duc de Richelieu au marquis d'Osmond (1816–1818),* Paris, Gallimard, 1939.
2. *Benoît Lacombe, propriétaire et négociant à Gaillac (1783–1819),* thesis by J. Cornette, June 1982, Paris, EHESS.
3. G. T. Mollien, *Voyage dans l'intérieur de l'Afrique aux sources du Sénégal et de la Gambie, fait en 1818, par ordre du gouvernement français,* Paris, 1820, 7 reprints from 1822 to 1967; *Histoire de Haïti. Statistique et moeurs,* ms. 1827–31, Bibliothèque municipale, Calais.
4. P. L. Courier, *Simple discours de Paul Louis, vigneron de la Chavonière ... à l'occasion d'une souscription proposée ... pour l'acquisition de Chambord,* Paris, 1821.
5. Anonymous, *L'Haïtiade,* 1827.
6. Abbé Grégoire, *Des peines infamantes à infliger aux négriers,* Paris, 1822.
7. L. de la Sarthe, *Mémoires,* Paris, 1829.
8. B. Constant, *Mélanges de littérature et de politique,* Paris, 1829.
9. S. Daget, *La traite des Noirs,* éd. Ouest-France, 1990.
10. V. Hugo, *Bug-Jargal,* n.p., 1819–26.
11. C. de Rémusat, *L'Habitation de Saint-Domingue,* new ed., Paris, Éditions du CNRS, 1977.
12. *Itinéraire de Paris à Jérusalem,* 1811, new ed., 1826. *Oeuvres complètes,* 'Discours', 8, 1859 [Eng. trans., F. Shoberl, *Travels in Greece, Palestine, Egypt, and Barbary, during the Years 1806 and 1807,* London, Henry Colburn, 1812].

13. M. Rodinson, *La fascination de l'Islam*, Paris, Maspero, 1980 [Eng. trans., R. Veinus, *Europe and the Mystique of Islam*, London, Tauris, 1988, p. 48].

14. G. Groc, 'Les premiers contacts de l'empire ottoman avec le message de la Révolution française', *Cahiers du CEMOTI*, 12, 1991.

15. A. de Vigny, *Héléna*, n.p.1822.

16. V. Hugo, *Les Orientales,* n.p., 1825–9.

17. On the expedition to Algiers and the conquest, the most relevant analyses are still: C. A. Julien, *Histoire de l'Algérie contemporaine*, Vol. 1, 1964; Y. Lacoste, A. Nouschi and A. Prenant, *Algérie, passé et présent*, n.p., 1960; A. Hamdani, *La vérité sur l'expédition d'Alger*, Paris, Balland, 1985.

18. Archives Affaires Étrangères, *Mémoires et documents*, 'Algérie', 4 and 5.

19. B. and L. Bennassar, *Les chrétiens d'Allah*, Paris, Perrin, 1989.

20. P. Dan, *Histoire de Barbarie, et de ses corsaires*, Paris, 1637.

21. F. Charles-Roux, *France et Afrique du Nord avant 1830*, Paris, 1832.

22. A. Thomson, 'Arguments for the conquest of Algiers in the late eighteenth and early nineteenth centuries', *Maghreb Review*, Vol. 14, Nos. 1 and 2, London, 1989.

23. J.-F. Guilhaume, *Les mythes fondateurs de l'Algérie française*, Paris, L'Harmattan, 1992.

24. F. J. L. de Montagnac, *Lettres d'un Soldat*, collected and published by his nephew in 1885, Paris, Plon, p. 225.

25. A. Foignet, *Quelques refléxions sur les colonies*, Paris, Auguste Auffray, 1831.

26. F. Patron, *De quelques questions relatives aux colonies françaises*, Paris, 1832.

27. E. Corbière, *Le négrier*, Paris, 1832.

28. Prince de Joinville, *Vieux souvenirs, 1818–1848*, 13th ed., Paris, Calmann Lévy, 1894 [Eng. trans., Lady M. Lloyd, *Memoirs, Vieux Souvenirs, of the Prince de Joinville*, London, W. Heinemann, 1895].

29. Schœlcher's writings against slavery: November 1830, 'Les nègres', *Revue de Paris*; 1833, *De l'esclavage des Noirs et de la législation coloniale*; 1840, *L'abolition de l'esclavage. Examen critique du préjugé contre la couleur des Africains*; 1841, *Colonies étrangères et Haïti*; 1842, 'Colonies françaises', 'Du droit de visite', *Revue du Progrès*; 1847, *Histoire de l'esclavage pendant les deux dernières années*.

30. A. de Lamartine, *Oeuvres complètes* and in particular 'Discours de 1844'; 'Les esclaves, fragment d'un tragédie', *Revue des Deux-Mondes*, 1843; *Histoire des Girondins*, 8 Vols, Paris, 1847 [Eng. trans., *History of the Girondists*, 3 Vols, London, Bohn, 1847]; R. David, *Lamartine, la politique et l'histoire*, Imprimerie Nationale, 1993.

31. Montalembert, 'Discours de 1831', *Oeuvres complètes*.

32. F. R. de Lamennais, *De l'esclavage moderne*, 1833.

33. F. R. de Lamennais, *Paroles d'un croyant*, 1834 [Eng. trans., *The Words of a Believer*, London, B.D. Cousins, 1834, p. 31].

34. F. R. de Lamennais, *Le livre du peuple,* 1837 [Eng. trans., J. H. Lorymer, *The Book of the People*, London, H. Hetherington, 1838, p. 7].

35. *Mémoires de la société académique de la ville de Saint-Quentin*, 1834–6, pp. 339–40.

36. *Bulletin de la Société des Arts, Lettres et Agriculture de l'Aisne*, 1836, A.D.A; *Annuaire de l'Aisne*, 1837–40, 1845–51, A.D.A.; G. Marival, *L'Aisne de le sucre*, A.D.A., 1992.

37. A. de Vigny, *Stello*, 1832.

38. R. Caillé, *Journal d'un voyage à Tombouctou … pendant les années 1824, 1825, 1826, 1827, 1828*, Paris, 1830 [Eng. trans., *Travels through Central Africa, and across the Great Desert, to Morocco, performed in the years 1824–1828*, London, H. Colburn & R. Bentley, 1830, 2 Vols].

39. E. Sue, *Atar-Gull*, 1831.

40. A. Dumas, *Quinze jours au Sinaï*, 1838 [Eng. trans., *Impressions of Travel in Egypt and Arabia Petraea*, New York, John S. Taylor, 1839].

41. A. Dumas, *Charles VII chez ses grands vassaux*, Paris, 1831.

42. A. Dumas, *Le Capitaine Pamphile*, 1839 [Eng. trans., J. Herald, *The Adventures of Captain Pamphile*, New York, New World Press, 1850].

43. A. Dumas, *Georges*, 1843 [Eng. trans., G. J. Knox, *George; or The Planter of the Isle of France*, Belfast, Simms and M'Intyre, 1846].

44. A. Dumas, *Le Véloce, ou Tanger, Alger et Tunis*, Paris, 1848–51 [partial Eng. trans., A. E. Murch, *Tangier to Tunis*, London, Peter Owen, 1959].

45. J.-A. Peyssonel, *Voyages dans les régences de Tunis et d'Alger en 1725*, Paris, 1838, new edition, La Découverte, 1986, manuscript at the Bilbliothèque Municipale, Avignon.

46. C. Mohamed Ibn Omar El Tounsy, *Voyage du Darfour*, Paris, 1845; and idem, *Voyage au Ouaday*, Paris, 1851.

47. A. de Lamartine, *Souvenirs, impressions, pensées et paysages, pendant un voyage en Orient*, 4 Vols, Paris, 1835, *Souvenirs, impressions*, Paris, 1845 [Eng. trans., T. Phipson, *De Lamartine's Visit to the Holy Land, or Recollections of the East*, 2 Vols, London, George Virtue, c. 1847].

48. V. Schœlcher, *L'Égypte en 1845*, Paris, 1846.

49. X. Yacono, *Un siècle de franc-maçonnerie algérienne, 1785–1884*, Paris, Maisonneuve & Larose, 1969.

50. B. P. Enfantin, *La colonisation de l'Algérie*, Paris, P. Bertrand, 1843.

51. L. Veuillot, *Les Français en Algérie. Souvenirs d'un voyage fait en 1851*, Tours, A. Mame & Co., 1862, p. 77.

52. Abbé L. Godard, *Soirées algériennes*, Paris, 1857.

Chapter 24

From Bug-Jargal to Toussaint Louverture: Romanticism and the Slave Rebel

Gérard Gengembre

IF WE ACCEPT the idea that French romanticism constitutes the literary revolution inscribing in literary texts certain ideals of the French Revolution, reformulating them and eliciting all of their contradictions, we might expect that it should take on board the character of the slave rebel, who ought to be among its favourite figures. But the major works devoted to the events in Saint-Domingue can be counted on the fingers of one hand.[1]

Colour, or the Indelible Difference

The figure of the black is indeed present in the literature of the Romantic age. Compared to the treatment in eighteenth-century novels, what we see here is a deepening of the theme of difference, the tragedies that it involves and the barriers that it erects between human beings. Among other significant examples, we shall mention *Ourika* by Madame de Duras (1778–1828), published in 1824, which was hailed by Goethe and became a European-wide success. Leaving aside fashion, which was so taken with the novel that it invented 'Ourika-style' bonnets, the narrative focused on a topic common in Madame de Duras's stories – the illusory happiness of a privileged childhood brutally thwarted by a world without exit, followed by a fall into solitude, sickness and death.

Ourika, a young Senegalese woman raised in refined circumstances by the wife of Marshal de Beauvau, enjoys the pleasures of fashionable life. But she overhears a conversation between the marshal's wife and the marchioness of ——, which reveals her true isolation in society. Eaten up with a secret sorrow, she is overwhelmed by the massacres in Saint-Domingue, occurring during a revolution that had awakened so many hopes. The marshal's wife's grandson and her childhood friend, Charles, Ourika and an old priest are devoted to the marshal's wife, who is imprisoned in her house in St Germain during the Terror. After Thermidor, they all taste the quiet joys of the countryside, soon interrupted by the imperatives of a rediscovered fashionable life. Charles becomes engaged and Ourika pines away. Charles's marriage and the birth of his son make Ourika wish for death. The marchioness of —— then compels her to look clearly into her heart: she loves Charles. Feeling desperately guilty because of this love, which she has been repressing, Ourika is converted by the priest who has come to administer her the last rites. She takes refuge in the convent and, before she dies, is able to tell her sad story to the doctor, whose care proves in vain.

In this long novel, which is actually a psychological drama, Madame de Duras privileges one image of woman. Devoted to the cause of happiness – once experienced in harmony close to the one she loves, unaware of it though she may be – Ourika, a nostalgic figure, incarnates the dream of an impossible return to the unity of separate consciousnesses. In Madame de Duras, the heroes internalize the hostility of the world, symbolized by racial difference or social inferiority. Thus, the marchioness appears to Ourika in a dream: 'It was before me like the reflection of my own form. Alas! I see now too clearly that it was only the shadows of the chimeras that haunted me.' As they suffer, so they look to self-destruction. The deterioration has but one respite, the dream of a life stopped, of a love without tensions. Such a personal myth leads to religion and its consolations directly associated with death, the convent becoming a tomb, the sole place where Ourika can think of Charles. Perhaps, too, it refers to a drive for self-punishment by survivors, a mark of the Revolutionary trauma, or some female overinvestment in love after tragic trials in which women have engaged their energy, only afterwards to be returned to the futilities of fashionable life, as many other novels of the same period seem to suggest, thus developing a female version of the *mal de siècle*. The heroine dies a victim of a history that has failed to abolish difference.

To this well-known text we might add a work by the youthful Balzac, *Le Nègre*, a melodrama in three acts, rejected by the Gaîté Theatre in 1823, the reading committee deeming the investment 'too risky, too dangerous even'. It involves the love of a black man for a white woman, with Balzac clearly taking up the theme of *Othello*. 'African blood courses' through the veins of the hero, who loathes France and describes his condition in these terms: 'Bent under the yoke in my homeland, I was happy in my misfortune, it is the gentleman who bought me, who transported me to a country where the most insulting laugh taught me that I was a being outside humanity.' A slave, he hopes so to be in love, adjuring the one he loves in these words: 'Follow me, we will go far, far away, into the desert, to the ends of the world, wherever you want. There, unnoticed and content, you will find in me the slave, yes, the most attentive and most devoted slave.' Jealous and humiliated, he stabs her with a dagger and then kills himself. Here again, the difference that excludes is at the heart of the work.

We will end this very incomplete survey with *Georges*, a historical novel by Alexandre Dumas, published in 1843, which passed almost unnoticed. This novel, in which are combined extreme exoticism and romanticism, is the story of a heroic individual struggling against prejudice – a fine Romantic figure, who bears the same forename as Balzac's hero – and of an exemplary couple who overcome the barrier of race.

Dumas portrays a rich mulatto on the Île-de-France (now Mauritius). As a child, in 1810, Georges Munier resolved 'to kill all by himself the prejudice that no man of colour had dared to fight'. As a student in Paris, and of a colour so fair that he can pass for white, he becomes a perfect man of the world. He has understood 'that it was not enough to be, in everything, of the strength of ordinary men' and decided that 'in everything he would be superior to them'. Thus, superman returns to his homeland in 1824, falls in love with the young Creole Sara de Malmédie and reveals to her his origins. Sara's uncle refuses to allow the marriage. Georges then turns to force, leading a revolt by black slaves. Taken prisoner and condemned to death, he escapes with his beloved, just before his execution, thanks to the intervention of his father and brother, who have become pirate captains. The novel ends with a final battle at sea.

A mulatto like his creator, Georges Munier is one of the few persons of colour in Dumas's works, and the only one to take the principal role. Moreover, the novel gives blacks only a bare minimum fictional lot. Télémaque loyally serves his master Georges, Bijou is a drunkard and the gang of rebel slaves is soon neutralized by alcohol. Nazim, a runaway Negro, and his brother Laïza, both belonging to Mr de Malmédie, are exceptions to the rule. Nazim is recaptured and is about to be lashed. Laïza, who saved Sara from the jaws of a shark, begs for his pardon. Malmédie refuses, but, entreated by his niece, gives them both to Georges, who frees them. Like Ali de Monte-Cristo, Laïza will be devoted henceforth to Georges and will die trying to save him in the revolt. But then we learn that he is in fact the son of a chief, a mulatto with Arab blood. *Georges* is thus a more a mulatto novel than a black one.

We therefore have to reduce the significance of the story: it pleads for the abolition not of slavery but of discrimination by Creoles against free and talented mulattoes. Yet the description of conditions, the picture of a slave island, the analysis of racial and social relations are standard parts of a novel that is, of course, one of adventure, but is above all a situation novel. To the feeling of unfamiliarity, *Georges* adds the virtues of emotion. On the island in *Paul and Virginia*, he places a noble young woman with strong passions and a greatness of mind.

In sum, while this little survey has no statistical value at all, we have to admit that the figure of the black, whether slave or not, combines the extremes of exoticism, marginality and sufferings imposed on him by the contemptuous, uneasy and secretly fascinated gaze of a society that is the prisoner of its ignorance and its prejudices. According a central place to the excluded individual, romanticism encounters the black, exposes the drama of his alienating difference, unveils this dark zone of the human consciousness and highlights the cleavage that fractures humankind. Yet it does not accord him a potential as powerful as that available to the Romantic bandit, denouncing the social order. It is not really there that we must look for the literary portrayal of the rebel slave, incarnating an ideal of freedom, fighting for human dignity, taking the Revolution literally. Let us then turn to the two texts that we feel to be the most representative.

Bug-Jargal and Toussaint Louverture, Romantic Figures of the Rebel Slave

Victor Hugo's first novel – written in 1818, first published in May–June 1820 in *Le Conservateur littéraire*, and then, in a revised and enlarged version, in an anonymous volume in Paris by Urbain Canel, in February 1826 – *Bug-Jargal* (Eng. trans., *The Noble Rival; or The Prince of Congo*, London: George Pierce, 1845) is a visionary adventure novel in the framework of a historical subject: the black revolt in Saint-Domingue in 1791, a 'struggle of giants, with three worlds interested in the question, Europe and Africa as combatants, America as the battlefield' (1832, *Preface*).

In 1791, on a plantation in Saint-Domingue, the slave Pierrot is in love with Marie, his master's gentle and light-skinned daughter, who is engaged to Léopold d'Auverney. The latter sets off to find Marie, who has been carried off in a revolt on her wedding day. Pierrot has hidden Marie to save her from certain death. Captured by the insurgents, d'Auverney is saved from the hands of the ferocious Biassou and the hideous Habibrah by the leader of the insurgents, Bug-Jargal, who is none other than Pierrot. In fact, Bug-Jargal, taken prisoner, has been freed on parole to go and help d'Auverney, to whom he owes his life. But Sergeant Thadée, believing that his chief has died, has Bug-Jargal executed when he comes back to surrender his parole. D'Auverney takes in Rask, the black chief's dog.

If the first version stands as a military novel, in which Captain Delmar (who subsequently becomes d'Auverney) tells how he fell into Biassou's hands and was delivered by the leader of the uprising, Bug-Jargal, whose life he had once saved, freed on parole to free him and executed on his return, the final version of the novel is full of local colour, stressing both colonial enslavement and the realities of repression, and introduces the love story, as well as the fool Habibrah. This latter, who was once Léopold's uncle's fool, imposes the satanic outburst of his avenging hatred in a story that is full of *coups de théâtre*, in which Hugo plays ironically with melodramatic tricks, multiplying hyperbolic clichés and deploying the excesses of language, while already privileging his favourite device, antithesis.

So we have the love of a black man for a white woman, the friendship and rivalry of a black man and a white man, the contrast between the near-giant Pierrot and the dwarf Habibrah, good and evil, the slave status of Bug-Jargal, who is yet the son of an African king – all go together to dramatize the fiction. Like Jean Valjean and Javert, d'Auverney and Bug-Jargal give themselves up to each other and save each other; like Gauvain and Lantenac, the heroes of *Quatrevingt-treize*, they outdo each other in magnanimity. As a novel that is all about promises, about purity (of love, the heroes know only kisses, and Bug-Jargal dies a virgin like Jean Valjean, Enjolras and Cimourdain), about the tragic sentiment of life (d'Auverney seeks rest for his soul in death on the battlefield), about Manichaeism, in which the wicked dark strangers Biassou and Habibrah stand in contrast to the luminous figures of the heroes, *Bug-Jargal* already contains the myths of Victor Hugo.

Among the most interesting aspects of this novel, we would like to high-light the subtlety with which Hugo distributes his black figures, detailing the hierarchy among them based on their condition itself but also on their social origin, the degrees of alienation and degradation that mutilate them in different ways, the strength of the savagery engendered by exploitation and dehumanization. Hugo brings out, too, the stubborn resistance of the colonists and the planters, the contradictions between supporters of the old order and partisans of the Revolution. Exotic excesses, fascination with horror, indulgence with regard to the tumultuous spectacle are combined with the treatment of a complex reality. The sound and the fury do not prevent a certain lucidity.

Let us compare this work of youth – both Hugo's doubtless brilliant youth, and the youth of romanticism – with a text of maturity, Lamartine's *Toussaint Louverture*.

This drama in five acts in verse was first performed in Paris at the Porte de Saint-Martin theatre on 6 April 1850, and published in Paris by Michel Lévy the same year. Emerging from a project, *Les Noirs*, designed in 1839, completed in 1840 with the title *Haïti ou les Noirs*, partly lost, rewritten and published in two fragments in 1843 (*Les Esclaves*), bought by the publisher Lévy, put on by Frédéric Lemaître, reviled by the critics, better received by the public, *Toussaint Louverture* tells of the tragic confrontation between the France of the consulate and the Haitian republic in 1802.

To the sound of the 'Marseillaise noire' and at the foot of the tower where Toussaint is working, the arrival of Bonaparte's vessels is announced. In the tower, Toussaint talks of his fate, expresses his doubts, sees again Father Antoine, who once 'baptized him to freedom', and resolves to fight ('I can no longer doubt it. War or slavery!/I shall cover this shore with iron and fire'). To galvanize his people, he pretends to have foreseen the early defeats and explains to his niece Adrienne, a girl abandoned by her father, a white man, that he wants to disappear in order to prepare the revenge and prove his prophecy right: 'Haiti will be black, it is I who tell you so.' In their headquarters, Leclerc's French forces have brought with them the children that Toussaint had once entrusted to France. Pauline Bonaparte, Leclerc's wife, takes a poor blind man under her protection, unaware that he is in fact Toussaint. Leclerc wants to use him to carry peace proposals to the black leader. Moïse, a Haitian general, turns traitor and proposes to the French to take revenge on the 'tyrant'. Toussaint discovers him, kills him and flees.

We then move to the prison where Adrienne is held. This act, wholly taken up with family scenes, shows the reunion of Adrienne with Toussaint's children, including Albert, who loves her. Albert curses 'those who profaned her' and whom he had hitherto admired. Salvador, the unworthy father, a fanatical supporter of Bonaparte ('The consul, like God, wants everything to be his'), thinks he can escape his error by having the children, who have broken the irons of their 'sister', arrested and by entrusting Adrienne to Father Antoine, who, in fact, frees her. In Toussaint's camp, his sons bring him the condition laid down by the French: 'Between the whites and us complete equality,/Their flag alone covering liberty.' Albert has given his word. Torn apart, at the moment of choosing his father against France, he is taken away by Salvador's soldiers. Toussaint, in the depths of despair, surrenders ('You triumph, O whites!... I had a heart!'). Betraying their promise, the French now attack. Adrienne dies raising the flag of Haiti. Toussaint picks it up and issues the call to arms.

Cited twice in his *Histoire de l'art dramatique* by Théophile Gautier, first when discussing the crisis of romantic drama after the revival of *Ruy Blas* in 1842 ('Lamartine keeps his *Toussaint Louverture* in his wallet') and then when writing of the 1850 performance ('It was just like the great days of *Marion Delorme*, *Lucrèce Borgia* and *Antony*'), Lamartine's play illustrates some of the poet's major concerns. He wants to reach a wide popular audience, and the theatrical writing here expresses the same ambition as the novel-writing, for example *Geneviève, histoire d'une servante* (1851).

The choice of subject is obviously exemplary. It is at once a reminder of the humanist revolutionary message and a portrayal of a revolution that has become the guardian of the established order, of the affliction of the poor and the excluded, and of the contradictions of history, which sees the defenders of the rights of man in confrontation with those who ought to benefit from them. The dramatic poem is part of Lamartine's attempt to unite poetry, politics and action. The heroic figure of Toussaint Louverture speaks for suffering humanity in search of dignity. He thus has most of the dimensions of the Romantic hero.

As a hymn to the freedom of blacks ('Arise, children, arise, the black is man at last') and the family ('I am a father above all else', says Toussaint), the historical drama utilizes to the full all the resources of melodrama (betrayals, pathetic rifts, heightened emotions, etc.). Denouncing racism and the law of self-interest, the play vibrates with accents of Hugo to evoke the 'depths' of the slave, the monster whose soul is a 'night'. As a play that portrays a tragic breach in history, in which man is halted on the path to democratic fulfilment, *Toussaint Louverture* is designed as a missionary work, a fragment of a humanitarian-religious epic that looks to a providential future.

Perhaps we have here the work that romanticism took so long to produce. Let us stress the date: 1850. This means that Lamartine was writing after the abolition of slavery adopted through the actions of Victor Schœlcher. While the Romantic writers had been able to give vibrant voice to many a humanitarian cause, we can see the difficulty that they had in confronting the question of slavery. It did not happen until mid-century. But this relative disappointment is corrected if we look at what the end of the century would do with this theme.

A Fin-de-Siècle Vision of Slavery

We shall now look at *Les Nuits chaudes du Cap français*, a novel by Hugues Rebell, the pseudonym of Georges Grassal (1867–1905), published in *La Plume* starting on 15 September 1901. The book was published in 1902 (*La Plume*, imprimerie de Deverdun, Buzançais, Indre). Rebell later wrote a sequel to *La Plume*, entitled *L'Orgie noire*. It was never published following problems over publishing rights. We may consider that Hugues Rebell is here giving us his masterpiece, shot through with eroticism and voluptuous and libertine airs, replete with the corrupting perfume of tropical nights heavy with miasmas and storms.

The novel begins with 'An African vengeance' (which in the book would become 'The vengeance of an unknown hand'). During the Revolution, in Bordeaux, Thérésa de Fontenay, the mistress of the representative Tallien, receives flattering declarations of love from an unknown source that annoy her lover. But they are soon followed by abusive letters, which, from the writing, seem to come from the same correspondent. Public rumour attributes them to a rich merchant, Dubousquens, about whom nothing is known, except that he lives with a black woman recently brought from Le Cap Français in Saint-Domingue. He is arrested and summarily tried, and then guillotined. It is the black woman who has put this plot together in order to avenge herself on the man to whom she is bound by a passion that has become hatred, and who whips her until she bleeds.

The second part, 'Journal of a Creole lady', which is supposed to be a rediscovered manuscript, reveals the origins of this affair. At Le Cap Français, in May 1791, Mrs Gourgeuil is reputed as the most virtuous of women, but she is prey to an all-devouring sensuality. One evening, she takes in Mrs Lafon and her young unconscious daughter, who are fleeing the rebel slaves. Zinga, her black woman, persuades her to kill them so as to steal their belongings. Mrs Gourgeuil needs money to pay a blackmailer who has involved her in orgies with black men, but she nevertheless saves the little Antoinette and conceives a tender affection for her. The shipowner Dubousquens takes her from her, but Zinga, who loves her passionately, kills Antoinette. All flee, while the freed blacks put Le Cap to the torch.

A wonderfully told story of an exotic and dark affair, Les Nuits chaudes portrays a frivolous and self-centred society, preoccupied with its pleasures, carrying on a lush and lascivious life. To the spicy sensuality of the tropics, which terrifies the Creoles, are added the unrestraint of an overexcited flesh, in particular that of mulatto women, such as Dodue-Fleurie, and excesses of all sorts, where, in an ambience of revolution and fire, lust and death mingle together:

> Suddenly, the moon sailed free of the clouds, enveloped this turf with its luminous vapour, called forth from the shadows a thousand drunken and fierce faces, revealed hundreds of delirious couples, horrible couplings in which the teeth, the nails dig deep into the flesh, where the embrace and the kiss are like the slitting of a throat.

The novel is a tale of murders, plots and extravagances, combining hatred, desire and violence, and sets out in a few quick strokes portraits and landscapes, describing an atmosphere that is somewhat demonic in which the confessions of Mrs Gourgeuil to the complaisant Father Le Pouyade inscribe the murky charm of what is being confessed, in particular homosexual attraction. It is a celebration of the senses, of the temptation and fascination with evil made all aesthetic, the clash of races and colours, the strength of temperaments, in which everything provokes, but in which everything is caught in brilliant writing, which suggests trances without falling into excess, mastering the intemperance of situations and characters.

Slavery and the revolt of the oppressed are simply a pretext for voluptuous pictures and murky seductions. Now that it has been abolished, slavery can become a decadent theme, with sulphurous immoderation. Here we are indeed far from Toussaint Louverture.

* * *

This brief survey cannot go into all of the literary inscriptions of a specific memory of slavery, and it would be easy to multiply the references. We can nevertheless stress that French nineteenth-century literature was much more successful in erecting a Jean Valjean as a symbol than a slave, whether enslaved or in revolt. Celebrating or advocating the integration of people, of women or children, in a fraternal and harmonious humanity, Promethean, religious, preaching or protesting romanticism seeks to address the mass of humanity awaiting deliverance and to hasten that liberation. It is as if the slave was simply one of the components of a human race whose natural condition is enslavement, on its way to its universal assumption. The slave belongs to the shadows peopled with a whole suffering humanity. In short, romanticism – and more broadly the humanitarian nineteenth century – was quite capable of writing the drama of the human condition, of its moral, spiritual or physical slavery. But it did not really write slavery.

Notes

After this essay had been delivered and the text corrected, Jean-Paul Piquet drew my attention to the existence of a novel by Alexandre Dumas published in 1853, *Ingénue, un amour interdit de Restif de la Bretonne*, in which the novelist evokes the slave trade and enslavement of blacks. The work was reprinted by François Bourin in 1990.

1. We are limiting ourselves here to texts sufficiently well known to be regarded as representative, while not exhausting the list. Thus, it would of course have been necessary also to look at works such as Prosper Mérimée's *Tamango*. A more thorough inventory remains to be made. We should also like to point out that some of what is said here about *Ourika, Georges, Bug-Jargal, Toussaint Louverture* and *Les Nuits chaudes du Cap français* repeats the content of articles appearing in the *Dictionnaire des Oeuvres de langue française*, Paris, Bordas, 1994.

Part V

1848: The Suppression of Slavery – Debates and Modalities of Implementation

Preamble

Oruno D. Lara and Nelly Schmidt

THE CENTRE DE RECHERCHES CARAÏBES-AMÉRIQUES (CERCAM) was approached for part of the organization of this colloquy: the day on abolitions of slavery in the nineteenth century.[1]

CERCAM began as a priority research unit of the Université de Paris X-Nanterre in 1983. Some of its members currently teach the history of the Caribbean and co-ordinate research on international relations between Africa, the Caribbean, and Europe. One point needs to be made at the outset: the term 'abolition' of slavery may be convenient, but the expression 'process of destroying the slave system'[2] is a more accurate description of reality. It is a complex reality, inscribed in the long term of a century of emancipations, between the rebellion of the slaves in Saint-Domingue in 1791, the first abolition which was proclaimed there in 1793 and the last abolition decree promulgated in Brazil in 1888.

To deal with this complex, sometimes contradictory subject in the slave-owning nineteenth century calls for a comparative approach. Thus, from the Caribbean, we shall go to the United States and Africa.

Richard Hart (Jamaica) situates in a critical perspective the action of the abolitionists and the racism that appeared during the slave period and which lasted over the centuries in the British colonies in the West Indies. Emiliano Gil-Blanco (Alcalà de Henares University, Madrid) presents a synthesis of the abolitionist measures adopted in the Spanish-speaking colonies and notably the application of the Moret law, adopted by the Cortes in 1870.

Oruno D. Lara (Centre de Recherches Caraïbes-Amérique, CERCAM, Université de Paris-X) and Iñez Fischer-Blanchet (CERCAM) concentrate on justifying a fundamental terminological point. What we are dealing with here is a *process*, a process of destroying slavery, and not the successive coming into force of a series of discrete decrees. What country in the Caribbean can illustrate such an analysis better than Cuba?

While the British Act of 1833 was regarded as one of the key documents by all the colonial powers, the French law adopted by the Republican Government in 1848 also exercised a considerable influence. The work of the Commission for the abolition of slavery, which was chaired by Victor Schœlcher, determined French colonial policy in the long term. The decree itself and the measures that accompanied it, analysed by Nelly Schmidt (CNRS, Universités d'Aix-Marseille and Paris X) contained the seed of the economic and social evolution of the French colonies in the Caribbean for at least a century. The decree of 27 April 1848 was applicable in the trading posts in Senegal. Mbaye Gueye (Université Cheikh Anta Diop, Dakar) deals with the effects of the French decree in West Africa during the second half of the nineteenth century. Abdelhamid Largueche (Université de la Manouba, Tunis) examines the abolition of slavery in Tunis, the commitments of a social élite and the resistance of traditions.

The emancipation decrees and Schœlcher's action in 1848 gave birth to a powerful mythical construct whose effects are still felt today. Édouard Delépine (Martinique) and Serge Barcellini (Association Sonthonax) provide a survey of eyewitness accounts, still very relevant today, of events inscribed in the long term.

Finally, we should point out that while researchers at CERCAM engage in analysing documents, they have also worked on other forms of traces of the past. The items that Schœlcher brought back from his journeys in the American slave colonies and Africa were the object of an exhibition, mounted in cooperation with the Laboratoire d'Ethnologie of the Musée de l'Homme in Paris. The items on display were testimonies of slavery, of the everyday life of slaves and of the repression that dominated the a-social relations generated in the Americas, and they were the object of guided visits for the schoolchildren while the international colloquy was being held.[3]

Notes

1. The Centre de Recherches Caraïbes-Amériques was established in 1982. Its founder and present director, Oruno D. Lara (Guadeloupe) is a historian specializing in the Caribbean and Africa. He has written a 'Histoire générale des Caraïbes' which appeared under the title *Caraïbes en construction: espace, colonisation, résistance*, 2 Vols (Éditions du CERCAM, 1992).
2. See Oruno D. Lara, *Les Caraïbes* (Paris: P.U.F., 1986).
3. A catalogue of the exhibition is available on request to: CERCAM, B.P. 22, 93801 Épinay Cedex, France. The researchers at CERCAM have also published for the Centre National de Documentation Pédagogique the following booklets in the series 'Textes et Documents pour la Classe': 'L'esclavage' (1984), 'La galaxie caraïbe' (1993) and 'Les abolitions de l'esclavage. La longue marche' (1993). They also contributed to the October 1994 issue of *UNESCO Courier* devoted to 'Slavery'. Members of CERCAM have also published: Oruno D. Lara, *Les Caraïbes* (Paris: P.U.F., 1986); idem, *Le Commandant Mortenol, un officier guadeloupéen dans la 'Royale'* (Éditions du CERCAM, 1985); idem, *La Guadeloupe dans l'Histoire* (Paris: L'Harmattan, 1979); idem, *Caraïbes en construction: esclaves, colonisation, résistance*, 2 Vols (Éditions du CERCAM, 1992), articles on the Caribbean in *Encyclopaedia Universalis*; Nelly Schmidt, *Victor Schœlcher* (Paris: Fayard, 1994); idem, *La suppression de l'esclavage aux Caraïbes* (Publications de l'Université d'Aix-Marseille I, 1995). CERCAM has also published the collection *Cimarrons*, through Éditions J.M. Place, Paris.

Chapter 25

Slavery and the Roots of British Racism

Richard Hart

THE HORRORS AND CARNAGE engendered by the transatlantic slave trade and slavery in the plantations in the Caribbean have already been studied in great detail and do not need to be gone over again here. But the impact of the transatlantic slave trade and slavery on the formation and perpetuation of racist ideas has not been given the attention it deserves; that is the topic of this essay.

At the time when the demand for slaves for the British plantations in the Caribbean began to take off, in the mid-seventeenth century, slavery was not a notion familiar to British public opinion: slavery there had ceased to exist four centuries earlier, long before the first English settlements in North America, a situation quite different from that of Spain in the early sixteenth century. But as the English transatlantic slave trade and colonial interests expanded, and the enormity of the human sacrifices that they involved became apparent, the need to find an acceptable justification for enslaving Africans became more and more obvious to those same interests. A humanitarian reaction in England against slavery had to be avoided at all costs.

The best means of achieving this was a sustained campaign to show that Africans were a lower variety of humanity, pagans, cannibals, whom Divine Providence had set aside to serve as beasts of burden for the use of the white man. The visible differences of physical type facilitated this campaign to win over opinion.

At the time when the slave trade was getting under way, the vast continent of Africa contained a great variety of nations at very different stages of development. Some African civilizations predated by several centuries European civilizations over which they had initially had an edge although they never had either gunpowder or firearms. Others were as primitive as the ancient Britons were in the eyes of Julius Caesar when he landed in Britain with his 'civilized' Romans. But the defenders of the slave interest were not much concerned with truth. Their task was to circulate and impose a stereotype of the black man which showed him as an inferior being.

This task they successfully accomplished in England. For at least a century and a half after the beginning of the English slave trade, slave traders met no effective resistance in the home country. It is true that in the eighteenth century there were a few philanthropists who felt touched by the oppression and suffering of the slaves, but they were few in number and, initially, lacked the resources to join battle with the slave traders in a campaign designed to work on public opinion. As a result, until the nineteenth century, this human-itarianism was in no position to counter pro-slavery and colonial propaganda.

Of course, in all the countries with colonies where slavery existed, colo-nial interests also needed to put about the same sort of derogatory image of blacks. But in those countries where the Catholic Church was dominant, they faced ideological obstacles that were absent in Protestant Britain. In the first place, the Catholic Church's doctrine clearly asserted the humanity of blacks. In those Catholic countries, it was not possible to argue with any chance of success that Africans were not human beings. In dealing with moral problems of this sort, the Catholic faithful had to follow their priests, who did not have the same freedom for personal interpretation as Protestant ministers. On the other hand, the Protestant faithful had much more freedom to deal directly with God on these problems without necessarily going through their minis-ters. These latter were themselves subject to much less strict discipline in doc-trinal matters; by the same token, they were much more sensitive to the economic interests of their flocks, who found themselves caught up in the slave trade and slavery as slave owners.

Furthermore, in the Iberian peninsula, slavery had had an unbroken exis-tence, unlike the situation in Britain. Since the end of the Roman occupation, the laws regarding the status of slaves, developed in Roman times and applied then to white slaves, had remained in force, subsequently strengthened by fea-tures of Muslim law; they were applied in the Spanish colonies in America.

A final point is that the political organization of British colonization was highly decentralized. The white slave-owners in the various colonies had the right to elect a representative assembly, and it was that body that passed legis-lation regarding slaves, and not the Parliament in England. It is true that these laws might be disallowed by the Government in England but the assemblies in the Caribbean colonies got round that difficulty by passing laws that were only valid for one year. That meant that the home Government did not have the time to annul one before it expired. At that point the local assembly would re-enact the law for another short period.

But in the first half of the nineteenth century, vast changes occurred in Great Britain following what has been called the industrial revolution. The rise of industrial capitalism brought into being a new social class. However, the ad-vance of this new class, factory-owners or financiers of these industrialists, required the dismantling of every last remnant of the rigid class structure inher-ited from feudalism. This new order needed to replace social hierarchies based on birth and ownership of large estates by the freedom of social mobility resting on wealth accumulated in industry or trade. It needed freedom for the working classes to move from the countryside to the towns; it needed the removal of price and wage controls and of all restrictions on employment; it needed free-dom of contract between employers and workers. Although in fact, in the new industrial cities of nineteenth-century England, freedom of contract more often than not meant, for the worker, a choice between accepting the conditions laid down by the factory owner and starving to death, employers waxed lyrical about the many virtues of freedom of contract. Thus, at the beginning of the nineteenth century, the industrial bourgeoisie, although still under-represented in the British Parliament, was already becoming increasingly powerful and influential. This new class showed itself to be sensitive to anti-slavery ideals, which should come as no surprise. Slavery was a system of restrictions that inhibited the free movement of workers seeking employment, was opposed to the principle of freedom of contract, and, finally, was the most absolute negation of social mobility. From a more directly pragmatic standpoint, manufacturers and businessmen saw this unwaged forced labour as inhibiting the growth of purchasing power and the spread of the cash economy.

What all this meant is that, in the aftermath of the industrial revolution, the humanitarians opposed to slavery found new allies who could provide the abolitionist cause with the financial resources that it had hitherto lacked. Once this was assured, the abolitionists were in a position to provide an effective counter to colonial slave interests in the forum of public opinion. In 1807, thanks to their parliamentary spokesman, William Wilberforce, they succeeded in getting adopted an Act banning the importation of slaves throughout the British Empire, although slavery itself was not abolished.

In 1823, a society was founded popularly known as the Anti-Slavery Society but whose actual name was Society for the Gradual Abolition of Slavery. And this name is revealing of the socio-economic background of the British abolitionist movement at that time. These were men attached to the defence of property who wanted an end to the slave system, but were anxious to avoid social disruption. They were particularly most anxious not to see any repetition of revolutionary events such as those that had occurred in the former French colony of Saint-Domingue (Haiti). These abolitionist leaders had absolutely no desire to alter the social structure of the colonies, they wanted simply the substitution of wage labour for slave labour. They did not consult with the slaves themselves, they simply tried to convince them to leave everything in the hands of their British benefactors.

The first motion for the gradual abolition of slavery, adopted in 1823 by the House of Commons, with the backing of the Abolition Society, would have taken at least fifty years for abolition to be completed. But in the interim, the slaves themselves made their voice heard in a series of uprisings culminating in the biggest one, which occurred in Jamaica in 1831–2; this obliged Parliament urgently to reopen the debate. The slaves had brought the timetable forward.

The Reform Act of 1832 had just given the British industrial cities, hitherto not or scarcely represented in the Commons, the right to be represented in proportion to their population, while the rotten boroughs dominated by landowners were eliminated. This left the path open for the adoption of the act abolishing slavery in 1833. It replaced slavery with a sort of part-time servitude known as apprenticeship, which was itself abolished in 1838.

The abolitionist cause had finally carried the day, but major after-effects remained simply because, for some one hundred and fifty years before the nineteenth century, the formation of public opinion in this area had been monopolized by the slave interest. Their campaign to exclude Africans from humanity had been pervasive and conducted at every level, from caricatures and tracts aimed at the general public to literary pseudo-scientific works.

For example, one of the most widely read writers was the planter-historian Edward Long. This is what he had to say about the humanity of the Negro:

> In general, they are void of genius, and seem almost incapable of making any progress in civility or science. They have no plan or system of morality among them. Their barbarity to their children debases their nature even below that of brutes.... When we reflect on the nature of these men, and their dissimilarity to the rest of mankind, must we not conclude, that they are a different species of the same genus?... That the orang-outang and some races of black men are very nearly allied, is, I think, more than probable ... nor, for what hitherto appears, do they seem at all inferior in the intellectual faculties to many of the Negroe race; with some of whom, it is credible that they have the most intimate connexion and consanguinity. The amorous intercourse between them may be frequent ... an orang-outang ... has in form a much nearer resemblance to the Negroe race, than the latter bear to white men....

As to the advantages that slavery secured to the Negroes (according to him), Long wrote:

> This brutality somewhat diminishes, when they are imported young, after they become habituated to cloathing and a regular discipline of life; but many are never reclaimed....

As for God's will, Long concluded:

> Let us not then doubt, but that every member of the creation is wisely fitted and adapted to certain uses, and confined within the certain bounds to which it was ordained by the Divine Fabricator. The measure of the several orders ... of these Blacks may be as compleat as that of any other race of mortals; filling up that space, or degree, beyond which they are not destined to pass; and discriminating them from the rest of men, not in *kind* but in *species*....[1]

Many British abolitionists were influenced by this image of blacks put about by their opponents, consciously or unconsciously. The result was that when they were in a position to undertake their own campaigns, they were unable to counter the challenge thrown at them by some of their enemies' basic concepts.

The arguments that many of them advanced rested less on the concept of the humanity of the slaves than on the idea that all God's creatures should be treated charitably. Their denunciations of the horrors of the slave trade had little to distinguish them from the demands of members of the Society for the Prevention of Cruelty to Animals. The image of the African as an ignorant creature without religion who needed the civilizing influence of the white man's Christianity was widely accepted among the English anti-slavery activists. Thus, when defending his motion for the abolition of the slave trade in 1792, Wilberforce expressed himself in these words: 'What aim would be more noble than that of alleviating the sufferings of our brothers, by introducing Christianity and civilization into this quarter of the inhabitable world!'

William Pitt, speaking in support of his friend Wilberforce's motion in the same debate, declared:

> I hope therefore that we shall hear no more of the moral impossibility of civilizing the Africans.... Grieved am I to think that there should be a single person in this country, who can look on the present uncivilized state of that continent, as a ground for continuing the slave trade, – as a ground ... for refusing to attempt the improvement of Africa.... We were once as obscure among the nations of the earth, as savage in our manners, as debased in our morals, as degraded in our understandings, as these unhappy Africans are at present.[2]

Granville Sharp, one of the most enlightened of the early abolitionists, was a deeply religious man, who based his rejection of the notion that blacks were sub-human on the biblical belief that all people with dark skins were descendants of Cush, son of Ham, son of Noah. He was therefore extremely disturbed when he learnt that Jacob Bryant, a well-known writer of the time, had argued that 'the negroes on the Gold coast, and below it, were not descended from Cush'. Having read Bryant's essay on *Egypt and the Shepherd Kings*, he wrote to him in October 1772 as follows:

> I had always supposed that black men in general were descended from Cush, because a distinction in colour from the rest of mankind, seems to have been particularly attributed to his descendants ... therefore I concluded that all negroes, as well east Indian as African, are entitled to the same general name of Cushim, as being, probably, descended from different branches of the same stock.... I am far from having any particular esteem for the negroes, but as I think myself obliged to consider them as Men, I am certainly obliged, also, to use my best endeavours to prevent their being treated as beasts, by our unchristian countrymen, who deny them the privileges of human Nature; and in order to excuse their own brutality, will scarcely allow that negroes are human beings.

Bryant's reply came as a great relief to Granville Sharp:

> All the inhabitants of this vast continent are assuredly the sons of Ham: but not equally descended from Chus [sic]. For though his posterity was very dark, yet many of the collateral branches were of as deep a die: and Africa was peopled from Ham, by more families than one.... We learn from scripture, that Ham had four sons, Chus, Mizraim, Phut and Canaan..... Phut passed deep into Africa, and, I believe, most of the nations in that part of the world are descended from him.[3]

Many Methodists, influenced by John Wesley, were supporters of the abolition of slavery. But many of them were influenced by the argument that the pagan Africans needed the civilizing influence of the Christian white man. They were thus sensitive to the argument that, in spite of everything, there was a positive aspect to the enslavement of Africans. This comes out in the writings of the missionary Thomas Coke, as the following extract shows:

> Among those strange and mysterious events which take place through the permission of God, the case of the Africans, who have been torn from their native land, transported across the vast Atlantic, and are now held in bondage by the nations of Europe, claims our particular regard.... And yet it is not an improbable case, that even this most abominable traffic, (for the abolition of which every Christian will bless the God of love,) and this condition in which human nature appears, in one of its most degraded and unhappy forms, may be made subservient to those wise designs, which we shall not be able fully to unravel on this side an eternal world. We are not sufficiently acquainted with the extent of sin, nor with the vast designs of God, to pronounce these things absurd, or even improbable. Thus, even the slavery of the human species (though so directly contrary to the spirit of Christianity) we plainly perceive is now overruled by the unerring wisdom of God; and, strange as it may appear, myriads without all doubt will rejoice eternally that ever they were taken into the western world.
>
> It may be asked, 'Why did not God convey the same gospel to Africa, which he has conveyed to the West Indies? Why did he not bring them into the liberty of his children without shackling them first with chains?'
>
> We have already observed that the judgments of God are unsearchable, and his ways past finding out. The conduct which he pursues, leads invariably to the same important issue, though we cannot trace the path through which that conduct moves. His ways are just, though incomprehensible....[4]

Can this fact – that all through the period of slavery, the Anglo-Saxon populations of England and its colonies in North America were subjected to a sort of racist indoctrination that was much more effective than that endured by the essentially Roman Catholic populations of the Latin countries – not fail to have had long-term consequences after that period came to an end? Is it not therein that is to be found the explanation for that other fact that anti-black prejudice is much more deeply entrenched in the mind of people of Anglo-Saxon origin than among those of Latin origin?

Notes

1. E. Long, *The History of Jamaica*, 3 Vols, London, 1774, pp. 351–6, 365, 370–1, 374–7.
2. *Parliamentary History*, 2 April 1792.
3. G. Sharp, *The Just Limitation of Slavery in the Laws of God*, London, B. White in Fleet Street, 1776.
4. T. Coke, *A History of the West Indies*, 3 Vols, Liverpool, 1808 [reprinted 1969], Vol. 1, p. 38.

Chapter 26

Spanish Policy towards the Abolition of Slavery in the Nineteenth Century

Emiliano Gil-Blanco

Introduction

Slavery can be defined as a situation where the individual human being is simply a thing and as such subject to the power of a person who exercises over him rights of ownership. Slavery was extraordinarily widespread in the classical ancient world where it formed the basis of economic organization. Enslavement arose generally from people having been prisoners of war or the fact of being born of a mother who was a slave; escape from it was by way of manumission. But both the sources of enslavement and the actual condition of the slave have varied over history.

In ancient Spain, slavery undeniably existed. It is believed that at that time there were state slaves belonging to the various cities who farmed the common lands. In Rome and, subsequently, in Romanized Spain, slavery involved the loss of any legal personality; the slave enjoyed no legal protection, he could neither acquire property nor make contracts. His master could do with him as he wished, even kill him without the least criminal liability. Deprived of any legal capacity, including any family rights, the slave could not marry, and unions between slaves were nothing more than concubinage with no legal standing. Doubtless this situation improved somewhat over the centuries. In the later Roman Empire, the influence of Christianity began to be felt and there were other improvements, with the Church imposing severe punishments on inhuman masters. In the later empire, slavery declined in importance as there was a move to another social structure, the colonate, with serfs who were assigned land to farm. But by the time of the Visigoths, there were still many slaves in Spain, and their condition was much as it had been under the later Roman Empire. In Christian Spain at the time of the *reconquista*, slavery declined in importance, and it must be clearly distinguished from serfdom. It was supplied essentially by Muslim prisoners of war while, in Arab Spain, slaves were Christian prisoners of war. Their fate was regulated by official legal provisions (*Fueros*). In modern times, slavery practically disappeared in Spain, apart from a few cases of personal servitude following the continuing wars in North Africa.

Slavery in America

Slavery in America existed among the various peoples in the regions conquered by the Spaniards in America. Christopher Columbus was the first person to undertake to make his discoveries pay by using indigenous slaves.

But the Spanish monarchy always had a paternalistic attitude towards the indigenes, and it therefore prohibited the enslavement of the Indians through legislation designed to protect them (the 'new laws' of 1542 and the Code of the Laws of the Indies collected under Philip II). Exceptions were cases of war or rebellion or where a people itself maintained the institution. But the need for labour led to other 'institutions' such as the *repartimientos* or concessions (*encomiendas*) regulated by the monarchy which took action against those in breach of the regulations. These protective provisions and the shortage of labour in America led to the introduction after 1501 of black labour. In the beginning, it was Genoese and Portuguese, who already had experience of the slave trade, who engaged in this type of trade, with licences issued to individuals by the Spanish Crown in exchange for a duty on each black imported. After 1525, the so-called *asiento* system (or monopoly contracts) was established, of which the Portuguese were the first beneficiaries, followed by the Germans, the French and the English. With the Treaty of Utrecht in 1713, the British gained a monopoly of it, which they also used to bring in prohibited goods. This monopoly lasted until 1753, when King Carlos III revoked it.

The condition of the African slave was in all respects well below that of the Indians. Masters were officially required to see to his material and spiritual welfare but, in general, his life was an extremely harsh one. In 1785, Carlos III undertook to improve the condition of slaves in Spanish America with the promulgation of the Código Carolino which, while it did not abolish slavery, did mark the beginning of its decline.

The Process of Abolition in Spain and America

This abolition was belated because of the interests of the local Creole oligarchies who deemed the maintenance of slavery vital to keeping labour on their plantations, and for those plantations to remain profitable. So the first countries where abolition took place were those where slavery was not necessary economically, where it was a sort of luxury. But where slaves constituted a significant proportion of the labour force, abolition occurred only later, and not without resistance from slave-owning interests; that was the case in Brazil and Cuba.

The abolitionist movement originated in the wars of independence of the Spanish colonies, and already outside either party; it was also influenced by the abolition of the slave trade enacted by Britain in 1807 (won by a long established abolitionist movement and which ended in 1834 with the abolition of slavery in the British colonies. In France, slavery was first abolished in 1794, restored by Napoleon in 1802 and finally abolished in 1848). Also, the Anglo-Spanish treaty concluded between George III and Fernando VII envisaged the suppression of the slave trade and the means of controlling it, but as events showed, it was not very effective.

British influence was felt through the proximity of its colonies in the Caribbean, notably Jamaica; one sign of it can be seen in the slave insurrection in Cuba in 1844, which was brutally suppressed. Cuba was to be the last bastion of the Spanish presence in America. Here the process of abolition was delayed by the already mentioned opposition of the Creole oligarchy and the ten-year long wars of independence.

In Spain, at the beginning of the nineteenth century, there was as yet no anti-slavery social awareness, except for a handful of very isolated figures, such as J. Marchena, I. Antillon, A. Argüelles, J. M. Blanco White and the count of Toreno.

At the time of the Cortes of Cadiz of 1812, a parliamentary commission was established to study the possibility of abolishing the slave trade with the Spanish colonies. It followed on from a proposal put forward by two deputies, one from Mexico and the other Spanish, who had themselves witnessed the British process of abolition: Alcocer and Argüelles. But the commission must never have reported since we are not aware of any result of its labours.

Later, at the time of the liberal Cortes of 1821, another parliamentary commission looked into the same problem, with equally meagre results. In the dark decade that followed, from 1823 to 1833, this sort of debate and the work of commissions were buried since slavery and the slave trade continued.

Dates of Abolitions in America

Country	Beginning	Final abolition
Chile	1811	1823
Argentina	1813	1853
Peru	1821	1854
Central America	1824	
Mexico	1825	
Venezuela	1850	
Colombia	1851	
United States	1862	1865
Cuba	1868	1886
Brazil	1871	1888
Puerto Rico	1873	

In 1845, following the 1835 Treaty with Britain and the Vatican's stand against the slave trade, a law to abolish slavery and suppress the slave trade was promulgated. But it provided for only light penalties that were not very effective against law-breakers and it included exceptions and restrictions to its application which reduced its impact. In any case, from this time on, within some sectors of Spanish society, a public debate began between supporters and opponents of abolition. Among the former, mention should be made of Castelar, Rivero and Orenses, who engaged in a lively discussion in the press and in the Cortes with the 'moderates', in other words the defenders of slavery and Spanish interests in Cuba. This shift in public opinion in Spain was also influenced by the American Civil War of 1861–5, and the abolition proclamations issued by Lincoln in 1863 and 1865, as well as by the Anglo-American treaty on the same subject in 1862. The Spanish Abolitionist Society formed in 1865 by Viscarrondo out of the Free Economic Society headed up this whole movement. The whole liberal class of the country participated in it and, among others, future presidents of the First Spanish Republic, such as Salmeron and Castelar, as well as Sagasta, Olozaga, Valera, Moret and C. Arenal.

The results of this movement appeared with the revolution of 1868, which took up the task of abolition, as was clear in the Cortes of 1869. Out of that came the Morel law of 1870, which the abolitionists however deemed inadequate. In 1873, the government of Ruiz Zorilla passed a law abolishing slavery in Puerto Rico, which the pro-slavers (the 'moderates' in the Assembly) violently opposed going so far as to launch a campaign of denigration against the Abolitionist League and its sympathizers. As regards Cuba, abolition was more difficult because of the already-mentioned opposition of the Creole oligarchy and wars for independence fought between 1868 and 1878. Finally, in 1880, the Canovas government got the Cortes to approve a new law which provided for the gradual abolition of slavery in Cuba, over eight years, through a new institution known as the *patronato*, with extremely harsh rules. Finally, in 1886, a decree of the liberal government abolished this provision and final abolition was achieved. This decree was proof that Spain was the last European country to abolish slavery in its possessions. From that date, there was a shift in Spanish anti-slavery policy which showed itself in participation in every diplomatic meeting aimed at the total suppression of slavery, and notably through the signing of a new treaty with Britain in 1890 and Spain's presence at the Brussels anti-slavery conference in 1889–90.

Bibliography

DIAZ SOLER, L. M. *Histoire de l'esclavage des Noirs à Porto-Rico.* Rio Negras, 1969.

DOMINGUES ORTIZ, A. 'L'esclavage en Castille à l'âge moderne'. In: *Estudios de Historia Social de Espana.* Vol. 2. N.p., 1952.

FRANCO SILVA, A. *L'esclavage à Séville jusqu'à la fin du Moyen Âge.* Seville, 1979.

KLEIN, H. S. *L'esclavage agricole en Amerique latine et dans les Caraïbes.* Madrid, Alianza American, 1986.

MARRERO, L. *Cuba, économie et société. Le sucre, savoir et conscience (1763–1868).* Madrid, Editorial Playor, 1983–4.

MORALES CARRION, A. *Essor et decadence de la traite négrière à Porto-Rico (1820–1860).* Rio Piedra, 1978.

SANCHEZ ALBORNOZ, N. *La population de l'Amérique latine depuis l'époque préecolombienne jusqu'à l'an 2000.* Madrid, Alianza Universitad, 1977.

SOLANO, F. de. *Études sur l'abolition de l'esclavage.* Supplements to *Revista de Indias*, 2. Madrid, 1986.

VILA VILAR, E. *L'Amérique espagnole et le commerce de esclaves, l'Asientos portugais.* Seville, École des études hispano-américaines, 1977.

Chapter 27

Abolition or Destruction of the Slave System?

Oruno D. Lara and Iñez Fischer-Blanchet

A NUMBER OF CULTURAL AND ARTISTIC EVENTS were organized to mark the bicentenary of the abolition of slavery in France (1794–1994). There were films, music, plays, round tables, debates, exhibitions, colloquies and so on and so forth. For some, it was a celebration, for others, a commemoration. For some, a tour round a few heroes (Sonthonax, Schœlcher, Sarda Garriga). For others, the music of a rediscovered memory. An apocryphal contemplation.

For researchers at the Centre de Recherches Caraïbes-Amériques, it was an opportunity to reflect on our history in a context of everyday struggle, far away from the festival lights.

In 1793, the armed insurrection of the blacks in the Plaine du Nord of the colony of Saint-Domingue, which had erupted in August 1791, forced the French authorities to decree the abolition of slavery there and then. The civil commissioners, with their backs against the wall, on the defensive, took the decision to promulgate the emancipation of the slaves in North province (29 August), West province (21 September) and South province (7 October). This belated promulgation, endorsed by the Convention in February 1794, did not prevent the war from spreading. The blacks of Saint-Domingue did not fall into the trap laid for them. The principal enemy was not Britain or Spain, as they were being led to believe, but France, colonial France. They got the right target and committed themselves irreversibly to war – France's first colonial war – which ended in the total defeat and rout of the French troops in 1803 and the independence of Haiti on 1 January 1804.

As of 1994, the Caribbean was still being rocked by seismic shocks, the epicentres of which are in Haiti, Cuba, Guatemala, Nicaragua, El Salvador or Guadeloupe. Two centuries after 1793, the Caribbean stands out as a maritime, insular and mainland area where the number of conflicts is on the increase and rulers and ruled are on a collision course. It is a region of the globe where colonization is continuing its corrosive and pitiless activity – in Guadeloupe, in Martinique, in French Guyana, in the Virgin Islands, in Puerto Rico, in Montserrat, for example – a region where democracy is finding it extremely difficult to put down permanent roots.

Recent research, over the last two decades, has enabled us to clarify the prospects, the opponents and the stakes. In this Caribbean of History into which oppositions and conflicts are projected, it is necessary to make one's position clear, to make a clear distinction between the camps.

Our research has been chiefly focused on mastering our history. We have neither the desire nor the impertinence to write chapters on the history of France or Europe, simply the determination to *construct* the history of the Caribbean. We want, using all due rigour, to take part in writing our history, a history in which Carib, blacks and indigenes of the Americas are the principal actors and not passive subjects, held on a leash, far removed from external centres where decisions are made.

This posture – very different, granted, from that of 'Creolist' writers, those exotic creatures which fashion latches onto for a time – determines our research approaches, our methods of investigation, our concern with clarity and simplicity in exposition, without glossing over the difficulties or obliterating the complexity of the Caribbean.

* * *

The suppression of slavery in Haiti and the Spanish colonies – except for Cuba and Puerto Rico – occurred in a context of war. In truth, Haiti was a unique case: blacks fought victoriously, broke their chains and seized their independence. They inaugurated a *process of destroying the slave system*. The colonial war against France set off a chain reaction that could not be halted. After Haiti, it was the turn of the Spanish colonies to be engulfed. The war against the Spaniards, won by military leaders such as Bolivar, ensured their independence and shook the slave system. In Venezuela, Bolivar's abolition decrees of 23 May, 2 June and 6 July 1816 envisaged the enlistment of blacks in the army and their front-line participation in the 'revolutionary' war. However, the congress of Angostura, in 1819, marked the beginning of a process of reconstructing slave relationships in Venezuela. The black caudillo Manuel Carlos Piar, shot on 16 October 1817, summoned his brothers to other battles. The slave system gradually disintegrated in the institutional framework of the new republics (Chili in 1823, Bolivia in 1826, Mexico in 1829, Colombia in 1851 and Venezuela in 1854). The American Civil War led to the disappearance of slavery in the United States in 1865, while in Cuba the destruction occurred in the course of the armed struggle of 1880–6.

The suppression of slavery took different forms in the territories in the Caribbean where the colonial system remained in place. In the French, Dutch and Danish colonies, the slave-based colonial system was replaced by the colonial system without slavery, sometimes with violence, but without war. The transition took the form of a series of legal measures and abolition laws. These laws transformed the slave blacks into *emancipated* blacks, but they did not make the colonized disappear. The term *abolition* suggests the brevity of an instant operation: a law is enacted and slavery goes, disappears forever.... *Abolition*: a rite of passage towards general emancipation involving one or more abolitionists who cut the Gordian knot of slavery: John Penn, William Wilberforce, Granville Sharp, Thomas Clarkson, James Ramsay, James Stephen and Zachary Macaulay, names of 'saints' whom colonial history honours in Britain. William Lloyd Garrison, Abraham Lincoln, Frederick Douglass in the United States. A single mythical figure stands out in France, placed in the Panthéon of great men: Victor Schœlcher. But moving from a colonial slave society to a set of social actors who have freely chosen to constitute a society does not happen just like that. Numerous slave revolts undermined the slave system but they did not succeed in dismantling it as in Haiti.

The slave system did not vanish, its imprint remained in the mode of production, in social relations and in the heads of the colonized. Such a mark must either be crushed or extirpated. Everything still remains to be done when slavery has been declared 'abolished'. The process of destroying the slave system, a concept that it is preferable to use, makes it possible to pose the problem of those colonized territories which have to try, in the long run, to rid themselves of slavery. Analysis of these *abolitions*, in the colonies, poses complex problems. It means rejecting a solidly established historiographical tradition. The colonial powers have in fact manipulated history in their possessions, endeavouring to mask the real problems, seeking essentially to maintain production and control the population.

The general insurrection of the blacks in Saint-Domingue and the independence of Haiti inspired untold terror in the slave-owners of the Caribbean. After the fall of Napoleon, the contradictions between European merchants, Creole planters, free blacks or coloureds and slaves, measures indicative of mistrust or aimed at repression led to disturbances, plots and revolts. A process of resistance by free blacks and slaves developed leading up to the suppression of slavery in the island and mainland colonies of the Caribbean.

In France, the supporters of maintaining slavery denounced the colonial failure in Saint-Domingue and the error of having granted the immediate abolition of slavery. They feared Haiti's influence over the colonial territories in the Caribbean. The smaller numbers of those in favour of suppressing the slave system deplored the mismanagement of Haiti, and its international isolation. Victor Schœlcher went to the island in 1841 to assess the situation of the country on the spot. Those in charge of colonial administration took steps designed to limit contagion spreading from the freedom proclaimed in Haiti. These protective measures did not prevent that influence from reaching the colonized territories, as witness two examples. The *separatist* tendency which appeared in Guadeloupe in 1848 at the instigation of Marie-Léonard Sénécal was harshly put down by the central government.[1] The Governor of Jamaica, Edward Eyre, violently cracked down on a rebellion at Morant Bay in 1865. He was recalled to London and justified himself by explaining his fears of seeing a repetition in Jamaica of what had happened in Haiti.

In the Danish colonies of the Virgin Islands (St Thomas, St Croix and St John), the slave system was severely shaken by slave revolts between 1846 and 1848. They led to the suppression of the 'peculiar institution'. The blacks' revolt in St Croix in October 1878 convinced the Danes to get rid of their islands. They decided to sell them to the United States, on 17 January 1917, for 25 million dollars.[2]

* * *

It is undeniably in Cuba, in the second half of the nineteenth century, that the problem of abolition can best be studied. This concept of *abolition* used by colonial historiography, like that of *emancipation*, is not suitable. A look at the Cuban case gives a better understanding of the process of destroying the slave system. This process began at the time of the Ten Years' War in Cuba and has continued down to the present day at varying speeds. The Ten Years' War – which for some was the first war of liberation and for others was not one at all – began on 10 October 1868 with a meeting of the *manzanilleros* commanded by Carlos Manuel de Cespedes on his estate of La Demajagua and the proclamation of a manifesto entitled *Manifiesto de la Junta Revolucionaria de la Isla de Cuba dirigido a sus Compatriotas y a todas las Naciones*. It followed a series of slave uprisings and disturbances caused by maroon blacks and *apalencados*. Maroon blacks and *palenques* were involved in the Yara revolution in 1868. They were chiefly located in the mountainous regions of the Vueltabajo (Campanarios, Cabezadas, Rio San Cristobal, Guacamayas) and in the other provinces: La Havana, Las Villas (Trinidad mountains), Camagüey and Oriente. The revolutionary movement in Cuba from a very early date was associated with attempts at liberation embarked on by the oppressed of the slave system to break their chains. At the end of the eighteenth century, those involved in the Bayamo plot discovered in 1795 had revolutionary objectives. The revelations of the *retinto* Negro Nicolás Morales, the leader, and his fellow plotters left no doubt on this point and deserve a deeper analysis of Cuban history. As do all the slave uprisings which became more numerous in the 1840s and 1850s (the 1843 conspiracy of La Escalera, for example) which have never been seriously studied by Cuban historiography. The experience of these maroon blacks and defenders of the palenques was decisive during the ten years of war of the *Mambises*, decisive in terms of the revolution.[3]

Historians who refuse to see the Ten Years' War as a war of liberation support their views by referring to the uncertainty and ambiguity of the political aspirations formulated by the leaders, the tepidness of their abolitionist sentiment and above all the limits of their strictly economic demands. One has only to read the *Manifesto* of October 1868 launched by Cespedes and his friends to understand the reality and importance of the contradictions that undermined the movement from its birth. The fraction of the ruling classes that led the war failed to go beyond its class interests. It got itself trapped in the political alternative: real independence or final break with Spain. This hesitation ended in negotiations with the representatives of the Spanish army in 1878 (*Convenio del Zanjon*) and sealed the end of the war (pact of Zanjon, 10 February 1878).

What was the position of these owners of the means of production faced with the problem of slavery? How did they behave towards their own slaves?

The Junta's *Manifesto* was disturbingly vague on this point. After stating 'venerable principles', such as that 'all men are equal' and spoken of justice and tolerance, they declared: 'We respect the life and property of all peaceful citizens, including those of Spaniards living on this territory;… we desire gradual emancipation accompanied by compensation for slavery.'[4] In addition, the rebels of 1868 were firm advocates of exclusively white immigration into Cuba. On the very day that they launched their insurrection, Cespedes and some of his slave-owning neighbours decided to free their slaves and invite them to help them in the struggle. The *caudillo* was very afraid of the other slave-owners on whom he was counting to gain freedom from Spanish rule. The contradictions were not overcome and the decree of 28 December 1868 signed by Cespedes at Bayamo clearly illustrates these internal difficulties.[5] On the other hand, the region of Camagüey decreed the total abolition of slavery in February 1869. A distinction in fact needs to be made between Oriente, an area dominated by the sugar industry (and thus dependent on slave labour), and Camagüey, a cattle-raising region where slave labour was not preponderant. But the limits of the insurrectionary movement are best measured in economic terms. At the beginning of the war, a fraction of the masters of the slave labour force which was fighting to obtain a reduction of tax on income from capital won out. The war aims were chiefly limited to economic demands with no political programme, as indicated above. The 1868 *Manifesto* ended with a decision of the revolutionary Junta to abolish taxes.

As the war ground on over ten years, it considerably modified the economic and social situation by inaugurating a process of destruction of the slave system, precipitating a transformation of economic structures and the shift from colonial capitalism to imperialism and finally promoting the appearance of class parties, which were manifestations of an original form of class struggle that was sharpened in the course of this period.

During the Ten Years' War, large numbers of plantation slaves, maroons and runaways from the palenques gained the *manigua* and fought to alter the direction and significance of the war. This war ended in 1878 after the Spanish army had given in to the demand of Antonio Maceo, the leader of the slaves under arms, on the principle of the right of rebel slaves henceforward to be completely free. It is possible to follow the progress of this disappearance of slave relations, from the constitution of Guiamaro adopted on 10 April 1869 to the freedom of the rebel slaves recognized by the Pact of Zanjon (10 February 1878) and beyond the war in the decade 1878–88 which saw the collapse of the last remaining traces of slave relations in Cuba.

Cuban blacks, guns and machetes in hand, were thus the real artisans of their liberation. One aspect of this problem must be underlined. For four centuries, slaves of African origin had made the white colonists of Cuba tremble. It is enough still to read José Antonio Saco's *Ideas sobre la Incorporacion de Cuba en los Estados Unidos*, written in Paris in 1848, to understand retrospectively the impact of those 500,000 slaves and 200,000 free people of colour who were at that time outnumbered the whites.[6] The spectre that was haunting the owning class was clearly Saint-Domingue, which had become Haiti in 1804.

How could it be possible to fight against Spain without calling on the blacks and without ending slavery? How could they be prevented from gaining the upper hand, being numerically the larger group, and transforming the island into a second black republic, like Haiti? This was the dilemma faced by Cespedes and his supporters who declared: 'Cuba libre es incompatible con Cuba esclavista' (*Manifesto* of 27 December 1868) but showed themselves incapable of proceeding to the destruction of the slave nexus. There appeared to be two solutions to this conflict: the creation of a revolutionary movement capable of building on the popular classes and in particular on all those Cuban blacks liberated from their chains by their action during the Ten Years' War, or the intervention of a foreign power – the United States in this case – which would stifle the revolutionary forces and the black threat and line up the Cuban bourgeoisie relieved of Spanish tutelage behind it. These two solutions followed one another in Cuba with the appearance of the Cuban Revolutionary Party and the outbreak of the Spanish-American War which enabled the United States to grab Cuba with the consent of the racist bourgeoisie. The Ten Years' War also provoked a total transformation of the economic infrastructure by carrying through a redistribution of productive forces brought about by the ending of the slave mode of production and by destroying the whole financial base of masters who had lost their *labour-capital*. They had to honour their debts accumulated since the 1850s and 1860s – a time when colonial capitalism in Cuba was accelerating. They were thus forced to hand over to their creditors much of their means of production (plantations, factories etc.). A large sum of cash (finance capital) and productive capital (factories, plantations) arising from these debts were concentrated in the hands of American financiers. Thus, the domination of the financial trusts that marked the transition from colonial capitalism to imperialism, completed around 1880–90, was reinforced. In addition to these economic shifts, there were the financial consequences of the increasing tax burden of the colonial state apparatus on incomes from capital, after the war, which affected the process of redistributing productive forces.

The Spanish Government loaded the Cuban proprietors with tax, which caused the disappearance of the island's social capital and put former masters in a difficult situation. As José Marti predicted, the Ten Years' War played a political role since it made it possible to go beyond certain social contradictions by precipitating the formation of class parties which were distributed across the political stage as the Party of Constitutional Union, the Reformist Party, the Autonomist Party and the Cuban Revolutionary Party.

The Spanish-Cuban War, 1895–1898

The conflict which broke out in February 1895 pitted Spain against the revolutionary forces. What were the numbers on either side? When hostilities began, the Spaniards thought that they would be able put down the rebellion with 100,000 soldiers. When the fighting started, Spain had 21,777 soldiers in the island. A few months later, in October 1895, Madrid sent 80,000 soldiers and was ready to send 35,000 more, commanded by generals Marin and Prado. By June 1896, there were estimated to be 150,000 Spanish troops. The troops were at that time commanded by three lieutenant-generals (Marin, Prado and Valera), ten major-generals and twenty-five brigadiers. By December 1896, 300,000 men were involved. If we compare this figure with the total population of Cuba estimated at 1,800,000 inhabitants, then there was one soldier for every six inhabitants. That is a record unequalled in the world history of repression. What is more, this number made the Spanish army, which usually had 100,000 men under arms in peace-time, the leading military power to cross the Atlantic in terms of numbers. How many were there on the side of the revolutionaries? Until 1896, the Cuban guerilla remained divided into highly mobile small groups which must have grown from 10,000 to 40,000 men. A rural and urban militia which acted clandestinely complemented the action of the revolutionary army.

The Spanish-American War

For almost four years, the Spanish-Cuban war tragically disrupted Cuban society. What is its position today in Cuban historiography compared to that of the Spanish-American War which lasted just three months? The war of 1895–8 pitted Spaniards – and all the institutions of the colonial state – against Cuban revolutionaries. Behind Spain, other powers such as the United States, Britain and France were interested in the conflict and participated more or less directly in it. The Spanish-American 'blitzkrieg' saw a confrontation in a singular joust – one that was more verbal than real – between the United States, which was unmasking its colonial design, and Spain, which was abdicating, only too content to get out so cheaply after a severe military defeat caused not by the forces of the United States but by Cuban revolutionaries.

Behind Spain lay Britain and above all France which had invested vast amounts of capital in Spain; it too backed United States intervention, thinking that the Americans would pay and that it would recover what it was owed. In this international game, the Cubans were marked as the losers. But a distinction must be made between those who despaired at seeing their nation subjected to the United States and others who were supporting an intervention that some had called for. The Cuban revolutionary movement in fact found a great deal of support in the United States, as a result of the intense propaganda put out by José Marti and his Cuban friends. They held meeting after meeting, throughout the Union, collecting large sums of money which were used to purchase weapons, powder and ammunition that were then sent to the island.

At first, United States intervention was limited to the exercise of policing the seas through patrols between the United States and the Cuban coasts to arrest any expedition to Cuba. The United States also took it upon itself to gaol anyone who helped the Cuban Revolutionary Party in any way at all. At the beginning of 1896, the Spanish Government had to choose among three solutions: to put down the insurrection by force and maintain Spanish rule, to sell Cuba or to grant it self-government, which would maintain Spanish sovereignty. Madrid was in fact counting on using a strategy of intervention by the United States to its own ends which would take the form of a rejection of help from the US Government, so that it would be forced to intervene in the conflict without Spain's agreement and under cover of a war with Spain.

The explosion of the *Maine* on 15 February 1898 in Havana harbour triggered this process. The decision for direct United States military intervention was taken by President McKinley on 11 April 1898. It was justified by three essential principles: Spain's inability to put an end to the conflict between it and the insurgents in the island, the imminent eventuality of the proclamation of Cuban independence and the alleged inability of Cubans to govern themselves. The explosion of the *Maine* in fact suited all opponents of the Cuban revolution, Spain, the United States and France in particular, as well as a large fraction of the Cuban bourgeoisie. The masquerade began by giving itself a mask of reality. Spanish officers chorused the usual revenge-filled justifications, suggesting that the war would be long and hard-fought. In Spain there was talk of destroying United States vessels, and even of an invasion of the United States (General Weyler). Piracy and freebooting reappeared in the imaginary of the time, becoming for Spain a weapon that was as effective as it had ever been.

The United States set up a commission of enquiry which was sent to Havana in the hope of avoiding any conflict with Spain. The report sent to Washington established that the ship had been destroyed by the explosion of a submarine mine but counted on a further enquiry by the Spanish Government to maintain friendly relations between the two governments. However, Madrid, looking for a fight, recalled its ambassador to Washington on 11 February and raised the tension to destroy the United States' commitment to peace. The Spanish Government was in fact pursuing a systematic policy of provoking the United States by winning the support of the European powers. With the help of France, Spain won the support of Russia, Britain, Austria-Hungary, Italy and Germany. These countries refused to intervene individually in the conflict which seemed imminent but agreed to offer Spain collective support in April 1898.

Hostilities began, without any prior declaration of war, with a few cannon shots fired from a fort in Havana, to which the North Americans did not respond. At sea, Spanish vessels engaged in incomprehensible battles, all becoming phantom vessels, despite the departure of squadrons from Cape Verde and of reserves in April and June.

The grouping of European powers discovered the imperialism of the United States. As for Spain, it had been successful in the first phase of its disengagement from Cuba: to remove the spectre of revolution. It now started on the second: to bring about the replacement of powers in Cuba. On 19 July 1898, France's mediation was made official. On 22 July, the Duke of Almodovar, Spanish Minister of State, told the French ambassador the terms Spain was demanding in the negotiations. Spain was in fact basing the transactions not on a possible independence of Cuba but on annexation of the colony by the United States. That suited France, anxious to recover its debts. The negotiations continued in Paris, conducted by Jules Cambon. They ended in the Treaty of Paris which ensured the transition from the Spanish colonial state to the North American colonial state in Cuba. On the spot, once master of Santiago, General Shafter began by banning armed Cubans from entering the city. He kept the Spanish authorities in their jobs.

Notes

1. See I. Fischer-Blanchet, 'Troubles paysannes en Guadeloupe à l'époque de l'émancipation: le procès Sénécal à Basse-Terre', *Cimarrons*, I, Guadeloupe, Institut Caraïbe de Recherches Internationales en Sciences Sociales and Paris, Éditions Jean-Michel Place, 1981.
2. On the process of destroying the slave system, see O. D. Lara, *Caraïbes en construction: espace, colonisation, résistance*, 2 Vols, Éditions du Centre de Recherches Caraïbes-Amériques, 1992, B.P. 22, 93801, Épinay Cedex, France, Vol. 1, chaps. 5 to 7, 'Destruction du système esclavagiste', 1, 2, 3; and chap. 8, 'Lutte armée à Cuba'.
3. See J. L. Franco, 'La presencia negra en el Nuevo Mundo', *Cuadernos de la Revista Casa de las Americas*, 7, 1968; J. L. Riverend, *Histoire économique de Cuba*, Havana, Instituto del Libro, 1967 [Eng. trans. M. J. Cazoba and H. León, *Economic History of Cuba*, Havana, Ensaya Book Institute, 1967]; and R. Guerra, *Manual de Historia de Cuba*, Havana, 1962.
4. H. P. Vinals, *Documentos para la Historia de Cuba (Epoca colonial)*, Havana, Editora Universitaria, 1965, pp. 378–9.
5. Ibid., pp. 381–3.
6. J. A. Saco, *Ideas sobre la incorporacion de Cuba en los Estados Unidos*, Paris, 1848, p. 347.

Chapter 28

The Drafting of the 1848 Decrees: Immediate Application and Long-Term Consequences

Nelly Schmidt

THE HISTORY OF THE FRENCH DECREE abolishing slavery is full of paradox. The decree is ignored in most school textbooks, yet it seems conversely to be a well-known text for many, a republican sanction imposed without debate on an old colonial regime that was thereby finally defeated. The text adopted by the provisional government in 1848 legally abolished slavery in the French colonies with immediate effect. Unlike in the neighbouring British colonies, where emancipation had been spread over the period 1833–8, it settled the issue in one blow. Often, in discussing the second French emancipation, that is as all that is said; the year 1848 is seen as the year of emancipation, a positive, humanitarian aspect of action by the Government that had emerged from the revolutionary days of February.

One man, Victor Schœlcher, a well-known abolitionist, was the author of a republican decree which was itself perceived as a direct emanation of the French Revolution and the principles of 1789, with its promises of political assimilation – at the time regarded as revolutionary. Promulgation of the decree was seen as having led to falling production, workers walking off the job and political disturbances. What was remembered of it then was only an impression of confusion and the work of local political construction was seen as beginning only after 1871.

To see things in this way was to overlook many aspects of the decree itself, its drafting, the influences on that drafting, the resistance it aroused, the international context in which it was occurring and, of course, the long- and short-term effects of the actual document. There is of course no question of attributing to a mere decree an exaggerated impact with no relation to a historical reality that was nothing if not complex. A reading of the proceedings of the commission that drafted it and then a close examination of its content will however help to bring out the broad lines of post-abolitionist French colonial policy.

I propose to look at the following points:
- the distinct objectives that the abolition commission set itself, the influences to which it was subjected and the enquiries that it carried out;
- a brief analysis of the resistance that appeared inside the commission when it submitted its first reports to the Ministry of the Navy and the Colonies;
- a survey of the decisions that it took and the recommendations that it made to colonial administrators and the ministry;
- the initial procedures for implementation of the decree and the *annexed* decrees that accompanied it and the initial instructions that the general commissioners of the Republic carried with them; and
- finally, the short- and long-term consequences of implementation of the decree in the French colonies in the Caribbean.

* * *

First, I shall review the sequence of events, since a brief chronological framework is important for our understanding of the problems that arose in a context of very high social tension, accentuated over the previous fifteen years by the promulgation of emancipation in the neighbouring British colonies:

3 March 1848: interview by Victor Schœlcher with François Arago, Minister of the Navy. He told him that to maintain slavery as he had agreed to do under pressure from delegations of colonists would lead to incidents similar to those in Saint-Domingue/Haiti a few decades earlier;

4 March: the Provisional Government adopted the principle of abolishing slavery in the colonies;

5 March: Arago appoints Schœlcher as under-secretary of state for the Colonies and president of the Commission on the abolition of slavery whose members he appointed, at once taking good care (itself something unheard of in the history of commissions looking into colonial affairs) that no colonist or former senior official of the Ministry of the Navy who had become a colonial governor was a member;

27 April: the decree is signed by the minimum number required of members of the Provisional Government to be adopted and published in *Le Moniteur*;

26 July: the commission is dissolved. It submitted two reports to the ministry which contain all its recommendations. It drafted a series of decrees to be annexed to the decree of 27 April.

Meanwhile, the general commissioners of the Republic had left for Guadeloupe, Martinique, French Guyana and Réunion. They were carrying the decree and the instructions drawn up by Schœlcher for its implementation. These instructions provided that an interval of at least two months should elapse between their arrival and the coming into force of the decree, which is what happened, except in Martinique and Guadeloupe. In Martinique, the decree was promulgated by Governor Claude Rostoland on 23 May following serious incidents and rioting by slaves in Saint-Pierre and Fort-de-France. The sharp social tension prevailing in Guadeloupe forced Governor Jean-François Layrle to proclaim freedom there too before the official arrival of the decree, on 27 May 1848.[1] The general commissioners of the Republic, Perrinon in Martinique and Gatine in Guadeloupe, reached their destinations only on the following 3 and 5 June respectively.

Objectives of the Commission

Schœlcher set out the objectives at the very first working meeting. They were: (1) to agree on the terms of the decree that would free the slaves, and (2) to propose the most considered means to ensure that work continued after freedom.

The first task facing its members was to collect significant documents on:

- the debates in the Convention on abolition in 1794;
- the preparation of the British abolition act;
- reports and memorials on the initial effects of this measure when it was implemented in the British West Indies;
- existing reports, particularly in London, on developments in Haiti since 1804; and
- preparing a questionnaire to be submitted to all the delegations that the commission might receive, in particular delegations of representatives of the colonists and *armateurs* (outfitters) in the Atlantic ports.[2]

An analysis of the work of the first sessions provides a reasonably compete breakdown of the topics which may be summarized as follows.

- How to get the new freedmen to provide regular labour on the plantations?
- What wages to pay them? How would they survive outside the periods of the sugar cane harvest?
- What electoral system should be used to constitute the local assemblies which were to succeed the colonial councils?
- How to improve the marketing of cane sugar on the French market?
- Should this emancipation be gradual, as in the British colonies, or immediate? This was an echo of the reservations and considerable timidity of the proposals of the Société pour l'abolition de l'esclavage which, since its establishment in 1834, had only envisaged extremely gradual emancipation accompanied by a long apprenticeship.

The last questions to which the commission had to reply in the light of the opinions of the delegates received also deserve mention.

- Did the members of the commission judge that the colonies were 'a burden for France'?

• Finally, would what was then called the 'freed class' have some 'representatives of its interests' in various local bodies and the assembly?

These questions make it possible to assess the state of 'social death' in which the colonies languished, a situation that has been well described by historians and sociologists such as Oruno D. Lara and Orlando Patterson.[3]

Right from the outset, Schœlcher had laid down as one of the basic principles of the resolutions that the commission should reach that 'the "regenerated" colonies would be entering the great French family and it is right that they should enjoy without delay the right of representation in the National Assembly'. Also, with this aim of modifying the relations of power, he quickly secured acceptance of the principle that the colonial councils should be dissolved and the official delegation of colonists to the ministry and the representation of colonists in the Assembly be eliminated. And this was achieved against the advice of the man who was to be on the same list as him in the elections that followed in the colonies, François-Auguste Perrinon, of Martinican origin, appointed commissioner of the Republic in Martinique, who had pointed out to the commission that the slaves in the French colonies seemed to him to be less well prepared for public life than those in the neighbouring British colonies. Mestro, also a member of the commission, and an administrator in the Ministry of the Navy, had also expressed fears as to how the elections that were to be organized in the colonies would actually work. He felt that the enforced proximity of masters and former slaves that would arise in the exercise of the right to vote was particularly perilous for public order.

Here we might remember a fact that is not sufficiently well known: until February 1848, the majority of the delegates of the colonial councils and many other planters in Guadeloupe and Martinique were the subjects of enquiries and trials for illegal punishment of slaves and had sent a plethora of justificatory files to the ministry. Most of these trials ended in acquittals or discharges. That gave some indication of how difficult social relations immediately after promulgation of emancipation would be. Masters still had the right of life and death over their slaves, away from prying eyes on the plantations, on the eve of the promulgation of the decree abolishing slavery. Colonial justice only became cognisant of illegal punishments inflicted on slaves when the matter was serious and had got beyond the limits of the plantation.[4]

A historiographical point must be stressed here: the theory that slavery had become *less oppressive* in the years just before emancipation in 1848 is one of those illusions that has been around for a long time. If it is true, how are we to explain the virulence of the protests of the colonists in Martinique and Guadeloupe when, in 1848, Schœlcher dared to expose certain legal affairs of this sort which they had hoped to keep virtually secret? How are we to explain those interminable lists, still preserved in the Archives Nationales, of cases of punishments that went beyond the fifteen lashes allowed by an ordinance of June 1846?

In fact, the delegates of the colonists had laid before the commission all the conditions that they set on any abolition of slavery.

They called for a whole range of precautionary measures to maintain public order, and in particular for an ongoing numerical increase in the number of naval artillery forces. With the same persistence, they asked for financial compensation for slaveowners. They also expressed the social fear they all had at the idea of immediate freedom, of a potential wage labour force of slaves and of the right to vote that was to be granted to the new freedmen/new citizens. In particular, they wanted only those free before 1848 to have the right to vote, and not those recently emancipated. Many of them asserted that these latter ought to be regarded by the commission as 'big children, unaware of their rights and duties'.[5]

The work of the commission proceeded in two stages. It took the following decisions in April 1848: abolition would be immediate; the colonists would be compensated; indentured labour in Senegal would be abolished; the colonists would lose their representation to the central government; the colonies would be represented in the National Assembly through election of their candidates by universal suffrage. It continued to sit until July 1848 and finally agreed on a set of decrees that would be annexed to the emancipation decree that would organize the practical aspects of a new social life in the colonies.

The main recommendations of these annexed decrees covered the following areas:

- the organization of education, which was entrusted by Schœlcher, the atheist, the anti-clerical, to the Brothers of Christian Instruction of Ploërmel;
- the organization of justice;
- new labour legislation and in particular the establishment of a diversified and comprehensive system of bonuses for the best workers;
- the protection of sick or aged slaves and orphan children by the opening of hospices; and
- finally, the creation of savings banks.

The commission also pronounced itself in favour of the rapid industrialization of sugar production, improved marketing of colonial sugars in Europe and resort to European (and not African or Indian or Chinese) labour in the event of a shortage of labour, Schœlcher having already denounced the contracts for bringing this so-called free labour into the Caribbean colonies as a second slave trade and a second slavery.[6]

From Theory to Colonial Constraints

The Provisional Government did not sign the decree of 27 April 1848 in a burst of unanimity. Schœlcher had to betake himself to the home of some of its members to obtain their signatures on an individual basis. Three of the measures that he had proposed were rejected by the commission and then by the government:

- extending indemnity to former slaves;
- granting a plot of land to these latter as damages; and
- expropriating land deemed to have been usurped by the families of planters since the beginnings of colonization.

We ought to spell out a few of the conditions in which the emancipation decree was put into force in terms of the socio-economic context in which it was proclaimed.

- It did not lead to a sudden and lasting crisis of the sugar economy, but a temporary diminution of production which by 1854 had recovered the level of the years 1845–7.
- But the abolition of slavery did lead to a social crisis, which arose particularly, on the one hand, from difficulties in paying regular wages and, on the other, from problems raised by the transformation of human relations. The colonists found it very hard to accept the immediate freedom of their slaves and their status as *new citizens*.
- The indemnity envisaged by Article 5 of the decree of 1848 began to be paid only three years later. The colonial banks that were also envisaged by the commission only opened their doors in 1853.
- Particularly harsh labour regulations were introduced in May 1848 by the commissioners of the Republic, which in fact affected all areas of social life.

It is worth recalling a few examples of this.

- In the Directorate of the Colonies in the Ministry of the Navy, plans were initially afoot to get rid of elements in the so-called 'population of colour' who were deemed to be 'dangerous' through emigration to other colonies (Algeria and sub-Saharan Africa in particular). Numerous reports requested by the colonial administration even as early as 1848 contained such a proposal. The plan was to replace part of the freed population by either European workers or Chinese or African contract workers. That seemed to be the price to be paid for social peace and labour in the sugar cane fields.
- Access to primary education was limited by a system of fees;
- An internal passport was made compulsory for movement from one commune to another, as well as a passbook for every job;
- Crops other than sugar cane or coffee were subjected to taxes, which soon led to shortages and the setting of maximum prices for food staples by the colonial administration, in Guadeloupe for example;
- The political rights and freedoms of expression that the commissioners of the Republic had brought with them were rapidly restricted by the commissioners themselves, within two weeks of their arrival in the colonies: the political clubs opened in virtually every commune were closed and the press muzzled or even banned.[7]

A Decree, from One Century to the Next

The emancipation decrees in the French colonies, and above all the observations and recommendations made in the course of their drafting, contained in fact the broad outlines of what would subsequently develop over the following half-century or more. I shall mention in particular the following.

- Labour legislation very similar to that of the slave system was introduced. Local bylaws made by the 'labour police' were described twenty years later as 'attacks on individual freedom' by Schœlcher himself, who, it will be recalled, was forced into exile under the Second Empire.
- Schœlcher's proposal for the industrial development of sugar monoculture was realized.
- The resort to labour, brought in under conditions very much like the slave trade and slavery, from the coast of Africa, the Indian trading post, China and even Japan.
- The development of a model of a 'good colonial citizen', grateful to the 'liberating republic' – a worker in the sugar mills, respectful of order and devoid of ambition. I shall recall in particular that the commission suggested the writing of special textbooks for the colonies, highlighting the virtues of agricultural labour.
- The new colonial citizen should become, as Schœlcher had planned and promised, a new consumer.
- The decree made the 'new free men' 'new citizens', who were entitled, in the case of men aged 21 and over, to elect their representatives by universal suffrage. This aspect of the provisions introduced into the debates on colonial affairs that were to continue down to the end of the century a long and vigorous argument between supporters and opponents of colonial assimilation, which had appeared in 1848 as a truly revolutionary measure that was unique in the international history of colonies;
- Results and assessments made when bonuses were granted to the best workers show distinct similarities with the judgements made of slaves. Until the 1880s, workers who got the bonuses were those who kept a low profile, did not ask for their wages too insistently or had demonstrated cast-iron loyalty to their former master-owner.

We should also stress the impression of ineffectiveness that emerges from an analysis of the French abolitionist movement, its interventions and the stands it took in 1848, just when the emancipation which it had come into being to achieve was being effected. At a time when the Société pour l'abolition de l'esclavage was envisaging only delayed and very gradual abolition, when social tension was running high in Guadeloupe and Martinique and when the republican government itself was initially deciding to postpone any decision on abolition in the colonies, Schœlcher secured the adoption of this measure relatively rapidly and, it might be said, furtively, provoking opposition and criticism from many republicans. Moreover, at the end of his life he wrote that the interests at stake in the colonies and in the Atlantic ports were such in mid-century that only a 'measure taken revolutionarily'[8] could impose a solution. Any parliamentary debate would have postponed such a decision.

Several of the contradictory aspects and paradoxes of the economic, social and political development of the colonies concerned were thus inscribed in the decree itself, the annexed decrees and the recommendations made to the central government by the abolition commission. Here I shall mention the intensive industrialization of the colonies, ending three short decades later in a crisis of overproduction from which they have not recovered even today. Such industrialization was of course the effect in the colonial empires of the industrial revolution then under way in Europe. The abolition commission itself was responsible for initiating the construction of a series of central factories which took no account of the irreversible spread of beet sugar production in Europe.

It was also at the time of the promulgation of the emancipation decree in 1848 that a lasting mythical construct took root, which has survived down to the present day, cobbled together from the following themes.

- The abolitionist *ex machina*, who would resolve all problems by his action of freeing some 75 per cent of the colonial population from the yoke of slavery. This is the myth of the abolitionist which of course glosses over a much more complex historical reality, and simply erases centuries of resistance by slaves and social tensions of all sorts.
- The myth of colonial assimilation, a principle inherited from the French Revolution and the decisive interventions of Boissy d'Anglas in 1795,[9] which took ambiguous forms in the century and a half after 1848. The first effect of this assimilation was to engender the distinction between two Frances, that of the colonists, slave-owning, anxious not to share his civic rights, and that of the republicans, to which a cult without limit was to be paid by the 'new citizens' of the colonies. But, in Paris, in political circles or in the National Assembly, colonial questions after the 1880s were the ones on which the most constant consensus prevailed, from left to right. Associated with the myth of assimilation, another myth developed after 1848 around colonial representation in parliament. How otherwise can we describe the gap that appeared in mid-century between political leaders, the elected representatives who, at first, expressed themselves through the voice of Schœlcher and then at the end of the century, became owners of press organs hardly read by the bulk of the population, which in fact felt itself little involved in the debates in which they engaged. It is worth recalling that while electoral participation reached 75 per cent in Guadeloupe and Martinique in 1848, it was only 11 per cent in 1871 with the restoration of the republican regime and universal suffrage.

Notes

1. See N. Schmidt, *La suppression de l'esclavage aux Caraïbes*, Publications de l'Université d'Aix-Marseille I, 1995.
2. For the work of the commission, see N. Schmidt, *Victor Schœlcher*, Paris, Editions Fayard, 1994; and idem, 'Continuités et ruptures dans la politique coloniale aux Caraïbes. L'apport de documents mal connus, les travaux des premières commissions coloniales post-esclavagistes, 1848–1875', in *Sources. Travaux historiqes*, Histoire au présent (Paris), Vol. 13, 1988.
3. See O. D. Lara, *Caraïbes en construction: espace, colonisation, résistance*, 2 Vols, Éditions du Centre de Recherche Caraïbes-Amériques, 1992; and O. Patterson, *Slavery and Social Death: A Comparative Study*, Cambridge, Mass., Harvard University Press, 1982.
4. See the notes on judicial proceedings for illegal punishments inflicted on slaves by colonists in Guadeloupe and Martinique preserved in the Centre des Archives d'outre-mer, Aix-en-Provence, and N. Schmidt, *La suppression de l'esclavage*.
5. Remark by Froidefonds-Desfarges, delegate of the colonists of Martinique, Centre des Archives d'outre-mer, sitting of the commission of 7 March 1848, Généralités C 162 d 1326 (proceedings of the commission).
6. See O. D. Lara and N. Schmidt, *Les abolitions de l'esclavage. La longue marche*, Paris, Centre National de Documentation Pédagogique, Collection 'Textes et Documents pour la Classe', 1993.
7. See N. Schmidt, *Victor Schœlcher*, pp. 122–7.
8. Private Victor Schœlcher funds, Carnets, 1870–80.
9. On the debates on the planning of European colonial policy towards the Caribbean colonies, see O. D. Lara, op. cit., Vol. 1, pp. 348–460.

Chapter 29

22 May 1848: Against 'Tropical Neo-revisionism'

Édouard Delépine

THIS COLLOQUY PROVIDES an opportunity to put forward ideas which if not new at least are seminal ideas that run counter to an opinion that tends to prevail in Martinique and to a lesser extent in Guadeloupe.

The most basic accepted facts about abolition, in particular the role of Victor Schœlcher, are being challenged by a 'tropical neo-revisionism'. That makes it important to set out the view of those who feel that we must not give ammunition to those who see our discipline as

> the most dangerous product developed by the chemistry of the intellect, a sort of artificial paradise which makes peoples drunk, engenders false memories in them, keeps open their old wounds, torments them in their sleep, leads them to delusions of grandeur or delusions of persecution and renders nations bitter, unbearable and vain.... (Paul Valéry)

The purpose of this essay is to try and understand how in the last few years in Martinique and Guadeloupe there has been a questioning and even a reversal of the values that have been the staple components of our collective memory for more than a century. The second purpose is to suggest a few lines of research that might help us to answer the questions that arise about the circumstances of the abolition of slavery, not only in Martinique and Guadeloupe but also in French Guyana and the other colonies where there were no events in May 1848.

The debate that has been taking place these last few years is bound to have a major impact. It began with what was originally a perfectly anodyne debate on which was the proper date to commemorate the abolition of slavery: 27 April or 22 May. Then it was continued by a much more serious debate about abolition itself. That debate has assumed such proportions today that history, at least in Martinique, might not emerge from it unscathed, if there was not, *at the highest level*, and, first and foremost, of course, at the level of the Université des Antilles et de la Guyane, whose responsibility it is, a vigorous reaction against an irresistible regression of our historical knowledge about slavery.

Originally, the debate was between the supporters of a traditional history of slavery, focused more on the metropole than on the colonies, and the advocates of a more open approach to the history of abolition.

The former attributed little importance to the black slaves in their emancipation, the latter gave the slaves a much important role in it.

For the former, the historical initiative could not but lie with the colonial power, in this case with the provisional government that emerged from the February revolution. For this school, the act that granted freedom to the slaves was the decree of 27 April 1848 adopted by the provisional government at the instigation of Victor Schœlcher whom we very early on in the Antilles made the main, if not the sole, author of the abolition of slavery.

For the latter, things were more complex: the February Revolution had, undoubtedly, been the key factor in abolition, but the decree was not yet known in Martinique when slavery was effectively abolished there on 23 May.

For one side, all was said on 27 April. For the other, everything began on 22 May.

For many years, the first group had been so dominant in Martinique, particularly in education, that there was a veritable cult of Victor Schœlcher. This cult is all the more remarkable because other abolitionists, such as Wilberforce, Stephen or Clarkson, do not seem to have enjoyed such favour in the countries they helped to liberate themselves.

Naipaul writes that for the Trinidadian people, Wilberforce was at most a name in the history books, whereas in Martinique the name of Schœlcher cannot be avoided.

Those familiar with Martinique know that not only is there a town bearing the name of Victor Schœlcher, but in the capital there is a Lycée Schœlcher, a Schœlcher library and a statue of Schœlcher and that in every one of the 34 communes of Martinique, there must be a road named after Schœlcher or something that recalls Schœlcher.

Leaving aside a very small group of direct descendants of the slave-owning colonists, those whom Victor Schœlcher called the 'incorrigible ones', and, perhaps, too, a small group of followers of Cyrille Bissette, Victor Schœlcher has undoubtedly enjoyed an aura that has made him an absolutely unavoidable reference point across the whole political spectrum, including the far left.

Until about twenty years ago, it was customary to claim Victor Schœlcher as our own. There are probably two of us in this room who took part in a street demonstration, a confrontation even during which communists and Gaullists each claimed the sole right to honour the memory of Victor Schœlcher. That was in February 1948, for the commemoration of the centenary of the February Revolution. That indicates that this admiration was universal until twenty or so years ago.

I still remember that in 1974, at one of the last big strikes in Martinique, the main demand of the principal Martinican trade union federation was to make 27 April a paid public holiday. Finally, I remember that in 1959, the communist mayor of Pointe-à-Pitre, Henri Bangou, made 21 July, Victor Schœlcher's birthday, a holiday, thus restoring an old colonial tradition that had fallen into disuse.

That gives some indication of the scale of the cult devoted to or that used to be devoted to Victor Schœlcher in our part of the world. Sometimes that cult blinded us, as Charles André Julien once remarked amiably to Aimé Césaire. Our cult of Victor Schœlcher prevented us from seeing those who were working alongside him and to appreciate fully the importance of the achievements of the abolitionist movement in France.

Today, the situation is quite different, and, probably from ignorance of his work, Victor Schœlcher is blamed for the fact that we Caribbeans have not given sufficient place to the slaves in abolition. The fact is that for many years Martinicans did not treat the events of 22 May with the importance accorded them today.

On this I should like to say two things from two documents.

One serves as a Bible for the neo-revisionists, who derive all the arguments and facts from it but never cite their source and the name of their author. This document is the report of a colonist who was driven out of Martinique during the events of May 1848 and had to take refuge in Puerto Rico while awaiting better times.

This colonist, whose name was Huc, sent a long report to the Minister of the Colonies to inform him of what had happened, according to him, in Martinique in May 1848. Huc's Martinique is a Martinique of fire and blood, a Martinique delivered over to the torch of incendiaries and the cutlass of assassins, not to mention the ambitions of the mulattoes. Martinicans long had a painful memory of that day.

This document was rediscovered a century later, in the light of the fires of decolonization. The document, which has become the charter of the neo-revisionists, being used to show that there was indeed a revolution on 22 May 1848 in Martinique and that Victor Schœlcher had nothing to do with it, was written by a colonialist and a slave-owner. Léo Elisabeth has clearly set out the facts on this question.

But there is more to come.

The second document, the one that precipitated the events of 1848, is the 'Husson proclamation'. This document drawn up by a close collaborator of the governor announced the forthcoming freeing of the slaves. Written in French and Creole, it was posted up, to the fury of the colonists, in places to which slaves had access.

All that the slaves remembered of the proclamation were the words 'Freedom is coming'. Each vessel that arrived raised the temperature. As one incident followed another, the point was reached where there was virtually an insurrection in May. Faced with the threat of the insurrection spreading, the governor proclaimed the abolition of slavery.

We may make fun of this debate. A young Martinican linguist, L.-F. Prudent, has made a complete study of the bilingual text and concluded that, in the absence of black generals who had defeated Napoleon's armies, Martinicans now have an ersatz little home-grown national festival that fits in very nicely with 14 July, since 22 May is a public holiday in Martinique.

But it would be wrong to treat all that lightly and not probe further into the reasons for a defeat of the spirit. If academia does not take care and does not take the debate seriously or treats it complacently, it is adding a suicidal attitude to the history of our part of the world.

What is needed is above all *to move on from this debate*: that means we should cease contemplating our own navels, and give up making abolition in the French Antilles an essentially Franco-Martinican affair. Ten or fifteen years after emancipation in the British West Indies, how could abolition in the French Antilles be understood other than as part of a single and complex abolitionist and anti-slavery process involving the colonies as much as the metropoles, developing unevenly and at speeds varying from one colonial area to another, from one colonial empire to another.

The triumph of abolitionist ideas in France can be separated only with difficulty from the long struggle of British abolitionists or from the countless slave revolts which, especially after the Haitian revolution, distinguish the history of the colonies.

What was the impact of emancipation in the British West Indies on the movement of ideas in the French colonies and in France itself? What was the effect on public opinion of the development of marronnage by Martinican and Guadeloupian slaves to St Lucia, Dominica and Antigua, which in the late 1930s became lands of refuge? On this level too, Victor Schœlcher was a remarkable precursor and probably one of the best comparative historians of slavery in the Caribbean colonies.

If we want to avoid quarrels over nothing that obscure the true problems which are, in the last analysis, those of the mutual influence between the anti-slavery struggles in the colonies and the abolitionist struggles in the metropoles, it is perhaps that itinerary that we ought to be exploring, but having constantly in mind what the old combatant of the Commune, P. O. Lissagaray, wrote: '[H]e who tells the people false revolutionary legends, he who amuses them with pretty stories is as criminal as the geographer who prepares misleading maps for the navigator.'

Chapter 30

From Definitive Manumissions to the Emancipation of 1848

M'Baye Gueye

Abolition by Custom

In Africa, slaves had been able to obtain their full and absolute freedom long before the decree of 27 April 1848 was implemented in France's African possessions. Such manumissions were due either to the generosity of masters or to purchase by mutual agreement or to the intervention of custom which, in certain circumstances, could declare slaves free.

Albinos were manumitted at birth. Twins automatically enjoyed the same privilege, along with their mother. Christian captives received their deed of manumission at the time of their baptism.[1] Among the Muslims, literate slaves did not even need to ask for their freedom. Masters granted it to them the day they passed 'their reading and writing tests'.[2] Children who were destined to be educated were freed the day they were born.

The notarial deeds of Gorée and St Louis provide many cases of voluntary liberation of captives by their masters, expressing their satisfaction with the outstanding services that they had given them. But the succession to a captive who had been manumitted and who died without heirs born subsequent to his freeing reverted as of right to his former master according to the custom of the country.[3] Children born prior to the manumission of their mother, and who had not been emancipated, could not inherit from their mother, since they remained in a state of slavery.

On 19 January 1829, *dame* Jeannette Lefèvre manumitted her two captives, Espérance and Bigué, both aged 15. These children were however obliged to remain with their former owner and to serve her until her death. Old and blind, Jeannette Lefèvre, feeling the approach of death, performed this act of benevolence to make her servants more willing to accept her authority and above all to obtain remission of her sins.[4]

On their return from Mecca, some pilgrims voluntarily freed the captives who had accompanied them to the Holy Places of Islam.[5] Some masters provided in their wills that at their death all their captives should be freed. On 3 March 1832, Aimé-Désirée and Amélie de Grigny freed Gracia Faye and her four-year-old daughter who were part of the estate of *dame* Marie-Gabriel Roussin. This manumission was done in accordance with the wish expressed by the deceased shortly before her death.[6]

At first sight everything seems to suggest that these deeds of manumission were only issued to old and decrepit persons who were no longer of any great use to their owners. But in fact, captives of all ages and both sexes benefited from the generosity of owners. We are unfortunately unable to put a figure on the numbers, especially as some manumissions were not registered with the notary.

This was in part because tradition ratified any manumission of captives declared before notables. So as not to have to pay the fees to which notarial deeds were subject, most owners were content with that procedure. In the interior of the continent, manumissions of this sort were probably less common. Freedmen who left their owner's house risked being re-enslaved at any time.

Captives who saved could purchase their freedom with the consent of their masters. The right of self-purchase was not recognized for slaves and any master could perfectly well refuse to negotiate with his captive, even if the latter was offering a price for his manumission much higher than his actual value. For self-purchase, the captive had to obtain the consent of his master on the principle. Once that had been given, the captive might well be able to secure his freedom, since, by immemorial custom which had the force of law, captives were required to hand over to their master only half what they earned.[7]

The Restoration Government, which sought to eliminate slavery in the French possessions without precipitating serious social unrest, asked the governor to gather the opinion of the population on the eventuality of granting slaves the right to self-purchase. Arranging the project gave rise to heated discussions. Pellegrin, Mayor of St Louis and spokesman of the slaveowners, declared the proposed measure inopportune as it threatened to harm the slaves. Its adoption 'would diminish the universal benevolence which masters felt towards their captives'.[8] It would also ruin the masters since captives would be guided by the sole concern to free themselves and they would stop giving anything to their masters.[9]

Butignot, chairman of the tribunal, replied to them that the project would lead to a positive change in the way people behaved. It would make captives save money if they wanted to obtain their manumission. They would be more self-disciplined, and that would act as preparation for them for their future life as free men.[10] Some councillors opined that these philanthropic speculations threatened to undermine the good rapport that prevailed in relations between masters and slaves, and replace it with a climate of suspicion.

For the administration, it was a matter of defending the principle that acknowledged every man's right to freedom. Since slaves would enjoy the right to own property, captive parents would be able to purchase their children aged under 12 and masters would no longer have the right to separate mother and child.[11] Putting this project into effect would make the transition from slavery to freedom easier for captives. But the masters dug their heels in. They saw granting slaves the right of self-purchase whether their masters were willing or not as an attack on property. Despite this stubborn opposition, the council adopted a draft ordinance recognizing slaves' right to purchase their own freedom.[12]

Purchase was in no way an attack on property rights. The purchase price had to be calculated according to the actual value of the captive. In other words, his fitness for work would be taken into account. To avoid the desire to acquire freedom encouraging the inclinations of some captives towards theft, those seeking manumission would have to prove that their savings were legitimately come by. There would be penalties that would forbid or postpone the manumission of anyone who resorted to dishonest means to gain their freedom. This would only be earned by saving and good behaviour. The desire to earn it would necessarily produce an improvement in slaves' morale.[13]

On 12 July 1832, a royal ordinance set out the formalities to be followed in manumissions. It was promulgated on 2 February 1833 in Senegal.[14] This law simplified the procedures for acquiring manumission by eliminating the tax on freedom that had been in force since 1786. It provided that every slave manumitted, whether by an act of generosity or by redemption, was only to be handed his freedom certificate six months after the fact, in case there were protests. The public prosecutor's department was empowered to oppose it whenever it thought that the freedman was not in a position to provide for his own subsistence.[15]

In the French settlements there was a relatively high number of manumissions. In 1835, there were eleven manumissions by voluntary redemption in Gorée. In 1840 and 1847, the registers of civil status in St Louis record 576 cases of freedom by redemption. These figures are less than the true figures. The president of the St Louis court of appeal was complaining as early as 1838 that masters did not always feel the need to have certificates issued by the authorities to captives who had purchased their freedom.[16]

Manumission by voluntary purchase in fact concerned only slaves who had skills: *laptots* and craftsmen. It was thus illusory to think that slavery would be eliminated in the French possessions using this method. Labourers, along with most women and children, had no means of regaining their freedom personally. A radical measure was therefore needed to eliminate slavery.

The French administration found itself caught in a cleft stick. On the one hand, it had to respect the rights of owners over their slaves. On the other, it wanted the gradual end of captivity. The only way to put an end to this conflict between law and morality was to abolish the institution of slavery.

This equivocal situation had not escaped the French Government, which, as early as 1819, said that everything ought to move towards the disappearance of slavery in the French possessions in Africa. The trick was to achieve that without provoking social unrest.[17] In September 1823, Governor Roger banned the introduction of any more captives into the French possessions. But on 29 January 1836, *ordonnateur* (quartermaster-treasurer) Guillet made a report to the Conseil privé against the abolition of slavery. The elimination of slavery would, he said, be disastrous for all classes of society, even if the masters were well compensated. The purchase price 'would be immediately wasted in the hands of those who were not very skilful and not good at managing their affairs'. The owners would be left with nothing but poverty.

The many aged or sick captives would probably be put out from under their master's roof. There would be no one to help them, and the French settlements would suffer morally as a result. There would also be a breakdown of morality as masters ceased to have any personal interest in keeping an eye on young women captives.

Such emancipation would also disrupt the good relations that existed between the French possessions and the surrounding countries. They would become a refuge for every captive in the interior dissatisfied with his lot. That would lead their masters to use reprisals against French subjects. The governor for his part advocated acting cautiously and with 'with deliberate slowness' in order to avoid upsets.[18]

In short, the administration recognized that general emancipation was not something that was going to happen soon. The failure of agricultural colonization had removed from masters any other means of making a living than through the work of their captives. Slavery was above all an economic matter. It could not be abolished without first ensuring that masters were in a position to earn their living without resort to slave labour.

Failing an alternative product to the slave trade, owners opposed any innovation that might be a step in the direction of the suppression of this institution hallowed by time and enshrined in custom. They regarded slavery not only as the fundamental underpinning of social organization, but also as a natural institution which could not be altered without overthrowing the very structures of society. For them, slavery was 'one step on the social ladder, like fortune and honour in the various classes of European society'.[19]

Such owners simply could not suddenly convert to the idea that all men are equal. They refused to accept this idea which was foreign to them in every sense of the word. The administration refused to allow itself to be discouraged by the negative attitude of masters, and continued to try to get them to accept at least the principle of general emancipation with compensation. A census was conducted of the captive population in the French possessions. But the announcement of the news started a panic among the slaveowners. Some of them, determined to hold on to their property, left the French settlements for the countries in the interior.[20]

There was a danger that such departures might become general, if the administration remained determined to want to abolish slavery, and they seemed to provide proof conclusive that emancipating the slaves was not a possibility in the French settlements. At the first sign, the black inhabitants deserted the trading posts for places beyond the reach of the French administration.[21]

As soon as he came into office, in 1843, Governor Bouet-Villaumez attacked the institution of slavery. The commission of enquiry which he set up to determine how attached the people were to slavery came up with very surprising results. Skilled slave workers were all for immediate emancipation. They were convinced that slaves who refused to work, because they were sure of being fed by their masters, would find themselves compelled to find work in order to survive.[22] Conversely, labourers and women captives, worried about this leap into the unknown, wished to remain under their master's roof, and bound to slavery.[23]

Some black owners were disposed to grant their captives freedom in exchange for fair compensation. But the indigenous women and the mulattoes vigorously protested against any measure of manumission, even if there were to be compensation. Force of habit prevented them from accepting innovations. The marabouts for their part stressed that the Quran provided only for temporary captivity and that any slave who embraced Islam automatically had a right to freedom.[24]

Abolition by Law

These frequent discussions on the problem of slavery had the end-result that the population of the French settlements became convinced that the institution of slavery could not be maintained indefinitely. The French Government would suppress it as soon as circumstances seemed right. In January 1848, the governor noted that emancipation, in the French possessions, was now no more than child's play that concerned the authorities not in the least. The whole population was expecting it and was perfectly well prepared for it.[25] The abolition of slavery was the work of the provisional government that emerged from the revolution of 24 February 1848.

The decree of 27 April 1848 abolished slavery in the French colonies. It was promulgated in Senegal on 23 June 1848. In two months, on 23 August, all the slaves in the French possessions in Africa would be free. Du Château, commissioner of the Republic in Senegal, took advantage of this interval to prepare people and to take measures for its implementation. This governor did not have much experience of the country, but he went to great lengths to get masters and slaves to conform to the provisions of the decree.

He urged slaves to be on their best behaviour: they were bound to continue working for their masters until 23 August. He exhorted owners to accept the new order with dignity. For despite the kindness with which they treated their captives, slavery was still an offence to humanity. Now that it had been abolished, all men had the same dignity and the same rights.

Despite the promise of compensation made by the governor, the affected interests were too important for all the masters to resign themselves to losing their slaves. When the decree was promulgated, some owners, especially the *signares*, protested violently and even threatened to sell their slaves before the decree came into force.[26] Slavery was a natural institution that had to be safeguarded whatever the cost: to interfere with it was to strike at the very structures of society. Many masters could not accept that their slaves should enjoy the same rights as them.

Others contemplated going into exile in the interior out of reach of the law. This movement was not new. In 1842, when a ministerial despatch asked the administration to count the whole slave population, some slave-owners had seen in it the intention to abolish slavery and had gone to settle in Walo a few kilometres from St Louis. There they devoted themselves to cattle-raising and agriculture.[27]

In 1848, a similar exodus was prevented by a ministerial despatch which instructed Du Château to ban slaves from leaving the colony if their masters attempted to leave with them before 23 August.[28] The masters, fearing that the compensation would be inadequate, had the idea of sending their captives to be sold in the trading posts along the river. Governor Baudin forestalled such sales by ordering the officers commanding the trading posts to examine carefully any slaves that might be brought in, and to warn the chiefs on both banks that they must not buy those who were legally now only ex-slaves.[29]

The slaves welcomed the emancipation decree joyfully. Assured that freedom was just around the corner, many refused to obey their masters, whom they now regarded as their equals. Some owners even asked the governor to bring forward the date when the decree would come into force, as being the only means, they said, for them to recover their battered authority. Du Château asked them to be patient, taking the view that it was natural for slaves to adopt such an attitude on the eve of their freedom.

Some slaves thought that the time had come to settle some scores. One twenty-year old young captive in St Louis violently struck his mistress and threatened to kill her. She had many slaves in St Louis.[30] Du Château was obliged to come down hard. The guilty party was imprisoned and a proclamation issued reminding the slaves that until the moment of their freedom they must continue to respect their masters.

Despite the ban imposed in the decree on inflicting corporal punishment on slaves, there were masters who refused to abdicate their rights and to acknowledge the changes that the decree had made in the condition of slaves. Two or three masters accused of excessive punishment were taken before the courts. And the sentence of one of them, Agui Samba, almost provoked disturbances in St Louis.

Agui Samba had been a slave. But, through his labour, he had been able to purchase his freedom, and then acquire houses to a considerable value and even many slaves. In July 1848, despite the exhortations of Du Château, Agui Samba brutally struck one of his men and, in addition, publicly bragged about it. This former slave ought to have appreciated the value of freedom. But, perhaps jealous at seeing his slaves freed without having to pay a penny, or seized with regret at not having profited enough from their labour, he declared that he refused to accept the decree. He was sentenced to five days in prison.

Naturally, he could not understand why he was going to prison for giving a few blows to one of his slaves: so he appealed. It was on the occasion of this second trial that there were almost serious disturbances.

Worrying rumours began to circulate. Slaveowners agreed together to use force to prevent the sentence imposed on Agui Samba being carried out if it was confirmed on appeal. On 7 August, on the eve of the verdict in appeal, the government was officially informed by Alin, Mayor of St Louis, that a lot of arms and ammunition had been collected by traders in Agui Samba's quarter, and that they were determined to prevent his imprisonment. The mayor, a merchant himself, only broke ranks with the merchants' group because he feared the consequences of rebellion.

The governor took his precautions. He secretly had the garrison troops held at the ready. The verdict was to be given on 8 August between 2 and 3 p.m.

The slaves feared the victory of Agui Samba's clan. At about 3 p.m., some 400 of them met behind the battery, opposite the seat of government. They delegated five of their number to go to Du Château and tell him that they were making their forces available to him to help him to ensure respect for law and justice. Du Château saw that if he issued arms to these slaves, they might use them against masters outside Agui Samba's clan. In any event, he feared a general panic in the town; he felt that the troops would be enough to contain any attempt at rebellion and dismissed the delegates without accepting their help.

At 4 p.m., doubtless to calm things down, the court of appeal of St Louis acquitted Agui Samba. This verdict, as we may well imagine, was received differently by different groups. The slaves were afraid that this acquittal might give masters new strength and postpone the date of liberation. The supporters of Agui Samba, mulattoes and slaveowners, noisily demonstrated their joy, but ordinary people, convinced that the administration must come out on top, protested energetically against this outrageous verdict. Calm eventually returned without the troops having to intervene.

Apart from these isolated, one-off incidents, the social transformation initiated by the decree of 27 April 1848 began in Senegal without upsets. The slaves welcomed it joyously, while the masters resigned themselves to this new situation. Calm and decorum prevailed everywhere.[31] That the change occurred without clashes was possible thanks to the gentle manner in which owners had treated their slaves.

At 8 a.m. on the morning of 23 August 1848, a proclamation posted and published by the drums made all slaves free citizens.

Right from dawn, many freedmen went to bathe in the sea. They hoped in so doing to leave their old soul in the water since, according to local beliefs, not only did bathing in the sea purify but, in some circumstances, it conferred immunity. Thus, the condemned man who went directly for a bathe in the sea as soon as he came out of prison, would not return to prison again. After their bathe, the slaves were sure that they would never again return to slavery.

At eleven o'clock, a large number of new freedmen met in front of the grill enclosing the seat of government. Flags, a sign of joy and freedom, waved over the thousands of heads. Some delegates of 'these new citizens' asked Du Château for permission to enter the courtyard to show their gratitude to France.

A few moments later, a delirious crowd was pressing against government house. Cries of 'Long live France! Long live freedom!' were repeated again and again. Then the dancing began. All the drums in the town were there. No human tongue could express 'the cries of joy, and the deafening shouts of joy and gratitude that the sight of the French flag inspired in this tide of men, happy, perhaps, for the first time in their life'.[32]

The rest of the day went by like the morning without the least disturbance and amid the old free population which generally joined in the happiness of the new citizens.

Emancipation gave rise to a problem which required an immediate solution. In effect, when masters saw that they could no longer get any profit from their people, they refused to feed them and put them out of the house. Du Château had a tent camp put up behind the battery and two hundred freedmen found shelter there while awaiting the construction of brick huts on the site of the old cemetery.

The provisional government had thought that compensation was fair. That presupposed an accurate census of former slaves. That was a difficult task. Many indentured workers had been fraudulently classified as slaves. An enquiry would thus have to check the origin of all those who were slaves or alleged to be slaves. Registers would keep a list of any 'who had been brought in illicitly or who were children of parents of such people. Blacks in this category would be deducted from the total number of captives, ownership of whom by each master, at the moment of emancipation, will give entitlement to a share of the compensation'.[33] This ministerial order thus excluded from compensation the many slaves brought into the colony after the act of 1823 which prohibited their entry. There would only be compensation in respect of slaves who fell within the law.

The first census of the slave population, for the share-out of the compensation, initially established that there were 10,075 slaves giving an entitlement to compensation living in Senegal. This revealed the scale of the fraud. This number was exaggerated. Most of them must long since have benefited from the advantages of freedom. These were indentured servants claimed as slaves for life.

In Gorée, the census of 18 July 1848 counted 1,991 slaves, whereas the claims for compensation lodged by 195 owners listed 3,043 slaves or indentured servants. The commission of enquiry eliminated 364 names of whom two had been freed before emancipation, one had died before the same date, 24 were not in the census and 337 had already run away before 27 April.[34]

In St Louis, 2,033 slaves appeared on the freedom registers in August 1848. Claims for compensation from 671 owners listed 4,524 slaves or indentured servants. The commission discovered a large number of frauds: 484 already freed before 27 April, 1 self-purchased with his own money, 7 deceased, 89 run away before emancipation, 2 children born since April 1848, 5 residing abroad, 364 not listed in the census, 175 indentured servants brought in contrary to the provisions of the order of 18 January 1844 and 77 double counts.

Thus, the commission had finally accepted only 6,259 slaves or indentured servants giving a right to compensation: 3,230 in St Louis, 3,029 in Gorée.

It is true, of course, that captives had always been running away, but that 426 should have done so on the eve of their liberation is hard to understand.

Possibly, despite the vigilance of the authorities, some masters had succeeded in selling some of their slaves to foreigners. Subsequently, some of them returned to St Louis or Gorée to claim their freedom, but the children sold, of whom there must have been a large number because of the incomplete way in which the July 1848 census had been compiled, could not so easily deceive the vigilance of their new masters, and come and ask for the freedom granted by the decree of 27 April 1848. However that may be, the number of slaves for whom their masters were compensated in the end amounted to 6,703. What happened was that the commission ended up applying the principle of compensation both for the benefit of owners who had legally acquired indentured servants and for that of owners who, in good faith, had fallen foul of the ordinance of 18 January 1844.[35]

Thus, the census of slaves in the French possessions in Senegal in the end confirmed the right to immediate emancipation and without compensation of 3,372 individuals illegally detained in slavery.

On 4 September 1848, the share of Senegal in the compensation fund was fixed at 1,245,000 francs. Then it was raised to 2,215,572 francs, which represented 10,075 slaves presumed to give the right to compensation. But the commission had not yet revised the lists supplied by the owners. Taking account of these first lists, each slave would have been compensated at 219.90 francs. After corrections, each slave yielded 2,330.15 francs to his master. If an average ever has any meaning, the owners of St Louis received 1,650.75 francs each, those of Gorée 4,952.25 francs.

Radical emancipation would have been truly harmful if the end-result had been to throw masses of freedmen into poverty. Vagrancy and pilfering would have been the natural means of keeping themselves supplied with food to eat. Work therefore had to be found for them. And that the administration endeavoured to do.

Notices put up before the coming into force of the decree announced that the directorates of civil engineering and engineering and the general works department were offering jobs to any who asked for them. The pay they received for their labour would enable the freedmen to stay out of poverty.[36]

On 24 May 1849, Governor Baudin, who had replaced Du Château, asserted that emancipation had changed nothing in the life of the colony. The freedmen were carrying on their trades as they had when they were slaves. But whereas under slavery they shared their pay with their masters, now they kept it all. Of course, most of the new freedmen had left their master's house, but many others remained attached to them, continued to serve them and received food, lodging and clothing as before.

Under slavery, the houses of the signares were full of young women captives employed in domestic activities. They were closely watched by their mistresses who had every interest in doing so as they waited for them to reach marriageable age to make the most out of them. The fact that the freedwomen now had to be given a wage deterred the signares from employing them in large numbers. It was feared that the girls who had been freed, that is left to their own devices, with no work and no resources, would turn to prostitution. But that did not happen. Generally, the women found an income either as sorters or as gum pounders at harvest time or by remaining in the trading posts as laundrywomen or domestics. The girls easily found husbands among the freedmen. That was their best bet for the future.[37] There were grounds for hoping that a few former slaves, whose resources had doubled since emancipation, would succeed in a few years in following the example of Samba Agui or Fara Birame, who had been able to buy very expensive houses.

But all masters did not have the same number of slaves. Some, such as the Valentins, the Laboures or the Pellegrins, had dozens of them. Others, of more modest means, had only one or two domestics. They made up the vast majority of former masters. They had been living only on the income they derived from hiring out their slaves. They were therefore the first ones to be ruined by emancipation.[38]

The petty traders also had their difficult moments. The slaves used to help them in their businesses. Suddenly, emancipation had forced them to employ only wage-earners. Thus, the price of hiring *laptots* rose and traders' profits fell sharply. General emancipation had thus hit part of the population of St Louis and Gorée very hard, and the stagnation in business led to widespread impoverishment. To meet their needs, families had to sell their gold jewellery.[39] On 29 November 1849, the governor asked the minister to grant higher compensation than what had been voted by the French Parliament. According to this authority, at least 500 francs was needed to avoid the ruin of a large number of inhabitants who, in Gorée especially, could not replace the product of the labour of their former captives by any other means.[40]

In 1854, poverty was still widespread in the French settlements. Emancipation and population growth meant that more people were sharing the income from gum. Profits became inadequate, not only to feed the old luxury, but also to meet the needs of everyday life.[41] Many former masters had large debts, a new form of their decline. Their future was bleak.

To relieve the impoverishment of their former masters, freedmen spontaneously gave them some of their earnings.[42] But that was only a palliative.

Article 6 of the abolition decree provided that 'purged of slavery, the colonies and the possessions in India shall be represented in the National Assembly'.[43] It was silent on the local populations' right to vote, and perhaps it was originally only intended for Europeans resident in the colonies.

The regulation drawn up by the provisional government in execution of the decree of 5 March 1848 provided some clarification. Promulgated in Senegal, it comprised 43 articles. In Article 6, the only one where there was mention of the indigenes, it was provided that the indigenes of Senegal and its dependencies, who had been resident for more than five years, would be exempt from any proof of naturalization. It thus acknowledged the right to vote of all the indigenes living in the French trading posts and outposts from Saint-Louis to the Melacorie who met that criterion. But the Commissioner of the Republic restricted its scope to the islands of St Louis and Gorée alone. The elections of 30 October 1848 saw the victory of Durand-Valentin.

It is easy to imagine the joy which then ran through the ranks of the freedmen, when they went with their ballot paper to realize, at least legally, equality with their former masters.

Of course, the Constitution of 1852 abolished colonial representation. But when it was restored in 1871, it was applied in the spirit of 1848. Then as formerly the freedmen or their descendants exercised the same rights as those who were of free descent.

After emancipation, the philanthropists could admire their handiwork in the French trading posts and wax lyrical about a society without divisions. As early as 17 May 1848, Minister Arago rejoiced at the idea that the whole population of Senegal was to be combined in a single feeling of fraternity and nationality.[44]

Notes

1. D. Boilat, *Esquisses sénégalaises*, Paris, Bertrand, 1853, p. 213.
2. L.-G. Binger, *Du Niger au Golfe de Guinée par le pays de Kong et le Mossi*, Paris, Société des Africanistes, 1980 [1892], p. 45.
3. Archives nationales de la France d'Outremer à Aix en Provence (ANFOM), Notariat de Saint-Louis, 21 May 1827.
4. ANFOM, Notariat de Saint-Louis, 19 January 1829.
5. Paulet, 'Rapport sur la captivité dans le cercle de Tivaouane', 1904 (Arch. K17).
6. ANFOM, Notariat de Saint-Louis, 3 March 1832.
7. Conseil privé de Saint-Louis, session of 1 April 1819 (Arch.3E2).
8. Conseil privé de Saint-Louis, session of 4 May 1829 (Arch.3E8).
9. Ibid.
10. Ibid.
11. Ibid.
12. Continuation of discussion, session of 28 September 1829 (Arch.3E8).
13. Governor to minister, 5 April 1832 (Arch.2B15).
14. ANFOM, Sénégal XIV-13, Gallois, 'Rapport sur les affranchissements'.
15. L.-M. Bajot, *Annales maritimes et coloniales: recueil des lois*, Paris, 12 July 1832.
16. ANFOM, Sénégal XIV-13, Gallois Mont Brun, 3 July 1838.
17. Conseil privé de Saint-Louis, 1 April 1819 (Arch.3E2).
18. 'Rapport de l'ordonnateur Guillet', 29 January 1836 (Arch. K7).
19. 2B18, folio 143, Governor to minister, 15 February 1842.
20. 2B20, folio 13, Governor to minister, 1 April 1842.
21. Ibid.
22. ANFOM Sénégal XIV, Dossier de l'émancipation, 23 January 1844.
23. Ibid.
24. ANFOM, Sénégal I, 33a, Baudin to minister, 10 January 1848.
25. Ibid.
26. 2B27, folio 114, Governor to minister.
27. 2B18, folio 144, Governor to minister, 15 February 1842.
28. 1B48, folio 261, Minister to governor, 7 May 1848.
29. K8, Baudin to director of external affairs.
30. 2B26, folio 154, Du Château to minister, 8 September 1848.
31. 2B26, folio 154, Governor to minister, 8 September 1848.

32. 2B27, folio 134, Du Château to minister, 23 August 1848.

33. 1B48, folio 258, Minister to governor, 7 May 1848.

34. 3B21, Conseil privé, sitting of 25 October 1849.

35. Ibid.

36. 2B26, folio 137, Governor to minister, 24 August 1848.

37. 1B51, folio 208, Minister to governor, 13 December 1849.

38. L. Faidherbe, *Le Sénégal: la France dans l'Afrique occidentale*, Paris, Hachette, 1889, pp. 115–16.

39. Carrère, 'Notes sur le Sénégal', Sénégal, II-4, 9 January 1854.

40. 2B27, folio 145, Governor to minister, 29 November 1849.

41. F. Carrère and P. Holle, *De la sénégambie français*, Paris, Didot, 1855, p. 15.

42. Faidherbe, op. cit., p. 115.

43. Ibid.

44. 1B48, folio 257, Arago to governor, 17 May 1848.

Chapter 31

The Abolition of Slavery in Tunisia:
Towards a History of the Black Community

Abdelhamid Larguèche

THE HISTORY OF THE ETHNIC, religious and linguistic minorities in Tunisia largely remains to be written. Until now, only the Jewish community has been recognized as a minority by virtue of its religious and linguistic differences from the Muslim majority.[1] The minority of African origin has only belatedly begun to interest researchers.[2] This essay will focus on that community. To give some idea of the importance of this initiative, we should recall that slavery was finally abolished in Tunisia in 1846, whereas it was only in 1984 that it was abolished in Mauritania. Tunisia was thus one of the first homes of the *Nahda*, the renaissance, in the Arab world, along with Egypt. Of course, Egypt experienced the renaissance on a much larger scale, given its position in the 'centre' of the Arab world, but, in the mid-nineteenth century, Tunisia too was involved in the era of reform. It was first the shock of colonialism in Algeria, and then the coming to power of an élite that was particularly well aware of the changes that had occurred in Europe, that sparked the era of reforms. One of the particular features of those reforms is that they came 'from above': the state was the principal designer and mover in every social, political and constitutional reform in Tunisia in the mid-nineteenth century. This constituted the basis of a theory of 'the advanced state' in a 'backward society', the state being resolutely at the centre of reform.[3]

The importance of the abolition of slavery lies first in the chronology of the reform process. Socially, the first reformist measure was the abolition of slavery, while at the level of state institutions, it was the establishment of the École Polytechnique, with a dominant military role. The state, approaching reform from a *technicist* viewpoint, felt that it was above all necessary to modernize the army, a focus which cost society very dear, through the added tax burden, while deepening the gulf between society and the state, the latter seeing modernization as the sole guarantee of maintaining its sovereignty and independence. The problem of reform was thus clear from the outset: to borrow from the West in order to be protected against the threat from that same

West. For us, it is also a starting point for criticizing a colonialist historiography which sought to portray every reform as simply the result of pressure from the European (especially the British and French) consuls then present in Tunisia. There were internal factors at work and from the earliest years a small élite emerged and played an important role in the actual practice of reform, in the design of an overall plan and in the first attempts to theorize this reform. Among the earliest reformists, there was the Minister Khayr al-din, who is more or less the equivalent of the better-known Tahtawi in Egypt. Before embarking on these reforms, Khayr al-din had travelled widely and studied all over Europe and with great scientific curiosity he summarized all his impressions, described the new constitutions and tried to popularize new concepts, in particular that of freedom, using a new language and style. In the cultural tradition of Islam, the major concept in the management of the political affairs of the *Umma* is that of *badel*, justice. Khayr al-din introduced the concept of *hurriya*, freedom, which is the protector and guarantor of that justice.

To study the process of the abolition of slavery is to replace a measure, which socially and sociologically concerned a minority, in its global context. That requires a presentation of the black minority in Tunisia in the mid-nineteenth century.

Over the long run, that history blends with the history of such an old institution as the slavery of blacks and the slave trade in blacks across the Sahara to North Africa.[4]

Recent research in African anthropology has increasingly stressed the exchanges and close human and cultural links that have for centuries existed between the north and south of the African continent.[5]

The fact is that the whole of Africa from north of the Sahara to the Atlantic was inhabited in prehistoric times by a variety of Nigritic elements. It is therefore quite natural that there should be multiple processes of cultural interaction consequent upon the mixing and movements of people in these regions.

All the research in historical demography and on non-indigenous groups in Tunisia agrees that during the Roman Empire there were growing numbers of black slaves in Tunisia. Thus, the processes of mixing and accumulation led to blacks mixing with indigenous strata of the population at every level especially through manumission, which developed along with slavery itself.[6]

The modern period did not represent a break. On the contrary, while the economic vitality of commercial routes may have declined markedly, the movement of people continued in various guises, the most of important of which were slavery and the regular caravans that criss-crossed the Sahara, linking the main North African cities, including Tunis, with trading centres in sub-Saharan Africa.[7]

Social history thus enables us to approach the question of the black minority in a wider setting that includes both the long term and the short term, and that takes account of the political factor and the relationship between the minority and the state without making that the sole viewpoint. It is also one that takes on board other levels of analysis such as those relating to inter-ethnic relations, the general and even seasonal morphology of these groups, their practices and cults, religious life and collective psychology as well as the phenomenon of acculturation and integration into the host society.

The socio-historical approach thus coincides with the anthropological approach in seeking to obtain an overall scientific portrait of the social group and borrows tools and notions perfected in the scientific field of social and cultural anthropology.

In this way, by reconstructing the main stages of the social and cultural evolution of this community, it becomes possible to analyse the mechanisms of acculturation of an ethnic group brutally cut off from its geocultural environment and integrated by force into the lowest echelons of traditional Arab society.

However, the cultural aspects of such a reality cannot be envisaged and analysed without a global perspective that takes into account the social, economic and political status of such a minority.

At once the question of sources arises.

We historians are used to a precise type of sources, for the most part written (archival or literary) or archaeological sources. Using oral history and fieldwork, another type, originating in field ethnography, proves to be not only useful but indispensable. Not only does it fill the gaps in the written documentation but it is also the sole method that gets into the vagaries of collective memory in order to grasp how mythical and historical time are organized, the dimension of the sacred, the levels of functional, cultural and linguistic integration, and the changes made to ensure better group adaptation to changes in the social, economic, cultural and political environment,

Using a combination of sources and a variety of methods will enable us to ask more questions and probe more deeply into the subject.

As soon as we attempt to get a clear picture of the minority we are faced with the difficult issue of numbers at the time. How can we quantify these groups at a time when chroniclers were little concerned with figures? The available archives only rarely give numbers of slaves or freedmen in this or that region, and in any event not in Tunis.

The question of the legal status of the community alone raises several problems. The status of slave coexisted with other specific statuses, some permanent, some temporary, such as domestic, freeman or *chouchane*. Over his life-time, a slave might therefore have a number of different statuses leading up to his manumission which often, while freeing him legally, did not free him socially.

So we must not lose sight of the fact that there were blacks all over Tunis and at all levels of society, from the bey's court to the *fondouk*, the most deprived suburb, by way of the homes of the well-off and the houses of the urban masses. And it is precisely there that the whole problem of marginality arises taken as a relative, shifting, internally differentiated and non-static state within a single group.

The integration of the black did not exclude secondary unspoken and subtle forms of secondary exclusion that were more or less apparent and made him a marginal figure: these included exclusion through marriage strategies or the negative social perception that relegated him, whatever his function or legal status, to an inferior position, an object of contempt in the scale of values.

Following the life of black groups in Tunis is thus not simply a matter of reconstructing the historical trajectory from slavery to emancipation and the forms of social integration or rejection which determined how they lived.

To refine our knowledge of this milieu we must bring out and analyse how these originally uprooted groups developed in the context of slavery and how they adapted their basic cultural traits and identities.

Black Minority and Slavery

The available archival documents offer a range of scattered and insufficient information, which relates mainly to freed slaves at a late period following the abolition of slavery.

In this general overview of the status of blacks before and after emancipation, we shall restrict ourselves to a description, based on the sources, of the state of this social category, the treatment suffered by black slaves before 1846, the date of abolition and their social mobility in relation to the emancipation that was common before 1846.

The slaves in Tunis came from a very wide area south of the Sahara from West Africa to Lake Chad. The Kingdoms of Bornu and the Fezzan region provided the bulk of them. Most groups were reduced to slavery as a consequence of the interminable local wars between rival tribes or as a result of kidnapping.[8]

According to Dr Louis Frank, 'most of the Negroes who were sold in Tunis came from the Kingdom of Bornu, Hawnia and the Fezzan.... I saw some from Houffeh who can mainly be recognized from the way in which they are accustomed to sharpen the incisors in their upper jaw'.[9]

The caravan routes terminating in Tunis came from several sub-Saharan centres. In addition to Ghadames, which linked the regency to the Fezzan, Morzuk and the Kingdom of Bornu, Timbuktu was in regular contact with the Regency by the caravan route through Mzab and Djarid, which put the country in touch with African ethnic groups over a wide area including Bambara country, the city of Jenne and several regions in central West Africa.

The names of slaves or freedmen that we have found in the archives confirm this diverse origin. Alongside frequent names such as 'Burnaoui' (from Bornu), 'Ghdamsi (from Ghadames), 'Ouargli' (from Ouargla), there are names suggesting an origin in other centres in West Africa such as 'Jennaoui' (from Jenne) or 'Tombouctaoui' (from Timbuktu).

The variety of the names of the houses of the black brotherhoods in Tunis confirm that their members came from a wide variety of regions of Africa.

How many slaves were there in Tunis in the nineteenth century, on the eve of emancipation and what was their role in economic life?

Number and Status of Blacks and How They Were Organized

Although quantitative data are lacking for the eighteenth century, some partial censuses conducted from the mid-nineteenth century have made possible some rough estimates of the total number of black slaves for the whole country. Lucette Valensi concluded with an estimate of some 7,000 slaves or descendants of slaves for the whole country.[10] We feel that this figure is on the low side. No systematic count of the black population was conducted for several reasons. The abolition of slavery came ten years before the date of the first census registers of the population subject to the *mejba* (head tax introduced in 1856), and, as a result, many of these groups scattered at various levels of urban or even rural society thereby escaped the old system of control.

The frequent collective manumissions of black slaves on the occasion of the death of a prince or a princess reveals quite high numbers. In 1823, 177 slaves were freed in Tunis on the occasion of the death of a princess.[11]

To try to reach an overall estimate, we need more than the few partial censuses carried out in various localities. These figures need to be combined with data provided by studies of the caravan trade as a whole.[12]

We observe that for the modern period, the sole sources available for the caravan trade come from travel literature and consular correspondence. The situation is quite different with the transatlantic slave trade where historical studies over time have had the advantage of abundant quantitative documentation.

Basing himself on data provided by travellers, Ralph Austen proposed averages for the eighteenth and nineteenth centuries. He concludes with the following overall estimates:[13]

Tunisia:	100,000
Algeria:	70,000
Morocco:	520,000
Tripoli:	430,000
Egypt:	800,000

Yet the distribution of blacks varied from region to region. In the southeast, the proportions were quite high especially in the oases. Some villages had a large majority of blacks, like those to the south of Gabès and in the region of the oases. In Tunis, despite continuous arrivals, this group probably remained a minority of no more than a few thousand.

Social organization in traditional society offered a specific organizational framework to the black slaves of Tunis.

The archival documents give us information on the forms of organization of the slaves in Tunis and the leader responsible for the group. The *agha* of the blacks was generally the bey's chief eunuch; in the documents he is often called *Hakim al kichra assouda*, which literally means the *magistrate of the black skin*; it was his job to ensure order within the group and to settle any disputes that might arise between masters and slaves or among the blacks themselves.

These data and other evidence confirm the relative autonomy of organization that the slaves in Tunis enjoyed, as well as the protection given them by the political authorities; a protection that, while conforming to the rules for the proper treatment of slaves laid down by Islam, revealed an acute sense of the political. By protecting a minority, were not the political authorities by the same token ensuring that minority's unconditional loyalty to them? Above all, the bey's guards had for many years been recruited from among the blacks.

Alongside this half-political, half-administrative organization, the blacks had of course their own specifically religious forms of organization such as the brotherhoods whose functions went beyond simply ministering to the mystical and affective life of the group. The brotherhood also performed many social functions.

This social role became especially apparent after a slave had been manumitted. Such manumission generally meant for the slave a shift from the tutelage of a master to that of a brotherhood which for him replaced his extended family or his absent tribe. Accommodation, work and marriage were all usually settled in the brotherhood which constituted in the context of exile the moveable homeland of the black in his new world.

What were the social and economic roles of slaves in Tunis? From the censuses of the *ma'atig* freed groups for the payment of the *mejba*, we can conclude with Lucette Valensi that the areas where black slaves were concentrated were in Tunis, the Sahel and the south-east.[14]

What is immediately apparent is that slaves were features of urban society. Slavery essentially met the needs of urban society. Was there then a demand for slave labour in the economic sectors of pre-colonial Tunisian cities?

A look at the main trade guilds in the city of Tunis, which have been widely studied in research and books, has not shown any particular recourse to black slaves, even in sectors that were very labour-intensive.[15] The main traditional guilds such as weaving, *chechia* or leather remained the preserve of local urban labour. Work in the guilds thus remained the work of freemen, and slavery cannot be explained in terms of economics.

Slavery for economic purposes has been reported for some regions in the Maghreb, such as in early modern Morocco, but it was already a phenomenon that was disappearing.[16]

Conversely, the sources are unanimous as to the domestic character of black slavery in the pre-colonial Maghreb. It is this feature that gives the Maghrebi form of slavery its originality and enables us to evoke the peculiarities of the way of life of the upper classes in Tunisian cities and especially the capital. Ownership of black slaves was a necessary mark of high status in the city.

The almost systematic resort to one or more slaves for domestic tasks inside and outside the home testified to a rather pronounced tendency to look down on physical labour, a traditionally well-known characteristic of aristocratic and especially urban attitudes.

Some practices that were widespread in the courts of the rulers of the Maghreb must have helped to make this tradition and this attitude take root. Blacks from Africa often formed élite corps in royal guards. From the time of the Hafsids down to the Husseini beys, the princes of Tunis systematically employed black guards in the palaces and recruited large numbers of blacks as servants and valets in their harems.

On the death of the bey of Tunis in 1835, six hundred freed black slaves followed the funeral cortege brandishing their letters of manumission.

By integrating blacks into the machinery of court life and making this an institution, the political leadership raised resort to black slaves to the level of a model to be followed in aristocratic circles as a whole living close to the court and from them by every urban notable.

But while such domestic slavery was the rule in urban society, it must not obscure the fact that there were some forms of slavery that integrated blacks into economically productive activities.

In the oases of southern Tunisia, staging-points on the caravan routes, black groups were employed in the agrarian economy and especially in irrigation work. The archival sources are full of evidence of the economic ways in which slaves were exploited as field labour and in other tasks in the oases and regions in the south. It is moreover in the south of the country that we have been able to observe survivals of slavery after abolition in 1846 and until the beginning of the twentieth century.

Viviana Pâques has noted similar phenomena:

> In the oases, the slave was above all used either as a domestic or to dig wells and irrigation canals. He also worked from dawn to dusk and in return would receive a plate of couscous. When he became *chouchane*, his status was that of a *khammas* (one-fifth share-cropper) and he was entitled to a percentage of the harvest, but his work remained the same.[17]

Slavery was abolished throughout the country in 1846. In Tunis, where it was the model of the prince who was the essential model of behaviour and reference point for all the well-off classes, it did not survive abolition. By the end of the century there were no significant survivals of slavery. But, in the south, where slaves were integrated into the production process, there were various forms of resistance, which justified in colonial times, in 1890, what the French like to call the *second abolition*. Colonial historiography has erased from memory the first abolition, which was more important, and has highlighted the *second abolition* as being the real abolition. But this second abolition was attacking only survivals. It was a decree which provided for monetary sanctions (in the form of fines) and even penal sanctions (in the form of imprisonment) for those who continued to supply the slave trade or to keep their black servants and domestics in slavery.

Effective abolition moved at two speeds because the nature of slavery was different in the urban centres from what it was in the economic centres of the oases in the south.

At another level, one that is no less important (and here I am touching on the cultural problem), it is the practice of manumission which makes for an interesting comparative approach. Manumission was a tradition which preceded abolition as a political act. According to Islamic traditions, if we go back to the sacred texts, a good Muslim was supposed to free his slaves if it was within his means to do so. Such manumission was in fact practised not by those groups nor by the *ulemas*, the scholars of official Islam, but by institutions of cultural Islam.

After Abolition

During the second half of the nineteenth century, that is several years after abolition, most of the blacks that we meet, freedmen, men or women, in fact constituted an urban sub-proletariat eking out an existence from petty jobs, or no job at all, living in makeshift accommodation, in the *fondouks* of the popular suburbs.

Often the black was a petty bread-seller, a hawker, a masseur in a Moorish bath, a free domestic, or simply a vagabond wandering in the dark streets of the city, an easy prey for the municipal police for drunkenness or petty theft.

We have estimated that up to 10 per cent of the prostitutes in the city were black women. A legendary figure in black folklore in Tunis, *Boussâadia*, even gave her name to a cul-de-sac given over to prostitution in the southern part of the city.[18]

It was thus following complete emancipation and abolition that a process of pauperization and social marginalization of the blacks became widely observable.

Manumission ensured the legal but not the social emancipation of the slave.

Another equally important aspect of the cultural history of these minorities has to do with the question of the cults and beliefs specific to these groups.

The black minority in Tunis had its own cults, organized in brotherhoods which gave it a framework in which to express its particular identity. These elements are today part of a folklore that is in the process of disappearing but which in fact relate to a heritage linked to the Afro-Maghrebi cultural life of the black groups of Tunisia and North Africa.

The *Stambali* (black music group), the *Boussâadia* (folk figure of the black community who performs masked dances and wears animal skins), the *diwan des ouarglia* (meeting of black community leaders), *bouri* (state of ecstasy and possession of blacks), possession dances, the sacrifice of the black ox in the shrine of *Sidi Saâd* at the *Mornag* or of *Sidi Frej* in Carthage – these have all been features of the everyday experience of the black brotherhoods and groups in Tunis all through their history.

The black groups had a particular cult for *Sidi Saâd*, a famous black saint around Tunis. An annual festival of the *Stambali* was celebrated in his honour each autumn. But a big festival was held at the end of every October.

The festival of *Sidi Saâd* brought together blacks from all the 'houses' in Tunis who went on the pilgrimage to slaughter a black bull and hold the *Diwan*; the blacks of *Sidi Frej* also took part in this festival, arriving according to various reports with a dressed bull, after having held a preliminary three-day festival in honour of their saint. They would then go to *Sidi Mehrez* (patron saint of the city of Tunis), to slaughter a bull as an offering to the descendants of the saint. Study of this intense religious life brings us back to the theme of the acculturation of groups from Africa in a traditional Muslim Arab environment. Such acculturation was not by any means a smooth uninterrupted process.

And this is why we can no longer speak of a 'silent minority' because, often, the black community in Tunis, unlike other communities, such as the Jewish community, which is particularly active, is regarded as a 'silent minority', There was no revolt, no open struggle for the abolition of slavery. What we find is a different path, the path of holiness, integration, resistance in silence, in acceptance of the model; or how the black minority was able to forge, within the culture in which they lived, two references which made it possible to prepare the whole society ideologically, culturally and mentally to accept manumission as a necessary path. This minority succeeded in getting manumission accepted, and manumission functioned significantly in the nineteenth century, even before the state, conforming to the model that was dominant in Europe, abolished slavery. In the framework of these marabout institutions, the black minority was able to protect itself socially.

On this point I should like to mention something touched on in earlier essays: flight by slaves. *Marronnage* of slaves in the Caribbean offers a bleak picture. Flight was a practice which functioned not only for the slave but also for women who sinned, for murderers, for those avoiding the state tax. In the context of cultural Islam, in the shrine of the saints they found the right of asylum; in the sacred space of the shrine, the right of asylum was an island of freedom, which enabled all those who were more or less marginalized, who feared the state, or for a slave running away from a violent or harsh master – there are also stories about white mistresses who fell in love with their black slave; shrines acted as a space where runaway slaves found protection. So much so that runaway and slave became one in the imaginary. Another level of analysis has to do with the cultural and religious anthropology of these minorities: they were able to keep intact animist forms and cults imported from sub-Saharan Africa, while giving them a veneer of superficial Islamization. It was an acculturated black who had become a scholar in Tunis, who wrote a letter to the bey, at the beginning of the nineteenth century, to inform him that this minority on which he relied, from among whom he recruited his bodyguard, was continuing to profess heresies. This is a valuable document, put to use by all anthropologists who want to analyse the forms of animism: how the black Muslim in Tunis continued in his underground temples to profess a religion that was decidedly African. It was a warning to the state, and the ruler of the time, who was an open man, had to come down hard on the so-called 'animist' practices; there was a sort of rooting out of idolatrous practices, but using non-violent methods. No black was put to death; it was the temples that were burned, and the bey issued a decree compelling blacks to conform to Islamic precepts, under the responsibility of Muslim sheikhs chosen by the *ulemas*.[19]

From the mid-nineteenth century, there was then a collective forgetting precipitated by the state. Of all these rituals, what remained at the end of the nineteenth century was the ritual of possession for therapeutic purposes. Blacks were the great specialists of possession therapy, through dance. These rituals have equivalents in cultural Islam: the functionality of these rituals enabled them to survive and be accepted into the Muslim embrace.

Thus, study of the black minority in Tunisia is a fascinating and complex scientific undertaking.

A multifaceted approach that avoids privileging the political or institutional domain makes it possible to grasp this community history in a global dynamic perspective. At the political and economic levels it throws light on the relationship between the state and élites and slavery and these minorities, and at the social and cultural levels on inter-ethnic relations and forms of adaptation, integration and resistance.

Thus, the history of minorities might constitute a total history that throws light on the whole social organization.

Notes

1. A. Allagui, *La Minorité juive en Tunisie à l'époque coloniale*, thesis, Tunis, 1994.
2. A. Temimi, 'Pour l'écriture de l'histoire sociale de la minorité africaine en Tunisie', *Revue d'Histoire maghrébine* (Tunis), 45–6, June 1987.
3. A. Larguèche, *L'Abolition de l'esclavage en Tunisie à travers les archives, 1841–1846*, Tunis, Alif, 1990.
4. See H. Clapperton, D. Denham and W. Oudney, *Voyages et découvertes dans le nord et les parties centrales de l'Afrique*, Paris, 1826 [Eng. orig., *Narrative of Travels and Discoveries in Northern and Central Africa in the Years 1822, 1823, and 1824*, Boston, 1826].
5. *Cahiers d'études africaines*, 119, Paris, 1990.
6. M. Ammar, 'Les allogènes en Tunisie à l'époque ancienne', in *La démographie historique en Tunisie et dans le monde arabe*, Tunis, CERES, 1993.
7. M. Abitbol, *Tombouctou et les armes*, Paris, 1979, pp. 178–217.
8. L. Valensi, 'Esclaves chrétiens et esclaves noirs à Tunis au XVIIIe siècle', *Annales E.S.C.*, 6, 1967.
9. L. Frank, *Histoire de Tunis*, 2nd ed., Tunis, 1987.
10. L. Valensi, op. cit., p. 1278.
11. Archives Nationales de Tunisie, Série historique, dossiers relatifs aux familles princières, document 58188.
12. A. Larguèche, 'La minorité noire à Tunis au XIXe siècle', in *Être marginal au Maghreb*, Paris, C.N.R.S., 1993, pp. 139–40.
13. R. Austen, 'The Trans-Saharan Slave Trade: A Tentative Census', in H. A Gemery and J. S Hogendorn, *The Uncommon Market: Essays in the Economic History of the Atlantic Slave Trade*, New York, Academic Press, 1979.
14. L. Valensi, op. cit., p. 1286.
15. P. Pennec, *La Transformation des corps de métiers à Tunis sous l'effet d'une économie de type capitaliste*, Tunis, ISEA, 1964.
16. O. D. Lara, 'Esclavage et révoltes négro-africaines dans l'empire musulman du haut Moyen Âge', *Présence Africaine*, 1976, p. 95.
17. V. Pâques, *L'Arbre cosmique dans la pensée populaire et dans le vie quotidienne du nord-ouest africain*, Paris, 1964.
18. D. Larguèche and A. Larguèche, *Marginales en terre d'Islam*, Tunis, CERES édition, 1993.
19. See A. Larguèche, 'La minorité noire à Tunis au XIXe siècle', pp. 145–53.

Chapter 32

Two Memories in the Present: Léger Félicité Sonthonax, Victor Schœlcher

Serge Barcellini

BY DESIGNATING THEM as the 'first abolitionists', history has united Léger Félicité Sonthonax and Victor Schœlcher. It was through them that the Enlightenment advanced. Memory has broken that union. For in the collective memory, that reading of history in the present, Léger Félicité Sonthonax and Victor Schœlcher do not have the same qualities.

Since 1949, the body of the latter has lain in the Panthéon, but the body of the former, buried in 1813 in the village of Oyonnax where he was born, disappeared when the cemetery was closed in the late nineteenth century. These graves, one of light for Schœlcher, one of darkness for Sonthonax, symbolically translate the place of these two memories in the present.

The 1980s, marked by the development of the ideology of human rights and the celebration of the bicentenary of the Revolution, did little to alter this situation. And it is that decade that I shall be focusing on.

On 21 May 1981, in the Panthéon, the new President of the French Republic, François Mitterand, laid a rose on the tombs of three great Frenchmen: Jean Jaurès, Jean Moulin and Victor Schœlcher. This simple ceremony, one man alone moving forward towards the Panthéon, sought to give direction to the 'septennat' that was beginning. Jean Jaurès represented homage to the social struggle, loyalty to commitment. Jean Moulin represented the memory of the Resistance, the desire to inscribe the new septennat in the continuity of de Gaulle's Fifth Republic. Victor Schœlcher represented the opening to a new ideology, that of Human Rights.

For the presidential rose opened a new period in the use of the memory of Schœlcher. After being pressed into the service of a policy of cohesion of the French Union, that memory was becoming a vector of the ideology of Human Rights. The actor of colonial times was being transformed into the precursor of Human Rights.

Victor Schœlcher died during the night of 25–26 December 1893, at the age of 90. As soon as news of his death arrived, his friends in the Republican

Union group in the Senate sought the honour of a state funeral for him. The bureau of the Senate rejected that request.

The interment took place on 5 January 1894. The funeral ceremony was organized symbolically. Two Caribbean students walked in front of the hearse, while two young black officers – Commander Lecournet and Lieutenant Commander Mortenol – held the ropes of the pall.

Of the latter, Schœlcher had written shortly before: 'We know a young Negro, Mr Mortenol, a graduate of the École Polytechnique, who is now a midshipman on the *Bison*.... Do you see any white Creole declaring that his instincts and his education protest against any assimilation of this young man to him?'[1]

Schœlcher's burial prefigures the type of use that would be made of the memory of the abolitionist hero. That memory would be pressed into the service of a policy of assimilation directed at both Caribbean blacks and black African élites.

In 1894, groups were formed with the aim of preserving Schœlcher's memory. Each year, on 22 July, the hero's birthday, a ceremony was organized on the tomb in Père Lachaise cemetery. Alongside this annual ceremony, the odd monument and column were erected at Houilles, on the square near his house, on 22 July 1904,[2] and at Fort-de-France, place Barre, the same year.

The arrival on the political stage of the black Caribbean Gaston Monnerville made it possible to get this policy of memory out of the grip of a very narrow circle in which it had developed.

On 5 January 1938, Gaston Monnerville, Secretary of State in the Chautemps Government, gave his approval to a project to transfer Schœlcher's ashes to the Panthéon.

The project was in abeyance during the Occupation but was back on the agenda in 1947, when preparations were being made to celebrate the centenary of the 1848 Revolution. In April 1948, at the Sorbonne and the Opéra, there were big ceremonies marking the centenary of the abolition of slavery presided over by Gaston Monnerville, then President of the Council of the Republic.

A few days earlier, on 4 March 1948, the Assembly of the French Union had unanimously approved a motion to transfer Schœlcher's ashes to the Panthéon. On 28 June 1948, the motion was adopted without debate by the National Assembly followed on 1 July 1948 by the Council of the Republic.

On 14 July, the law providing for the transfer of the remains of Victor Schœlcher to the Panthéon was promulgated. But this transfer would not be done alone: in addition to the remains of his father,[3] Victor Schœlcher would only enter the Panthéon accompanied by Félix Éboué.

In deciding on this double pantheonization,[4] the government sought to make this ceremony focus on the defence of the French Union. The explanatory memorandum accompanying the bill tabled by the government at the June 1948 session reflected this desire 'at a time when the whole French Union is solemnly celebrating the centenary of the 1848 revolution', it is right to honour the man who in our times has best incarnated in his person Black Africa and France: Governor General Félix Éboué, 'France owes to this spiritual son given it by the Empire a solemn consecration'.

On 20 September 1948, the National Assembly unanimously approved the government bill. In the name of the Commission on National Education, Deputy Finet congratulated 'the government for taking the initiative to bring together in a single ceremony the memories of Schœlcher, the promoter of the idea of the French Union, and Governor Éboué, one of those who contributed most to achieving it'.

On 19 May 1949, at 6 p.m., the two coffins, one containing the remains of Victor and Marc Schœlcher and the other the remains of Félix Éboué, were placed under the Arc de Triomphe, near the tomb of the unknown soldier. The choice of this site for the first stage gave the pantheonization a patriotic and national aspect. The two coffins were then transferred to a temporary mausoleum erected in the Luxembourg gardens. This second stage recalled the place of the Senate in Victor Schœlcher's career. Until midnight, the public was admitted to file past the two catafalques.

On 20 May at 10:30 a.m., the ceremony organized in the same garden began, presided over by the President of the Republic, Vincent Auriol. Forty black soldiers belonging to the colonial infantry formed an honour guard for Schœlcher's coffin and forty students from the École Nationale de la France d'outre-mer for Félix Éboué's.

Two speeches set out the orientation that the government sought to give these two pantheonizations. The first was made by Coste-Floret, Minister for Overseas France:

> The grateful mother-country today welcomes into the temple of glory two precursors of the French Union: Victor Schœlcher, who did the preparatory work by dedicating his life to the emancipation of the slaves, which he had the great honour of seeing enshrined in positive legislation; and Félix Éboué, a pure Frenchmen of the black race, who built its solid foundations by calling his black brothers to fight for the liberation of the mother-country in chains.
>
> Nearly a century separates the high points of the life of these two great Frenchmen. April 1848, final abolition of slavery. August 1940, Chad's decision to go over to the Free French government. Yet who cannot see a clear causal connection between the work of the first, of the white man dreaming of the liberation of black humanity which he pursued until it was achieved, and that of the second, the son of those blacks whom the other had emancipated, setting across the seas the example of the most lucid and most upright patriotism and, despite the setbacks to our armies, of faith in final victory!…
>
> To the work achieved by Schœlcher for his racial brothers, almost a century earlier, Éboué responded with the most magnificent testimony, that of faithfulness in misfortune and continuity of faith in France. To the desire for a better humanity that Schœlcher had, to the sentiment of justice which had inspired everything he did. Éboué in turn signified that the time was come when the black man could speak as a free man, fully responsible for his action, his strength, his justice and his duty.

The second speech was made by the President of the Council of the Republic, Gaston Monnerville.

An act that is unique in the history of the world is being accomplished in Paris.

The man who devoted his life to the fight for the liberation of men: Victor Schœlcher, and one of the sons who is most representative of the effects of that liberation, Félix Éboué, are being solemnly interred in the Panthéon, by the will of the French people.

In a few moments, Victor Schœlcher and Félix Éboué will be united, on the same day, in a single procession to the sanctuary on the Sainte-Geneviève hill, by the will of the grateful mother-country.

Two Frenchmen, very great and very noble.

Two men, worthy of the fine name of man.

Two pure symbols of faithfulness to human dignity.

When the speeches were over, the catafalques borne by the students and the infantrymen who had mounted the guard of honour moved to the Panthéon, which the procession entered at 11.45 a.m.[5]

The two coffins were then placed on a shelf occupied by a single tomb, that of Jean Jaurès.

A journalist from the *Semaine de Guyane* offered a parallel between the three men:

JAURÈS – ÉBOUÉ – SCHŒLCHER

The three liberators have deserved well of the mother-country. Schœlcher who freed us from the shame of slavery, Jaurès who died to deliver us from war and hatred, and finally Éboué who, showing us the path of honour and national recovery, freed us from the shame of defeat and servitude.

Thirty-two years later, the presidential roses, replacing Félix Éboué with Jean Moulin, effaced the assimilationist cast given to the double pantheonization of 1949 and symbolically opened the time of Human Rights.

* * *

The celebration of the bicentenary of the Revolution of 1789 was a continuation of that opening. In a manner similar to the celebration of the centenary of the Revolution of 1848, which highlighted the act of abolishing slavery, celebration of the bicentenary was constructed around a series of tributes paid to the actors in the first abolition.

Among those actors, Léger Félicité Sonthonax, who was the man who initiated abolition, enjoyed no homage. No ceremony was organized to recall the memory of this Jacobin revolutionary, no column was raised, no plaque was put in a street, no reference to his name was made in the articles published in the French dailies and weeklies on the occasion of the pantheonization of the abbé Grégoire.

Léger Félicité Sonthonax appears as one of the great forgotten figures of this bicentenary. This forgetting was not quite total. Three patches of light were lit.

The first has the form of a book, *Léger Félicité Sonthonax – The Lost Sentinel of the Republic,* by Robert Louis Stein, published in 1984 by Dickinson University Press in Toronto, Canada. In 234 pages, the author has transformed our knowledge of this individual and has broken with the negative views that had developed since the beginning of the nineteenth century both by 'Dr' Bacon-Tacon, a fellow-citizen of Oyonnax who published a pamphlet against the Sonthonax family in 1802, and by the colonists of Saint-Domingue, who were deeply hostile to the commissioner of the Republic. But because this book was not widely disseminated,[6] it never wholly achieved what it set out to achieve.

When Pierre Pluchon published a book about Toussaint Louverture in 1989, he did so without having read Stein's book.[7]

> Sonthonax had not been instructed to prepare for the gradual abolition of slavery. His unexpected initiative, which destroyed white rule abruptly and not gradually, led to his being arraigned by the Convention!
>
> For the time being, the commissioner, with a fatuousness that nothing could stop, pursued his demonstration on two levels, in which the true lie and the false truth joined together to drive their way through the labyrinth of a derisory rhetoric. 'We are speaking the truth, citizens, slavery was then essential, both for getting work done and for preserving the colonists. Saint-Domingue was still in the grip of a horde of ferocious tyrants who publicly preached that skin colour should be the sign of power or reprobation.'
>
> For reasons we know not, what was true in May was no longer so in August: 'today circumstances have greatly changed; the slavers and the man-eaters are no more. Some perished from their impotent rage, others sought their salvation in flight and immigration. The whites who remain are the friends of French law and principles, and, carried away by the surging flow of what he was saying, the lawyer called to the new citizens: do not forget 'that of all the whites in the world, the only ones who are your friends are the Frenchmen in Europe'.
>
> The general abolition of slavery, proclaimed on 29 August 1793, was a trick, a derisory deceit: it granted a regulated freedom to men who had conquered the full possession of their fate by violence! The revolution of French whites, even when it was apparently being driven to the very threshold of illegality, remained the enemy of blacks, it confiscated from them ownership of property and sovereignty.
>
> The deep faith that inspired Sonthonax, a faith he never abjured, did not cloak itself in philanthropic generosity for the wretched victims, but wore the mantle of hatred: hatred of the colonists. More than the freedom of the slaves the lawyer wanted the destruction of the caste of planters.
>
> In what he wrote, Sonthonax, the man from the metropole, the son of provincial merchants, did not hymn the happiness of the state of freedom, but in his crude hand-writing, set out a negative vision of the action and the future. He had no wish to build anything new in the light of new thinking. No, he was settling scores: his pathological hatred of the planters commanded him to do so. In that, he succeeded: in their thousands, the property owners of Saint-Domingue fled, seeking refuge nearby, in the United States in particular, or died the victims of legitimized murder. The son of Oyonnax, as if inspired by some egalitarian envy, sought to annihilate the immediate beneficiaries of the slave regime, not to attack the system that made them rich. Sonthonax is not the liberator of the blacks,

whom he scorned: if everything went as they would have wished, these enemies of modern progress would plant a backward Guinea in the middle of the Caribbean Sea. Even less was he the destroyer of a mode of exploitation: he sought to save it from its death throes, to restore it to life. Finally, the commissioner was satisfied with little: he wallowed in the satisfaction of decapitating the class of colonists. Betraying the ideas that he claimed to be inspired by, the man was without rigour in thought, without greatness.

The second spot of light was lit in Haiti on the occasion of the celebration of the bicentenary. The year 1989 marked the real reappearance of Sonthonax in Haitian memory. This reappearance took the forms of a portrait, a poster and a circular.

In 1988, a portrait of Léger Félicité Sonthonax – an oil painting on canvas measuring 58.17 cm x 77 cm – was discovered in a storeroom of the Musée du Panthéon national haïtien on the occasion of the transfer of this museum into the mausoleum that was intended to receive the remains of President Duvalier, known as 'Papa Doc'. The painting was restored and is now on public view. Experts attribute it to either David or one of his pupils. It was probably painted in France in 1795–6 and brought to Saint-Domingue by Sonthonax himself in 1796. In this portrait Sonthonax is a young man (he was 33) decidedly on the fat side. In one hand he is holding the declaration of 29 August 1793, which replaced the *Code Noir*, the torn pieces of which are scattered before him.[8]

In 1989 a poster was designed by the Haitian committee for the bicentenary. It shows two profiles of Sonthonax and Toussaint Louverture and treats the two heroes equally. This poster was widely disseminated in Haitian educational institutions.

Finally, a circular addressed to the heads of secondary schools in the Republic of Haiti by the directorate-general of the Ministry of National Education, Youth and Sports called on

directors, teachers and pupils to devote some moments on 5 April to reflect on the life and political action of this great historical figure (Sonthonax) and to comment on certain articles in the Proclamation of the general freedom of slaves of 29 August 1793.

The third spot of light was lit in the town where Sonthonax was born. In Oyonnax, in 1989, at the suggestion of members of the local section of the *Ligue des Droits de l'Homme*, an association was formed called 'Mémoire de Léger Félicité Sonthonax'. This little association has been behind three important initiatives.

The first was the painting of a portrait of Léger Félicité Sonthonax by the Haitian painter Édouard Duval-Carrié. This full-size portrait, 180 cm x 200 cm, was shown at the 'La Révolution française sous les Tropiques' exhibition organized at the Musée National des Arts Africains et Océaniens in 1989.[9] Strongly influenced by the portrait in the Musée du Panthéon National Haïtien, the work of the painter Duval-Carrié marks an important stage in the history of Haitian naive painting. It is actually the first portrait of a white by a Haitian artist.[10]

The second is the placing of a plaque in Port-au-Prince. This plaque was unveiled by the French ambassador to Haiti, Jean-Raphaël Dufour, on 6 December 1989 in the sole building from colonial times still standing in Port-au-Prince, the former cathedral.[11] Its inscription was intended to be educational:

On 29 August 1793
Léger Félicité Sonthonax
Commissioner of the French Republic
abolished slavery
and proclaimed the general freedom
of the population
of the island of Saint-Domingue

The third was the organization of a colloquy on 7–8 September 1990 at the Musée des Arts Africains et Océanien in Paris. This colloquy was opened by Jean-Noël Jeanneney, President of the Mission du Bicentenaire de la Révolution and the closing speech was made by Jean-Raphaël Dufour, French ambassador to Haiti, and Serge Vieux, Haitian ambassador to France. The chairpersons of the various sessions were *maître* Yves Jouffa, President of the Ligue des Droits de l'Homme, Jean Metellus, a Haitian writer, Jean-René Suratteau, President of the Société des Études Robespierristes, and Jean Peyrot, President of the Association des Professeurs d'Histoire et Géographie. Fifteen papers discussed in detail the life and work of Sonthonax.[12] The scholarly conclusions of the colloquy were highlighted by Michel Vovelle, director of the Institut d'Histoire de la Révolution Française. Michel Vovelle stressed that Sonthonax was neither someone unknown to history nor a *monstre sacré*. In the gallery of Frenchmen in the Caribbean at the time of the Revolution, Sonthonax offers the anti-Rochambeau, the anti-Victor-Hugues:

Sonthonax was both a man of conviction and a strategist who, within the limits of his own conceptual framework, was to be compelled to go beyond himself; this man of law, this innocent confronted with the reality of the world, took on the stature of those through whom proclamations are made that change the world. For that very reason, Sonthonax was truly the precursor, the man who went farther than the prudent strategies of the Société des Amis des Noirs, beyond compromise solutions of gradual emancipation. For that reason, Sonthonax deserves not to be forgotten.

Thus, the action of the association born in the narrow confines of the commune of Oyonnax has developed essentially on the stage of Paris and Haiti.[13]

* * *

Despite these three spots of light, the celebrations of the bicentenary left the memory of Sonthonax in a deep shadow.

He was not the only person who benefited from the first abolition of slavery. Another was Toussaint Louverture.

The 1980s completed the slow shift in the perception of the historical role played by Toussaint Louverture in the Haitian revolution. The father of independence became the actor in abolition. This shift was begun by the Martinican writer Aimé Césaire in his book on Toussaint Louverture in 1960.[14] In July 1989, Aimé Césaire was 'celebrated' at the Avignon festival. On that occasion, he stated to the newspaper *Libération* of 10 July: 'Toussaint Louverture was the man who helped the French revolution to bring forth what it contained as a principle within it, but precisely only in the state of a principle.'

> Toussaint Louverture came to take at its word the Declaration of the Rights of Man, to show that in it there is no marginal country; that no people is excepted. It was to incarnate and particularize a principle; in other words to give it life. In history and in the area of human rights, he was, for the blacks, the operator and the intercessor. That gives him his place, his true place. Toussaint Louverture's fight was this fight to transform formal law into actual law, the fight for the recognition of man and that is why he inscribed himself and inscribed the revolt of the black slaves of Saint-Domingue in the history of universal civilization. If there is a negative side to the man – hard to avoid given the situation – it is there that it lies: to have been more attached to deducing the existence of his people from an abstract universal than to grasping the singularity of his people to promote it to universality.

Echoing Aimé Césaire, François Mitterand stated on 31 March 1987, during an official visit to Franche-Comté as he paid his respects at the château de Joux in Toussaint Louverture's cell:

> Toussaint is one of the great men of his time, he is the symbol of the emancipation of black slaves, but also of the emancipation of all.[15]

The year 1989 accentuated this re-reading of the work of Toussaint Louverture. The black hero had become omnipresent in exhibitions.

In the catalogue of the exhibition put on by the town of Palaiseau, 'Esclavage, Révolution, Droits de l'homme, 1789–1989', Sonthonax is cited seven times, Toussaint Louverture thirty-five times.[16] In the catalogue of the 'Images de la Révolution aux Antilles' exhibition mounted in Basse-Terre, Guadeloupe, in March 1989, Toussaint Louverture appears in fourteen of the ninety-two items on display.[17] Similarly, thirteen portraits of Toussaint Louverture, as against one of Sonthonax, appear among the 104 documents of the exhibition put on in Port-au-Prince at the Musée d'Art Haïtien of the *collège* Saint-Pierre.[18]

This reassessment complements that of the work of Victor Schœlcher. On 10 September 1989, the City Council of Massy inaugurated a square and a statue. The name of Victor Schœlcher was given to the square, while the bronze statue, 2.63 metres high, was that of Toussaint Louverture.[19] The inauguration took place in the presence of Gaston Monnerville. By putting Victor Schœlcher and Toussaint Louverture together, this Council was part of the process of transforming the black hero into a popular hero.

By the same token, it was furthering the work of the S.O.S. Racisme association which in 1989 placed its traditional Fête des potes (Festival of mates) organized at Vincennes under his patronage.[20]

In another area, but with the same aims, a major show was put on in 1989, 'Toussaint Louverture ou la révolution d'un esclave africain devenu général de la République'. Financed by the French Government and placed under the patronage of President Diouf of Senegal, this Puy-du-Fou-type spectacle was put together by Claude Moreau.[21]

Eleven individuals appear in the booklet:[22] Toussaint Louverture, the abbé Grégoire, General Laveaux, Louis XVI, Dessalines, Barnave, Mirabeau, Ogé, Robespierre, the abbé Maury and a pro-colonist deputy. Sonthonax is forgotten. His work is attributed to General Laveaux. This is the show that President Mitterand attended in Dakar on 25 May 1989, along with all the heads of state meeting for the Francophone summit.[23] The following month, this show was put on in Lille.

In the office of the President of the Republic and the Ministry of Culture there were advisers who thought of giving this tabloid-style hero treatment a republican 'sanctification'. A proposal to pantheonize Toussaint Louverture was dreamed up. Since the body of the Haitian hero had disappeared at Fort Joux, such a symbolic pantheonization required only the agreement of the Haitian Government. Was that agreement sought? We do not know. The project was soon abandoned in favour of a replacement, the abbé Grégoire.

The abbé Grégoire is the second beneficiary of the disappearance of Sonthonax from the collective memory. He comes a close second to Toussaint Louverture in colloquies and exhibition catalogues.

In the catalogue of the exhibition organized at the Musée d'Architecture in Liège from 19 February to 9 April 1989, on the theme 'Les Droits de l'homme et la traite des Noirs' (Human rights and the slave trade),[24] the abbé Grégoire is portrayed as the true initiator of abolition: 'Supported by Danton, he extracted the first abolition of slavery in the colonies.'

At the international history colloquy organized in Port-au-Prince from 5 to 8 December 1989, four papers were devoted to him as against five to Toussaint Louverture and none to Sonthonax.[25]

The same competition appears in the special issue of *Différence*, the bulletin of the M.R.A.P. (Mouvement contre le racisme et l'antisémitisme) devoted to the abolition of slavery. Two articles are devoted to the abbé Grégoire and one to Toussaint Louverture. By making numerous references to both heroes, the interview with Minister of Culture Jack Lang restores the balance.[26]

This balance was upset on 18 April 1989 by the announcement, by the President of the Republic, of the pantheonization of Gaspard Monge,[27] Condorcet and the abbé Grégoire. *France-Soir* justified the choice of the abbé Grégoire by stressing that 'he got the abolition of slavery adopted and contributed to the emancipation of Jews in France'.[28] The announcement of the pantheonization led to the publication of a series of works on the abbé Grégoire.[29] As in 1948, the choice of those to pantheonize reflected the spirit of the times.

The three heroes had a consensual view of the Revolution. Gaspard Monge is presented as a scholar, the founder of the École Polytechnique, Nicolas Condorcet as a philosopher and a mathematician who, as deputy to the Legislative Assembly and the Convention, was the author of a project to reform public education, and finally the abbé Henri Grégoire as the deputy of the clergy who on 20 June 1789 joined the third estate and fought to put an end to the exclusion of Jews and slaves. They were 'revolutionaries of tolerance'.[30] This choice was part of the development of the ideology of human rights which was the engine of the commemorations of the bicentenary. But the consensus was partly challenged by the Church of France which abstained from taking part in the pantheonization ceremony[31] and by the Société Robespierriste which expressed its regret 'that one of the most significant figures of the Revolution should have been left out of the homage of the Nation'.[32]

On 12 December, the ceremony of pantheonization concluded the year of the bicentenary.[33] The ceremony was deliberately restrained.

A procession bearing an enormous painted canvas ('Aux grands hommes, Condorcet, Grégoire, Monge, la patrie reconnaissante') moved towards the Panthéon. It was made up of 48 people: 12 young people from the Lycée Condorcet in front, on the side students from the École Normale Supérieure and the École Polytechnique (Monge helped to found the former and created the latter), and at the back twelve Africans whose presence recalled the action of Condorcet and Grégoire in favour of the abolition of slavery.

Forty-nine drums from the three services and the gendarmerie headed the procession; the same number brought up the rear. A few steps from the monument the procession halted. Three voices rang out one after the other: a text by each of those to be pantheonized was read by an actor. Then Minister of Culture Lang made a speech paying his respects which, true to the form of such speeches, was a paean to men sent by providence: 'Condorcet and Grégoire made history move.' Finessing the first abolition, Lang stressed 'that it took fifty more years for slavery to be abolished'.

* * *

Sonthonax thus appears as the 'great forgotten' of this 12 December 1989 event despite the fact that the three men being pantheonized had direct contacts with him. Monge was Minister of the Navy and the Colonies at the time of the first civilian commission to Saint-Domingue, while Condorcet and Grégoire were, like Sonthonax, members of the Société de Amis des Noirs.[34]

The year of the bicentenary will thus have contributed to the development of the 'forgetting' of the man whom the slaves of Saint-Domingue had christened 'the Good Lord'.

Let us then ask ourselves about the 'construction of forgetting' in the collective memory.

The mechanisms of constructing memory are today well known and analysed – with their heritage component (the construction of monuments, columns and commemorative plaques, the creation of ceremonies at dates conceived to ring memory bells), their scholarly component (the publication of books and research, the organization of colloquies), and finally their pedagogical component (the creation of museums, exhibitions, the writing of school textbooks, educational packages, etc.) but the mechanisms of constructing forgetting have never been studied.

By becoming the subject of such a study, Sonthonax might perhaps take his revenge on forgetful memory.

Notes

1. On Schœlcher's burial, see J.-A. Debray, *Victor Schœlcher*, Perrin, 1983, 360 pp., especially chap. 13: 'Tel qu'en lui-même enfin l'éternité 1894–1981'.
2. This bronze bust, the work of Marguerite Syamours, was removed by the Germans in February 1942. A new bust was unveiled on 4 July 1948 in a ceremony presided over by Gaston Monnerville.
3. In his will, Victor Schœlcher had asked to be buried alongside his father Marc. This testamentary instruction embarrassed the government, which had to have a law providing for the transfer of the remains of Marc Schœlcher to the Panthéon passed as an emergency measure by the two assemblies.
4. Chronology of the pantheonization of Félix Éboué:

    - 30 January 1944: Brazzaville conference.
    - 17 May 1944: death of Félix Éboué.
    - 20 January 1946: resignation of General de Gaulle as prime minister.
    - July–August 1946: 'états-généraux de la colonisation' in Paris.
    - 7 April 1947: creation of the RPF by General de Gaulle (Rassemblement du Peuple Français – Rally of the French people).
    - 15 May 1947: unveiling in Bordeaux of a plaque in memory of Félix Éboué by General de Gaulle who in his speech set out his view of the French Union.
    - 11 March 1948: the socialist-led government decides to inter Félix Éboué in the Panthéon.
    - 10 July 1948: decision of the Council of Ministers.
    - 20 September 1948: vote by the National Assembly.
    - 24 September 1948: vote by the Council of the Republic.

    The pantheonization of Félix Éboué was an issue of memory disputed between de Gaulle (and the RPF) and the Third Force government (especially the SFIO).
5. On the ceremony of pantheonization, see E. Castor and R. Tarcy, *Félix Éboué*, Paris, L'Harmattan, 1984, 357 pp.
6. This book has not been translated into French. There is no copy in the Bibliothèque Nationale.
7. Pierre Pluchon published his first, 400-page book about Toussaint Louverture in 1979 (P. Pluchon, *Toussaint Louverture – De l'esclavage au pouvoir*, Port-au-Prince, Éditions Caraïbes, 1979), at a time when the author was cultural adviser to the French embassy. A second 654-page work on the same subject was published by Fayard in Paris in 1989. The quotations about Sonthonax are taken from this latter work (pp. 89, 90 and 91). The negative picture of Léger Félicité Sonthonax in Pierre Pluchon's book was used as the basis for a play by young secondary school pupils at the French *lycée* in Jamel, Haiti.
8. Michel Philippe Lerebours, director of the École Nationale des Arts in Port-au-Prince, has studied this picture in his thesis on *Haïti et ses peintres*. The painting was displayed in the exhibition devoted to the bicentenary of the Haitian revolution, mounted at the Musée d'Art Haïtien of the Collège Saint-Pierre in Port-au-Prince from 6 to 16 December 1989.

9. The catalogue of the exhibition was published by the Tipe press in Montreuil (74 pp.).
10. The painter Édouard Duval-Carrié is regarded as one of Haiti's up-and-coming painters. Today the picture is in the collection of a Californian art-lover.
11. This magnificent eighteenth-century building was in the process of being restored in 1989. It was completely destroyed by a fire during the demonstrations marking the failure of the attempted coup by Roger Lafontant against the elected president, Father Aristide, on 9–10 January 1991. The plaque did not survive this destruction.
12. The entire proceedings were published as follows: *Léger-Félicité Sonthonax: la première abolition de l'esclavage,* ed. M. Dorigny, St Denis, Société française d'histoire d'outre-mer (SFHOM), 1997.
13. A study using the files on Sonthonax held by the Archives Départementales de l'Ain and the cadastral archives deposited at Nantua enabled the association to locate precisely the house where Sonthonax was born. Situated on the main road in Oyonnax (rue Anatole-France), this house is still standing. A plaque was to be put up on this building in 1995.
14. A. Césaire, *Toussaint Louverture – La Révolution française et le problème colonial,* Paris, Éditions Présence Africaine, first published 1960. On the back cover of the 1981 edition, it is stated: '[R]eissue of the work that altered the historical analysis of colonial societies by basing itself on a political and cultural project which still retains all its force for the third world today.'
15. Quoted in R. Lambalot, *Toussaint Louverture au château de Joux,* Office du Tourisme de Pontarlier, 1989, a 52-page brochure subtitled 'the extraordinary fate of a former slave of Saint-Domingue who became governor general and symbol of the emancipation of blacks'.
16. The abundantly illustrated 94-page catalogue of the exhibition was published by the Palaiseau town council.
17. The catalogue of the exhibition reproduces ninety documents making up the Marcel-Chatillon collection, the catalogue printed at the Union press in Paris.
18. Catalogue of the exhibition published by the Henri Deschamps Press in Port-au-Prince.
19. In 1992, the municipality of Nantes named a square after Toussaint Louverture.
20. On this occasion, the cartoon strip made by Pierre Birens and Nicolas Saint-Cyr and published by Hachette in 1985 as *Le Napoléon Noir, Toussaint Louverture* became known to a wider audience.
21. 'The director Claude Moreau, a former advertising executive, designer of the productions of the Abaque and the extension group, specializes in this sort of show which has taken him from Cuba to Bercy, from Rodez to Dakar ...' (G. Dumur in *Le Nouvel Observateur,* 27 May 1989).
22. The text of the show was published in a 68-page booklet, designed by Typofilm Company.
23. Several articles were devoted to this show in *Le Monde du bicentenaire,* 8, *Le Nouvel Observateur* and *Le Monde.* In the last paper, an article by J.-P. Peroncel-Hugoz denounced 'the text, with its third-worldist manichaeism that has been out of date for twenty years with good blacks on one side and dirty whites on the other ...'.
24. Catalogue printed by the Lemaire press in Liège, 88 abundantly illustrated pages.
25. Titles of the papers devoted to the abbé Grégoire: 'Grégoire et Haïti'; 'le rôle de l'abbé Grégoire; 'l'abbé Grégoire humaniste'; 'textes de l'abbé Grégoire'.
26. *Différences,* March 1989. Titles of articles: 'L'abbé Grégoire, les Juifs et les hommes de couleur' [The abbé Grégoire, the Jews and people of colour], by Mgr G. Huberlot, Bishop of Évry-Corbeil; 'Le combat de Toussaint Louverture' [Toussaint Louverture's combat]; 'Points de vue de personnalités diverses sur l'abbé Grégoire et Toussaint Louverture' [Viewpoints of various figures on the abbé Grégoire and Toussaint Louverture], with remarks by J. Lang, Minister of Culture and the Bicentenary.
27. Announcement made on the occasion of the inauguration of the exhibition 'Les savants et la Révolution', organized at the Cité des Sciences de la Villette.
28. *France-Soir,* 19 April 1989.
29. G. Hourdin, *L'abbé Grégoire, évêque et démocrate,* Paris, Desclée de Brouwer, 160 pp.; B. Plongeron, *L'abbé Grégoire ou l'Arche de la Fraternité, 1750–1831,* Paris, Letouzey et Ané, 1989, 109 pp.; idem, *Lettre de M.-J. Dufraise à Grégoire* (same publisher, 100 pp.); abbé Grégoire, *Essai sur la régénération physique morale et politique des juifs* (reprint), Paris, Stock, 1896.

30. P. Boggio, 'Les révolutionnaires de la tolérance', *Le Monde*, 14 December 1989. Also, 'Trois lumières à l'aube de la République', *Libération*, 12 December 1989.

31. 'La conception de l'Église de l'abbé Grégoire, celle de la religion nationale, est contraire à la tradition catholique' (interview with Cardinal Lustiger, *Le Monde*, 8 December 1989) and article by A. Mandouze, 'L'abbé et le cardinal', *Le Monde*, 16 December 1989.

32. J. Suret-Canale, 'Exclus du Panthéon', *Révolution*, 12 January 1990; M. Vovelle, 'Et Robespierre?', *L'Humanité*, 12 December 1989; B. Peuchamel, 'L'Incorruptible dans la fosse commune', *L'Humanité*, 13 December 1989.

33. The year of the twentieth anniversary of the liberation of France concluded on 10 December with the pantheonization of Jean Moulin.

34. In 1799, Sonthonax chaired the meeting that the Société des Amis des Noirs devoted to the fifth anniversary of the abolition of slavery.

Afterword: On the Abolition of Slavery by the First Republic

Samir Amin

I INTEND TO DEVELOP two themes that definitely run counter to the dominant ideas of our day.

I. CAPITALISM, LIKE ALL MERCANTILE SOCIAL FORMATIONS, IS NOT INIMICAL TO SLAVERY; ON THE CONTRARY, IT FREQUENTLY EMBRACES IT AMONG THE MODALITIES FOR EXTRACTING SURPLUS LABOUR WHICH IT CONTROLS.

1. Slavery does not constitute a stage in general history that is more or less 'necessary' or even common. This thesis assumes that there is a determined, relatively strong relationship between the form of labour exploitation that it represents and a given stage of the development of productive forces. Marx's hasty thesis on the subject is well known: '[T]he hand-driven mill produces slavery, the water mill serfdom, the machine wage labour.'

In fact, slavery as the dominant form of social relations is only rarely met with in periods preceding modern times (capitalism). Yet precisely because it is found in that position in ancient Greece and Rome, the Eurocentric distortion that dominates modern social thought has encouraged the view that slavery is indeed a stage, overtaken by feudalism (serfdom) and then capitalism (wage labour).

2. But slavery is commonly found in various societies (various in terms of their level of productive development) that have one common denominator: the importance of mercantile relations.

This was indeed the case of ancient Greece and some regions of the Roman Empire. This association between slavery and density of mercantile relations has unfortunately escaped Eurocentric analyses. Moreover, this same association can be found in other circumstances. For example, in sub-Saharan Africa slavery appears much more common when the society is strongly marked by mercantilization.

Conversely, in societies that are little mercantilized, slavery loses its importance, disappears from the principal area of production and is relegated, when it subsists (or exists) to domains not directly linked to production (domestic slavery, slavery in armies, etc.). There are even examples where slavery becomes a social relationship internal to the dominant class (Mamluks in the Islamic Orient), thereby subjecting the bureaucratic class-state to the supreme ruler.

This hypothesis may well better account for the absence of slavery in the historical trajectory of the peoples of ancient Egypt, China, etc. than the one formulated in the preceding section.

It may also explain better than the association between 'slavery and hand mills' the decline of slavery in the Middle Ages in the West (parallel to the retreat of mercantile relations) and its replacement by serfdom.

Nevertheless, and still complementing the Eurocentric view dominated by the generalization of the slavery-serfdom-capitalism succession in the (artificially constructed) space of 'Europe' (thereby artificially linking Greece and Rome to the continent north of the Alps), the absence of slavery in other parts of the world has been 'explained' by the theory of the Asiatic mode of production – and has done so by a sleight of hand, since in this way the concept of slavery as a stage is retained by speaking of those 'Asiatic' societies in terms of 'generalized slavery'. By thus opposing the concept of private property (and hence 'private' slavery) to that of its absence (and hence 'generalized' slavery), are we not projecting onto the past a key modern concept, that of private (capitalist) property?

3. The intensification of mercantile relations that accompanied the birth of capitalism was marked by a massive extension of slavery.

Atlantic mercantilism was largely based on the generalization of slavery in the peripheries that it constituted for itself (the Americas); that slavery was the origin, after the extermination of the Indians, of the transatlantic slave trade. But this slave relationship was decisive in the constitution of the dominant mercantile capital (sixteenth-eighteenth century), the necessary prelude to the industrial revolution. It even survived significantly, after this last revolution, in countries such as the United States and Brazil until almost the end of the nineteenth century.

It is true that the extension of slavery occurred on the periphery of the system, whether the Atlantic peripheries of America or the new periphery of Eastern Europe. The 'second serfdom' (an attenuated form of slavery) which reappeared there in the eighteenth century (and which itself survived until late in the nineteenth century) was closely associated with the mercantilization of the agrarian economies of Eastern Europe. Conversely, not only has slavery not existed in modern Europe, the centre of the new system, but serfdom itself shrank with growing mercantilization and capitalist expansion. It is that concomitance that encouraged the thesis of the opposition capitalism/slavery. But is there not another explanation for this phenomenon? I suggest here that the bourgeoisie, struggling to assert itself against the feudal classes of the Ancien Régime, needed, in order to triumph, the support of peasant struggles. And it was they that made serfdom retreat.

4. It is not desirable to stretch the meaning of words beyond certain limits. It is useful – necessary, even – to distinguish between slavery as a mode of production (even if integrated into a capitalist social formation) and the 'unequal statuses' among individuals that are a feature of all pre-modern societies. The idea of equality of status is in fact a product of bourgeois ideology, not only because that equality 'frees the proletariat' (and compels it to sell its labour power), but also because the bourgeoisie needed this new idea to combat the privileges of feudalism. And even so we should be clear that inequality in the statuses of women persists down to the present day.

The 'unequal statuses' in pre-capitalist societies fulfilled various functions, that are not reducible to those associated with the exploitation of labour. In lineage societies, intermediate between the most archaic communitarian modes and the constitution of the general form that I call 'tributary', these inequalities were essential for the organization of social power (which was not yet a state power), not for the exploitation of labour. That is also the reason why the inequality of statuses is generalized in all these 'tributary' (state) forms, in close relationship with the organization of power.

Capitalism, on the other hand, in its development, encourages the reduction (or even the abolition) of status inequalities associated with the organization of power, while at the same time constantly generating new status inequalities, which it then associates directly with the exploitation of labour. The most marked of these unequal statuses are to be found in the peripheries. Apartheid is one example of it. Of course, apartheid, odious thought it is, is not slavery, any more than 'forced labour' in the colonies was. The discourse developed by 'liberal' sociologists who claim that apartheid was a hindrance to capitalism, I never found convincing. I have shown on the contrary that it fulfilled functions that were 'useful' to the dominant capital, indispensable even in the case of South Africa, and that its calling into question is not the 'natural' product of capitalist logic, but on the contrary that of struggles waged against that logic.

5. The ideology fashionable today claims to establish a one-to-one relationship between the market and democracy (which implies, I suppose, the abolition of status inequalities, including the most violent one of all, slavery). No market without democracy, no democracy without the market.

History shows rather the contrary. By the duration and the number of people affected, the extension of the market was rather associated with the extension of status inequalities, including slavery. Even today, the brutal expansion of the market is accompanied by the re-creation of new status inequalities that were barely thinkable just a few years ago.

Status inequalities sometimes retreated, it is true, and the abolition of slavery is a fine example of it. But such advances are not the 'natural' and even less the spontaneous product of the working of the logic of the system (of the market, of capitalism) but on the contrary the result of struggles against that logic, even if, quite obviously, the 'system' adapts itself to that progress.

II. IN THE MOMENTS WHEN THEY ARE RADICALIZED, REVOLUTIONS FULFIL FUNCTIONS THAT ARE INDISPENSABLE TO THE PROGRESS OF HUMANITY, NOT BY REVEALING THE OBJECTIVE DEMANDS OF THE IMMEDIATELY FOLLOWING STAGE, BUT BY GOING AHEAD OF THEM, THEREBY PREPARING LATER ADVANCES

1. It is fashionable today to devalue revolutions (the 'great' ones, that is), whether it be the Russian revolution (which led – *inevitably* led, according to this fashionable thesis – to 'totalitarianism' and failure), the Chinese revolution or the French revolution (long live Deng Xiaoping, long live Bonaparte and the Restoration!). Conversely, the moderate revolutions-as-evolution – the English (1688, of course!) or the American – are lauded. These latter are seen as establishing 'true democracy' directly, that is, the democracy of rich minorities. No mention is made of the fact that the American revolution did not abolish slavery, the direct source of the wealth of half the States making up the Union. This assessment is always accompanied by much talk of Greek democracy, which was also based on slavery.

Simultaneously, the 'utopia' of the great revolutions is highlighted: the Jacobin project of equality and rationality, the Bolshevik project of Communism, the Chinese Cultural Revolution. Yes, they are indeed utopias in the sense that these projects did not respond to the 'objective needs' of the societies at the time these revolutions were being made. They were rather creative, positive utopias with ideas in advance of their time, but which constitute beacons capable of enlightening the long periods of later struggles. The utopia of the moment becomes reality much later. In that sense, the great revolutions all experience these moments of paroxysm that are decisive for history, and then those of their retreat. After the Jacobins came the Directory, after Lenin, Stalin, after Mao, Deng.

2. The French Revolution was in advance of its time. 'Objectively', France only needed to quit the old habits of the Ancien Régime to make possible a full flowering of capitalist relations. That required only 'freedom of trade', the establishment of a democracy of the rich (with a property qualification), but neither equality (except the limited equality of the abolition of all status inequalities, necessary to break the political power of the nobility and the clergy), nor even less fraternity and the abolition of slavery in the colonies.

The Jacobin moment went far beyond these 'objective' demands. It proposed to establish a people's democracy and then discovered that freedom of trade was the enemy of that democracy. It formulated this discovery in the astonishingly modern slogan '[economic] liberalism is the enemy of democracy'. Two centuries ahead of its time, it thus gave the response to today's discourse ('capitalism is democracy').

It is in this framework that we must place the abolition of slavery. Abolition did not respond to capitalism's 'objectively necessary' need. Capitalism needed colonies, and colonies needed slaves. But the Jacobins were logical with themselves; 'equality and universality' implied that abolition. We might add, 'at whatever the immediate economic price' (if the slave is necessary for sugar, let us do without sugar, wrote Condorcet).

Because the French Revolution was in advance of its time, the utopia that it proposed failed for the time being. The Directory and the Empire re-established the priority of economic liberalism over equality and people's democracy, and so restored slavery, while the Restoration set the rules of property-based democracy.

3. The advances of the great revolutions, like their later retreats, are not mysterious products of the movement of thought, swinging between unrealism and realism. They have their material explanation.

In the case of the French Revolution, the bourgeoisie was forced to make an alliance with the people (peasants, petty urban groups) to face up to the internal adversary and the stubbornness of its external allies.

The bourgeoisie was overtaken on the left. Just as, in other circumstances, the Russian and Chinese revolutions went beyond the 'true' demands of Russia and China: to escape from underdevelopment, and little more. The intervention of the popular classes and their crystallization in alliances animated by the communist parties of the time put the 'building of socialism' (of a society without classes) on the agenda.

The abolition of slavery by the French Revolution was also, in the same spirit, the obvious product of the revolt of the slaves in Saint-Domingue and its alliance with the metropolitan revolutionary left.

4. The material explanation – that is, by the dynamic of the social struggle – does not abolish the importance of ideas. On the contrary, it makes it stand out, making ideas material forces, as has already been said.

The French Revolution – and the abolition of slavery – are thus equally the product of the long maturation that the Enlightenment had prepared. The left wing of the Enlightenment took the themes of human universalism, freedom and equality seriously. It discovered the horrors of the reality of the capitalism of its time (mercantilism), the human qualities of so-called primitive peoples (the Indians of North America, the Polynesians), and how those qualities are eroded by the social exploitation of 'more advanced' societies, and thus naturally came to denounce the genocide of the Indians and the transatlantic slave trade.

5. The 'question of slavery' allows me then to plead the cause of the creative utopia of the great revolutions, and to rehabilitate the concept of progress, so much denigrated today.

To conclude, I make a parallel between the two great moments of human progress, constituted by a series of successive great revolutions.

The first of these moments extended from the time between 500 BC and 650 AD, which saw the constitution of the series of great philosophies and religions that invented the concept of universality and took humankind out of the provincialisms of narrow spaces. Confucius, Buddha and Zoroaster (all three at exactly the same time, 500 BC) were followed by the Hellenistic philosophy, which crystallized in the encounter with the societies of the ancient Middle East (Egypt, Babylonia, Persia, Phoenicia and Greece, which belonged to this region as Europe did not then exist), and then by Christianity and Islam. These first vast cultural revolutions were all in advance of their time. They proposed the universalism that objective conditions made it impossible to realize, and, in their fatal withdrawal before this fact, established the legitimacy of what I have called the tributary systems embracing the great cultural areas, and no more. But the affirmation of the universalist concept which underpinned them remains very much alive, giving those carrying it a remarkable flexibility that enables these great religions to survive and adapt to the objective evolution, and even sometimes to intervene actively in that evolution.

In this spirit, I have proposed that some stress should also be placed on the continuity that links this first wave of progress to the second, initiated by the French Revolution and continued by the Russian and Chinese ones. The Enlightenment gave renewed vigour to the concept of universalism, which had fallen into disuse by the decline of the Christianity of the feudal Churches. I have called attention here to the invention by the French Revolution of a concept of the nation which goes beyond ethnic mediocrity (the nation based on the social contract – the 'French' concept of the nation – in contrast to the 'ethnic' nation of the German *Gemeinschaft*). Today, it is true, it is very fashionable to laud any and every 'communitarianism' (religious, ethnic or para-ethnic), because it responds precisely to the logic of the system of exploitation (dividing and multiplying 'differences' while claiming to respect them, etc.), not to the need to abolish it and move forward.

The second moment thus integrates in a continuous movement the advances of the French Revolution and the crystallization of socialist thought. This appeared – not then by chance – in and from the French Revolution (Babeuf), and thus well ahead of the 'objective conditions'. That is the socialist 'utopia' which is no less the always necessary creative utopia. The Russian and Chinese revolutions were pursuing the same objective, realizing new advances – always utopian because they were contradicted by later retreats.

Of course, in this always incomplete movement, the abolition of slavery is not an 'interesting epiphenomenon'. It is one of its essential cornerstones. And for this, we should be ever grateful to the Revolution that proclaimed it.

Appendix: Summary Chronology of Abolitions of the Slave Trade and Slavery

Yves Bénot

1770	The Quakers of New England ban their members from owning slaves.
1772	In England, Somerset case: a slave taken to England is free there.
1776	*April*: The Congress of the rebels in North America suspends the slave trade. *4 July*: United States Declaration of Independence – nothing on slavery.
1777	In Vermont, law for gradual abolition (children born of a slave mother are free, but must redeem themselves by working for a master until they are 21).
1780	In Pennsylvania, gradual abolition law (at age 28).
1783	In Massachusetts, a judgement outlaws slavery. In England, Quaker petition against the slave trade.
1784	Gradual abolition laws in Rhode Island and Connecticut.
1785	Foundation of a Society for Promoting Manumission in New York State.
1787	American Constitution: any discussion of the slave trade postponed for 20 years. *April*: Foundation in London of a Society for Effecting the Abolition of the Slave Trade.
1788	In Paris, foundation of the Société des Amis des Noirs. In England, flood of petitions to Parliament calling for abolition of the slave trade.
1789	In England, Wilberforce's first bill in the Commons for the abolition of the slave trade defeated. *31 August*: In Martinique, first slave insurrection under the French Revolution.
1791	*May*: In Paris, debates in the Constituent Assembly on equal rights for 'free men of colour and blacks'; adopted for those of the second generation only. *22–23 August*: Outbreak of the slave insurrection in the north of Saint-Domingue – continues until abolition.

1792	*March*: In Denmark, abolition of the slave trade, to take effect after 10 years.
	4 April: In France, law establishing equality of 'free men of colour and blacks'.
	April: In England, House of Commons votes for abolition of the slave trade with effect from 1796, but House of Lords postpones consideration.
1793	*1 February*: Beginning of the Franco-British war (1793–1801; 1803–14).
	29 August and 21 September: Abolition of slavery in Saint-Domingue by the civil commissioners Sonthonax and Polverel.
	September 1793–June 1794: The British occupy most of the coastal areas of Saint-Domingue and maintain slavery there.
1794	In Philadelphia, convention of all US abolition societies.
	4 February: In Paris, the Convention ratifies the abolition of slavery in Saint-Domingue and extends it to all the French colonies.
	6 May: In Saint-Domingue, Toussaint Louverture goes over to the French Republic.
	7 June: Abolition comes into force in Guadeloupe.
	14 June: Abolition comes into force in French Guyana.
1795–6	Slave insurrections in Grenada and St Vincent are put down. In St Lucia, slavery is abolished for a year following the French reconquest and restored in mid-1796 after the British reconquest.
1796	In the Mascarenes, white revolt against the commissioners sent to implement abolition: there is no abolition.
1796	England continues the slave trade.
1797	In Jamaica, insurrection of maroons in the Blue Mountains.
1798	In the United States, Georgia suspends the overseas slave trade. In Cuba, Morales conspiracy. In Saint-Domingue, the country is finally freed of British occupation.
1799	In New York State, act for gradual abolition.
	10 November: In Paris, General Bonaparte takes power.
1800	*30 August*: In Virginia, slave insurrection – 16 executions.
1801	*January*: Occupation of the Spanish part of Saint-Domingue by Toussaint Louverture extends abolition of slavery there.
	July: Constitution of Saint-Domingue.
	1 October: Preliminaries of peace between France and Britain.
	November: Insurrection in Guadeloupe, Governor Lacrosse is expelled, de facto autonomy. In Cuba, the Spanish governor recognizes the freedom of the maroons (*cobreros*) in Oriente province.
	December: Departure of the Leclerc expedition to reconquer Saint-Domingue.
1802	*February*: Leclerc lands at Le Cap and begins war against Toussaint Louverture, which lasts until May.
	27 March: Treaty of Amiens between France and Britain.
	May: Richepanse reconquers Guadeloupe – 10,000 dead.

20 May: Law restoring slavery and the slave trade promulgated in Paris.

16 July: Restoration of slavery in Guadeloupe.

October: In Saint-Domingue, war resumes throughout the formerly French part of the country.

November: In French Guyana, restoration of slavery. Danish abolition of the slave trade comes into force.

1803   *27 April*: Death of Toussaint Louverture in the fort of Joux.

        November: In Saint-Domingue, capitulation of Rochambeau.

1804   *1 January*: Proclamation of the independence of Haiti. In England, the Society for Effecting the Abolition of the Slave Trade, dormant since 1797, resumes its activity. In New Jersey, law for the gradual abolition of slavery. South Carolina resumes the slave trade.

1806   Slave insurrection in Trinidad.

        May: British Act prohibiting the introduction of new slaves into the conquered colonies.

        June: In London, Resolution in the Commons for the abolition of the slave trade.

1807   *2 March*: Slave Trade Abolition Act in the United States, effective 1 January 1808.

        25 March: British Act for the Abolition of the Slave Trade, effective 1 January 1808. Slaves freed on illegal slave ships to be bound apprentices for three years.

1808   Sierra Leone becomes a Crown Colony: liberated slaves to be transferred there.

        Christmas: Nazaré's insurrection in Brazil.

1809–10   The British seize all the French colonies and prohibit the slave trade there but maintain slavery.

1810   *December*: In Guadalajara, Mexico, Hidalgo proclaims the abolition of slavery, but he is defeated and killed.

1811   *January*: In Louisiana, slave insurrection. In independent Chile, law abolishing the slave trade aims for the gradual abolition of slavery.

        19 September: Slave insurrection in Martinique.

1812   *January–March*: In Cuba, Aponte's conspiracy. In Spain, in the Cadiz Cortes, abolition of the slave trade and slavery proposed by Varela and Arguëlles is defeated.

1813   In independent Argentina, the constituent assembly in Buenos Aires opts for gradual abolition. In Mexico, Morelos confirms Hidalgo's abolition, but he is defeated and killed.

1814   End of Napoleonic regime. Under the Treaty of Paris, France recovers French Guyana, Martinique, Guadeloupe, Senegal and Reunion; it maintains slavery there.

1815   In France, the 100 Days.

28 *March*: Napoleon decrees the abolition of the slave trade. The Congress of Vienna calls for the abolition of the slave trade.

July: Louis XVIII confirms the abolition of the slave trade, but it is not effectively enforced under the Restoration.

1815–16   Bolivar in Haiti; Pétion gives him his support, but asks him to abolish slavery.

1817   Anglo-Spanish treaty for the abolition of the Spanish slave trade within four years; it is not implemented.

1817   In Venezuela, at the Congress of the independentists, Bolivar calls for the abolition of slavery. In Argentina, the new constitution declares slavery abolished (but it continues to exist in part).

1818   The American Colonization Society acquires land on the coast of Africa (Liberia) to settle American ex-slaves there.

1821   In Peru, law prohibiting the slave trade and gradually abolishing slavery. In Gran Colombia, emancipation law. In Paris, foundation of the Société de la Morale Chrétienne which calls for abolition of the slave trade.

13 *October*: In independent Mexico, law prohibiting the slave trade and abolishing slavery (for those born in Mexico).

1822   In Martinique, slave insurrection. Annexation of Saint-Domingue to Haiti leads to the abolition of slavery there.

1823   In Chile, abolition law. In London, foundation of the Society for the Gradual Abolition of Slavery.

August: In Demerara-Berbice (British Guyana), slave insurrection – 250 killed in the repression.

1824   In Central America, abolition of slavery.

1825   Charles X's France recognizes the independence of Haiti in exchange for an indemnity of 150 million gold francs (reduced to 90 million under Louis-Philippe).

1829   Final abolition of slavery in Mexico.

1830   In Uruguay, slavery abolished. In England, relaunching of the abolition society, which becomes the Society for the Immediate Abolition of Slavery.

July: Revolution in Paris – Louis-Philippe.

1831   In Bolivia, slavery is abolished. Franco-British agreement for controlling the illegal trade (reinforced in 1833). In Britain, campaign of petitions for the abolition of slavery.

Christmas: Beginning of slave insurrection in Jamaica – 14 whites and 500 blacks killed.

1832   In France, equal rights for all free men in the colonies.

June: Limited electoral reform in Britain, followed by elections.

1833   In England, act abolishing slavery, to come into force in August 1834, combined with compensation for masters and compulsory apprenticeship for the newly freed slaves for six years.

1834   Foundation of the French abolition society.

1838	In the British West Indies, apprenticeship is abolished by local assemblies.
1842	In Paraguay, gradual abolition law.
1844	In France, petition for abolition: 7,000 signatures.
1845	In France, Mackau law 'mitigating' slavery.
1846	In Tunisia, abolition of slavery. In France, Louis-Philippe frees slaves on royal estates.
1847	In France, new petition for abolition: 11,000 signatures. In Africa, proclamation of the independence of Liberia, formed by American ex-slaves.
1848	*February*: Revolution in Paris, Second Republic.
	4 *March*: Decision of the provisional government setting up the Schœlcher commission to prepare abolition.
	27 *April*: Abolition decree in Paris (published 2 May).
	May: Slaves in Guadeloupe and Martinique abandon the plantations and free themselves.
	22 *May*: Bloody incident in Saint-Pierre de la Martinique.
	23 *May*: Governor of Martinique proclaims immediate abolition (before the arrival of the decree).
	27 *May*: Governor of Guadeloupe proclaims immediate abolition.
	May–June: Slaves in the Dutch colonies of St Martin, St Eustatius and Saba free themselves.
	2 *July*: Slave insurrection in the Danish island of St Croix.
	3 *July*: Governor of St Croix proclaims abolition.
	22 *September*: King of Denmark ratifies abolition in St Croix.
1849	In France, law for compensation of colonists. Foundation of Libreville (Gabon) where freed slaves are settled.
1851	Final abolition in Colombia.
1852	In the United States, publication of H. Beecher Stowe's *Uncle Tom's Cabin*.
1853	Final abolition in Argentina.
1854	In the United States, foundation of the Republican Party, opposed to Southern slave states. Final abolition in Venezuela.
1861–5	*April*: Civil War in the United States.
1863	Abolition in the Dutch colonies (Surinam-Curaçao).
1863–5	Abolition in the United States.
1865	14 *April*: Assassination in Washington of abolitionist President Abraham Lincoln.
1873	Abolition in the Spanish colony of Puerto Rico.
1880–6	Abolition in Cuba.
1888	Abolition in Brazil.

In 1860, despite the abolitions that had already been adopted, the number of slaves on the American continent must have been about double what it had been at the beginning of the century (United States, Cuba, Puerto Rico and Brazil combined).

List of Contributors

Lucien René Abénon, Université des Antilles
Samir Amin, Forum du Tiers-Monde, Dakar
Francis Arzalier, Institut universitaire de formation des maîtres de Picardie
Serge Barcellini, President de l'association 'Mémoire de L.-F. Sonthonax'
Jean Bart, Université de Bourgogne, Dijon
Yves Bénot, Paris
Jean-Marcel Champion, École des hautes études en sciences sociales, Paris
Jean-Charles Benzaken, Toulon
Jacky Dahomay, Université des Antilles
Édouard Delépine, Université des Antilles
Francis Démier, Université de Paris X
Doudou Diène, former Director, Division for Intercultural Projects, UNESCO
Marcel Dorigny, Université de Paris VIII
Jean Ehrard, Université de Clermont-Ferrand
Léo Élisabeth, Inspecteur de l'éducation nationale, Martinique
Prosper Ève, Université de la Réunion
Iñez Fischer-Blanchet, Université de Paris X
Harris Memel Foté, Université d'Abidjan
Bernard Gainot, Université de Paris I
Florence Gauthier, Université de Paris VII
Gérard Gengembre, École normale supérieure de Fontenay
Emiliano Gil-Blanco, Universidad de Alcala de Henares, Madrid
M'Baye Gueye, Université Cheikh Anta Diop, Dakar
Jean-Claude Halpern, Paris
Richard Hart, University of the West Indies, Jamaica
Laënnec Hurbon, CNRS
Oruno D. Lara, Université de Paris X
Abdelhamid Larguèche, Université de la Manouba, Tunis
Élise Marienstras, Université de Paris VII
Éric Mesnard, Université de Paris VIII
Nelly Schmidt, Université de Paris X
Philippe Steiner, École normale supérieure de Fontenay
Jean Tarrade, Université de Poitiers
Philippe Vigier, Université de Paris X
Michel Vovelle, Université de Paris I
James Walvin, University of York
Claude Wanquet, Université de la Réunion

Index of Personal Names

Dumas, Alexandre, 267, 270n, 271n, 273, 279n
Dumond, Dwight Lowell, 31
Dumont, Étienne, 125–6, 128, 131n
Dumouriez, 202
Dumur, Guy, 351
Duny, 178n
Dupin, André Marie, 254n
Dupont de Nemours, P.S., 142n
Duport, 188
Dupré, Marie-Thérèse, 210
Dupré, 210, 218
Dupuy, 232
Durand-Valentin, 327
Duras (de), 272–3
Dusaillant, J.B., 211
Dussaillant, Toussaint, 245
Duval-Carrié, Édouard, 345, 351n
Duvalier, 15, 345

Éboué, Félix, 341–3, 350n
Edwards, Jonathan, 84
Egret, Jean, 110n
Ehrard, Jean, 106, 110n, 111
El Tounsy, 268, 271n
Elgard, Thomas, 39n
Elisabeth, Léo, 148, 316
Élise, 214
Émilie, 211
Enfantin, 269, 271n
Engerman, S.-L., 116
Englethorp, John, 113
Enjolras, 275
Épinay, Adrien (d'), 205n
Eschassériaux, Joseph, 185–6, 188, 193, 195n
Estaing (Comte d'), 226
Ève, Prosper, 17
Eyre, Edward, 298

Fabulé, 45, 49
Faidherbe, 329n
Faiguet, 114
Falope, Josette, 46
Farmer, A., 98n, 238
Fayance, 149, 151–2
Faye, Gracia, 319
Fénelon (Marquis de), 93
Ferla, 27, 38n
Fernando VII, 293
Fiedmont, 109n
Finet, 342
Finkelman, Paul, 92, 97, 98n
Finley, Moses, 3, 16n
Fischer-Blanchet, Iñez, 283
Fitz-James, 278
Fogel, R.W., 97
Foignet, Alexandre, 270n
Fontenay, Thérésa (de), 278
Forbonnais, 115, 134, 143n
Ford, Paul L., 98
Formey, 115
Fourcroy, 193n
Foutard, Jean-Dominique, 149
Frank, Louis, 333, 339n

Franklin, Benjamin, 86–7, 97n, 136
Frémont, H. de, 53n
Frey, Sylvia R., 99n
Froidefonds-Desfarges, 313n
Frostin, C., 67–8n
Furetière, Antoine, 112

Gabaret, 46
Gainot, Bernard, 180, 203
Galbaud, 170
Galenne, 27
Gallois, Mont Brun, 328n
Ganilh, C., 138, 142n, 143n
Gareshé, 131n
Garnier, Claude, 24, 38n
Garnier, François, 24
Garnier, Jacques, 171
Garnot, Pierre, 171, 173
Garran de Coulon, 192n
Garriga, Sarda, 296
Gasparin, Adrien de, 253n
Gasparin, Agénor-Étienne de, 253
Gatine, 307
Gauthier, Florence, 167, 193n
Gautier, Théophile, 277
Gauvain, 275
Geggus, David, 226n
Gendron, François, 166n
Gengembre, Gérard, 272
Genty, J.-L., 148
Genty, Louis, 50
George, Carol V.-R., 99n
George III, 293
Georges, Joseph, 171
Gerteis, Louis S., 97n
Gil-Blanco, Emiliano, 291
Gillot, 199
Girard, 23
Giraud, 182
Girod, F., 67n
Gisler, Antoine, 65
Glissant, Édouard, 8, 16n
Godard, Léon (Father), 308
Godechot, Jacques, 195n
Goethe, 272
Goggi, G., 120n
Gonneau de Montbrun, 33
Gonneau, François, 22
Gouin, Amboise, 258
Gouly, Benoît, 179n, 192n, 205n
Gournay, 134, 143n
Gourran-Coulon, J.-P., 68n
Gouy d'Arsy, 148
Gradis, 149
Gramagnac, 128
Granet, 189–90
Grassal, Georges, 277
Greene, Lorenzo, 97n
Grégoire, Henri (Father), ix, 66, 125, 169, 189, 269n, 343, 348
Gresham, 218
Grigny, Amélie de, 319
Grimaud, Jean-Baptiste, 39n
Groc, Gérard, 270

Gros, 68
Gubillon, Antoine, 22
Guérin, Louis, 214
Guerra, Ramiro, 304n
Guichard, Germain, 30
Guigné de La Bérangerie, Joseph de, 21
Guilhaume, J.-F., 264, 270n
Guillemardet, 188
Guillemin de Vaivre, Jean-Baptiste, 109n
Guillet, 320, 328
Guilloteau, Victor, 220
Guiral, 253n
Guisan, 106
Guiton, 154
Guizot, François, 249
Guybre, 189
Guyomard, Pierre, 195n
Gyges, 7

Habibrah, 275
Hall, Prince, 99n
Halpern, Jean-Claude, 155, 185
Hamdani, Amar, 270n
Hamilton, Alexander, 90
Harding, Vincent, 132
Hart, Richard, 283
Hayot, E., 257
Hédouville, 185, 190
Heming, Sally, 98n
Henry, Patrick, 88
Hervieu, 210
Hesse, Philippe, 107, 110n
Hibon, Pierre, 32, 37n
Hidalgo, 361
Higginbotham, Leon A., 96n
Hilaire, Régine, 211
Hodgson, Adam, 142n
Hoffman, Ronald, 98n
Hohl, Claude, 236n
Holle, 329
Honoré, J.B., 211
Hopkins, Samuel (Reverend), 117
Hourdin, Georges, 351n
Howell, Samuel, 91
Huberlot (Mgr), 351n
Huc, 316
Hugo, Victor, 262, 269n, 270n, 275
Hugues, Victor, 9, 148, 190, 196n, 198, 202, 207–9, 213–5, 231
Humbert de la Meuse, 224
Humblot-Conté, 243
Hurbon, Laënnec, 16n, 55
Husson, 316
Hyrne, 199

Ibn Omar El Tounsy, Cheikh Mohamed, 271
Ibrahim, 268
Isambert, 257, 259

James, C.L.R., 16, 177n
Jan (Mgr), 67n